Published By:
Airlife Publishing Ltd
101 Longden Road
Shrewsbury SY3 9EB
England
Telephone: 01743 235651
Fax: 01743 232944

Produced wholly by Aerospace Publishing Ltd
and published jointly with Airlife Publishing Ltd

Author:
Günter Endres

Sub-Editor:
Karen Leverington

Design:
Robert Hewson

First published 1996

ISBN 1 85310 581 3

Printed in Hong Kong

Picture Credits

AIR: Back Cover, 94.
Aerospace: Cover, 18, 36, 38 (two), 59, 60, 78, 99.
Adrian Arzenheimer: 49
Airbus: Cover, 5, 7, 8, 13, 17, 23, 32, 34, 43 (two), 54, 61, 65, 67, 69 (two), 73, 74, 81, 83, 85, 86, 90, 95, 100, 101, 103, 106, 107, 111, 113, 120, Back Cover.
Austin J. Brown/Aviation Picture Library: Cover (3), 5, 9, 15, 16, 17, 42, 47, 48, 50, 60, 104, 115.
Boeing: Cover, 8, 21, 24, 25, 29, 36, 37, 38, 45, 50, 55, 57, 58, 70, 71, 74, 82, 83, 86, 89, 93,

112, 114.
Bombardier: 13, 22, 37, 52, 75, 87, 116.
Bill Brabant: 108, 109.
British Aerospace: 1.
Bill Crimmins: 108.
David Donald: 11.
Günter Endres: 19, 59, 66.
Fokker: Back Cover (two), 23, 26, 39, 41, 80, 91, 116.
Gary Gentle: 10, 11, 40, 117.
Robert Hewson: Endpapers, 1, 2 (two), 3, 6, 12, 14 (two), 19, 20, 25, 26, 28, 29, 30, 31, 32, 33, 35, 41, 44 (two), 45, 46, 47, 52, 53, 56, 57,

62, 63, 64 (two via RH), 66, 67, 68, 70, 76 (two), 77 (via RH), 78, 79, 84, 87, 88 (two), 92, 95, 96, 97 (two), 98, 100 (via RH), 102, 103, 105, 109, 110, 113, 118, Back Cover (two).
McDonnell Douglas: 21, 27, 51, 53, 62, 93, 119.
Saab: 27, 72.
Jim Winchester: 18, 30.

Special thanks also to: Eddy Gual, Dan Hagedorn and Robert F. Dorr.

THE VITAL GUIDE TO MAJOR AIRLINES OF THE WORLD

AUTHOR: GÜNTER ENDRES
EDITOR: ROBERT HEWSON

Airlife
England

Adria Airways (JP/ADR)

Adria Airways has weathered the break-up of Yugoslavia and civil war to emerge as the national carrier of independent Slovenia.

History: Founded as Adria Aviopromet in 1961, in Slovenia, then one of six republics and autonomous provences constituting Yugoslav Federation. Began flying mostly long-haul charters with four ex-KLM **DC-6B**s, and occasionally leased **DC-8-50**. Jet competition in European charter market forced Adria into realignment with Belgrade-based trading group Interexport, to guarantee financing for a new fleet. Airline renamed Inex-Adria Airways in 1968, but reverted to original title when association ended in May 1986. First **DC-9-32** entered service in April 1969, followed by inauguration of domestic

Ljubljana-Belgrade flights in 1970. Further fleet modernisation in 1981/82 with the **MD-81** permitted international scheduled expansion, first to Larnaca in November 1983 and Munich in 1984. Two **DHC-7**s acquired in 1984 to open up smaller domestic airports to tourist traffic. Next stage of fleet upgrade effected from May 1989 with delivery of first **A320-200**. On 28 June 1991, as a direct consequence

of the civil war in Yugoslavia, fighters of the Yugoslav air force attacked four Adria aircraft and facilities at Ljubljana Brnik Airport, causing severe damage. Moved base temporarily to Klagenfurt, Austria, but airline grounded on 25 October 1991, until Slovenia independence achieved in January 1992. Network gradually redeveloped, but with a reduced fleet.

Adria Airways today: European network including code-share and marketing agreement with Air France on Ljubljana-Paris route, Avioimpex on Skopje-Ljubljana, and Lufthansa between Frankfurt and Ljubljana.

Annual revenue: $100 million
Passengers: 0.5 million
Employees: 700

Adria Airlines fleet

Airbus A320-200	c/n	DHC-7-100	c/n	Douglas DC-9-32	c/n
S5-AAA	043	S5-ACA	90	S5-ABF	47239/466
S5-AAB	113	S5-ACB	92	S5-ABH	47570/684
S5-AAC	114				

Aer Lingus (EI/EIN)

History: Founded in April 1936 and began operations on 27 May when a **DH.84 Dragon** flew from Baldonnel, near Dublin, to Bristol. Service extended to London later that year. Fleet supplemented by two **DH.86B**s and a **DH.89A Dragon Rapide**, followed in June 1939 by two **Lockheed**

L.14. During war, operations confined to Dublin-Liverpool, with Manchester as alternative UK terminal as required. Single **Douglas DC-3** entered service on 7 May 1940. In immediate post-war years, concentrated on routes across Irish Sea, facilitated by Anglo-Irish Air Agreement

signed in April 1946, giving Aer Lingus exclusive rights. BEA took 30 per cent stake and BOAC 10 per cent. By 1948, network expanded to London, Liverpool, Glasgow, Manchester, the Isle of Man, Amsterdam and Paris. Fleet supplemented by several war surplus types, and 10 DC-3s (C-47s), seven **Vickers Vikings** and five new **Lockheed L.749 Constellations**. Aerlinte Eireann Teoranta formed in 1947 to concentrate on long-haul flights.

Bristol Freighters, Vickers V.700 and **V.800 Viscounts** and **Fokker F27-100**s added in mid-1950s. After twice cancelling plans for transatlantic services, routes from Dublin to Boston

Aer Lingus pioneered the use of the Airbus A330 on the North Atlantic when the type began to replace the airline's long-serving Boeing 747-100s in 1994.

Aer Lingus Commuter operates the Fokker 50 and BAe 146, having now disposed of its Saab 340Bs.

and New York, via Shannon, finally inaugurated in April 1958, using Seaboard & Western **L.1049H Super Constellation**s, pending delivery of own **Boeing 720** in November 1960. From 1 January 1960, Aer Lingus and Airlinte began operating under common marketing title of Aer Lingus-Irish International Airlines, and on 31 May 1964, Irish government acquired remaining BEA holding. Received first **Boeing 707-320C** in June 1964, followed by first of four **BAC One-Eleven 200**s in May 1965. Services to Chicago and Montreal inaugurated on 29 May 1966. On 10 January 1967 ordered two **Boeing 747-200C**, introduced on New York run on 5 April 1971. Fleet then also included eight **Boeing 737-200**, six 707-320C and four One-Elevens. Network expansion focused on UK and Europe. Purchased 75 per cent holding in cargo airline Aer Turas Teoranta on 5 August 1980, but sold stake as part of restructuring in 1994. Short-lived introduction of two **Boeing 767-300ER** in early 1990s. US/Irish bilateral changed October 1993 to permit direct flights to USA from Dublin, eliminating Shannon stopover. First of three **Airbus A330-300** entered service in June 1994. Last 747 withdrawn on 1 October 1995.

Aer Lingus today: Government-owned flag-carrier maintaining a domestic and European route system, together with transatlantic services to Boston and New York. European destinations inlude Amsterdam, Belfast, Birmingham, Bristol, Brussels, Copenhagen, Düsseldorf, East Midlands, Edinburgh, Frankfurt, Glasgow, Hamburg, London (Heathrow and Gatwick), Manchester, Milan, Newcastle, Paris, Rome, Stuttgart and Zürich. Domestic points on the network

are Cork, Dublin, Galway, Kerry, Shannon and Sligo. Code-share with Delta, and general co-operation with British Airways.

Annual revenue: $1,250 million
Passengers: 4.5 million
Cargo: 36,850 tonnes
Employees: 7,500

Associate carrier: *Aer Lingus Commuter,* which began flying on 1 May 1983, operates on Irish and UK routes with three **BAe 146-300**s and six **Fokker 50**s.

Aer Lingus fleet

Airbus A330-300	c/n	EI-BXB	24521/1788	EI-CDB	24919/1970
EI-CRK	070	EI-BXC	24773/1850	EI-CDC	24768/1975
EI-DUB	055	EI-BXD	24866/1867	EI-CDD	24989/1989
EI-JFK	086	EI-BXI	25052/2036	EI-CDE	25115/2050
EI-SHN	054	EI-BXK	25736/2269	EI-CDF	25737/2232
				EI-CDG	25738/2261
Boeing 737-400	c/n	**Boeing 737-500**	c/n	EI-CDH	25739/2271
EI-BXA	24474/1742	EI-CDA	24878/1939	EI-CDS	26287/2427

Aeroflot Russian International (SU/AFL)

History: Legal successor to Aeroflot-Soviet Airlines, retaining all international route rights transferred from former Soviet Union to new Russian Federation. Vastly reduced operations compared to old Aeroflot, which not only was world's largest airline, but was also responsible for all other aerial activities, airports and regulatory affairs. Operations were undertaken by 30 directorates, of which 27 divided were divided into geographical areas. The other three were the Moscow Transport Directorate, the Direc-

torate of Civil Aviation of the Central Regions and the Arctic (UGATsRIA), and the Moscow-based Directorate of International Air Routes (TsUMVS), which formed basis of present-day international airline. History goes

back to March 1923 and founding of Dobrolet with small fleet of **de Havilland**, **Junkers** and **Vickers** aircraft. In 1929 Dobrolet became Dobroflot when merged with Ukrainian company Ukvozduchput. After amalgamation of

Aeroflot Russian International is a far smaller operator, compared to its Communist heyday. Russian flags have replaced the 'hammer and sickle' and most aircraft have repainted grey tails.

Aeroflot Russian International Airlines

Soviet-era aircraft like this Tu-134 and An-124 still dominate Aeroflot, though Western airliners are being slowly introduced.

all civil aviation activities, with exception of Arctic services, Dobroflot reorganised in 1932 as Grazdansij Wozdusnyj Flot, better known as Aeroflot. First international service opened in 1936 between Moscow and Prague. Introduction of first jet, **Tupolev Tu-104**, between Moscow and Irkutsk on 15 September 1956, and **Tu-114** aircraft used to inaugurate long-haul service to Havana. Short-lived supersonic flights opened with **Tu-144** on 1 November 1977 from Moscow to Alma Ata. Aeroflot operated a several thousand-strong, almost entirely Soviet fleet of fixed-wing aircraft and helicopters. Network spanned world and every city in Soviet Union, transporting well over 100 million passengers. Following collapse of USSR, acquired its first Western aircraft: two (later five) **A310-300**s

in August 1992. **Il-96-300** joined fleet in 1994, as did **Boeing 767-300**. Became joint-stock company on 21 June 1994, with 51 per cent retained by government and remaining 49 per cent distributed among employees.

Aeroflot today: Extensive international network to 135 destinations in 100 countries, including Commonwealth of Independent States (CIS). In addition to serving most European and CIS capitals, flies intercontinental routes to Abu Dhabi, Accra, Addis Ababa, Amman, Anchorage, Antananarivo, Baghdad, Bamako, Bangkok, Beijing, Bombay, Brazzaville, Buenos Aires, Cairo, Calcutta, Casablanca, Chicago, Colombo, Conakry, Cotonou, Dacca, Dakar, Damascus, Delhi, Djibouti, Douala, Dubai, Hanoi, Harare, Havana, Hong Kong, Jakarta, Johannesburg,

Karachi, Kathmandu, Kuala Lumpur, Kuwait, Lima, Lomé, Los Angeles, Luanda, Lusaka, Mexico City, Miami, Montreal, Nagoya, Nairobi, New York, Osaka, Ouagadougou, Phnom Penh, Rio de Janeiro, San Francisco, Sana'a, Santiago, Sao Paulo, Seattle, Seoul, Shanghai, Sharjah, Singapore, Sydney, Tehran, Tel Aviv, Tokyo, Tripoli, Tunis, Ulan Bator and Washington. In Russia's Far East, services link Khabarovsk and San Francisco, and Irkutsk to Niigata and Shenyang. Code-share and block-space agreement with Austrian Airlines, Delta Air Lines and Finnair; joint service with Cyprus Airways on Larnaca-Moscow.

Annual revenue: $980 million
Passengers: 3.5 million
Cargo: 60,800 tonnes
Employees: 14,800

Fleet development: Five **Tupolev Tu-204C**s remain to be delivered and there are plans for further orders. Contract signed for four more **Airbus A310-300**. Expects to proceed with the acquisition of 20 Pratt & Whitney-powered **Il-96-300M** following agreement on a $1 billion loan facility from the US Eximbank.

Aeroflot Russian International Airlines fleet

Airbus A310-300	c/n							
F-OGQQ	592	RA-86512	3037314	RA-76473	0033448404	RA-65566	63952	RA-85639	771
F-OGQR	593	RA-86514	4037647	RA-76474	0033448407	RA-65567	63967	RA-85640	772
F-OGQT	622	RA-86517	3139732	RA-76476	0043451528	RA-65568	66135	RA-85641	773
F-OGQU	646	RA-86518	3139956	RA-76477	0043453575	RA-65623	49985	RA-85642	778
F-OGYM	457	RA-86520	1241314	RA-76478	0053459788			RA-85643	779
F-OGYN	458	RA-86522	2241536	RA-76479	0053460790	**Tupolev Tu-134A-3**	c/n	RA-85644	780
		RA-86523	2241647	RA-76482	0053460832	RA-65697	63307	RA-85646	784
Antonov An-124-100 c/n		RA-86524	3242321	RA-76488	0073479371	RA-65717	63657	RA-85647	785
RA-82069		RA-86531	4242654	RA-76750	0083485561	RA-65769	62415	RA-85648	786
RA-82070		RA-86532	4243111	RA-76751	0083487610	RA-65770	62430	RA-85649	787
		RA-86533	1343123	RA-76785	0093495863	RA-65781	62645	RA-85650	788
		RA-86534	1343332	RA-76795	0093498962	RA-65783	62708	RA-85661	811
Boeing 767-300ER c/n		RA-86558	4952928			RA-65784	62715	RA-85662	816
EI-CKD	26205/474	RA-86562	4831517	**Ilyushin Il-96-300**	c/n	RA-65785	62750	RA-85663	817
EI-CKE	26208/505	RA-86564	4934734	RA-96005	74393201002			RA-85665	819
		RA-86565	2546812	RA-96007	74393201004	**Tupolev Tu-154B-2**	c/n	RA-85668	826
Ilyushin Il-62M c/n		RA-86566	4255152	RA-96008	74393201005	RA-85363	363	RA-85669	827
RA-86474	3726952			RA-96010	74393201007	RA-85564	564	RA-85670	828
RA-86483	2829637	**Ilyushin Il-76T**	c/n	RA-96011	74393201008	RA-85570	570	RA-85810	824
RA-86485	3830912	RA-76460	0013431928	RA-96012	74393201009	RA-85592	592	RA-85811	831
RA-86488	4830345	RA-76519	093420599						
RA-86489	4830456			**McDonnell Douglas**		**Tupolev Tu-154M**	c/n	**Tupolev Tu-204C**	c/n
RA-86492	4149324	**Ilyushin Il-76TD**	c/n	**DC-10-30**	c/n	RA-85625	752	RA-64007	
RA-86497	1931253	RA-76467	0023440157	N524MD	46999/289	RA-85626	753	RA-64008	
RA-86502	3933345	RA-76468	0023441195			RA-85634	763	RA-64009	
RA-86506	1035324	RA-76469	0033444286	**Tupolev Tu-134A**	c/n	RA-85637	767	RA-64010	
RA-86510	1035213	RA-76470	0033445291	RA-65559	49909	RA-85638	768		

Aerolineas Argentinas (AR/ARG)

Ministro Pistarini (Ezeiza) and AP Jorge Newberry

History: Created by government decree in May 1949 through combining operations of four airlines: FAMA, international flag-carrier; Aeroposta Argentina, serving Patagonia and Punta Arenas; ALFA, covering Argentine Litoral, Asuncion and Montevideo; and ZONDA, operating to Santiago de Chile and Argentina's northern regions. Officially started operations on 7 December 1950 with inherited fleet of around 70 aircraft, including six **Douglas DC-6**s, 10 **DC-4**s, 25 **DC-3**s, five **Convair 240**s, five **Vickers Vikings**, six **Shorts Sandringham** flying-boats, and other types. In addition to regional and domestic flights, served Havana, New York, Frankfurt, Lisbon, London, Madrid, Rome and Paris. Development adversely affected by diversity of fleet and loss of monopoly situation from 1955. In April 1958, ordered six **de Havilland Comet 4**s and opened first jet service on South American continent on 16 April 1959 with flight to Santiago. Comets introduced on South Atlantic route on 19 May and to North America on 7 June. Modernisation of domestic fleet started with order for nine **HS 748**s in March 1961 and continued five months later with purchase of three **Caravelle VIN**s. Miami and Los Angeles added to network, and later Cape Town. **Boeing 707-320B** began to replace Comets from October 1966, and other aircraft progressively introduced, including **Boeing 737-200** from 1969, **Fokker F28-1000** from 1974, **Boeing 747-200B** from 1977, and **727-200** the next year. Service across South Pole to Auckland, New Zealand, but, like several other international flights, disrupted or suspended during

Above: Aerolineas' three PW4152-powered A310s were all once operated by Pan American.

Right: The airline's six Boeing 747-287Bs were delivered between 1979 and 1982.

Falklands conflict in 1982. On 27 December 1989, government authorised privatisation and on 21 November 1990, Iberia acquired 30 per cent stake, later increased to 83 per cent with further capital injection. Order placed for six **MD-88**s, first delivered in August 1992, followed in July 1994 by three **A310-300**.

Aerolineas Argentinas today: Flag-carrier responsible for regional and long-haul intercontinental passenger and cargo services, together with domestic trunk routes. International destinations are Asuncion, Auckland, Bogotá, Cape Town, Frankfurt, Johannesburg, La Paz, Lima, London, Los Angeles, Madrid, Miami, Montevideo, Montreal, New York-JFK, Paris, Rio de Janeiro, Rome, Santa Cruz, Sao

Paulo, Toronto and Zürich. Marketing alliance, code-share or block-space agreements with Iberia, Ladeco, Malaysia Airlines and VIASA.

Annual revenue: $900 million
Passengers: 3.9 million
Cargo: 40,550 tonnes
Employees: 6,345
Major shareholder: Iberia with 83 per cent, but the Spanish airline expected to sell its stake in 1996

Associate carriers: Holds 100 per cent of shares in local airline **Austral Lineas Aereas** (AU), founded in June 1971. Serves almost 30 destinations within Argentina with fleet of two **BAC One-Eleven 500**s, eight **DC-9-32**s, three **MD-83**s and two **MD-81**s.

Aerolineas Argentinas fleet

Airbus A310-300	c/n	LV-OLO	22604/1777	Boeing 737-200 Adv	c/n	Boeing 747-200B	c/n	LV-LOC	11083
F-OGYQ	453	LV-OLP	22605/1787	LV-JTD	20523/285	LV-MLO	21725/349	LV-LRG	11046
F-OGYR	456	LV-OLR	22606/1812	LV-JTO	20537/291	LV-MLP	21726/403		
F-OGYS	467			LV-LEB	20768/331	LV-MLR	21727/404	McDD MD-88	c/n
		Boeing 737-200	c/n	LV-LIV	20965/381	LV-OEP	22297/487	LV-VBX	53047/2016
Boeing 727-200 Adv	c/n	LV-JMW	20403/236	LV-LIW	20966/387	LV-OOZ	22592/532	LV-VBY	53048/2030
LV-MIM	21688/1415	LV-JMX	20404/243	LV-WGX	21358/498	LV-OPA	22593/552	LV-VBZ	53049/2031
LV-MIN	21689/1427	LV-JMY	20405/248					LV-VCB	53351/2043
LV-MIO	21690/1469	LV-JMZ	20406/261	Boeing 737-200C	c/n	Fokker F28-1000	c/n	LV-VGB	53446/2046
LV-OLN	22603/1732			LV-JND	20407/263	LV-LOA	11085	LV-VGC	53447/2064

5

Aero Lloyd (YP/AEF)

Aero Lloyd began life as a Caravelle operator and was one of the last in Europe. Today, it flies a mix of A320s and MD-80s.

leased from IIFC. First A320 delivered on 16 January 1996.

Aero Lloyd today: Inclusive-tour holiday flights to all Mediterranean and Canary Islands resorts, and to Egyptian and North African destinations.

Annual revenue: $375 million
Passengers: 2.45 million
Employees: 850
Major shareholders: Air Charter Market (52.25 per cent) and Jan Klimitz (42.75 per cent)

Fleet development: Delivery of total of six Airbus A320s in progress. First of 10 A321s due in March 1998.

History: Formed on 6 September 1979. Acquired three **Caravelle 10R** and began operations, from Frankfurt, Düsseldorf and Munich on 21 March 1980. Reorganised and restarted on 1 April 1981, adding four **DC-9-32**s. **MD-83** entered service in May 1986, and fleet expanded between 1987 and 1989 with four more **MD-83**s and four **MD-87**s. Added scheduled domestic routes on 31 October 1988, serving Frankfurt, Düsseldorf, Hamburg and Munich, and later Paris and London. Order placed for four **MD-11**s for delivery in 1991/92, but not taken up. MD-80 fleet increased instead to 20 aircraft. Growing competition forced discontinuation of scheduled services in April 1992. Signed contract for two **A320-200**s and four **A321**s on 12 April 1995 direct from Airbus, plus four more A320s and six A321s to be

Aero Lloyd fleet

Airbus A320-200	c/n	McDonnell Douglas MD-83		D-ALLP	53013/1738
D-ALAA	565	D-AGWB	49846/1581	D-ALLQ	53014/1740
D-ALAB	575	D-AGWC	49847/1585	D-ALLR	53015/1818
D-ALAC	580	D-ALLD	49402/1261	D-ALLU	49619/1483
		D-ALLE	49449/1354		
McDonnell Douglas MD-82		D-ALLF	49602/1435	**McDonnell Douglas MD-87**	
D-ALLS	49379/1205	D-ALLK	49769/1559	D-ALLG	49670/1453
D-ALLT	49440/1304	D-ALLL	49854/1601	D-ALLH	49671/1463
		D-ALLM	49856/1675	D-ALLI	49767/1587
		D-ALLN	49857/1687	D-ALLJ	49768/1595
		D-ALLO	53012/1736		

Aeromexico (AM/AMX)

History: Emerged in present privatised form after April 1988 bankruptcy of state-owned airline, originally founded on 15 September 1934 as Aeronaves de Mexico. Developed small local network until fleet upgraded to **Boeing 247D**, first service on 30 September 1941, and **Douglas C-39**, following acquisition of 40 per cent stake by Pan American Airways on 12 September 1940. First **DC-3** entered service in September 1946, supplemented by **DC-4** from November 1949. Acquired local operators LAMSA on 22 July 1952 and Aerovias Reforma on 16 October 1953. **Convair 340** bought to replace DC-3, and order placed on 31 May 1957 for two **Bristol Britannia 102**s, used to inaugurate first service to New York on 8 December 1957. Expansion into US previously frustrated by Pan American, whose holding finally acquired by Mexican government on 28 July 1959. Six **DC-6**s purchased from SAS and first **DC-8-30** jet delivered on 15 November 1960. Take-over of Aerovias Guest in August 1962 added new routes throughout Americas, together with service

Aeromexico operates a sizeable fleet of Mc Donnell Douglas DC-9s and MD-80s, including 'glass cockpit'-equipped MD-88s.

to Madrid, later extended to Paris. Marketing name changed to Aeromexico on 28 January 1972. Introduced two new aircraft, **DC-9-32** on 1 March and **DC-10-30** on 1 May 1974. Deteriorating national economy led to collapse of airline in April 1988. Privatised in September 1988 with Prevoisin Group becoming majority shareholder with 70 per cent. Acquired 55 per cent stake in Mexicana in 1993 and, together with Peruvian interests, a 70 per cent holding in Aero Peru.

Aeromexico today: Vast domestic network to 40 cities, together with scheduled services to USA and across Atlantic to Europe. International destinations are Atlanta, Dallas/Ft Worth, Houston, Madrid, Miami, Los Angeles, New Orleans, New York, Orlando, Paris, Phoenix, San Diego and Tucson. Marketing, code-share or block-space agreements with AeroPeru, Air France, Aeromar, America West, Austrian Airlines, British Airways, Delta Air Lines, Japan Airlines and Mexicana.

Annual revenue: $685 million

Passengers: 8.3 million
Cargo: 33,500 tonnes
Employees: 7,200
Major shareholders: Banco Mexicana (16 per cent), Banco Bancomer (14 per cent), Prevoisin Group (nine per cent), Banca Serfin/CINTRA (six per cent)

Associate carriers: *Aeromexpress* (QO), a wholly-owned subsidiary, provides scheduled cargo services with fleet of two **Boeing 727-200**s. Founded on 13 January 1994 and began flying on 9 June.

Aeromexico fleet

Boeing 757-200	c/n
N801AM	25624/541
N802AM	26270/558
N803AM	26268/590
N804AM	26271/592
N805AM	26272/594
N806AM	26273/597

Boeing 767-300ER	c/n
XA-RKI	26200/450
XA-RKJ	26204/464

Douglas DC-9-30	c/n
XA-AMA	48125/947
XA-AMB	48126/951
XA-AMC	48127/961
XA-AMD	48128/964
XA-AME	48129/968
XA-AMF	48130/976
XA-DEI	47650/771
XA-DEJ	47594/717
XA-DEK	47602/718
XA-DEL	47607/721
XA-DEM	47609/723

	c/n
XA-JEB	47394/458
XA-JEC	47106/235
XA-SDF	47006/99
N1003P	48150/1014
N1003U	48151/1017
N935ML	47549/639
N936ML	47501/571

Douglas DC-10-15	c/n
N10038	48275/358
N10039	48276/362

McDonnell Douglas MD-82	c/n
XA-AMP	49189/1173
XA-AMQ	49190/1180
XA-SFK	48068/1031
XA-SFL	48069/1032
XA-SFM	49149/1086
EI-BTX	49660/1445
EI-BTY	49667/1466
N10033	48083/1043
N1003X	48067/1028
N501AM	49188/1172

McDonnell Douglas MD-83	c/n
N831LF	53050/1704
N861LF	49826/1578
N881LF	53051/1718

McDonnell Douglas MD-87	c/n
XA-SFO	49673/1508
N803ML	49726/1610

McDonnell Douglas MD-88	c/n
XA-AMS	49926/1715
XA-AMT	49927/1716
XA-AMU	49928/1732
XA-AMV	49929/1741
N158PL	49761/1623
N160PL	49763/1626
N161PL	49764/1632
N162PL	49765/1645
N168PL	53174/1854
N169PL	53175/1868

Air 2000 (DP/AMM)

London-Gatwick Airport
Crawley, West Sussex, UK

History: Started charter operations on 11 April 1987 from Manchester with two **757-200**s. Then owned 76 per cent by Owners Abroad Group, but also operated on behalf of 40 other UK tour operators. Two more 757s acquired in 1988 and a **737-300** in 1989. Acquired four leased **A320-200**s for 1992 summer season. Scheduled passenger service from London-Gatwick to Paphos in Cyprus added in October 1993, supplemented with a similar connection from Birmingham.

Air 2000 today: Third-largest holiday charter airline in United Kingdom, serving all main European and North African resorts around Mediterranean and Canary Islands. Long-haul charter flights across Atlantic to Mexico and Caribbean, and to Sri Lanka and Thailand in Far East. Regular operations from 10 UK airports. Scheduled leisure routes to Paphos and Larnaca from London-Gatwick and Birmigham. During northern winter season sub-leases aircraft to Canada 3000.

Air 2000 is one of several UK charter airlines that adopted the Airbus A320 in recent years. Air 2000 opted for V2500-powered A320s and now has a fleet of four operating alongside its longer-ranged Boeing 757s.

Annual turnover: $430 million
Passengers: 4.2 million
Employees: 1,100
Ownership: Wholly-owned by First Choice Holidays

Associate carrier: *Canada 3000 Airlines* (2T), operating three **A320-200**s and five **Boeing 757-200**s on holiday charters for the group's Canadian tour operator Signature Vacations.

Air 2000 fleet

Airbus A320-200			
G-OOAA	291	G-OOOG	24292/219
G-OOAB	292	G-OOOI	4289/209
G-OOAC	327	G-OOOJ	24290/212
G-OOAD	336	G-OOOM	22612/114
		G-OOOS	24397/221
Boeing 757-200		G-OOOT	24793/292
G-OOOA	23767/127	G-OOOU	25240/388
G-OOOB	23822/130	G-OOOV	22211/74
G-OOOC	24017/162	G-OOOW	22611/75
G-OOOD	24235/180	G-OOOX	26158/526

7

Air Afrique (RK/RKA)

History: Established on 28 March 1961 as Air Afrique-Société Aérienne Africaine Multinationale. Eleven former French colonies each contributed six per cent of capital, and Paris-based Société pour le Developpement du Transport Aérien en Afrique (SODETRAF) remaining 34 per cent. Started operations on local routes with leased **DC-4** and **DC-6** aircraft on 1 August 1961. Longhaul route to Paris opened on 16 October 1961 with **L.1649A Starliner**. Jet services added with Air France **Boeing 707-320**, then by own **Douglas DC-8-33** in 1963. Route from Douala (Cameroon) to New York opened on 16 May by Pan American. Two **Caravelle 11R**s delivered on 18 September 1967, and new **DC-8-63CF** entered service on long-haul routes in 1970. Togo joined consortium in 1968, but Cameroon opted out in 1971. **DC-10-30** delivered in February 1973, with second added in August 1979, supplemented from May 1981 by **Airbus A300B4-200**. Constant financial struggle since early 1970s brought airline to brink of collapse on number of occasions,

Air Afrique has weathered severe financial storms to remain as the prime carrier to 11 African nations.

but radical restructuring and injection of capital with help of France in early 1994 has helped to stabilise situation. Embarked on fleet modernisation in 1990, acquiring first **A310-300**, with initial delivery in April 1991, and more recently two **A300-600R**s, delivered in 1995. Mali joined consortium in 1992 and Guinea-Bissau membership accepted, though not yet implemented.

Air Afrique today: Multinational flag-carrier of 11 states, providing scheduled passenger and cargo services, connecting capital cities of member states with each other and with long-haul destinations, centred principally on France. Cities served are Abidjan, Bamako, Bangui, Bissau, Bordeaux, Brazzaville, Conakry, Cotonou, Dakar, Douala, Jeddah, Johannesburg, Lagos, Libreville, Lisbon, Lomé, Lyon, Marseille, N'Djamena, New York-JFK, Niamey, Nouakchott, Ouagadougou, Paris, Pointe Noire and Rome.
Code-share and joint-service

agreements on specific routes with TAP, SAA and Swissair. Management contract and major co-operation in various activities with Air France. Cargo co-operation with DHL, which acquired 3.2 per cent equity stake in 1995.

Annual revenue: $500 million
Passengers: 0.85 million
Cargo: 45,500 tonnes
Employees: 4,400
Ownership: shared between Benin, Burkina Faso, Central African Republic, Chad, Congo, Ivory Coast, Mali, Mauritania, Niger, Senegal and Togo – totalling 70.4 per cent; Group Air France 12.6 per cent; Caisse Française de Developpement 9.1 per cent; West African Development Bank 4.7 per cent; DHL 3.2 percent

Associate carriers: Has 17 per cent stake in *Air Burkina* (VH), which flies a domestic network in Burkina Faso with one **EMB-110P2** and one **F28-4000**, and also feeds into Abidjan from Ouagadougou, Bobo Dioulasso, and Lomé in Togo.
Air Mali (L9), 46 per cent owned, flies one **EMB-110** and **Antonov An-24V** within Mali.
Air Mauritanie (MR), 20 per cent owned, uses one **F28-4000** on domestic services and regional flights.

Air Afrique fleet

Airbus A300B4-200			
TU-TAO	137	TU-TAD	651
TU-TAS	243	TU-TAE	652
TU-TAT	282	TU-TAF	671
		TU-TAG	
Airbus A300-600R		TU-TAR	435
TU-TAH	744		
TU-TAI	749	**Douglas DC-10-30**	
		TU-TAN	
Airbus A310-300		46997/288	
TU-TAC	571		

Air Algérie (AH/DAH)

History: Founded in 1946 as non-scheduled operator under title of Compagnie Générale de Transports Aériens (CGTA). Consolidated following merger with Compagnie Air Transport (CAT) on 23 May 1953 when present title adopted. First of four **DC-4**s delivered in March

1954 and two **Lockheed L.749A Constellation**s put on Paris route in 1956. Network established into Saharan communities in October 1954 with first flight between Algiers, Ghardaia and El Goléa. Acquired two **Noratlas** freighters in 1957. Major step forward taken on 13 March 1958

when ordered three **Caravelle III**s, which went into service on 12 January 1960 on links to French cities. After independence from France in 1962, Algerian government took majority 51 per cent holding in February 1963. Airline fully nationalised in 1972. In 1968, piston-engined aircraft

Boeing 727s and early-model 737s are still an important part of Air Algérie's current fleet.

replaced by four **Convair 640**s. **Boeing 727-200** arrived in April 1971, followed by the first **737-200** in December. Acquired small number of **Nord 262**s with integration of local carrier Société de Travail Aérien on 1 May 1972, and ordered three **F27-400**s for cargo flights.

Long-haul route established to Havana, after leasing **Airbus A300B4-200** from Lufthansa in 1981. First of **L.100-30 Hercules** delivered in March 1981.

New **A310-200** put onto main routes to France from August 1988. Suffered from growing political unrest, culminating in the cessation of all air services between Algeria and France in early 1995, when France accused Algerians of being behind terrorist acts.

Air Algérie today: State-owned flag-carrier operating scheduled passenger and cargo services to destinations in North and West Africa, Europe and Middle East. Cities served are Amman, Amsterdam, Athens, Bamako, Barcelona, Berlin, Beirut, Brussels, Cairo, Casablanca, Dakar, Damascus, Frankfurt, Geneva, Istanbul, Lille, Lyon, London, Madrid, Marseille, Moscow, Niamey, Nice, Nouakchott, Ouagadougou, Paris, Prague, Rome, Sharjah, Toulouse and Tunis. Extensive domestic network, together with aerial work and government flights.

Agreements on joint purchasing of services with Royal Air Maroc and Tunis Air.

Annual revenue: $330 million
Passengers: 3.4 million
Employees: 9,000

Air Algérie fleet

Airbus A310-200	c/n	7T-VEX	22765/1801	7T-VES	21287/486
7T-VJC	291				
7T-VJD	293	**Boeing 737-200 Adv**	**c/n**	**Boeing 767-300**	**c/n**
7T-VJF	295	7T-VEF	20759/332	7T-VJG	24766/310
7T-VJF	306	7T-VEG	20884/361	7T-VJH	24767/323
		7T-VEJ	21063/407	7T-VJI	24768/332
Boeing 727-200	**c/n**	7T-VEK	21064/409		
7T-VEA	20472/850	7T-VEL	21065/416	**Fokker F27-400M**	**c/n**
7T-VEB	20473/855	7T-VEN	21211/454	7T-VRJ	10547
		7T-VEO	21212/459	7T-VRK	10553
Boeing 727-200 Adv	**c/n**	7T-VEQ	21285/473	7T-VRL	10495
7T-VEH	20955/1075	7T-VER	21286/482	7T-VRQ	10526
7T-VEI	25053/1111	7T-VEY	22766/853	7T-VRR	10555
7T-VEM	21210/1204	7T-VEZ	22700/885	7T-VRU	10494
7T-VEP	21284/1233	7T-VJA	22800/897	7T-VRV	10543
7T-VET	22372/1662	7T-VJB	22801/900		
7T-VEU	22373/1664			**Lockheed L.100-30**	**c/n**
7T-VEV	22374/1711	**Boeing 737-200C Adv**	**c/n**	7T-VHG	4880
7T-VEW	22375/1723	7T-VED	20650/311	7T-VHL	4886

Airborne Express (GB/ABX)

Airborne Air Park
Wilmington, Ohio, USA

History: Formed on 17 April 1980 from merger of Midwest Air Charter and airline division of Seattle-based freight forwarder Airborne Freight Corp. Developed extensive overnight express parcels and courier services from main hub at Wilmington, Ohio, to nearly 100 cities across USA. Fleet included over 50 aircraft, headed by **DC-9-30**, **Sud-Aviation Caravelle** and **NAMC YS-11A**. Most piston and turboprop equipment phased out as more DC-9-30s and **DC-9-41**s added. Higher-capacity aircraft introduced from August 1985, building up to a large fleet of **DC-8-61/-62/-63** models by 1996.

Airborne Express today: Third-ranked US domestic courier operation after Federal Express and United Parcel Service. Operations centred on main hub at own airport in Wilmington, with regional distribution hubs main-

Airborne Express is an express package and overnight delivery airline that exclusively serves the US domestic market with a large fleet of DC-8 and DC-9 freighters.

Airborne Express

tained at Allentown PA, Providence RI, Roanoke VA, Atlanta GA, Orlando FL, Memphis TN, Waco TX, South Bend IN, Columbia MO and Fresno CA.

Fleet development: Ten more **DC-9-41**s destined for cargo conversion being acquired from SAS and JAS. Also acquiring 12 **767-200** for freighter conversion, plus possible 10-15 more, at a total cost of $600 million. First two to be delivered in 1997, followed by four each in 1998 and 1999, and two in 2000. Additional aircraft would join fleet between 2000 and 2004.

Annual revenue: $1,700 million
Shipments: 200 million
Employees: 6,350
Wholly-owned by Airborne Freight Corporation through ABX Air

Airborne Express fleet

Douglas DC-8-61	c/n								
N841AX	45908/296	N820AX	46155/529	N906AX	47072/270	N985AX	47522/606	N967AX	47509/643
N842AX	46015/405	N821AX	46116/518	N907AX	47203/401	N986AX	47543/654	N968AX	47499/568
N843AX	46017/418	N822AX	46079/476	N908AX	47008/98	N987AX	47364/484	N969AX	47464/575
N844AX	45848/285	N823AX	46122/506	N909AX	47148/246	N988AX	47084/179	N970AX	47494/601
N845AX	46157/541	N824AX	46141/533	N923AX	47165/260	N989AX	47314/279	N971AX	47497/604
N846AX	46158/543	N825AX	46115/530	N924AX	47403/507			N973AX	47511/677
N847AX	46031/435	N826AX	46061/480	N928AX	47392/447	**Douglas DC-9-30F**	c/n	N975AX	47512/678
N848AX	46032/436	**Douglas DC-8-63F**	c/n	N929AX	45874/351	N904AX	47040/172	N979AX	47492/559
N849AX	45891/305	N811AX	46113/521	N936AX	47269/371	N905AX	47147/208	N990AX	47493/562
N850AX	45894/297	N812AX	46126/524	N938AX	47009/152	N930AX	47363/445		
N851AX	45940/314	N814AX	46041/439	N939AX	47201/459	N931AX	47384/543	**NAMC YS-11A**	c/n
N852AX	46016/409	N815AX	46097/503	N941AX	47419/602	N932AX	47465/584	N910AX	2050
N853AX	46037/419	N816AX	46093/496	N942AX	47552/640	N933AX	47291/343	N911AX	2051
		N817AX	45928/334	N943AX	47528/617	N934AX	47462/564	N912AX	2952
Douglas DC-8-62	c/n	N819AX	45927/327	N944AX	47550/623	N935AX	47413/521	N913AX	2053
N801AX	46077/470			N945AX	47551/634			N914AX	2056
N802AX	46134/513	**Douglas DC-9-15**	c/n	N946AX	47003/86	**Douglas DC-9-40**	c/n	N915AX	2062
N803AX	45917/332	N925AX	45728/14	N947AX	47004/81	N951AX	47616/759	N917AX	2077
N804AX	45987/366	N927AX	45717/20	N948AX	47065/269	N952AX	47615/751	N919AX	2113
N805AX	45906/300			N949AX	47325/515	N953AX	47608/732	N920AX	2114
N808AX	45954/362	**Douglas DC-9-30**	c/n	N973ML	47074/376	N954AX	47612/736	N921AX	2117
		N900AX	47380/514	N980AX	47176/315	N955AX	47619/768	N922AX	2120
Douglas DC-8-63	c/n	N901AX	47381/519	N981AX	47273/347	N956AX	47620/777		
N813AX	46136/509	N902AX	47426/572	N982AX	47317/385	N957AX	47759/871		
N818AX	46075/484	N903AX	47427/573	N983AX	47257/386	N965AX	47498/566		
				N984AX	47258/387	N966AX	47510/645		

Air Canada (AC/ACA)

Montreal International Airport
Mirabel, Quebec, Canada

History: Established under title of Trans-Canada Airlines (TCA) on 10 April 1937. Services between Vancouver and Seattle begun in 1937 with **Lockheed L.10 Electras** and **L.14 Super Electras**, with passenger flights across Canada starting in April 1939. Outbreak of war limited expansion, but TCA operated Canadian government Trans-Atlantic Air Service with **Avro** Lancastrians between 1943 and 1945 to support Canadian troops in Europe. War-surplus **Douglas DC-3** added to fleet, supplemented in 1947 by first of 23 **Canadair DC-4M North Stars**, purposely built for intra-Canadian routes. Five **Lockheed Super Constellations** acquired in 1953 for growing North Atlantic network. Two years later TCA became first airline in North America to order the **Vickers Viscount**. **Vickers Vanguard** brought into service on 1 February 1961. First jet, **DC-8-41**, introduced on transcontinental routes on 2 April 1960, followed on 1 June to London. Stretched **DC-8-61** and **DC-8-63** acquired during next decade. On 1 January 1965 changed name to Air Canada to more accurately reflect expanded operations. First North American airline to fly to Soviet Union in 1966, and in same year introduced first of large fleet of Douglas **DC-9**s. Added **Boeing 747-100** in 1971, first ordered on 19 February 1968, but fuel crisis following year ended plans to order supersonic **Concorde**. Put first of 10 **Lockheed L.1011 TriStar**s on Toronto-Vancouver route on 15 March 1973. All-jet

Air Canada uses the Boeing 767-200 and -300 throughout its route network on domestic, transcontinental and transatlantic services.

During 1996, an Air Canada A320 adopted this special scheme in support of the newly-established **Toronto Raptors** *basketball team.*

operator in 1974 after retirement of Viscount. Jet fleet further modernised and enlarged with contract for **Boeing 767-200**, announced on 7 November 1979, with deliveries starting in October 1983. Large fleet of 34 **Airbus A320**s delivered between January 1990 and June 1993. Under Air Canada Act of 1977, airline became a direct subsidiary of government, but has been fully privatised since July 1989. Proposals for Air Canada and Canadian Airlines International to merge were rejected by latter, both subsequently creating partnerships with US airlines. Order placed in May 1994 for 25 **A319**s, plus 10 options, as major replacement programme for DC-9 fleet. Accelerating expansion into USA and/or international points following February 1995 Open Skies agreement between Canada and US, and a new international air transport policy.

Air Canada today: Canada's largest airline, providing, together with its regional airline partners, scheduled and charter services for passengers and cargo to 120 destinations from hubs at Calgary, Halifax, Montreal, Toronto and Vancouver. In addition to serving 90 cities in North America, also flies to Antigua, Bermuda, Bridgetown (Barbados), Brussels, Delhi, Düsseldorf, Fort-de-France (Martinique), Frankfurt, Glasgow, Hong Kong, Kingston, London, Manchester, Montego Bay, Nassau (Bahamas), Osaka, Paris, Pointe-a-Pitre (Guadeloupe), Port-au-Prince (Haiti), Port of Spain (Trinidad), Seoul, St Lucia, Tel Aviv and Zürich. Major strategic alliances with United Airlines, Lufthansa (from 1 June 1996), Continental Airlines and Korean Air, together with joint marketing and code-share agreements with

Air Jamaica, All Nippon Airways, British Midland, Cathay Pacific Airways, Czech Airlines, Finnair, Iberia, LOT, Royal Jordanian and Swissair. Has 19.6 per cent stake in Continental Airlines.

Annual revenue: $3,300 million
Passengers: 11.4 million
Cargo: 315,500 tonnes
Employees: 19,500

Fleet development: Airbus A340-300 deliveries due to be completed by 1997, with remaining **Canadair Regional Jets** to arrive during 1996. First delivery of 35 **A319**s on order to take place in December 1996 and continue until 1998. Two **767-300**s scheduled for 1997.

Associate carriers: Five wholly-owned regional airlines provide feeder services under collective *Air Canada Connector* umbrella. Includes *Air Alliance* (3J), which started operations

on 27 March 1988 and feeds Montreal and Quebec with 11 **DHC-8-100**s.

Air Ontario (GX), flying out of Toronto with 17 **DHC-8-100**s and six **DHC-8-300**

Air BC (ZX), operating from Calgary and Vancouver with six **BAe 146-200**s, 12 **DHC-8-100**s and six **DHC-8-300**s.

Air Nova (QK), based at Halifax in Nova Scotia, began flying in July 1986, became first Connector partner. Serves 21 destinations in eastern Canada and northeastern USA with five **BAe 146-200A** and 13 **DHC-8-100**.

NWT Air (NV) operates a network of passenger and cargo services centred on Yellowknife in Northwest Territories, using three **737-200C**s and a single **L.100-20 Hercules**.

Air Nova is an Air Canada Connector carrier which operates a mix of DHC-8s and BAe-146s.

Airbus A320-200	c/n							Airbus A340-300	c/n
C-FDQQ	059	C-FFWI		149	C-FKCR	290	C-FMSY	384	
C-FDQV	068	C-FFWJ		150	C-FKOJ	330	C-FNNA	426 C-FTNP	093
C-FDRH	073	C-FFWM		154	C-FKPO	311	C-FPDN	341 C-FTNQ	088
C-FDRK	084	C-FFWN		159	C-FKPS	310	C-FTJO	183	
C-FDRP	122	C-FGYL		254	C-FKPT	324	C-FTJP	233 **Boeing 747-100**	c/n
C-FDSN	126	C-FGYS		255	C-FMJK	342	C-FTJQ	242 C-FTOC	20015/144
C-FDST	127	C-FKAJ		333	C-FMST	350	C-FTJR	248 C-FTOD	20767/214
C-FDSU	141	C-FKCK		265	C-FMSV	359	C-FTJS	253 C-FTOE	20881/236
		C-FKCO		277	C-FMSX	378			

Air Canada

Boeing 747-200B *c/n*

Reg	c/n
C-GAGA	20977/250
C-GAGB	21627/355
C-GAGC	21354/314

Boeing 747-400 *c/n*

Reg	c/n
C-GAGL	24998/840
C-GAGM	25074/862
C-GAGN	25075/868

Boeing 767-200 *c/n*

Reg	c/n	Reg	c/n
C-FBEF	24323/250	C-GAUP	22521/66
C-FBEG	24324/252	C-GAUS	22522/75
C-FBEM	24325/254	C-GAUU	22523/87
C-FUCL	22681/18	C-GAUW	22524/88
C-FUCN	22682/60	C-GAUY	22525/91
C-GAUB	22517/16	C-GAVA	22526/92
C-GAUE	22518/22	C-GAVC	22527/102
C-GAUH	22519/40	C-GAVF	22528/105
C-GAUN	22520/47	C-GDSP	24142/229
		C-GDSS	24143/233
		C-GDSU	24144/234
		C-GDSY	24145/236
		C-GPWA	22683/36
		C-GPWB	22684/52

Boeing 767-300 *c/n*

Reg	c/n
C-FMWP	25583/508
C-FMWQ	25584/596
C-FMWU	25585/597
C-FMWV	25586/599

Canadair Regional Jet 100ER *c/n*

Reg	c/n
C-FRIA	7045
C-FRIB	7047
C-FRID	7049
C-FRII	7051
C-FSJF	7054
C-FSJJ	7058
C-FSJU	7060
C-FSKE	7065
C-FSKI	7068
C-FSKM	7071
C-FVKM	7074
C-FVMD	7082
C-FVKR	7083
C-FWJB	7087
C-FWJF	7095
C-FWJI	7096
C-FWJS	7097
C-FWJT	7098

Douglas DC-9-30 *c/n*

Reg	c/n	Reg	c/n
C-FTLH	45845/91	C-FTMH	47341/404
C-FTLJ	47019/113	C-FTMI	47342/418
C-FTLL	47021/133	C-FTMJ	47348/419
C-FTLM	47022/144	C-FTMK	47349/420
C-FTLO	47024/159	C-FTML	47350/431
C-FTLQ	47069/175	C-FTMM	47611/726
C-FTLR	47070/176	C-FTMO	47353/471
C-FTLS	47071/188	C-FTMP	47354/483
C-FTLT	47195/278	C-FTMQ	47422/576
C-FTLW	47198/302	C-FTMT	47546/655
C-FTLX	47199/321	C-FTMU	47554/658
C-FTLZ	47265/339	C-FTMV	47557/661
C-FTMA	47266/352	C-FTMW	47560/664
C-FTMB	47289/353	C-FTMX	47485/666
C-FTMC	47290/367	C-FTMY	47592/712
C-FTMD	47292/386	C-FTMZ	47598/719
C-FTME	47293/384		
C-FTMF	47294/402		
C-FTMG	47340/403		

Air China (CA/CCA)

Beijing Capital Airport
Beijing, China

Air China inherited the mantle of the People's Republic's primary international carrier from CAAC.

block-space arrangement with Finnair, and revenue sharing on specific routes with Asiana Airlines, Korean Air and Austrian Airlines.

Annual revenue: *$985 million*
Passengers: *5.3 million*
Cargo: *120,000 tonnes*
Employees: *14,000*

History: Established on 1 July 1988 following major structural reforms, which separated airline functions from administrative and regulatory functions of Civil Aviation Administration of China (CAAC). Tasked with taking over all CAAC international routes and domestic trunk services previously operated by Beijing Regional Bureau. Acquired status of independent trade group on 10 December 1993.

Air China today: Government-owned flag-carrier operating scheduled passenger and cargo services to 30 cities in 23 countries in all continents, except South America. International destinations are Addis Ababa, Ankara, Bangkok, Belgrade, Berlin, Bucharest, Cairo, Copenhagen, Dubai, Fukuoka, Hong Kong, Istanbul, Jakarta, Karachi, Kuwait, London, Melbourne, Milan, Moscow, New York, Osaka, Paris, Rome, San Francisco, Sendai, Seoul, Sharjah, Singapore, Stockholm, Sydney, Tel Aviv, Tokyo, Ulan Bator, Vancouver, Vienna, Yangon and Zürich. Apart from Beijing, or Chinese cities linked into international network, are Dalian, Shanghai, Guangzhou, Kunming and Xiamen. Extensive domestic route system also scheduled. Co-operation on

Fleet development: Three **Airbus A340-300s** ordered on 17 February 1996 for delivery starting in second half of 1997. Will replace four **Boeing 747SPs**. Order expected to be placed for 10 **Boeing 777s** and five **Boeing 747-400s**.

Air China fleet

Antonov An-12 *c/n*

Reg	c/n
B-3151	6344402
B-3152	8345303

Boeing 737-300 *c/n*

Reg	c/n
B-2531	233302/1224
B-2532	23303/1237
B-2535	25078/2002
B-2536	25079/2016
B-2580	25080/2254
B-2581	25081/2263
B-2584	25891/2385
B-2585	27045/2384
B-2587	25892/2396
B-2588	25893/2489
B-2598	27128/2493
B-2905	25506/2360
B-2906	25507/2373
B-2907	25508/2414
B-2947	25511/2599
B-2948	27361/2631
B-2949	27372/2650
B-2953	27523/2710
B-2954	27518/2768

Boeing 747SP *c/n*

Reg	c/n
B-2438	21933/455
B-2442	21932/433
B-2452	21934/467
B-2454	22302/473

Boeing 747-200B *c/*

Reg	c/n
B-2446	23071/591
B-2448	23461/628
B-2450	23746/670

Boeing 747-200F *c/*

Reg	c/n
B-2462	24960/814

Boeing 747-400 *c/n*

Reg	c/n
B-2443	25881/957
B-2445	25882/1021
B-2447	25883/1054
B-2456	24346/743
B-2458	24347/775
B-2460	24348/792
B-2464	25879/904
B-2466	25880/926

Boeing 767-200(ER)

Reg	c/n
B-2551	23307/126
B-2552	23308/127
B-2553	23744/155
B-2554	23745/156
B-2555	24007/204
B-2556	24157/253

Boeing 767-300 *c/n*

Reg	c/n
B-2557	25875/429
B-2558	25876/478
B-2559	25877/530
B-2560	25878/569

British Aerospace 146-100 *c/n*

Reg	c/n
B-2707	E1076
B-2708	E1081
B-2709	E1083
B-2710	E1085

Xian Y7 *c/n*

Reg	c/n
B-3461	04703
B-3462	04704
B-3463	04705

Xian Y7-100 *c/n*

Reg	c/n
B-3447	09702
B-3450	08710
B-3492	08703

Air France (AF/AFR)

History: Air France was founded on 30 August 1933 when Société Centrale pour l'Exploitation de Lignes Aériennes purchased assets of Compagnie Générale Aéropostale, which had achieved recognition for pioneering efforts across South Atlantic. Experimental flights across North Atlantic halted by advent of Word War II and salvaged fleet flown to North and West Africa to support Allied cause from bases at Algiers, Casablanca and Dakar. New company, Société Nationale Air France, set up on 1 January 1946 following nationalisation of French civil aviation after end of war. Network quickly re-established and services launched to Buenos Aires in June 1946 and to New York on 1 July. New aircraft included **DC-3, DC-4** and **S.E.161 Languedoc**, supplemented by **L.749A Constellation** from 1948 and later **L.1049G Super Constellation, L.1649A Starliner**, and **Breguet Deux Ponts**. Montreal added to network on 2 October 1950 and New York service extended to Mexico on 27 April 1952. First turboprop service flown in 1953, introducing **Vickers Viscount** on Paris-London route. First jet service followed with **de Havilland Comet 1A** between Paris, Rome and Beirut on 26 August 1953. **Sud-Aviation Caravelle** entered service on 6 May 1959, followed on 31 January 1960 by **Boeing 707**. Next 20 years marked by appearance of **Boeing 727** on 15 April 1968, **Boeing 747** on 3 June 1970, **Airbus A300** on 23 May 1974, and **Concorde** supersonic airliner on 21 January 1976. Caracas, Washington, New York and Mexico City added to initial supersonic route from Paris to Rio de Janeiro via Dakar, but only New York now served. Older jets taken out of service at time of delivery of first of 12 **Boeing 737-200**s on 15 December 1982. Large fleet of Airbus aircraft delivered over next 10 years, including **A310-300, A320-200** and **A340-200/-300**. On 12 January 1990, operations of all government-owned airlines, Air France, Air Inter, Air Charter and UTA merged into Air France Group. Air Charter and Air Inter continued operating in own names, but UTA was fully merged. European services and operations of domestic subsidiary Air Inter integrated into new airline, named **Air France Europe**.

Air France today: Government-owned flag-carrier serving 153 cities throughout world, with particularly strong presence in Europe and Africa, and French Overseas Departments. Strategic alliances with many airlines and minority equity stakes in Aéropostale (20 per cent), Air Afrique (12.6 per cent), Air Austral (34 per cent), Air Comores (6.3 per cent), Air Gabon (11.2 per cent), Air Madagascar (3.5 per cent), Air Mauritius (9.58 per cent), Air Tahiti (7.5 per cent), Air Tchad (33.7 per cent), Austrian Airlines (1.5 per cent), Cameroon Airlines (3.6 per cent), Middle East Airlines (28.5 per cent), Royal Air Maroc (4.0 per cent) and Tunis Air (5.6 per cent).

Group annual revenue: $10,150 million.
Passengers: 15.6 million.
Cargo: 650,000 tonnes.
Employees: 39,000

Together with Lufthansa, Air France was the launch customer for the Airbus A340. It was the first operator of the A340-300.

Fleet development: Renegotiated contract with Boeing, replacing orders for three **767-300ER**s, three **737-500**s and one **747-400F** with new order for seven 767-300ERs and eight 737-500s, for delivery between 1999 and 2001. Other types may be substituted as required. Eight 747-400s still to be delivered.

Associate carriers: Charter subsidiary **Air Charter** (SF), owned by Groupe Air France holding company, utilises aircraft from parent company, some with its own titles on European holiday charters from Paris-Orly. Aircraft used include **Airbus A300** and **A320**, and **Boeing 737-200** and **727-200** models.

L'Aéropostale, operated jointly with French post office, provides mail flights with fleet of 18 **737-200** and two **727-200**. Other types leased as required.

Air Inter has been absorbed and reorganised to operate under the Air France Europe banner.

13

Air France

Air France fleet

Aérospatiale/BAC Concorde 101	c/n
F-BTSC	203
F-BTSD	213
F-BVFA	205
F-BVFB	207
F-BVFC	209
F-BVFF	215

Airbus A300B2-100	c/n
F-BVGA	005
F-BVGB	006
F-BVGC	007
F-GBEC	104

Airbus A300B4-200	c/n
F-BVGG	019
F-BVGH	023
F-BVGI	045
F-BVGJ	047
F-BVGL	074
F-BVGM	078
F-BVGN	100
F-BVGO	129
F-BVGT	183

Airbus A310-200	c/n
F-GEMA	316
F-GEMB	326
F-GEMC	335
F-GEMD	355
F-GEME	369
F-GEMG	454

Air France Cargo

Asie is the Far Eastern department of the airline's sizeable freighter operation.

Airbus A310-300	c/n
F-GEMN	502
F-GEMO	504
F-GEMP	550
F-GEMQ	551

Airbus A320-100	c/n
F-GFKA	005
F-GFKB	007
F-GFKD	014
F-GFKE	019
F-GFKF	020
F-GFKG	021
F-GFKQ	002

Airbus A320-200	c/n
F-GFKH	061
F-GFKI	062
F-GFKJ	063
F-GFKK	100
F-GFKL	101
F-GFKM	102
F-GFKN	128
F-GFKO	129
F-GFKP	133
F-GFKR	186
F-GFKS	187
F-GFKT	188

F-GFKV	227
F-GFKX	228
F-GFKY	285
F-GFKZ	286
F-GKXA	287
F-GLGE	348
F-GLGG	203
F-GLGH	220
F-GLGI	221
F-GLGJ	222
F-GLGM	131
F-GLGN	132

Airbus A340-200	c/n
F-GLZD	031
F-GLZE	038
F-GLZF	043
F-GNIB	014
F-GNIC	022

Airbus A340-300	c/n
F-GLZA	005
F-GLZB	007
F-GLZC	029
F-GLZG	049
F-GLZH	078

Boeing 737-200 Adv	c/n
F-GBYA	23000/930
F-GBYB	23001/936
F-GBYC	23002/937
F-GBYD	23003/939
F-GBYE	23004/941
F-GBYF	23005/943
F-GBYG	23006/944
F-GBYH	23007/948
F-GBYI	23008/952
F-GBYJ	23009/958
F-GBYK	23010/959
F-GBYL	23011/971
F-GBYM	23349/1135
F-GBYN	23503/1256
F-GBYO	23504/1267
F-GBYP	23792/1397
F-GBYQ	23793/1426
F-GFLV	22597/773
F-GFLX	22598/792

Boeing 737-300	c/n
F-GFUA	23635/1436
F-GFUD	24027/1597
F-GFUJ	25118/2065
F-GHVM	24026/1595
F-GHVN	25138/2153
F-GHVO	24025/1556

Boeing 737-500	c/n
F-GGML	24785/1882
F-GHOL	24825/1894
F-GHUL	24826/2041
F-GHXM	24788/1921
F-GINL	24827/2243
F-GJNA	25226/2099
F-GJNB	25227/2108
F-GJNC	25228/2170
F-GJND	25229/2180
F-GJNE	25230/2191
F-GJNF	25231/2208
F-GJNG	25232/2231
F-GJNH	25233/2251
F-GJNI	25234/2411
F-GJNJ	25235/2428
F-GJNK	25236/2443
F-GJNM	25237/2464
F-GJNN	27304/2572
F-GJNO	27305/2574

Boeing 747-100	c/n
F-BPVB	19750/22
F-BPVF	20376/174
F-BPVG	20377/176
F-BPVH	20378/177
F-BPVJ	20541/200
F-BPVM	20799/227
F-BPVP	20954/252

Boeing 747-200B	c/n
F-BPVS	21326/303
F-BPVT	21429/313
F-BPVU	21537/333
F-BPVX	21731/364
F-BPVY	21745/370
F-BTDG	22514/518
F-BTDH	22515/521
F-GCBA	21982/428

F-GCBB	22272/463
G-GCBD	22428/503
F-GCBF	22794/558
F-GCBH	23611/656
F-GCBI	23676/661
F-GCBJ	24067/698

Boeing 747-200F	c/n
F-BPVR	21255/295
F-BPVV	21576/334
F-BPVZ	21787/398
F-GBOX	21835/388
F-GCBE	22678/535
F-GCBG	22939/569
F-GCBK	24158/714
F-GCBL	24735/772
F-GCBM	24879/822
F-GPAN	21515/337

Boeing 747-300	c/n
F-GETA	23413/632
F-GETB	23480/641

Boeing 747-400	c/n
F-GEXA	24154/741
F-GEXB	24155/864
F-GISA	25238/872
F-GISB	25302/884
F-GISC	25599/899
F-GISD	25628/934
F-GISE	25630/960
F-GITA	24969/836
F-GITB	24990/843
F-GITC	25344/889
F-GITD	25600/901
F-GITE	25601/906
F-GITF	25602/909

Boeing 767-300(ER)	c/n
F-GHGF	24745/355
F-GHGG	24746/378
F-GHGH	25077/385
F-GHGI	27135/493
F-GHGJ	27136/497
F-GHGK	27212/531

Air India (AI/AIC)

Bombay International Airport
Bombay (Mumbai), India

Air India operates the 747-200, -300 and -400 but, with nine in service, the 747-200 predominates.

and eight **Vickers Viking**s for expansion of domestic services, but received three **Lockheed L.749A Constellations**, with which it opened a Bombay-London service, via Cairo and Geneva on 8 June 1948. Route to Nairobi introduced on 21 January 1950. Nationalised on 1 August 1953 and given rights for international flights; domestic routes transferred to Indian Airlines. First **Super Constellation** delivered

History: Formed as Air India International on 8 March 1948 out of Air-India, which had been established on 29 July 1946 when Tata Airlines was reorganised. Air-India acquired **DC-3**s

on 6 June 1954 and put on London route. Network expanded to include Tokyo (1955), Singapore and Hong Kong (1954), Sydney (1956) and Moscow, inaugurated on 15 August 1958. Three **Boeing 707-437**s delivered in early 1960, permitting introduction of Bombay-New York service on 14 May. 'International' wording in airline title discontinued on 8 June 1962 by amendment to Air Corporations Act. Became world's first all-jet airline on 11 June 1962 following sale of nine Super Constellations. **747-200B** introduced on London route on 21 May 1971. Subsidiary Air India Charters formed on 9 September 1971. Network extended to Middle East and Africa, together with further terminals in Europe. Started Airbus services to Dubai on 18 June 1977 using aircraft leased from Indian Airlines. Own **Airbus A300B4-200** delivered in July 1982 for services to Gulf. Fleet renewal programme continued with delivery of eight **A310-300**s between April 1986 and August 1990. Also acquired **Boeing 747-300 Combi**s and ordered four **747-400**s for delivery in 1993/94.

Air India today: Government-owned international flag-carrier responsible for most regional and all long-haul services linking Bombay (renamed Mumbai) and Delhi to points in Europe, North America, and Middle and Far East. Destinations include Abu Dhabi, Amsterdam, Bahrain, Bangkok, Dar-es-Salaam, Dhahran, Doha, Dubai, Durban, Entebbe, Frankfurt, Geneva, Hong Kong, Jakarta, Jeddah, Johannesburg, Kuala Lumpur, Kuwait, London, Manchester, Nairobi, New York (through London), Osaka, Paris, Perth, Riyadh, Rome, Singapore, Tokyo and Toronto. Many international routes are also linked into other main Indian cities, including Bangalore, Calcutta, Madras and Trivandrum.

Annual revenue: $500 million
Passengers: 2.2 million
Employees: 17,700

Fleet development: Temporary fleet shortage overcome by leasing-in **TriStar** aircraft. Requirement for three more **Boeing 747-400**s and considering **Airbus A340** and **Boeing 777** for longer term.

Associate carriers: Minority holding of 8.82 per cent in Air Mauritius and involved in route development between India and Mauritius.

Air India fleet

Airbus A300B4-200	c/n	C-GCIT	455	Boeing 747-300	c/n
VT-EHN	177	C-GCIV	451	VT-EPW	24159/711
VT-EHO	180	V2-LEC	539	VT-EPX	24160/719
VT-EHQ	190	V2-LED	542		
				Boeing 747-400	c/n
Airbus A310-300	c/n	Boeing 747-200B	c/n	VT-ESM	27078/987
VT-EJG	406	VT-EBE	19960/130	VT-ESN	27164/1003
VT-EJH	407	VT-EBN	20459/185	VT-ESO	27165/1009
VT-EJI	413	VT-EDU	21182/277	VT-ESP	27214/1034
VT-EJJ	428	VT-EFJ	21446/318		
VT-EJK	429	VT-EFU	21829/390	Lockheed	
VT-EJL	392	VT-EGA	21993/414	L.1011 TriStar 500	c/n
VT-EQS	538	VT-EGB	21994/431	V2-LEJ	1246
VT-EQT	544	VT-EGC	21995/434	V2-LEK	1248
C-GCII	439	VT-ENQ	21936/401		
C-GCIO	449				

Air Jamaica (JM/AJM)

Norman Manley International Airport
Kingston, Jamaica

History: Founded in 1962 by Jamaican government, British Overseas Airways Corporation (BOAC) and British West Indian Airways (BWIA). Restructured as Air Jamaica (1968), with Air Canada taking 24 per cent minority stake and providing technical assistance. Started service with own equipment (three **DC-9-32**s) on 1 April 1969 from Kingston to New York and Miami. Over next five years added routes to Chicago, Detroit, Nassau, Philadelphia and Toronto, most also served from Montego Bay. Fleet grew to eight, including three DC-9-32s, three **DC-9-51**s, two **DC-8-61**s and one **DC-8-62**. Long-haul service to London-Heathrow inaugurated on 1 April 1974, but suspended in April 1981 and taken over by British Airways, when continuing losses forced cutbacks. Four **Boeing 727-200A**s added late in 1975 and DC-9s phased out. First two **A300B4-200**s delivered

in February 1983, heralding departure of DC-8s. Financial pressures and airline's deteriorating reputation for poor service standards left privatisation only option for government to ensure survival. Major restructuring and modernisation initiated after sale of 70 per cent on 15 November 1994. Prime route to London reactivated on 11 May 1996.

By the end of 1996 Air Jamaica was operating six A310s. The type was instrumental in reopening its transatlantic service to the UK.

Air Jamaica today: Operates over 100 flights a week on scheduled services from capital Kingston and Montego Bay to Atlanta, Baltimore/Washington,

Air Jamaica

Chicago, Ft Lauderdale, New York-JFK, Newark, Miami, Philadelphia, and across Atlantic to London, with Los Angeles, Toronto and San Francisco also to be reactivated.

Annual revenue: $160 million
Passengers: 1.0 million
Employees: 1,200
Shareholding: Jamaican government (25 per cent), chairman 'Butch' Stewart's Appliance Traders Group (35 per cent), Moo-Young family (15 per cent), National Commercial Bank (10 per cent),

Jamaica Hotel and Tourism Association (10 per cent) and employees (five per cent)

Fleet development: Six **A320-200**s to be delivered in late 1996, replacing four 727s.
Associate carrier: *Air Jamaica Express*, in which Air Jamaica Acquisitions Group (AJAG) acquired 55 per cent holding on 13 November 1995. Government retains 20 per cent. Provides domestic services with **Islanders** and **Trislanders**.

Air Jamaica fleet

Airbus A310-300	c/n
N836AB	660
N838AB	676
N839AB	678
N840AB	682
N841AB	686
N842AB	687

Boeing 727-200A	c/n
6Y-JMM	21105/1158
6Y-JMN	21105/1160
6Y-JMO	21107/1172
6Y-JMP	21108/117

AirLanka (UL/ALK)

Katunayake International Airport
Colombo, Sri Lanka

The Airbus A340 began to replace the TriStar in AirLanka service from 1994 onwards, when the first example was delivered.

History: Established in August 1979 as national airline to replace defunct Air Ceylon. Started operations on 1 September 1979 with two **Boeing 707-320B**s and one **737-200**, leased from Singapore Airlines which also provided technical assistance. Bought first two **Lockheed L.1011 TriStars** from All Nippon Airways (ANA) in November 1980, followed by two new **TriStar 500** in August 1982 and a fifth from ANA in March 1983. **737**s also leased from different sources. Route network expanded to 24 cities in 20 countries. Decision made in 1991 to replace its seven TriStars (two more had been leased from British Airways) with five **Airbus A340-300**s to refocus operations on long, high-yield routes in key European, Middle Eastern and Australian markets. First A340 delivered in September 1994. Two **A320-200**s also ordered and delivered in December 1992 and April 1993, replacing **737-200** fleet. Plan for restructuring and possible sale of 40 per cent stake to strategic partner announced in mid-1995.

AirLanka today: National flag-carrier serving 30 destinations in 23 countries in Europe and Middle East and Asia. Points serviced from capital Colombo include Abu Dhabi, Amsterdam, Bahrain, Bangkok, Bombay, Delhi, Dhahran, Dubai, Frankfurt, Fukuoka, Hong Kong, Jeddah, Karachi, Kuala Lumpur, Kuwait, London, Madras, Male, Muscat, Paris, Riyadh, Rome, Singapore, Tiruchirapalli, Tokyo, Trivandrum, Vienna and Zürich. Specific route code-share agreements with Gulf Air, Indian Airlines, Malaysia Airlines, MEA and Pakistan International Airlines.

AirLanka fleet

Airbus A320-200		Lockheed L.1011	
4R-ABA	374	TriStar 100	
4R-ABB	406	4R-ULC	1053
		4R-ULE	1062
Airbus A340-300			
4R-ADA	032	Lockheed L.1011	
4R-ADB	033	TriStar 500	
4R-ADC	034	4R-ULA	1235
		4R-ULB	1236

Air Liberté (VD/LIB)

Paris-Orly Airport
Paris, France

History: Founded in July 1987 and began inclusive-tour flights and charters with a fleet of **McDonnell Douglas MD-83**s, first delivered in April 1988. Flights undertaken from Paris, Lyon, Lille, Nantes and Basle/Mulhouse. Acquired two **A300-600R**s and one **A310-300** in spring 1990, and introduced long-haul services to Bangkok, Montreal, New York and Saint-Denis de la Réunion. Set up Air Liberté Tunisie in Monastir in March 1990, to feed Tunisian holiday resorts MD-83. Two **Douglas DC-10-30**s taken on in July and December 1994. Started short-lived schedule between Paris-Orly and London-Gatwick on 12 September 1994, but entered domestic market from Orly in spring 1995. Acquired scheduled routes and three **Boeing 737-200**s from Euralair in early 1996, in exchange for 10 per cent stake.

Air Liberté today: Domestic and European passenger services and long-haul flights to French Overseas Departments and Territories. From main hubs at Paris-Orly, Bordeaux and

Toulouse, services extend to Abidjan, Dakar, Faro, Fort de France, Lisbon, London-Gatwick, Montreal, Porto, Pointe-a-Pitre, Saint-Denis de la Réunion, Saint-Martin and Tunis. Fort de France and Pointe-a-Pitre in French West Indies also served from Nantes, Lyon and Mulhouse-Basel. Domestic network links Paris-Orly, Bordeaux, Lille, Montpellier, Nice, Strasbourg and Toulouse.

Air Liberté is an independent French airline which specialises in holiday charters around Europe and the Mediterranean. It also operates several scheduled routes from France.

Annual turnover: *$345 million*
Passengers: *1.0 million*
Employees: *1,450*
Shareholding: *divided between Banque Rivaud, Banque Indosuez, Club Méditerranée and International Lease Finance Corporation (IIFC)*

Associate carrier: *Nouvelair Tunisie* (BJ), formerly known as Air Liberté Tunisie, established in March 1990. Operates charter services between European points and Tunisian holiday resorts with three **MD-83**s. One more MD-83 on order.

Air Liberté fleet

Airbus A300-600R	c/n	Boeing 737-200	c/n	McDonnell Douglas	
F-GHEF	555	F-GCJL	19067/71	**MD-83**	c/n
F-GHEG	559	F-GCLL	19064/63	F-GFZB	47907/1487
		F-GCSL	19066/69	F-GHEB	49822/1539
Airbus A310-200	c/n			F-GHEC	49662/1429
F-GCOJ	217	**Douglas DC-10-30**	c/n	F-GHED	49576/1422
F-CPDJ	162	F-GPVB	47957/201	F-GHEI	49968/1668
		F-GPVD	47865/135	F-GHEK	49823/1540
Airbus A310-300	c/n	F-GPVE	46981/259	F-GHHO	49985/1838
F-GHEJ	535	N345HC	48265/345	F-GHHP	49986/1842

Air Malta (KM/AMC)

Luqa Airport
Malta

History: Registered by government on 30 March 1973. Assistance provided by Pakistan International Airlines, which took 20 per cent stake, with 51 per cent held by Maltese government. Government holding increased to 96.4 per cent by November 1980. Operations started on 1 April 1974 with **Boeing 720B** leased from PIA. Flights added in 1980s to Australia, first in association with Singapore Airlines, then Qantas. Purchased its first aircraft in 1978, Boeing 720B. Fleet eventually reached five of that type. After leasing three **737-200**s from Transavia in 1980, placed order with Boeing for three **Advanced 737-200**s, first delivered in March 1983. Two more added in 1987, and sixth in 1988. Three **737-300**s arrived in Malta in spring 1993 to join two **A320-200**s delivered in August 1990 and March 1992. Fleet further supplemented with four **Avro RJ70**s, which replaced 737-200A on 'one-for-one' basis from September 1994, and leased **A310-300** in December 1994, returned one year later.
Air Malta today: Government-owned flag-carrier providing

Air Malta's small but busy fleet maintains a network of schedules and holiday traffic routes throughout Europe.

scheduled passenger and cargo flights in Europe and to North Africa and Middle East. Additional seasonal schedules and charters.

Annual revenue: *$250 million*
Passengers: *1.0 million*
Cargo: *7,100 tonnes*
Employees: *1,700*

Associate carrier: *Malta Air Charter*, founded in May 1990 as wholly-owned subsidiary to provide helicopter link

between Malta and Gozo, and sightseeing tours of Maltese islands. First flight with single 24-seat **Mil Mi-8P**. Fleet since increased to four. Since 1994, all services operated under marketing name of *Gozo Wings*.

Air Malta fleet

Airbus A320-200		Boeing 737-200	
9H-ABP	112	**Advanced**	
9H-ABQ	293	9H-ABE	23847/1414
		9H-ABF	23848/1418
Avro RJ70			
9H-ACM	E1254	**Boeing 737-300**	
9H-ACN	E1258	9H-ABR	25613/2446
9H-ACO	E1260	9H-ABS	25614/2467
9H-ACP	E1267	9H-ABT	25615/2478

Air New Zealand (NZ/ANZ)

Auckland International Airport
Auckland, New Zealand

Air New Zealand introduced this new livery in 1996, replacing the previous, familiar, predominantly blue and green scheme.

History: Founded on 26 April 1940 as Tasman Empire Airways Ltd (TEAL) and started scheduled service across Tasman Sea between Auckland and Sydney on 30 April with two **Shorts S.30 'Empire Class'** flying-boat, then **Sandringhams** and later **Solents**. In May 1954 received first landplanes – three **DC-6**s – followed by first of five **Lockheed L.188C Electra**s in November 1959. Flying-boat era ended with last flight on 14 September 1960. Government acquired 100 per cent holding in 1961. Title Air New Zealand adopted on 1 April 1965. Ordered **DC-8-52**s to facilitate long-haul expansion. On 15 September 1970, contracted to buy three **DC-10-30**s which began operations on 3 February 1973. Absorbed New Zealand National Airways Corporation (NZNAC) and its subsidiary Safe Air with effect from 1 April 1978. In 1982 network expanded to Europe and UK with **747-200B**. Three **767-300ER**s ordered and four **747-400**s in July 1984. First **767** delivered in September 1985 followed by 747-400 in December 1989. 767 reordered in 1991 and new contract signed for six **737-300**s. Privatised in 1988. Winter service to Queenstown on South Island from Brisbane inaugurated on 1 July 1995.

Air New Zealand today: Flag-carrier providing international connections, together with domestic trunk services under brand name of Air New Zealand National. Domestic jet services supplemented by provincial feeder services operated under Air New Zealand Link banner. Main hubs at Auckland, Brisbane, Sydney, Los Angeles and Honolulu. Codeshare alliances with Eva Air, Japan Airlines, Korean Air, Mandarin Airlines, Polynesian Airlines, Qantas, and other marketing agreements with Air Pacific, Delta Air Lines, Midwest, Northwest Airlines, Lan Chile, Lufthansa, South African Airways, US Air and Virgin Atlantic.

Annual revenue: $1,550 million
Passengers: 5.8 million
Employees: 7,915
Major shareholders: Brierley Investments (41.9 per cent) and Qantas (19.4 per cent)

Fleet development: Six Boeing 737-300 on order for delivery from May 1998, with deliveries to be completed by end of same year; one more 767-300ER scheduled for June 1997 and another 747-400 due in September 1998.

Associate carriers: Has acquired a 50 per cent stake in Ansett Australia after gaining final approval in June 1996.

Air New Zealand Link feeder services flown by:

Air Nelson (NZ), based at Nelson in North Island with 12 **Saab 340A**s and eight **SA227AC Metro III**s.

Eagle Air (NZ), started flying on 15 November 1969. Operates from Auckland, Gisborne and Hamilton with nine **EMB-110P1**s and four **SA226AC Metro III**s.

Mount Cook Airline (NM), whose history goes back to 1920. Provides schedules on North and South Island, particularly serving tourist areas with seven **ATR72-210**s, two **DHC-6-300**s, three **BN-2B Islander**s and various smaller types.

Air New Zealand Link is the airline's affiliate domestic feeder operation. This ATR72 is flown by Mount Cook Airlines.

Air New Zealand fleet

Boeing 737-200 Advanced		Boeing 747-200B	c/n	Boeing 767-200(ER)	c/n
ZK-NAA	22638/858	ZK-NZV	22722/523	ZK-NBA	23326/124
ZK-NAB	22364/696	ZK-NZW	22723/527	ZK-NBB	23327/134
ZK-NAD	23040/955	ZK-NZX	22724/528	ZK-NBC	23328/149
ZK-NAF	23038/949	ZK-NZY	22725/563	ZK-NBI	23072/107
ZK-NAH	23039/954	ZK-NZZ	22791/568	ZK-NBJ	23250/113
ZK-NAI	22365/700				
ZK-NAT	23470/1186	**Boeing 747-400**	c/n	**Boeing 767-300(ER)**	c/n
ZK-NAU	23471/1189	ZK-NBS	24386/756	ZK-NCE	24875/371
ZK-NAV	23472/1194	ZK-NBT	24855/815	ZK-NCF	24876/413
ZK-NAW	23473/1197	ZK-NBU	25605/933	ZK-NCG	26912/509
ZK-NAX	23474/1199	ZK-SUH	24896/855	ZK-NCH	26264/555
ZK-NAY	23475/1203	ZK-SUI	24957/971	ZK-NCI	26913/558
ZK-NQC	22994/928			ZK-NCJ	26915/574

Airtours International (VZ/AIH)

History: Founded 10 October 1990 and began charter operations out of Manchester on 11 March 1991 with fleet of five **Mc Donnell Douglas MD-83**s. Part of Airtours Group which started life as small tour operator in North England in 1980. Initially three MD-83s based at Manchester, other two at Birmingham and London-Stansted. Cardiff-based Aspro Holidays plus operations and fleet of its in-house airline, Inter European Airways, fully merged into Airtours in November 1993, adding two **Airbus A320-200**s and two **Boeing 757-200**s. Two **767-300ER**s acquired in April 1994 for long-haul flights. Decision made at end of 1995 to replace MD-83 fleet with more A320s.

Airtours today: Inclusive-tour services to most popular holiday destinations in Mediterranean Basin, together with long-haul flights to United States and Caribbean, including Orlando, Las Vegas, Grand Cayman, Barbados, Montego Bay (Jamaica) and Antigua. Long-haul flights also operated to Gambia and Australia. UK departure points are Manchester, London-Gatwick, Belfast, Birmingham, Bristol, Cardiff, East Midlands, Glasgow, Humberside, Leeds Bradford, London-Stansted, Teesside, Liverpool and Newcastle.

Annual revenue: $1,000 million
Passengers: 2.8 million
Employees: 1,180
Ownership: Wholly-owned by Airtours Group

Airtours International began life as an MD-83 operator. This situation changed in 1993 after its merger with Inter European Airways, and a new Airbus A320 and Boeing 757/767 fleet was subsequently adopted.

Airtours fleet

Airbus A320-200		Boeing 757-200	
G-CRPH	424	G-CSVS	25620/449
G-DACR	349	G-JALC	22194/5
G-DRVE	221	G-LCRC	24636/259
G-HBAP	294	G-MCEA	22200/20
G-JANM	301	G-PIDS	22195/6
G-JDFW	299	G-RJGR	22197/8
G-RRJE	222		
G-SUEE	363	**Boeing 767-300ER**	
G-TPTT	348	G-DAJC	27206/952
G-YJBM	362	G-SJMC	27205/951

Air Transat (TS/TSC)

History: Founded in December 1986 by Transat A T and began operations flying international charters, initially with two **Lockheed L.1011 TriStars**. Acquired dominant position in Canada-UK market sector and boosted fleet with more TriStars, and three **Boeing 727-200** in May and June 1991. Activities expanded substantially following demise of biggest competitor Nationair, whose operating permits were suspended on 1 April 1993, plus purchase of large stake in Nationair's parent tour company. Fleet almost doubled with delivery of four **757-200**s between November 1992 and April 1993. Disposed of its 727s in 1994, and acquired additional TriStar.

Air Transat today: Regular and *ad hoc* charter services from Montreal, Toronto and Quebec

Montreal-based Air Transat operates holiday charter flights to numerous American and European destinations.

City to Mexico, Caribbean, US, Central and South America, and across North Atlantic to Europe. Main European countries served are France and United Kingdom where, in addition to London and Paris, other regional points include Glasgow, Leeds Bradford, Manchester, Newcastle, Marseille, Lyon, Nice and Toulouse. Other frequently served cities include Amsterdam, Athens, Frankfurt, Madrid and Rome.

Annual revenue: $265 million
Passengers: 1.4 million
Employees: 900

Air Transat fleet

Boeing 757-200		Lockheed L.1011	
C-GTSE	25488/471	**TriStar 150**	
C-GTSF	25491/511	C-FTNA	1019
C-GTSJ	24772/271	C-FTNB	1010
C-GTSN	24543/268	C-FTNC	1023
		C-FTNH	1049
		C-GTSX	1094
		C-GTSZ	1103

Air UK (UK/UKA)

History: Formed on 16 January 1980 through amalgamation of British Island Airways, Air Anglia, BIA/Air West and Air Wales. Air UK inherited large fleet comprising two **F28-4000**, 10 **F27-100/ 200**s, 19 **Handley Page Herald**s, four **BAC One-Eleven 400**s and five **EMBRAER Bandeirante**s, as well as 31-point domestic and European network. New international routes introduced in November 1981 from Stansted to Amsterdam but early years marked by route and fleet rationalisation including disposal of Fellowships, Heralds, Bandeirante and One-Elevens and acquisition of five **Shorts 360**. From 1984 international services added from many provincial cities to Amsterdam, Paris, Brussels, Copenhagen and others. KLM acquired 14.9 per cent holding in 1987, since increased to 45 per cent. Acquired five **Fokker 100**s in 1992, augmented in 1993 with four more. First of eight **Fokker 50**s entered service on 28 March 1994 from

Today's Air UK has a substantial fleet of F50 turboprops and F100 jets plus a long tradition of operating Fokker aircraft.

Norwich to Aberdeen/Edinburgh.
   Air UK today: UK's third-largest scheduled airline, with scheduled services from London-Stansted to 12 European destinations, Edinburgh, Glasgow, Guernsey, Jersey and Newcastle. Edinburgh and Glasgow also served from London-Gatwick, and Bergen and Stavanger in Norway

from Aberdeen. Channel Islands are served from six mainland airports. A large number of flights operate into Amsterdam, feeding part owner KLM.

Annual revenue: *$405 million*
Passengers: *2.6 million*
Cargo: *3,500 tonnes*
Employees: *1,600*
Ownership: *Wholly-owned by Air UK Group, whose shareholding divided between British Air Transport (Holdings) with 55 per cent and KLM with 45 per cent*

Associate carrier: *Leisure International Airways*, owned 60 per cent by Air UK and 40 per cent by Unijet. Started flying on 30 April 1988 as Air UK Leisure with two **Boeing 737-200**, but introduced **737-400** from October that year. Two **767-300ER**s acquired in 1993 and operated under Leisure International Airways name. Operation restyled in February 1996 and to be transferred to London-Gatwick in autumn 1996. Provides European and long-haul holiday charter flights with newly-acquired fleet of three **Airbus A320-200**s.

Air UK fleet

BAe 146-100	c/n	G-UKID	E3157	G-UKTH	20277	G-UKFI	11279
G-UKJF	E1011	G-UKRC	E3158	G-UKTI	20279		
		G-UKSC	E3125			**Fokker F27-200** *c/n*	
BAe 146-300	*c/n*			**Fokker 100**	*c/n*	G-BHMY	10196
G-BSNR	E3165	**Fokker 50**	*c/n*	G-UKFA	11246		
G-BSNS	E3169	G-UKTA	20246	G-UKFB	11247	**Fokker F27-500** *c/n*	
G-BTTP	E3203	G-UKTB	20247	G-UKFC	11263	G-BMXD	10417
G-BUHB	E3183	G-UKTC	20249	G-UKFD	11259	G-BNCY	10558
G-BUHC	E3193	G-UKTD	20256	G-UKFE	11260	G-BVOB	10366
G-UKAC	E3142	G-UKTE	20270	G-UKFF	11274	G-BVOM	10381
G-UKAG	E3162	G-UKTF	20271	G-UKFG	11275	G-BVRN	10427
G-UKHP	E3123	G-UKTG	20276	G-UKFH	11277		

Air Zimbabwe (UM/AZW)

History: Established as Air Rhodesia Corporation on 1 September 1967, following dissolution of multi-national Central African Airways (CAA) – which had served territories of Southern Rhodesia, Northern Rhodesia and Nyasaland – as a direct result of Rhodesia's Unilateral Declaration of Independence on 11 November 1965. Allocated fleet of three **Vickers Viscount**s

and three **DC-3**s. Domestic flights augmented with regional connections from Salisbury (now Harare) to Johannesburg, Durban, Beira, Lourenço Marques (now Maputo) and Blantyre. Met jet competition from South African Airways with purchase of three **Boeing 720B**, which arrived in Salisbury on 14 April 1973. Political unrest in Mozambique forced suspension of

routes to that country and Malawi, and airline also suffered badly from effect of international sanctions imposed against Rhodesia's racial policies. Renamed Air Zimbabwe in April 1980 following independence. Opening of intercontinental route to London in same month. Initially operated with leased **707-320C**, but acquired three of its **707-320B**s from Lufthansa in

Air Zimbabwe is one of Africa's more dynamic carriers operating a varied fleet over a wide network.

May 1981. Two more added next year and services opened to Frankfurt and Athens, supplemented with block-space agreement with Qantas to Perth and Sydney in Australia. Delivery of three **737-200**s from December 1986 and **BAe 146** in 1987. Fleet modernisation completed with replacement of 707 on Frankfurt and London routes by **767-200ER**s, delivered in November 1989 and October 1990. Domestic fleet upgraded with two **Fokker 50** in early 1995.

Air Zimbabwe today: State-owned flag-carrier operating long-haul services to Frankfurt, Larnaca, London, Perth and Sydney, and regionally to Cape Town, Durban, Gaborone, Johannesburg, Lilongwe, Lusaka, Manzini, Mauritius, Nairobi and Windhoek. Domestic flights from Harare to Bulawayo, Hwange, Kariba and Victoria Falls. Commercial agreement with Air Malawi, using Air Zimbabwe's

Boeing 737-200, and with Qantas, which operates Perth to Sydney service. Routes to Accra and Lagos in West Africa under consideration, as is eventual expansion to United States.

Annual revenue: $93 million
Passengers: 0.6 million
Employees: 1,850

Fleet development: Seeking finance for another 767

Air Zimbabwe fleet

British Aerospace 146-200		Boeing 737-200 Advanced		Z-WPF	24867/333
Z-WPD	E2065	Z-WPA	23677/1313		
		Z-WPB	23678/1405	**Fokker 50**	
Boeing 707-320B				Z-WPG	20104
Z-WKS	18923/435	**Boeing 767-200ER**		Z-WPH	20105
Z-WKU	18930/464	Z-WPE	24713/287		

Alaska Airlines (AS/ASA)

Seattle-Tacoma International Airport
Seattle, Washington, USA

History: Founded on 27 November 1937 with incorporation of Star Air Lines. On 10 November 1943, Star bought three small airlines and was renamed Star Alaska Airlines, and again on 6 June 1944 to Alaska Airlines. Began first route to destination outside Alaska in 1951 linking Anchorage and Fairbanks to Seattle with **DC-4**. First commercial flight over North Pole in December 1951. Bought first **DC-6** on 12 March 1958 and added two **L.100-30 Hercules** on 20 June 1966 for cargo flights in southeast Alaska. In October and November same year acquired its first two **727-100**s. **DHC Twin Otters** and **Grumman Goose** also operated to smaller communities in southeast. First charter flight to Siberia and Leningrad in 1970. Became launch customer for **MD-83** with order for six announced in March 1983. First delivered in 1984 and further orders in subsequent years brought MD-83s to 44. In 1985, Alaska Air Group formed as holding company, which acquired Horizon Air and Jet

America. Competitor Jet America merged in Alaska Airlines in October 1987. Placed order for 20 new **MD90-30**, plus 20 options; but competition and over-capacity in market forced cancellation of complete order in favour of just four **MD-83**s. Disposal of 23-strong 727 fleet also accelerated and completed by autumn 1994.

Alaska Air today: Low-cost, high-frequency service over an extensive north/south route network, extending from Barrow in Alaska to Puerto Vallarta in

Alaska Airlines has a substantial fleet of MD-83s in service alongside Boeing 737-200/-400s.

Mexico, and covering all major cities on US Western Corridor. More than 20 points scheduled with jet flights in Alaska. Also offers trans-Bering Strait flights to Russia, serving Vladivostok, Khabarovsk, Magadan and Petropavlovsk from Anchorage. Network centred on hubs at Seattle, Portland and Anchorage. Plans to extend services into Vancouver, Canada, from several

Alaska Airlines

Alaska Air affiliate Horizon Air was the launch customer for the Do 328 but has now decided to phase them out in favour of additional DHC-8s (seen here).

more cities from Alaska and US West Coast.

Group annual revenue: $1,400 million
Passengers: 8.9 million
Cargo: 57,000 tonnes
Employees: 6,500

Fleet development: Four MD-83s remain on order for delivery in 1996/97. Studying long-term transition to single-type, possibly new generation Boeing 737-600/700/800 family.

Associate carriers: Horizon Air (QX), founded in May 1981 and purchased by Alaska Air Group in 1986. Provides scheduled services to 39 destinations in Washington, Oregon, California, Idaho, Montana and Canada, from hubs at Boise, Portland, Seattle and Spokane, carrying 3.5 million passengers yearly. Fleet comprises 23 **DHC-8-100s**, 12 **F28-1000s**, 12 **Do 328s** and 18 **SA227AC Metro IIIs**. Metros being replaced by Do 328, with eight to be delivered.

Alaska Airlines Commuter services to communities within Alaska flown by **ERA Aviation** (7H) with two DHC-8-100s, nine **Twin Otters** and four **Convair 580**s from Anchorage and Bel; **LAB Flying Service** (JF) from Haines with two **BN Islanders**; and **Peninsula Airways (Penair)** (KS), in King Salmon, Kodiak, Dillingham, Dutch Harbor and Cold Bay markets, flown with seven Metro IIIs.

Alaska Airlines fleet

Boeing 737-200C Adv		N763AS	25100/2346	N783AS	25114/2666	N942AS	53052/1731	N960AS	53074/1976
N730AS	22577/760	N764AS	25101/2348			N943AS	53018/1779	N961AS	53075/1977
N740AS	22578/767	N765AS	25102/2350	**McDonnell Douglas**		N944AS	53019/1783	N962AS	53076/1988
N741AS	21959/610	N767AS	27081/2354	**MD-83**	**c/n**	N945AS	49643/1523	N963AS	53077/1995
N742AS	23136/1032	N768AS	27082/2356	N930AS	49231/1177	N946AS	49658/1461	N964AS	53078/1996
N743AS	21821/590	N769AS	25103/2552	N931AS	49232/1178	N947AS	53020/1789	N965AS	53079/2004
N744AS	21822/605	N771AS	25104/2476	N932AS	49233/1203	N948AS	53021/1801	N966AS	49104/1085
N745As	20794/346	N772AS	25105/2505	N933AS	49234/1204	N949AS	53022/1809	N967AS	49103/1083
N746AS	23123/1042	N773AS	25106/2518	N934AS	49235/1234	N950AS	53023/1821	N968AS	53016/1850
		N774AS	25107/2526	N935AS	49236/1235	N951AS	49111/1064	N969AS	53063/1851
Boeing 737-400	**c/n**	N775As	25108/2551	N936AS	49363/1275	N953AS	49386/1287	N972AS	53448/2074
N754AS	25095/2266	N776AS	25109/2561	N937AS	49364/1276	N954AS	49387/1288	N973AS	53449/2077
N755AS	25096/2278	N778AS	25110/2586	N938AS	49365/1277	N955As	48080/1022	N974AS	53450/2078
N756AS	25097/2299	N779AS	25111/2605	N939AS	49657/1459	N956AS	48079/1016	N975AS	53451/2083
N760AS	25098/2320	N780AS	25112/2638	N940AS	49825/1577	N957AS	49126/1080	N976AS	53452/2109
N762AS	25099/2334	N782AS	25113/2656	N941AS	49925/1616	N958AS	53024/1825	N977AS	53453/2112

Alitalia (AZ/AZA)

Leonardo de Vinci (Fiumicino) International Airport
Rome, Italy

History: Founded 16 September 1946 as Aerolinee Italiane Internazionali (Alitalia). Commenced operations 5 May on domestic routes with Fiat G.12 tri-motors. Service from Rome to London inaugurated 3 April 1948, with **Savoia Marchetti SM.95s**, followed 26 May with Rome-Rio de Janeiro-Sao Paulo-Montevideo-Buenos Aires route with **Avro Lancastrians**. Fleet supplemented by **DC-4** and **Convair 340** and **440** in early 1950s. On 8 October 1957 acquired routes and equipment of Linee Aeree Italiane, adding **DC-6**, **Viscount** and **DC-3**. DC-6s replaced by

DC-7C and **DC-8-40s** ordered, which inaugurated first jet service 1 June 1960. **Caravelle III**, later **VIN**, introduced 23 May. Set up Societa Aerea Mediterranea (SAM) in November 1960 as charter subsidiary, and Aero Trasporti Italiani (ATI) in December 1963 to handle domestic services. Placed orders for **DC-8-62**s and 28 **DC-9-32**s and became all-jet operator by January 1969. **Boeing 747** entered service on North American routes 5 June 1970, wide-body fleet later augmented between 1973 and 1975 with **DC-10-30**s. Other aircraft to join fleet were **727-200** in

1977 and **Airbus A300B-200** in 1980. Opened Rome-Delhi-Shanghai-Tokyo route 29 March 1987. Became first customer for new **A321**, contracting to buy 20 on 13 December 1989. **MD-11** entered service on cargo flights in early 1992.

Alitalia today: Government-owned flag-carrier providing passenger and cargo services from main hubs at Rome and Milan to more than 90 destinations across world, together with large domestic network. Undergoing major restructuring plan which will involve rationalisation of route structure and aircraft fleet.

Annual revenue: $4,500 million
Passengers: 20.9 million
Cargo: 270,000 tonnes
Employees: 18,600
Ownership: Owned 89.31 per cent by Italian government, 10.69 per cent held by TERZI

Fleet development: Thirty more A321s for delivery from late 1996 through 1998. DC-9-32 and A300 to be phased out.

Associate carrier: Avianova (RD), 45 per cent owned, operates domestic and European services. Fleet includes 11 **ATR42-300**s, three **ATR72-210**s and five **Fokker 70**s. Ten more for delivery in 1996/97.

Eurofly (EEZ), owned 45 per cent by Alitalia and 45 per cent by Olivetti. Started operations 26 February 1990. Provides charters out of Milan with fleet of two **DC-9-51**s and three **MD-82**s.

Air Europe (PE) – Alitalia has 27.45 per cent holding – also concentrates on holiday flights out of Milan-Malpensa with fleet of four **767-300**s. A 30 per cent stake is also held in Malév.

Above: Along with Lufthansa, Alitalia was the launch customer for the A321. Its first aircraft entered service in March 1994.

Right: Rome-based Avianova operates domestic and regional flights under the Alitalia banner. It has a total of 15 Fokker 70s on order.

Alitalia fleet

Airbus A300B4-100	c/n	Boeing 747-200B	c/n	I-RIFU	47433/526	I-DANL	53178/1994	I-DAVI	49430/1334
I-BUSP	067	I-DEMC	22506/492	I-RIFV	47533/641	I-DANM	53179/1997	I-DAVJ	49431/1377
I-BUSQ	118	I-DEMF	22508/499	I-RIFW	47575/680	I-DANP	53180/2002	I-DAVK	49432/1378
I-BUSR	120	I-DEMG	22510/533			I-DANQ	53181/2005	I-DAVL	49433/1428
		I-DEML	22511/536	**McDonnell Douglas**		I-DANR	53203/2007	I-DAVM	49434/1446
Airbus A300B4-200	c/n	I-DEMN	22512/542	**MD-11**	c/n	I-DANU	53204/2009	I-DAVN	49435/1504
I-BUSB	101	I-DEMP	22513/546	I-DUPB	48431/534	I-DANV	53205/2028	I-DAVP	49549/1544
I-BUSC	106	I-DEMS	22969/575	I-DUPC	48581/565	I-DANW	53206/2034	I-DAVR	49550/1584
I-BUSD	107	I-DEMT	23300/616	I-DUPD	48630/567	I-DATA	53216/2045	I-DAVS	49551/1586
I-BUSF	123	I-DEMV	23301/618			I-DATB	53221/2078	I-DAVT	49552/1597
I-BUSG	139	I-DEMY	21589/345	**McDonnell Douglas**		I-DATC	53222/2080	I-DAVU	49794/1600
I-BUSH	140			**MD-11F**	c/n	I-DATD	53223/2082	I-DAVV	49795/1639
I-BUSJ	142	**Boeing 747-200F**	c/n	I-DUPA	48426/468	I-DATC	53222/2080	I-DAVW	49796/1713
I-BUSL	173	I-DEMR	22545/545	I-DUPE	48427/471	I-DATD	53223/2082	I-DAVZ	49970/1737
I-BUSM	049			I-DUPI	48428/474	I-DATE	53217/2053	I-DAWA	49192/1126
I-BUSN	051	**Boeing 767-300(ER)**	c/n	I-DUPO	48429/500	I-DATF	53224/2084	I-DAWB	49197/1138
I-BUST	068	G-OITF	27908/578	I-DUPU	48430/508	I-DATG	53225/2086	I-DAWC	49198/1142
		G-OITA	27376/560			I-DATH	53226/2087	I-DAWD	49199/1143
Airbus A321-100	c/n	G-OITB	27377/561	**McDonnell Douglas**		I-DATI	53218/2060	I-DAWE	49193/1127
I-BIXA	477			**MD-82**	c/n	I-DATJ	53227/2013	I-DAWF	49200/1147
I-BIXB	524	**Douglas DC-9-30**	c/n	I-DACM	49971/1755	I-DATK	53228/2104	I-DAWG	49201/1148
I-BIXC	526	I-DIBA	47038/136	I-DACN	49972/1757	I-DATL	53229/2105	I-DAWH	49202/1170
I-BIXD	532	I-DIBE	47046/168	I-DACP	49973/1762	I-DATM	53230/2106	I-DAWI	49194/1130
I-BIXE	488	I-DIBI	47129/325	I-DACQ	49974/1774	I-DATN	53231/2107	I-DAWJ	49203/1174
I-BIXF	515	I-DIBL	47101/195	I-DACR	49975/1775	I-DATO	53219/2062	I-DAWL	49204/1179
I-BIXG	516	I-DIBM	47223/300	I-DACS	53053/1806	I-DATP	53232/2108	I-DAWM	49205/1184
I-BIXI	494	I-DIKM	47224/316	I-DACT	53054/1856	I-DATQ	53233/2110	I-DAWO	49195/1136
I-BIXL	513	I-DIKR	47228/355	I-DACU	53055/1857	I-DATR	53234/2111	I-DAWP	49206/1188
I-BIXM	514	I-DIZE	47502/574	I-DACV	53056/1880	I-DATS	53235/2113	I-DAWQ	49207/1189
I-BIXN	576	I-RIFE	47518/614	I-DACW	53057/1894	I-DATU	53220/2073	I-DAWR	49208/1190
I-BIXO	495	I-RIFG	47225/317	I-DACX	53060/1944	I-DAVA	49215/1253	I-DAWS	49209/1191
I-BIXP	583	I-RIFH	47128/210	I-DACY	53059/1942	I-DAVB	49216/1262	I-DAWT	49210/1192
I-BIXQ	586	I-RIFJ	47235/436	I-DACZ	53058/1927	I-DAVC	49217/1268	I-DAWU	49196/1137
I-BIXR	593	I-RIFM	47544/676	I-DAND	53061/1957	I-DAVD	49218/1274	I-DAWV	49211/1202
		I-RIFP	47438/545	I-DANF	53062/1960	I-DAVF	49219/1310	I-DAWW	49212/1233
		I-RIFS	47229/356	I-DANG	53176/1972	I-DAVG	49220/1319	I-DAWZ	49214
		I-RIFT	47591/706	I-DANH	53177/1973	I-DAVH	49221/1330		

All Nippon Airways (NH/ANA)

Tokyo-Haneda Airport
Tokyo, Japan

Beijing, Brisbane, Dalian, Frankfurt, Guam, Hong Kong, Kuala Lumpur, London, Los Angeles, Moscow, New York, Paris, Rome, Shanghai, Singapore, Sydney, Vienna and Washington.

Annual revenue: *$9,250 million*
Passengers: *35.8 million*
Employees: *13,600*

History: Formed 1 December 1957 through merger of Japan Helicopter and Aeroplane Transport (JHAT) and Far East Airlines. Received authority to compete with Japan Air Lines on trunk routes and started Tokyo-Osaka route in April 1959. Turboprop services with leased **Viscount** inaugurated on 25 June 1960, prior to obtaining own Viscount and **Fokker F27** fleet. First jet service with **Boeing 727** introduced in May 1964. **YS-11** added in September 1965. Delivery of 21 **TriStar**s between 1973 and 1978. **Boeing 747SR** entered service in January 1979, and order placed for 25 **767**s same year for introduction in 1983.

Japan's All Nippon Airways has been a strong Boeing customer for many years. This is one of 63 Boeing 767s in ANA service.

Deregulation in December 1985 enabled international expansion in 1986 to US West Coast with **Boeing 747-200B**s. Europe reached in April 1989. Fleet expanded with introduction of **747-400** in November 1990, **Airbus A320** in March 1991 and **Boeing 777** in December 1995. **All Nippon Airways today:** Japan's biggest domestic airline, with 51 per cent of market serving 30 major cities and other trunk routes. Overseas cities served from Tokyo are Bangkok,

Fleet development: Deliveries, to be completed between 1996 and 2000, include 10 **A321**s, five **A340-300**s, two **747-400**s, four **767-300ER**s and 16 **777-200**s. Follow-up order for stretched **777-300** signed in September 1995 for delivery from 1998.

Associate carriers: *Air Nippon*, until spring 1987 known as Nihon Kinkiyori Airways, formed 13 March 1974 by ANA, JAL, Toa Domestic and others, to provide subsidised feeder services. Operates in and from northernmost island of Hokkaido with three **737-500**s, nine **737-200**s, 18 **YS-11A**s and two **DHC-6**s. *Nippon Cargo Airlines* (NCA), formerly Nippon Air Cargo, formed by ANA and several shipping companies in September 1978. Operates scheduled cargo services with four **747-200F**s.

All Nippon Airways fleet

Airbus A320-200	c/n	JA8139	21925/422	JA8957	25642/927	JA8483	22789/67	JA8323	25654/463
JA8300	531	JA8145	22291/453	JA8958	25641/928	JA8484	22790/69	JA8324	25655/465
JA8313	534	JA8146	22292/456	JA8959	25646/952	JA8485	23016/80	JA8342	27445/573
JA8381	138	JA8147	22293/477	JA8960	25643/927	JA8486	23017/82	JA8356	25136/379
JA8382	139	JA8148	22294/481	JA8961	25644/975	JA8487	23018/84	JA8357	25293/401
JA8383	148	JA8152	22594/511	JA8962	25645/979	JA8488	23019/85	JA8358	25616/432
JA8384	151	JA8153	22595/516	JA8963	25647/991	JA8489	23020/96	JA8359	25617/439
JA8385	167	JA8156	22709/541	JA8964	27163/996	JA8490	23021/103	JA8360	25055/352
JA8386	170	JA8157	22710/544	JA8965	27436/1060	JA8491	23022/104	JA8362	24632/285
JA8387	196	JA8159	22712/572	JA8966	27442/1066			JA8363	24757/300
JA8388	212					**Boeing 767-300**	c/n	JA8368	24880/336
JA8389	219	**Boeing 747-200B (LR)**		**Boeing 767-200**	c/n	JA8256	23756/176	JA8567	25656/510
JA8390	245	JA8174	23501/648	JA8238	23140/106	JA8257	23757/177	JA8568	25657/515
JA8391	300	JA8175	23502/649	JA8239	23141/108	JA8258	23758/179	JA8569	27050/516
JA8392	328	JA8181	23698/667	JA8240	23142/110	JA8259	23759/185	JA8578	25658/519
JA8393	365	JA8182	23813/683	JA8241	23143/114	JA8272	24002/199	JA8579	25659/520
JA8394	383	JA8190	24399/750	JA8242	23144/115	JA8273	24003/212	JA8664	27339/556
JA8395	413	JA8192	22579/514	JA8243	23145/116	JA8274	24004/218	JA8669	27555/567
JA8396	482			JA8244	23146/121	JA8275	24005/222	JA8670	25660/539
JA8400	554	**Boeing 747-400**	c/n	JA8245	23147/123	JA8285	24006/223	JA8674	25661/543
JA8609	501	JA8094	24801/805	JA8251	23431/143	JA8286	24350/245	JA8677	25662/551
JA8654	507	JA8095	24833/812	JA8252	23432/145	JA8287	24400/269		
		JA8096	24920/832	JA8254	23433/167	JA8288	24351/271	**Boeing 777-200**	c/n
Boeing 747SR	c/n	JA8097	25135/863	JA8255	23434/171	JA8289	24415/276	JA8197	27027/16
JA8135	21606/360	JA8098	25207/870	JA8480	22785/51	JA8290	24416/280	JA8198	27028/21
JA8136	21922/393	JA8099	25292/891	JA8481	22786/54	JA8291	24417/290		
JA8137	21923/395	JA8955	25639/914	JA8482	22787/58	JA8322	24755/295		
JA8138	21924/420	JA8956	25640/920	JA8483	22788/61		25618/458		

American Airlines (AA/AAL)

History: Organised 13 May 1934 as direct successor to American Airways. Initial fleet included **Curtiss Condor** and a few **Douglas DC-2**s. Famous **DC-3** built to airline's specification and entered service between Chicago and New York on 25 June 1936. Biggest US domestic airline by end of decade. During World War II, half of fleet operated by Air Transport Command. First of 50 **DC-6** entered service in 1947, followed by **Convair 240** in 1948. Between 1945 and 1950 operated transatlantic division, American Overseas Airlines, serving number of European cities, but sold out to Pan American in September 1956. In 1953 pioneered non-stop transcontinental service across US with **DC-7**. Introduced **Lockheed L.188A Electra** in January 1959 and on 25 January same year operated first non-stop jet service between New York and Los Angeles with **707-120**. Turbofan-powered **707-320** went into service 12 March 1961. As jets added to fleet – **Convair 990A** in March 1962 and **Boeing 727** in 1964 – piston-engined aircraft phased out by December 1966. Order placed with Boeing for **747-100** and with McDonnell Douglas for **DC-10**. Latter went into service on 5 August 1971 on Los Angeles-Chicago route. Swapped transpacific routes for Pan Am's Caribbean authority in June 1975. First **747-200F** freighter service inaugurated 5 November 1974. Phase-out of 60 **707**s accelerated, replaced by 30 **767-200** ordered in November 1978. First 767 service in 1982. **MD-82** joined fleet in 1983 and in 1984 ordered 67 MD-82s, plus 100 options in what was then largest-ever single aircraft purchase in US. Opened service to Frankfurt and Paris and started American commuter feeder network same year. In 1987, announced acquisition of 25 **Airbus A300-600R**s for Caribbean services, and 15 **767-300ER**s for international routes, and in 1988 placed order for 50 **757-200**s.

American maintains a huge domestic network through its American Eagle feeder operation which stretches to every corner of the United States.

Acquired TWA route rights into UK, Continental's Miami-London route and Eastern Airlines' Central and South American network in 1990. First of 19 **McDonnell Douglas MD-11** entered service in spring 1991.

Annual revenue: $16,900 million
Passengers: 81.1 million
Cargo: 640,000 tonnes
Employees: 83,900

Fleet development: Two **757-200**s to be delivered. **MD-11**s for sale, 12 to be delivered to FedEx between 1996 and 1999. FedEx has options on remaining seven aircraft.

Associate carriers: Plans to enter into major alliance with British Airways. Vast local feeder services operated by four subsidiaries under **American Eagle** banner, providing more than 1,800 flights daily. These include:

Executive Airlines (NA), American Eagle carrier since 1 June 1986, flying two distinct networks, one from San Juan, Puerto Rico to the Caribbean,

American Airlines was one of the pioneers of transatlantic ETOPS (Extended Twin-engined OPerations) using its 767 fleet.

and other from Miami, within Florida and to nearby Bahamas.

Wings West Airlines (RM), founded in 1981 and American Eagle carrier since 1 June 1986. Purchased by AMR Corporation in August 1988. Provides network of services based on hubs at Los Angeles and Dallas/Ft Worth.

Flagship Airlines (8N) joined system 16 April 1986 and became subsidiary 31 December 1987. Operates out of Nashville, Miami, New York and Raleigh/Durham.

Simmons Airlines (MQ) founded in 1978, joined Eagle system 1 October 1985, and purchased on 8 August 1988. Main bases at Chicago-O'Hare and Dallas/Ft Worth. Combined fleet includes 28 **ATR72**s, 46 **ATR42-300**s, 52 **Jetstream 31**s, 100 **Saab 340B**s, 16 **Saab 340A**s and 29 **Shorts 360**s.

American Airlines fleet

Airbus A300-600R *c/n*

N91050	423
N50051	459
N80052	460
N14053	420
N70054	461
N7055A	462
N14056	463
N80057	465
N80058	466
N19059	469
N11060	470
N14061	471
N7062A	474
N41063	506
N40064	507
N14065	508
N18066	509
N8067A	510
N14068	511
N33069	512
N90070	513
N25071	514
N70072	515
N70073	516
N70074	517
N3075A	606
N7076A	610
N14077	612
N34078	615
N70079	619
N77080	626
N59081	639
N7082A	643
N7083A	645
N80084	675

Boeing 727-200 Adv

N701AA	22459/1742
N702AA	22460/1746
N703AA	22461/1750
N705AA	22462/1751
N706AA	22463/1755
N707AA	22464/1758
N708AA	22465/1761
N709AA	22466/1763
N710AA	22467/1765
N712AA	22468/1766
N713AA	22469/1769
N715AA	22470/1771
N716AA	20608/891
N717AA	20610/893
N718AA	20611/894
N719AA	20612/928
N720AA	20613/929
N721AA	20729/955
N722AA	20730/956
N723AA	20731/957

N725AA	20732/963
N726AA	20733/964
N727AA	20734/965
N728AA	20735/973
N729AA	20736/974
N730AA	20737/976
N731AA	20738/977
N6813	19488/588
N6818	19493/657
N6819	19494/661
N6822	19700/673
N6823	19701/677
N6835	20188/730
N843AA	20984/1121
N844AA	20985/1123
N845AA	20986/1125
N846AA	20987/1126
N847AA	20788/1141
N848AA	20989/1144
N849AA	20990/1184
N850AA	20991/1185
N859AA	21086/1248
N860AA	21087/1250
N861AA	21088/1255
N862AA	21089/1263
N863AA	21090/1267
N864AA	21369/1275
N865AA	21370/1276
N866AA	21371/1277
N867AA	21372/1278
N868AA	21373/1279
N869AA	21374/1280
N870AA	21382/1304
N871AA	21383/1324
N872AA	21384/1328
N873AA	21385/1331
N874AA	21386/1333
N875AA	21387/1335
N876AA	21388/1345
N877AA	21389/1349
N878AA	21390/1361
N879AA	21391/1367
N880AA	21519/1459
N881AA	21520/1461
N882AA	21521/1463
N883AA	21522/1465
N884AA	21523/1467
N885AA	21524/1473
N886AA	21525/1475
N887AA	21526/1476
N889AA	21527/1477
N890AA	22006/1636
N891AA	22007/1643
N892AA	22008/1646
N893AA	22009/1649
N894AA	22010/1650
N895AA	22011/1653
N896AA	22012/1655

N897AA	22013/1659
N898AA	22014/1663
N899AA	22015/1666

Boeing 757-200 *c/n*

N601AN	27052/661
N602AN	27053/664
N603AA	27054/670
N604AA	27055/680
N605AA	27056/682
N610AA	24486/234
N611AM	24487/236
N612AA	24488/240
N613AA	24489/242
N614AA	24490/243
N615AM	24491/245
N616AA	24524/248
N617AM	24525/253
N618AA	24526/260
N619AA	24577/269
N620AA	24578/276
N621AM	24579/283
N622AA	24580/289
N623AA	24581/296
N624AA	24582/297
N625AA	24583/303
N626AA	24584/304
N627AA	24585/308
N628AA	24586/309
N629AA	24587/315
N630AA	24588/316
N631AA	24589/317
N632AA	24590/321
N633AA	24591/324
N634AA	24592/327
N635AA	24593/328
N636AM	24594/336
N637AM	24595/337
N638AA	24596/344
N639AA	24597/345
N640A	24598/350
N641AA	24599/351
N642AA	24600/357
N643AA	24601/360
N644AA	24602/365
N645AA	24603/370
N646AA	24604/375
N647AM	24605/378
N648AA	24606/379
N649AA	24607/383
N650AA	24608/384
N652AA	24610/391
N653A	25611/397

Nineteen-seat BAe Jetstream 31s are used by several American Eagle operators.

N654A	24612/398
N655AA	24613/402
N656AA	24614/404
N657AM	24615/409
N658AA	24616/410
N659AA	24617/417
N660AM	25294/418
N661AA	25295/423
N662AA	25296/425
N663AM	25297/432
N664AA	25298/433
N665AA	25299/436
N666A	25300/451
N667A	25301/459
N668AA	25333/460
N669AA	25334/463
N670AA	25335/468
N671AA	25336/473
N672AA	25337/474
N681AA	25338/483
N682AA	25339/484
N683A	25340/491
N684AA	25341/504
N685AA	25342/507
N686AA	25343/509
N687AA	25695/536
N688AA	25730/548
N689AA	25731/562
N690AA	25696/566
N691AA	25697/568
N692AA	26972/578
N693AA	26973/580
N694AN	26974/582
N695AN	26975/621
N696AN	26976/627
N697AN	26977/633
N698AN	26980/635
N699AN	27051/660

Boeing 767-200 *c/n*

N301AA	22307/8
N302AA	22308/19
N303AA	22309/23
N304AA	22310/25
N305AA	22311/34
N306AA	22312/44
N307AA	22313/72
N308AA	22314/73

Boeing 767-200ER *c/n*

N312AA	22315/94
N313AA	22316/95
N315AA	22317/109
N316AA	22318/111
N317AA	22319/112
N319AA	22320/128
N320AA	22321/130
N321AA	22322/139

American Airlines introduced the first of its 95 Fokker 100s in July 1991.

N322AA	22323/140
N323AA	22324/146
N324AA	22325/147
N325AA	22326/157
N327AA	22327/159
N328AA	22328/160
N329AA	22329/164
N330AA	22330/166
N332AA	22331/168
N334AA	22332/169
N335AA	22333/194
N336AA	22334/195
N338AA	22335/196
N339AA	22336/198

Boeing 767-300(ER)

N351AA	24032/202
N352AA	24033/205
N353AA	24034/206
N354AA	24035/211
N355AA	24036/221
N39356	24037/226
N357AA	24038/227
N358AA	24039/228
N359AA	24040/230
N360AA	24041/232
N361AA	24042/235
N362AA	24043/237
N363AA	24044/238
N39364	24045/240
N39365	24046/241
N366AA	25193/388
N39367	25174/394
N368AA	25195/404
N369AA	25196/422
N370AA	25197/425
N371AA	25198/431
N372AA	25199/433
N373AA	25200/435
N374AA	25201/437
N7375A	25202/441
N376AN	25445/447
N377AN	25446/453
N378AN	25447/469
N379AA	25448/481
N380AN	25449/489
N381AN	25450/495
N382AN	25451/498
N383AN	26995/500
N384AA	26996/512
N385AM	27059/536
N386AA	27060/540
N387AM	27184/541
N388AA	27448/563
N389AA	27449/564
N390AA	27450/565
N391AA	27451/566

Douglas DC-10-10 *c/n*

N126AA	46947/247
N127AA	46948/249
N128AA	46942/250
N129AA	46996/270
N130AA	46989/271
N131AA	46994/273
N132AA	47827/294

N133AA	47828/319
N134AA	47829/321
N135AA	47830/323
N147AA	46702/18
N160AA	46710/70
N162AA	46943/163
N166AA	46908/95
N167AA	46930/112
N168AA	46938/153

Douglas DC-10-30 *c/n*

N137AA	47847/116
N143AA	46555/91
N144AA	47848/136
N163AA	46914/195
N164AA	46950/242

Fokker 100 *c/n*

N1400H	11340
N1401G	11352
N1402K	11353
N1403M	11354
N140AD	11355
N1405J	11356
N1406A	11359
N1407D	11360
N1408B	11361
N1409B	11367
N1410E	11368
N1411G	11369
N1412A	11370
N1413A	11376
N1414D	11377
N1415K	11385
N1416A	11395
N1417D	11396
N1418A	11397
N1419D	11402
N1420D	11403
N1421K	11404
N1422J	11405
N1423A	11406
N1424M	11407
N1425A	11408
N1426A	11411
N1427A	11412
N1428D	11413
N1429G	11414
N1430D	11415
N1431B	11416
N1432A	11417
N1433B	11418
N1434A	11419
N1435D	11425
N1436A	11426
N1437B	11427
N1438H	11428
N1439A	11434
N1440A	11435
N1441A	11436
N1442E	11437
N1443A	11446
N1444N	11447
N1445A	11448
N1446A	11449
N1447L	11456
N1448A	11457
N1449D	11458
N1450A	11459
N1451N	11460
N1452B	11464
N1453D	11465
N1454D	11466
N1455K	11467

N1456D	11468
N1457B	11469
N1458H	11478
N1459A	11479
N1460A	11480
N1461C	11481
N1462C	11482
N1463A	11483
N1464A	11490
N1465K	11491
N1466A	11498
N1467A	11499
N1468A	11501
N1469D	11502
N1470K	11506
N1471G	11507
N1472B	11514
N1473K	11515
N1474D	11520

McDonnell Douglas MD-11 *c/n*

N1750B	48419/450
N1752K	48421/452
N1753	48487/469
N1754	48489/492
N1755	48490/499
N1756	48491/503
N1757A	48505/462
N1758B	48527/504
N1759	48481/482
N1760A	48550/526
N1761R	48551/527
N1762B	48552/530
N1763	48553/531
N1764B	48554/535
N1765B	48596/537
N1766A	48597/540
N1767A	48598/550
N1768D	48436/483

McDonnell Douglas MD-80 *c/n*

N76200	53290/2013
N76201	53291/2019
N76202	53292/2020
N203AA	49145/1097
N205AA	49155/1103
N207AA	49158/1106
N208AA	49159/1107
N210AA	49161/1109
N214AA	49162/1110
N215AA	49163/1111
N216AA	49167/1099
N218AA	49168/1100
N219AA	49171/1112
N221AA	49172/1113
N223AA	49173/1114
N224AA	49174/1115
N225AA	49175/1116
N226AA	49176/1120
N227AA	49177/1121
N228AA	49178/1122
N232AA	49179/1123
N233AA	49180/1124
N234AA	49181/1125
N236AA	49251/1154
N237AA	49253/1155
N241AA	49254/1156

American Eagle is the single most inportant customer for the Saab 340.

N242AA	49255/1157
N244AA	49256/1158
N245AA	49257/1160
N246AA	49258/1161
N248AA	49259/1162
N249AA	49269/1164
N251AA	49270/1165
N253AA	49286/1175
N255AA	49287/1176
N258AA	49288/1187
N259AA	49289/1193
N262AA	49290/1195
N266AA	49291/1210
N269AA	49292/1211
N271AA	49293/1212
N274AA	49271/1166
N275AA	49272/1167
N276AA	49273/1168
N278AA	49294/1213
N279AA	49295/1214
N283AA	49296/1215
N285AA	49297/1216
N286AA	49298/1217
N287AA	49299/1218
N288AA	49300/1219
N289AA	49301/1220
N290AA	49302/1221
N291AA	49303/1222
N292AA	49304/1223
N293AA	49305/1226
N294AA	49306/1227
N295AA	49307/1228
N296AA	49308/1229
N297AA	49309/1246
N298AA	49310/1247
N400AA	49311/1248
N70401	49312/1249
N402A	49313/1255
N403A	49314/1256
N70404	49315/1257
N405A	49316/1258
N406A	49317/1259
N407AA	49318/1265
N408AA	49319/1266
N409AA	49320/1267
N410AA	49321/1273
N411AA	49322/1280
N412AA	49323/1281
N413AA	49324/1289
N33414	49325/1290
N415AA	49326/1295
N416AA	49327/1296
N417AA	49328/1301
N418AA	49329/1302
N419AA	49331/1306
N420AA	49332/1307

N77421	49333/1311
N422AA	49334/1312
N423AA	49335/1320
N424AA	49336/1321
N70425	49337/1325
N426AA	49338/1327
N427AA	49339/1328
N428AA	49340/1329
N429AA	49341/1336
N430AA	49342/1337
N431AA	49343/1339
N432AA	49350/1376
N433AA	49451/1388
N434AA	49452/1389
N435AA	49453/1390
N436AA	49454/1391
N437AA	49455/1392
N438AA	49456/1393
N439AA	49457/1398
N440AA	49459/1407
N441AA	49460/1408
N442AA	49468/1409
N443AA	49469/1410
N73444	49470/1417
N445AA	49471/1418
N446AA	49472/1426
N447AA	49473/1427
N448AA	49474/1431
N449AA	49475/1432
N450AA	49476/1439
N451AA	49477/1441
N452AA	49553/1450
N453AA	49558/1451
N454AA	49559/1460
N455AA	49560/1462
N456AA	49561/1474
N457AA	49562/1475
N458AA	49563/1485
N459AA	49564/1486
N460AA	49565/1496
N461AA	49566/1497
N462AA	49592/1505
N463AA	49593/1506
N464AA	49594/1507
N465A	49595/1509
N466AA	49596/1510
N467AA	49597/1511

N468AA	49598/1513
N469AA	495995/1515
N470AA	49600/1516
N471AA	49601/1518
N472AA	49647/1520
N473AA	49648/1521
N474	49649/1526
N457AA	49650/1527
N476AA	49651/1528
N477AA	49652/1529
N478AA	49653/1534
N479AA	49654/1535
N480AA	49655/1536
N481AA	49656/1545
N482AA	49675/1546
N483A	49676/1550
N484AA	49677/1551
N485AA	49678/1555
N486AA	49679/1557
N487AA	49680/1558
N488AA	49681/1560
N489AA	49682/1562
N490AA	49683/1563
N491AA	49684/1564
N492AA	49730/1565
N493AA	49731/1566
N494AA	49732/1567
N495AA	49733/1607
N496AA	49734/1619
N497AA	49735/1635
N498AA	49736/1640
N499AA	49737/1641
N501AA	49738/1648
N33502	49739/1649
N44503	49797/1650
N70504	49798/1651
N505AA	49799/1652
N7506	49800/1660
N3507A	49801/1661
N7508	49802/1662
N7509	49803/1663
N510AM	49804/1669
N90511	49805/1672
N7512A	49806/1673
N513AA	49890/1686
N7514A	49891/1694
N3515	49892/1695
N516AM	49893/1696
N7517A	49894/1697
N7518A	49895/1698
N7519A	49896/1707
N7520A	49897/1708
N7521A	49898/1707
N7522A	49899/1722
N59523	49915/1723
N70524	49916/1729
N7525A	49917/1735
N7526A	49918/1743
N7527A	49919/1744
N7528A	49920/1750

American was an early MD-11 customer but is now selling its fleet to FedEx.

American Airlines (fleet)

Reg	c/n	Reg	c/n	Reg	c/n	Reg	c/n	Reg	c/n
N70529	49921/1752	N7543A	53025/1802	N557AN	53087/1841	N571AA	49353/1387	N585AA	53248/1903
N7530	49922/1753	N7544A	53026/1804	N558AA	53088/1852	N572AA	49458/1406	N586AA	53249/1904
N7531A	49923/1758	N16545	53027/1805	N559AA	53089/1853	N573AA	53092/1864	N587AA	53250/1907
N7532A	49924/1759	N7546A	53028/1813	N560AA	53090/1858	N574AA	53151/1866	N588AA	53251/1909
N7533A	49987/1760	N7547A	53029/1814	N561AA	53091/1863	N575AM	53152/1875	N589AA	53252/1910
N7534A	49988/1768	N7548A	53030/1816	N562AA	49344/1370	N576AA	53153/1876	N590AA	53253/1919
N7535A	49989/1769	N7549A	53031/1819	N563AA	49345/1371	N577AA	53154/1878	N591AA	53254/1920
N7536A	49990/1770	N7550	53032/1820	N564AA	49346/1372	N578AA	53155/1883	N592AA	53255/1932
N7537A	49991/1780	N14551	53033/1822	N565AA	49347/1373	N579AA	53156/1884	N593AA	53256/1933
N7538A	49992/1781	N552AA	53034/1826	N566AA	49342/1374	N580AA	53157/1885	N594AA	53284/1966
N7539A	49993/1782	N553AA	53083/1828	N567AM	53293/2021	N581AA	53158/1891	N595AA	53285/1989
N7540A	49994/1790	N554AA	53084/1830	N568AA	49349/1375	N582AA	53159/1892	N596AA	53286/2000
N7541A	49995/1791	N555AN	53085/1839	N569AA	49351/1385	N583AA	53160/1893	N597AA	53287/2006
N7542A	49996/1792	N556AA	53086/1840	N570AA	49352/1386	N584AA	53247/1902	N598AA	53288/2011

American Trans Air (TZ/AMT)

Indiana International Airport
Indianapolis, Indiana, USA

Universally known as 'Amtrans', American Trans Air has replaced its former simple blue and gold scheme with this lively livery.

History: Established in August 1973, initially to provide contract flying for Ambassadair Travel Club, flying firstly **Boeing 720**s. **707-120B**s added in 1980. Obtained charter certificate and began programme of expansion in March 1981. Fleet quickly built up through acquisition of **707-320C**s, single **DC-10-40** and seven **Boeing 727-100**s. Rapid increase of charter activity continued in 1985, facilitated by purchase of nine Lockheed L.1011 TriStars, all delivered in 1985, making airline biggest US charter company. Fleet modernised with six **Boeing 757-200** between 1990 and 1992, all leased from IIFC. Entered scheduled passenger market with low-fare leisure routes to a number of Florida destinations, and to Arizona and Nevada. Eight **Advanced 727-200**s added during 1993, replacing older 727-100.

American Transair today: Scheduled and charter service for leisure travellers from Boston, Chicago-Midway, Indianapolis, Milwaukee and Philadelphia to several destinations in Florida, including Fort Lauderdale, Fort Myers, Orlando, St Petersburg and Sarasota/Bradenton, and to Las Vegas, Nevada, and Phoenix, Arizona. Additionally, strong charter-only business within United States, to Caribbean, and across North Atlantic to Europe.

Annual revenue: $580 million
Passengers: 4.3 million
Employees: 2,750
Owned by: AmTran Corporation

Fleet development: Four more **757-200** on order for delivery in late 1996 and 1997.

American Trans Air fleet

Boeing 727-200 Advanced	c/n			Lockheed L.1011 TriStar 50	c/n
N307AS	22000/1583	N774AT	21510/1359	N185AT	1052
N760AT	21954/1525	N775AT	21511/1439	N186AT	1074
N762AT	22162/1717	N776AT	21608/1426	N187At	1077
N763AT	22983/1806	N778AT	22005/1651	N188AT	1078
N764AT	22984/1813	N779AT	22091/1706	N189AT	1081
N765AT	23014/1816	N780AT	22295/1622	N190AT	1086
N766AT	21999/1581	N782AT	21972/1637	N191AT	1084
N767AT	22001/1585			N192AT	1057
N768AT	21996/1571	**Boeing 757-200**		N193AT	1071
N769AT	21998/1577	N512AT	25493/523	N196AT	1076
N770AT	21953/1516	N514AT	27971/690	N763BE	1082
N772AT	22003/1629	N515AT	27598/692		
N773AT	22004/1631	N516AT	27972/694		
		N750AT	23126/45		
		N751AT	23125/44		

Additional fleet:

Boeing 757-200	c/n	Lockheed L.1011 TriStar 1	c/n
N752AT	23128/48	N178AT	1008
N754AT	24964/424	N179AT	1120
N755AT	24965/438	N181AT	1125
N756AT	27351/639	N183AT	1153
N757AT	23127/47	N194AT	1230
		N195AT	1041

America West Airlines (HP/AWE)

Sky Harbor Airport
Phoenix, Arizona, USA

History: Incorporated September 1981 and began operations out of Phoenix, Arizona 1 August 1983 with three **737-200**s. Initial destinations Colorado Springs, Kansas City, Los Angeles and Wichita. Network extended across US and second hub established at Las Vegas. Took delivery of first **737-300** on 28 February 1985; 737-200 fleet expanded to 21 aircraft. Service initiated to Edmonton in March 1985. By December 1986, 737 fleet grown to 46. First **DHC-8**

America West was one of the airline sucess stories of the 1980s in the US, but it fell foul of the serious slump in the market and is only now recovering.

delivered on 27 February 1987, followed by **757-200** on 1 May 1987. On 11 August 1987, Ansett Airlines of Australia purchased 20 per cent stake, since relinquished. Started Honolulu service on 16 November 1989. Placed order for four **747-400**s in 1990 and announced intention to acquire 74 **A320-200**s. Opened service from Honolulu to Nagoya in February 1991. First Airbus service flown 10 days later. Filed for Chapter 11 protection in June 1991, heavily in debt. Restructured and emerged from Chapter 11 in August 1994. Fleet cut by 25 per cent and standardised on three types. **747** fleet disposed of following withdrawal of transpacific operations.

America West today: Flies to 90 cities and communities in 36 states and District of Columbia, providing low-fare full-service operation. Network extends right across US and to Mexico and Canada. Main hubs at Sky Harbor International Airport, and McCarran International Airport, Las Vegas; with mini-hub at Port Columbus (Ohio) Airport. Codeshare with Aeromexico, Mesa Air and Northwest Airlines on specific routes. Major marketing

Reno, Nevada, is an important 'Amwest' destination as evidenced by this special scheme.

agreement and code-share with Continental Airlines between 59 US airports.

Annual revenue: $1,550 million
Passengers: 21.4 million
Employees: 10,000
Major shareholders: TPG Partners, LP (43.1 per cent), Continental Airlines (17.7 per cent) and Mesa Air Group (7.6 per cent)

Associate carriers: Feeder system operated under market-

ing name of **America West Express**. Participants are Desert Sun Airlines and Mountain West Airlines, both divisions of Mesa Air Group.

Mountain West Airlines (HP) flies **Beech 1900C/D**s, **DHC-8**s and **EMB-120RT Brasilia**s. Mountain West also operates as United Express carrier.

Desert Sun Airlines (HP) flies two **Fokker 70**s from Des Moines to Phoenix and Las Vegas, and from Phoenix to Spokane.

America West Airlines fleet

Airbus A320-200	c/n	Boeing 737-100	c/n	N186AW	22653/832	N169AW	23630/1312	N327AW	23507/1252
N304RX	304	N708AW	19771/212	N187AW	22654/862	N172AW	23631/1337	N328AW	23377/1320
N620AW	052			N188AW	22655/872	N173AW	23632/1344	N509DC	23636/1438
N621AW	053	Boeing 737-200	c/n	N189AW	22656/876	N174AW	23633/1421	EI-CKV	23747/1363
N622AW	054	N144AW	19074/95	C-GAPW	20922/370	N175AW	23634/1423		
N624AW	055	N145AW	20194/196	C-GBPW	20958/391	N302AW	24009/1578	Boeing 757-200	c/n
N625AW	064			C-GCPW	20959/395	N303AW	24010/1606	N901AW	23321/76
N626AW	065	Boeing 737-200				N304AW	24011/1608	N902AW	23322/79
N627AW	066	Advanced	c/n	Boeing 737-300	c/n	N305AW	24012/1612	N903AW	23323/80
N628AW	067	N137AW	23148/1059	N150AW	23218/1076	N306AW	24633/1809	N904AW	23566/96
N629AW	076	N138AW	22792/887	N151AW	23219/1090	N307AW	24634/1823	N905AW	23567/97
N631AW	077	N141AW	21955/659	N154AW	23776/1417	N308AW	24710/1825	N906AW	23568/99
N632AW	081	N147AW	22630/860	N155AW	23777/1419	N309AW	24711/1843	N907AW	22691/155
N633AW	082	N149AW	22575/749	N156AW	23778/1455	N311AW	24712/1869	N908AW	24233/244
N634AW	091	N178AW	22645/768	N157AW	23779/1457	N313AW	23712/1336	N909AW	24522/252
N635AW	092	N179AW	22646/778	N158AW	23780/1459	N314AW	23733/1345	N910AW	24523/256
N636AW	098	N180AW	22647/785	N160AW	23782/1496	N315AW	23734/1359	N913AW	22207/35
N637AW	099	N181AW	22648/789	N164AW	23625/1283	N316AW	23714/1345	N914AW	22208/38
N638AW	455	N182AW	22649/801	N165AW	23626/1284	N322AW	25400/2112	N915AW	22209/40
N639AW	471	N183AW	22650/806	N166AW	23627/1302	N323AW	23684/1353	N916AW	24291/215
N640AW	448	N184AW	22651/819	N167AW	23628/1304	N324AW	23261/1157		
		N185AW	22652/831	N168AW	23629/1311	N325AW	23260/1146		

Ansett Australia (AN/AAA)

Ansett's three Boeing 747-300s have been leased from Singapore Airlines since 1994/95. They offer a massive increase in capacity.

History: Founded by Reginal M. Ansett as Ansett Airways and began operations 17 February 1936, flying Hamilton-Melbourne service with a **Fokker Universal**. After June 1942, when war reached Pacific, maintained only Melbourne-Hamilton flight, alongside transport operations for US Air Force. Full commercial operations resumed on 5 February 1945. Introduced war-surplus **DC-3** fleet in June 1946. Passing of government's new Civil Airlines Agreement Act, popularly known as two-airline policy, on 18 November 1952, shared out main market between new government airline Trans-Australia Airlines (TAA) and private company Australian National Airways (ANA), and left Ansett out in cold. Nevertheless, was able to expand through acquisition of regional airlines, finally becoming Australia's biggest privately-owned airline on 4 October 1957 with purchase of struggling ANA. New enlarged airline initially known as Ansett-ANA, but ANA name dropped in June 1969 in favour of Ansett Airlines of Aus-

tralia. Post-war fleet of six DC-3s and two **Sandringham** flying-boats augmented in 1954 by two **Convair 340**s and eight **Convair 440**s delivered in 1957 and 1958. Four **L.188 Electra**s entered service 10 March 1959, before introduction of jet equipment, first with **Boeing 727** on 2 November 1964 then **Douglas DC-9** in January 1967. Regional expansion towards end of 1959 with purchase of South Pacific Airlines, promptly renamed Ansett of New Zealand. By end of decade controlled most private airlines and continued its development along equal lines with TAA. In 1980, taken over by Rupert Murdoch's News Ltd, with other shares acquired subsequently by TNT. **Boeing 767-200** introduced on trunk routes in June 1983, and became launch customer for **Fokker 50** on 12 February 1985 with order and options for 15 aircraft. Signed another contract later that year for eight **Airbus A320**s, all delivered between September and December 1988. Acquired Eastwest Airlines, fully

integrated 31 October 1993. Won route authority for international routes in March 1993, inaugurated 11 September 1993 with flight to Bali. Further expanded into international arena in September 1994, flying leased **Boeing 747-300** between Sydney, Hong Kong and Osaka.

Ansett today: Largest privately-owned airline operating throughout Australia from main hubs at Sydney, Melbourne and Perth. Also regional and international services to Denpasar (Bali), Hong Kong, Jakarta, Kuala Lumpur and Osaka. Rights granted to Singapore and Taipei.

Annual revenue: $2,100 million
Passengers: 11.3 million
Employees: 17,000
Ownership: divided between News Corp. (50 per cent) and Air New Zealand which purchased stake from TNT in 1996

Associate carriers: Ansett New Zealand (ZQ), wholly-owned by parent, although agreement reached for sale of 25 per cent to Air New Zealand. Started operations in 1986 as Newmans Air and renamed in 1987. Operates mix of trunk and commuter services throughout New Zealand, with eight **BAe 146-300**s, one **146-200QC** and three **DHC-8-100**s. Code-share agreements with Malaysia Airlines and United Airlines.

Skywest Airlines (YT), founded in 1963, serves 19-point network centred on Perth with four **BAe Jetstream 31**s and three **Fokker 50**s.

Kendell Airlines (KD) operates out of Adelaide, Melbourne and Sydney with seven **Metro 23**s, six **Saab 340A**s, three **340BPlus**; has two **Saab 2000**s on order.

Aeropelican Air Services (PO), founded 23 October 1968, uses four DHC **Twin Otters** between Belmont (Newcastle) and Sydney Mascot.

Ansett New Zealand operates in New Zealand on behalf of its Australian parent, while Air New Zealand now owns 50 per cent of Ansett Australia.

Ansett Australia fleet

Airbus A320-200	c/n	Boeing 727-200F	c/n						
VH-HYA	022	VH-RMX	20551/1054	VH-CZV	23831/1471	VH-JJT	E2098	VH-FNJ	20115
VH-HYB	023			VH-CZW	23832/1473	VH-JJU	E2116		
VH-HYC	024	**Boeing 737-300**	**c/n**	VH-CZX	24029/1601	VH-JJW	E2110	**Fokker F28-1000**	**c/n**
VH-HYD	025	VH-CZA	23653/1260			VH-JJX	E2127	VH-FKA	11021
VH-HYE	026	VH-CZB	23654/1273	**Boeing 747-300**	**c/n**			VH-FKC	11025
VH-HYF	027	VH-CZC	23655/1274	VH-INH	23026/580	**BAe 146-200QT**	**c/n**	VH-FKE	11040
VH-HYG	029	VH-CZD	23656/1279	VH-INJ	23029/590	VH-JJY	E2113	VH-FKF	11008
VH-HYH	030	VH-CZE	23657/1280	VH-INK	23028/584	VH-JJZ	E2114		
VH-HYI	140	VH-CZF	23658/1281					**Fokker F28-3000**	**c/n**
VH-HYJ	142	VH-CZG	23659/1292	**Boeing 767-200**	**c/n**	**BAe 146-300**	**c/n**	VH-EWF	11143
VH-HYK	157	VH-CZH	23660/1294	VH-RMA	24742/303	VH-EWI	E3171	VH-EWG	11151
VH-HYL	229	VH-CZI	23661/1314	VH-RMD	22692/24	VH-EWL	E3177		
VH-	543	VH-CZJ	23662/1316	VH-RME	22693/28	VH-EWM	E3179	**Fokker F28-4000**	**c/n**
VH-HYO	547	VH-CZK	23663/1323	VH-RMF	22694/32	VH-EWR	E3195	VH-EWA	11195
		VH-CZL	23664/1326	VH-RMG	22695/35	VH-EWS	E3197	VH-EWB	11205
Boeing 727-200 Adv		VH-CZM	24302/1618	VH-RMH	22696/100			VH-EWC	11207
VH-ANA	22641/1753	VH-CZN	24303/1620	VH-RMK	22981/79	**Fokker 50**	**c/n**	VH-EWD	11208
VH-ANB	22642/1759	VH-CZO	24304/1622	VH-RML	22980/71	VH-FNA	20106	VH-FKI	11183
VH-ANE	22643/1762	VH-CZP	24305/1641			VH-FNB	20107	VH-FKJ	11186
VH-ANF	22644/1768	VH-CZS	24030/1654	**BAe 146-200**	**c/n**	VH-FNC	20108	VH-FKO	11212
VH-RMN	21695/1481	VH-CZT	27454/2703	VH-JJP	E2037	VH-FND	20129		
		VH-CZU	27267/2600	VH-JJQ	E2038	VH-FNE	20110		
				VH-JJS	E2093	VH-FNI	20114		

Asiana Airlines (OZ/AAR)

Kimpo International Airport
Seoul, South Korea

History: Established as Seoul Air International 16 February 1988. Signed contract with Guinness Peat Aviation for lease of six **Boeing 737-400**s, later increased to eight. Renamed as Asiana Airlines 11 August 1988. Began domestic services 23 December and contracted with Boeing for two **767-300**s with options for two more. Orders placed for five **737-400**s in April 1989 and for two **747-400**s in May. Two **737-500**s leased from Ansett in June. International routes inaugurated to Japan in January 1990. Massive new order concluded in September 1990 covering purchase of eight more Boeing 737-400s, eight additional **767-300ER**s and seven more **747-400**s.

Asiana today: Extensive and growing regional/domestic network, plus long-haul flights to Europe and US, serving 56 cities.

Code-share agreement with Northwest Airlines, and revenue sharing flights with Air China and China Eastern Airlines. Joint services with THY.

Annual revenue: $995 million
Passengers: 7.7 million
Employees: 5,820
Ownership: Kumho Group

In just eight years, South Korea's Asiana Airlines has grown to become one of the most important Far Eastern carriers.

Fleet development: Ordered 18 185-seat **Airbus A321**s at 1996 Farnborough air show for delivery in 1998-2005. Requirement for up to 75 new aircraft.

Asiana Airlines fleet

Boeing 737-400	c/n	HL7256	24314/1680	HL7250	25769/2737	HL7418	25780/1035	HL7264	24798/331
HL7227	25764/2314	HL7257	24469/1749	HL7261	24786/1898				
HL7228	25765/2335	HL7258	24493/1751	HL7262	24787/1900	**Boeing 747-400F**	**c/n**	**Boeing 767-300(ER)**	
HL7231	25766/2543	HL7259	24494/1757			HL7419	25781/1044	HL7249	26265/570
HL7235	26308/2665	HL7260	24520/1803	**Boeing 747-400**	**c/n**	HL7420	25783/1064	HL7266	25347/399
HL7251	23869/1639			HL7413	25405/880			HL7267	25404/411
HL7252	23976/1651	**Boeing 737-500**	**c/n**	HL7414	25452/892	**Boeing 767-300**	**c/n**	HL7268	25132/417
HL7253	23977/1655	HL7230	24778/1816	HL7415	25777/946	HL7247	25757/523	HL7269	26206/487
HL7254	23978/1659	HL7232	25767/2614	HL7416	25778/983	HL7248	25758/582	HL7286	26207/503
HL7255	23980/1667	HL7233	25768/2724	HL7417	25779/1006	HL7263	24797/328	HL7505	27394/572

Atlas Air (5Y/GTI)

Atlas Air has taken advantage of the low acquisition cost of early-model Boeing 747s to rapidly build up a large fleet of freighters on its all-cargo network.

History: Founded in 1992 to provide *ad hoc* cargo charter, supplementary or scheduled services and sub-contracts, with single **747-200F**. Fleet expanded rapidly with more 747-200Fs, and single **747-100F**.

Atlas Air today: Fast-growing cargo charter operator, providing *ad hoc* and contract charter flights across world. Frequent and regular destinations include Amsterdam, Anchorage, Bangkok, Buenos Aires, Caracas, Chicago, Dallas/Ft Worth, Delhi, Dubai, Frankfurt, Hong Kong, Khabarovsk, Lima, Los Angeles, Luxembourg, Manaus, Mexico City, Miami, Panama City, San Francisco, Santiago, Sao Paulo, Seoul, Singapore and Taipei.

Fleet development: Signed agreements with Lufthansa for purchase of four **747-200B**s with options on three more, and with Thai for six 747-200Bs. Plans to have fleet of 35-40 aircraft by 1998/99.

Atlas Air fleet

Boeing 747-100			
N3203Y	19751/39	N507MC	21380/320
		N508MC	21644/356
		N509MC	21221/299
Boeing 747-200B		N512MC	21220/294
N505MC	21251/296	N516MC	22507/497
N506MC	21252/297	N517MC	23300/613
		N518MC	23476/647
		N808MC	21048/253
		Boeing 747-200F	
		N747MC	23348/625

Austrian Airlines (OS/AUA)

Austrian's newly-delivered 186-seat Airbus A321s are soon to be joined by 144-seat A320s.

History: Founded 30 September 1957 and started operations 31 March 1958 between Vienna and London with four **Vickers V.700 Viscount**s. Larger **V.800 Viscount**s entered service 1 March 1960. Five **Caravelle VI-R**s delivered between February 1963 and May 1966. From 1 May 1963, three **DC-3**s replaced Viscounts on domestic network, but themselves replaced by two **HS 748**s from 5 June 1966. Short-lived transatlantic service inaugurated 1 April 1969 over Vienna-Brussels-New York route with **Boeing 707-320B** leased from SABENA. Order placed for nine **DC-9-32**s entering service on 22 June 1971. First of five **DC-9-51** arrived in Vienna 14 September 1975. Network expanded in 1976 to include Cairo, Dusseldorf, Stockholm and Helsinki. On 13 October 1977 decision made to order eight **MD-82**s; made first commercial flight between Vienna and Zurich 26 October 1981. Subsidiary *Austrian Air Services* (AAS) began internal flights with two **SA226TC Metro II**s on 1 April 1980. Further fleet expansion and modernisation initiated with orders for four **MD-87**s, two **Airbus A310-300**s and two **Fokker 50**s (for AAS). Inaugural flight with new A310 between Vienna and New York on 26 March 1989. Vienna-Moscow-Tokyo in co-operation with Aeroflot and ANA followed on 16 June. Joined with Finnair, SAS and Swissair on 3 May 1990 to form European Quality Alliance. In same year made largest investment in its history with order for 13 **Airbus A320/A321**s plus 13 options.

Austrian Airlines today: National flag-carrier serving 82 destinations in 46 countries throughout Europe, and to North America, Africa, and Middle and Far East, with particular strength in Central and Eastern European market. Long-haul flights connect Vienna with Almaty, Beijing,

Johannesburg, New York, Osaka, Tehran, Tokyo and Washington. Code-share agreements on specific routes with Aeroflot, Air China, Air France, All Nippon Airways, British Midland, Czech Airlines, Delta Air Lines, Finnair, Iberia, KLM, LOT, Lufthansa, Malév, SAS, South African Airways, Swissair, Tarom and Ukraine International. New co-operation agreement being initiated with Lauda Air.

Annual revenue: $910 million
Passengers: 2.5 million
Cargo: 35,500 tonnes
Employees: 3,750.
Major shareholders: Austrian government (51.9 per cent), Swissair (10.0 per cent), All Nippon Airways (9.0 per cent) and Air France (1.5 per cent)

Associate carriers: Austrian **Airtransport** (AAT), owned 80 per cent by Austrian Airlines and 20 per cent by Oesterreichische Verkehrsbüro, undertakes inclusive-tour and charter flights with aircraft leased from parent

company as required. Established on 15 February 1964.

Acquired 42.85 per cent of Innsbruck-based **Tyrolean Airways** (VO) on 16 May 1994. Serves 29 destinations in Europe from hubs at Graz, Innsbruck, Linz and Salzburg, carrying 1 million passengers. Fleet of eight **de Havilland Canada DHC-8-100**s, nine **DHC-8-300**s, four **Fokker 70**s along with five

Canadair Regional Jets. Two more DHC-8-300s on order.

Fleet development: Delivery of seven Airbus A320-200s imminent for completion spring 1997. Three more A321-100s due in 1997 and 1998. Two **Airbus A340-300**s on order for delivery in 1997 and 1999. Three more Fokker 70s were due to be delivered in autumn 1996 and early 1997.

Austrian Airlines fleet

Airbus A310-300	c/n	Fokker 70	c/n	OE-LDY	49115/1135
OE-LAA	489	OE-LFO	11559	OE-LDZ	49164/1182
OE-LAB	492	OE-LFP	11560	OE-LMA	49278/1183
OE-LAC	568	OE-LFQ	11572	OE-LMB	49279/1230
OE-LAD	624	OE-LFR	11568	OE-LMC	49327/1252
				OE-LMD	49933/1837
Airbus A321-100	c/n	McDonnell Douglas MD-80		OE-LME	53377/2057
OE-LBA	552	OE-LDP	48015/924	OE-LMU	49741/1630
OE-LBB	570	OE-LDR	48016/941		
OE-LBC	581	OE-LDS	48017/958	McDonnell Douglas MD-87	
		OE-LDT	48018/995	OE-LMK	49411/1412
Airbus A340-200	c/n	OE-LDU	48019/1001	OE-LML	49412/1424
OE-LAG	075	OE-LDV	48020/1045	OE-LMM	49413/1681
OE-LAH	081	OE-LDW	48059/1047	OE-LMN	49414/1682
		OE-LDX	48021/1078	OE-LMO	49888/1692

Balkan Bulgarian (LZ/LAZ)

Sofia International Airport (Vrajdebna)
Sofia, Bulgaria

History: Established in late 1948 as joint Bulgarian/Soviet airline as Trasportno Aviatsionno Bulgaro-Sovietsko Obshchestvo (TABSO). Initial operations with eight **Lisunov Li-2**s used on domestic network from Sofia. Soviet Union's 50 per cent holding reverted to Bulgarian state in October 1954. Re-opened Sofia-Prague service, suspended in 1950, via Budapest. Delivery of **Ilyushin Il-14** in 1956 permitted expansion to Berlin, Belgrade, Moscow, Vienna and other European cities. Three **Il-18**s introduced in 1962 and used to open routes to North Africa, and in 1965 to London. Fleet expanded and modernised with acquisition of **Antonov An-24** in 1966 and its first jet, **Tupolev Tu-134**, in 1967. Name changed to Balkan Bulgarian Airlines 1 February 1968. Bought large fleet of **Tu-154** jets between 1985 and 1987, permitting long-haul expansion as far as Luanda and Ho Chi Minh City. Began transition to Western equipment in 1990 with lease of two **Boeing 737-500**s and in late 1991 took delivery of first of four **Airbus A320-200**s replacing early-model

Tu-154s. Two **767-200ER**s leased from Air France in May 1992 to service long-haul routes.

Balkan today: National flag-carrier providing international services from capital Sofia to Algiers, Amsterdam, Athens, Bahrain, Bangkok, Barcelona, Beirut, Berlin (Schönefeld), Brussels, Budapest, Cairo, Casablanca, Colombo, Copenhagen, Damascus, Doha, Dubai, Frankfurt, Harare, Istanbul, Johannesburg, Kiev, Kuwait, Lagos, Larnaca, London, Madrid, Male, Malta, Milan, Moscow, Munich, Nairobi, New York, Ohrid, Paris, Prague, Rome,

Balkan is finding it difficult to finance new Western-built aircraft, like this A320, and may be a prospective customer for the Tupolev Tu-204.

Stockholm, Tel Aviv, Tunis, Vienna, Warsaw and Zürich. Domestic flights to Bourgas and Varna. Code-shares with Air France, THY, Iberia and Hemus Air.

Annual revenue: $200 million
Passengers: 0.8 million
Cargo: 27,500 tonnes
Employees: 3,900
Ownership: government-owned but with advanced plans for privatisation

Balkan Bulgarian Airlines

Fleet development: State Fund for Reconstruction and Development is making available $45 million loan to enable airline to embark on much-needed fleet modernisation for short to medium routes. Under consideration are three 50- to 60-seat aircraft, with new **Ilyushin Il-114** one likely candidate. Acquisition of two **Antonov An-12** freighters under consideration.

Balkan Bulgarian International fleet

Airbus A320-200	c/n	Boeing 767-200ER	c/n	Tupolev Tu-134A-3	c/n		
LZ-ABA	257	F-GHGD	24832/316	LZ-TUG	49858	LZ-BTO	258
LZ-ABB	271	F-GHGE	24854/326	LZ-TUM	3351906	LZ-BTP	278
LZ-ABC	308			LZ-TUT		LZ-BTR	320
LZ-ABD	314	**Ilyushin Il-18D**	c/n	LZ-TUV	1351408	LZ-BTS	422
		LZ-BEA	188010802	LZ-TUZ	1351503	LZ-BTT	483
Antonov An-12	c/n	LZ-BEH	186008905			LZ-BTU	484
LZ-BAC	343708			**Tupolev Tu-154B**	c/n	LZ-BTV	569
LZ-BAE	402001	**Ilyushin Il-18E**	c/n	LZ-BTA	026		
LZ-BAF	402408	LZ-BEW	185008601	LZ-BTC	036	**Tupolev Tu-154M**	c/n
		LZ-BEZ	185008603	LZ-BTE	073	LZ-BTH	754
Antonov An-24RV	c/n			LZ-BTF	077	LZ-BTI	706
LZ-ANK	17307005	**Ilyushin Il-18V**	c/n	LZ-BTG	095	LZ-BTN	832
		LZ-BEI	181002805	LZ-BTJ	270	LZ-BTW	707
Antonov An-24V	c/n	LZ-BEU	183005905	LZ-BTK	144	LZ-BTY	800
LZ-ANB	67302710			LZ-BTM	209	LZ-BTZ	781

Additional c/n column:

Reg	c/n
LZ-ANC	67302808
LZ-AND	77303301
LZ-ANF	77303407
LZ-ANG	77303408
LZ-ANL	67302206
LZ-ANM	77302905
LZ-ANO	87304406
LZ-ANP	97305402
LZ-ANR	07306001
LZ-ANS	07306006
LZ-ANT	27307903
Boeing 737-500	c/n
LZ-BOA	24881/1945
LZ-BOB	24921/1962
LZ-BOC	25425/2177

Biman Bangladesh (BG/BBC)

Zia International Airport
Dhaka, Bangladesh

Biman has begun to modernise its long-haul fleet through the acquisition of two A310-325s, supplementing its DC-10-30s.

History: Established as semi-autonomous state enterprise 4 January 1972, three weeks after country gained its independence from Pakistan 16 December 1971. Started operations 5 March 1972 with regular charter flights to London using leased **Boeing 707** equipment. Acquired two **Fokker F27-200**s from Indian Airlines and inaugurated domestic flights 9 March 1972, connecting Dacca with Chittagon, Jessore and Sylhet. Began own scheduled service to London on 18 June 1973, first with leased **707-320** and from December with own **707-320C**. Acquired four more F27s and two more 707-32Cs and expanded network to Dubai, Bangkok, Karachi, and 6 April 1977 to Singapore. Two **Fokker F28-4000**

Fellowships added in autumn 1981 for domestic and regional flights. First two **McDonnell Douglas DC-10-30**s delivered on 16 August 1983, followed by third in October, all three bought from Singapore Airlines. Placed order for two **Airbus A310-300** for delivery during 1996, as first step in fleet re-equipment.

Biman today: Government-owned flag-carrier maintaining international route network, and domestic services to all major points. International services link capital Dhaka with Abu Dhabi, Amsterdam, Bahrain, Bangkok, Bombay, Brussels, Calcutta, Delhi, Dubai, Doha, Frankfurt, Hong Kong, Jeddah, Karachi, Kathmandu, Kuala Lumpur, Kuwait, London, Muscat, New York, Paris, Rome, Riyadh, Singapore, Tokyo and Yangon. Some flights to Middle East also operate out of Chittagong's Potenga International Airport. Services planned to Amsterdam, Ho Chi Minh City and Jakarta. Domestic schedules to Barisal, Chittagong, Cox's Bazaar, Ishurdi, Jessore, Rajshahi, Saipur and Sylhet.

Employees: 5,960

Fleet development: Two **Airbus A310-300**s delivered in April and September 1996.

Biman Bangladesh Airlines fleet

Airbus A310-300	c/n	Douglas DC-10-30	c/n	Fokker F28-4000	
S2-ADE	698	S2-ACO	46993/263	**Fellowship**	c/n
S2-ADF	700	S2-ACP	46995/275	S2-ACH	11172
		S2-ACQ	47817/300	S2-ACJ	11180
British Aerospace ATP		S2-ACR	48317/445		
S2-ACX	2026	S2-ADB	47818/305		
S2-ACY	2027				

Braathens SAFE (BU/BRA)

History: Founded by Ludvig G. Braathen 26 March 1946 as Braathens South American and Far East Air Transport, soon abbreviated to Braathens S.A.F.E. Began charter flights in December 1946 with **DC-4**, to Hong Kong, New York and Johannesburg. Awarded concession for Far Eastern routes 3 February 1949, officially opened 5 August and flown to Hong Kong and Bangkok. Granted licence for Oslo-Tonsberg-Stavanger route and acquired two **de Havilland Heron**s. In December 1952 ordered two **L.1049C Super Constellation**s, but never delivered as result of cancellation of Far East scheduled licence 25 March 1954. After initial struggle to obtain authority for more routes, domestic network expanded steadily, helped by introduction of **Fokker F27-100**, in December 1958. Inclusive-tour operations started January 1961 with **DC-6**. Two **Boeing 737-200**s and five **F28-1000**s ordered in 1967; both types delivered in early 1969. Last DC-6B service operated 18 September 1973. Took delivery of first of two **767-200**s 18 March 1984 for inclusive-tour flights, but acquired its first international route licence for 35 years in August 1988, and 2 May 1989 inaugurated service to Billund in Denmark. Domestic market share boosted following deregulation of market 1 April 1994.
  Braathens today: Biggest domestic operator in Norway with 50 per cent of total market,

serving 15 major cities. Main operations centred on Oslo, Bergen and Trondheim. International flights scheduled to Alicante, Billund, Jersey, London-Gatwick, Malaga, Newcastle, Nice and Rome from Oslo; London-Gatwick from Bergen; and to Murmansk, in association with Aeroflot, as extension of Tromso service. European charter flights also undertaken. Route specific agreement with Finnair.

Annual revenue: *$525 million*
Passengers: *4.7 million*

Norway's Braathens SAFE operates an all-Boeing 737 fleet, including this 737-400, and holds the distinction of being the launch customer for 737-500.

Employees: *3,290*
Major shareholder: *Braathens Rederi with 69 per cent*

  Fleet development: Three more Boeing 737s, expected to be **737-500** models, on order. One delivery in 1997 may be changed to 737-400. Three options not yet decided.

Braathens SAFE fleet

Boeing 737-400	c/n	LN-BRD	24651/1842	LN-BRT	25789/2229
LN-BRA	24270/1726	LN-BRF	24652/1917	LN-BRU	25790/2245
LN-BRB	24271/1738	LN-BRG	24272/1923	LN-BRV	25791/2351
LN-BRE	24643/1860	LN-BRH	24828/1925	LN-BRW	25792/2353
LN-BRI	24644/1938	LN-BRJ	24273/2018	LN-BRX	25797/2434
LN-BRP	25303/2137	LN-BRK	24274/2035	LN-BRY	27155/2449
LN-BRQ	25348/2148	LN-BRM	24645/2072	LN-BUA	26297/2578
LN-BUB	24703/1828	LN-BRN	24646/2138	LN-BUC	26304/2649
		LN-BRO	24647/2143		
Boeing 737-500	**c/n**	LN-BRR	24648/2213		
LN-BRC	24650/1792	LN-BRS	24649/2225		

Britannia Airways (BY/BAL)

History: Formed 1 December 1961 by Universal Sky Tours under name of Euravia (London) and began flying with two **L.049 Constellation**s 5 May 1962. Six more Constellations added before end of year. Present name adopted in 1964, when re-equipping with **Bristol Britannia 102** aircraft, which operated first service 6 December 1964. By summer, five Britannias in operation and all Constellations withdrawn. Became part of Thomson

Organisation 26 April 1965. First European charter airline to operate **Boeing 737-200**, taking delivery of first aircraft 8 July 1968. 737 fleet built up to eight and last Britannia taken out of service at end of 1970. Two **707-320C**s operated on transatlantic and Far East charters between 1971 and 1973. Short-haul fleet expanded over next 20 years to total 29 737s. Another European first achieved with delivery of **Boeing 767-200** in February 1984.

  In August 1988, Thomson acquired Horizon Travel and its East Midlands-based airline Orion Airways which, together with its seven **737-300**s, was fully integrated into Britannia in November 1988. Announced major fleet review focused on **Boeing 757**, introduced in April 1992, and 767. Last Boeing 737 withdrawn in 1994.
  Britannia today: Largest inclusive-tour charter operator in world, flying from its main bases

35

Britannia Airways

Britannia adopted its name from the Bristol Britannias it once flew. Today the airline operates an all-Boeing fleet.

Tunisia, Malta and Canary Islands. Long-haul routes to Maldives, India, Sri Lanka, Australia, New Zealand, Kenya, United States, Mexico and Caribbean.

Annual revenue: *$900 million*
Passengers: *7.5 million*
Employees: *3,100*
Wholly-owned by: *Thomson Travel Group*

at Luton, London-Gatwick and Manchester, and 14 other UK provincial airports. Serves over 100 regular destinations through-

out Europe and Mediterranean Basin, taking in all main resort areas of Portugal, Spain, Italy, Greece, Cyprus, Turkey, Egypt,

Fleet development: Expects to add further four **767-300ER**s, one a year from 1997 to 2000.

Britannia Airways fleet

Boeing 757-200		G-BYAJ	25623/528	G-BYAS	27238/604	G-BNYS	24013/210	Boeing 767-300(ER)	
G-BYAC	26962/440	G-BYAK	26267/538	G-BYAT	27208/606	G-BOPB	24239/243	G-OBYA	28039/612
G-BYAD	26963/450	G-BYAL	25626/549	G-BYAU	27220/618	G-BPFV	24457/256	G-OBYB	28040/616
G-BYAE	26964/452	G-BYAM	23895/132	G-BYAW	27234/663	G-BRIF	24736/296	G-OBYC	28041/621
G-BYAF	26266/514	G-BYAN	27219/596	G-OAHF	24136/169	G-BRIG	24757/299	G-OBYD	28042/623
G-BYAG	26965/517	G-BYAO	27235/598			G-BYAA	25058/362		
G-BYAH	26966/520	G-BYAP	27236/600	Boeing 767-200(ER)		G-BYAB	25139/373		
G-BYAI	26967/522	G-BYAR	27237/602	G-BNCW	23807/184				

British Airways (BA/BAW)

London-Heathrow and -Gatwick Airports
UK

Seven Concorde 102s serve as prestigious flagships for British Airways. They are due to keep flying well into the next century.

History: Established as Imperial Airways 31 March 1924 through amalgamation of four airline companies – Handley Page Transport, Instone Air Line, Daimler Airways and British Marine Air Navigation. Inherited cross-Channel routes and motley collection of 18 aircraft, but focus realigned towards establishing eastern Empire routes. Aircraft progressed from **de Havilland DH.66 Hercules** to **Shorts S8 Calcutta** flying-boats, **Handley Page HP.42** and **Armstrong-Whitworth Atlanta**. Expansion into Africa saw pas-

senger service to Cape Town established 27 April 1932. Ordered 28 **'C' Class** four-engined flying-boats from Shorts to serve ambitious Empire Air Mail Scheme, inaugurated on 29 June 1937 and in full operation by 1938. Opening of transatlantic and South American routes forestalled by advent of war. Government decided to merge operations of Imperial Airways and British Airways, latter formed on 30 September 1935 to develop domestic and European services, using fleet of **DH.84**, **Junkers Ju 52/3m** and

Lockheed Electra and **Super Electra** aircraft. Merger under British Overseas Airways Corporation (BOAC) name became effective from 1 April 1940. Emerged from war with fleet of 175 aircraft, made up of 11 landplane and seven flying-boat types. Australian routes resumed 31 May 1945 in association with Qantas. **L.049 Constellations** acquired for New York service, opened 1 July 1946, and **Boeing Stratocruisers**, **Handley Page Hermes** and **Canadair Argonaut** equipment, before withdrawal of last flying-boat 7 November 1950. British European Airways (BEA) division formed 1 January 1946 charged with developing European network, initially with **DC-3** and **Vickers Viking** aircraft. Began world's first scheduled jet service with **de Havilland Comet 1** on London-Johannesburg route 2 May 1952 and, after problems with Comet solved following two disastrous crashes, opened first transatlantic jet service between London and New York with improved **Comet 4** on 4 October 1958. Both BOAC and BEA operated mostly British aircraft up to 1970s, including Comet 4, **Bristol Britannia**, **Vickers VC 10** and **Super VC 10**, and on short-haul routes **Comet 4B**, **Vickers Viscount** and **Vanguard**, **Hawker Siddeley Trident** and **BAC One-Eleven**. Two state corporations merged on 1 April 1972 under British Airways name. **Concorde** supersonic service introduced on 21 January 1976 to Bahrain. Shift to US, and specifically Boeing-built aircraft, begun with delivery of first **Boeing 747** on 22 May 1970, consolidated since then with acquisition of **737** (1980), **757** (1983), **767** (1990) and **777** (1995), interrupted only by **Lockheed TriStar** in 1974. 1987 saw controversial take-over of British Caledonian Airways and share flotation. Since then has become one of most profitable airlines in world. In January 1993 bought 24.9 per cent of stock in USAir for $300 million, and 25 per cent in Qantas in 1995 for around $440 million.

British Airways today: World's largest international passenger network, serving 169 destinations in 80 countries on all continents, from main hubs at London's Heathrow and Gatwick airports, Birmingham, Glasgow and Manchester. Also links 15 points in UK, including high-frequency Super Shuttle services between London-Heathrow and Glasgow, Edinburgh, Manchester and Belfast; and between London-Gatwick and Newcastle, latter flown by franchise partner CityFlyer Express. Code-share with Aeromexico and joint cargo flights with Korean Air on London-Seoul route.

Annual revenue: *$11,200 million*
Passengers: *35.7 million*
Cargo: *510,000 tonnes*
Employees: *53,000*

Fleet development: All TriStars out of service and stored in Mojave desert. Last remaining **767-300ER** on order due for delivery in February 1997. Three more **747-400s** to be delivered in 1997, with remaining 25 of type on order to follow in subsequent years. Sixth 777 due in December

Deutsche BA's first jet equipment was three leased Boeing 737-300s, later replaced by its own 737-300s in 1992.

1996, to be followed by further two each in January and February 1997. Remaining five aircraft to follow in 1998. Has requirement for up to 30 new regional jets plus 30 options, covering three sizes for 80, 100 and 120 passengers. A request for proposals has been issued to manufacturers. Delivery required from January 1997 through 1999.

Associate carriers: Major alliance proposed with American Airlines. Equity shareholdings in Qantas (25 per cent), USAir (24.6 per cent), Air Mauritius (12.8 per cent), Deutsche BA (49 per cent) and TAT (100 per cent).

Deutsche BA (DI), formed in April 1978 as Delta Air and acquired by BA and German banks in March 1992, operates domestic schedules in Germany, plus cross-border flights, from hubs at Munich, Berlin/Tegel and Friedrichshafen. Fleet comprises eight **737-300s**, five **Fokker 100s**, five **Saab 2000s** and three **Saab 340s**.

TAT European Airlines (IJ), formed in 1968, flies throughout France and Europe with current-fleet of seven **ATR42-300s**, seven **ATR72-200s**, six **737-200s**, seven **Fokker 100s** and 11 **F28s**.

Franchise operators include following: *Brymon Airways*

(BA), flies domestically from Plymouth and Bristol with **DHC-7** and **DHC-8-300** aircraft.

CityFlyer Express (FD), based at Gatwick, operates within UK and to Europe with fleet of seven **ATR42-300s** and four **ATR72-200s**.

GB Airways (GT), serves North Africa from London and Manchester with two **Boeing 737-200s** and two **737-400s**.

Loganair (LC), serves Scottish destinations with five **BN Islanders**, one **DHC-6** and eight **Shorts 360s**.

Maersk Air (VB), formerly Birmingham European Airways, serves European points with six **BAC One-Elevens** and one **Jetstream 31**.

Manx Airlines Europe (JE), operates with 11 **Jetstream 41s** and six **ATPs** in British Airways colours on domestic and European services.

Also *Sun-Air* (Scandanavia) and *Comair* (South Africa).

Brymon Airways operates as a British Airways Express carrier with a fleet of DHC-7s and DHC-8s.

British Airways

Airbus A320-100 *c/n*
G-BUSB 006
G-BUSC 008
G-BUSD 011
G-BUSE 017
G-BUSF 018

Airbus A320-200 *c/n*
G-BUSG 039
G-BUSH 042
G-BUSI 103
G-BUSJ 109
G-BUSK 120

BAe/Aérospatiale Concorde *c/n*
G-BOAA 206
G-BOAB 208
G-BOAC 204
G-BOAD 210
G-BOAE 212
G-BOAF 214

British Aerospace ATP
G-BTPA 2007
G-BTPC 2010
G-BTPD 2011
G-BTPE 2012
G-BTPF 2013
G-BTPG 2014
G-BTPH 2015
G-BTPJ 2016
G-BTPK 2041
G-BTPL 2042
G-BTPM 2043
G-BTPN 2044
G-BTPO 2052
G-BUWP 2053

Boeing 737-200 Advanced *c/n*
G-BGDA 21790/599
G-BGDB 21791/626
G-BGDD 21793/635
G-BGDE 21794/643
G-BGDF 21795/645
G-BGDG 21796/648
G-BGDH 21797/684
G-BGDI 21798/658
G-BGDJ 21799/660
G-BGDK 21800/661
G-BGDL 21801/669
G-BGDN 21802/670
G-BGDO 21803/677
G-BGDP 21804/686
G-BGDR 21805/697
G-BGDS 21806/699
G-BGDT 21807/710
G-BGDU 21808/712
G-BGJE 22026/644
G-BGJF 22027/684
G-BGJH 22029/662
G-BGJI 22030/693
G-BGJJ 22031/722
G-BGJM 22034/751
G-BKYA 23159/1047
G-BKYB 23160/1053
G-BKYC 23161/1055
G-BKYE 23163/1058
G-BKYF 23164/1060
G-BKYG 23165/1064
G-BKYH 23166/1067
G-BKYI 23167/1074
G-BKYJ 23168/1077

G-BKYK 23169/1081
G-BKYL 23170/1086
G-BKYM 23171/1088
G-BKYN 23172/1091
G-BKYO 23225/1102
G-BKYP 23226/1105

Boeing 737-400 *c/n*
G-BPNZ
G-BSNV 25168/2210
G-BSNW 25169/2237
G-BUHJ 25164/2447
G-BUHK 26289/2486
G-BUHL 25134/2083
G-BVBY 25844/2514
G-BVHB 25860/2545
G-BVNM 24163/1700
G-BVNN 24164/1702
G-BVNO 24167/1736
G-DOCA 25267/2131
G-DOCB 25304/2144
G-DOCC 25305/2147
G-DOCD 25439/2156
G-DOCE 25350/2167
G-DOCG 25408/2183
G-DOCH 25428/2185
G-DOCI 25839/2188
G-DOCJ 25840/2197
G-DOCK 25841/2222
G-DOCL 25842/2228
G-DOCM 25843/2244
G-DOCN 25848/2379
G-DOCO 25849/2381
G-DOCP 25850/2386
G-DOCR 25851/2387
G-DOCS 25852/2390
G-DOCT 25853/2409
G-DOCU 25854/2417
G-DOCV 25855/2420
G-DOCW 25856/2422
G-DOCX 25857/2451
G-DOCZ 25858/2522
G-GBTA 25859/2532
G-TREN 24796/1887

Above: BA was the launch customer for the GE90-powered version of the Boeing 777.

Below: BA still has many so-called 'Classic 747s' in service alongside its 747-400s.

Boeing 747-100 *c/n*
G-AWNA 19761/23
G-AWNB 19762/41
G-AWNC 19763/48
G-AWNE 19765/109
G-AWNF 19766/111
G-AWNG 20269/150
G-AWNH 20270/169
G-AWNJ 20272/183
G-AWNL 20284/187
G-AWNM 20708/210
G-AWNN 20809/220
G-AWNO 20810/222
G-BBPU 20953/248
G-BDPV 21213/281

Boeing 747-200B *c/n*
G-BDXA 21238/292
G-BDXB 21239/302
G-BDXC 21240/305
G-BDXD 21241/317
G-BDXE 21350/321
G-BDXF 21351/323
G-BDXG 21536/328
G-BDXH 21635/365
G-BDXI 21830/430
G-BDXJ 21831/440
G-BDXK 22303/495
G-BDXL 22305/506
G-BDXM 23711/672

G-BDXN 23735/674
G-BDXO 23799/677
B-BDXP 24088/697

Boeing 747-400 *c/n*
G-BNLA 23908/722
G-BNLB 23909/730
G-BNLC 23910/734
G-BNLD 23911/744
G-BNLE 24047/753
G-BNLF 24048/773
G-BNLG 24049/774
G-BNLH 24050/779
G-BNLI 24051/784
G-BNLJ 24052/789
G-BNLK 24053/790
G-BNLL 24054/794
G-BNLM 24055/795
G-BNLN 24056/802
G-BNLO 24057/817
G-BNLP 24058/828
G-BNLR 24447/829
G-BNLS 24629/841
G-BNLT 24630/842
G-BNLU 25406/895
G-BNLV 25427/900
G-BNLW 25432/903
G-BNLX 25435/908
G-BNLY 27090/959
G-BNLZ 27091/964
G-CIVA 27092/967
G-CIVB 25811/1018
G-CIVC 25812/1022
G-CIVD 27349/1049
G-CIVE 27350/1051
G-CIVF 25814/1058
G-CIVG 25815/1059
G-CIVH
G-CIVI

Boeing 757-200 *c/n*
G-BIKA 22172/9
G-BIKB 22173/10
G-BIKC 22174/11
G-BIKD 22175/13
G-BIKF 22177/16
G-BIKG 22178/23
G-BIKH 22179/24
G-BIKI 22180/25
G-BIKJ 22181/29
G-BIKK 22182/30
G-BIKL 22183/32
G-BIKM 22184/33
G-BIKN 22186/50
G-BIKO 22187/52
G-BIKP 22188/54
G-BIKR 22189/58
G-BIKS 22190/63
G-BIKT 23398/77
G-BIKU 23399/78
G-BIKV 23400/81

G-BIKW 23492/89
G-BIKX 23493/90
G-BIKY 23533/93
G-BIKZ 23532/98
G-BMRA 23710/123
G-BMRB 23975/145
G-BMRC 24072/160
G-BMRD 24073/166
G-BMRE 24074/168
G-BMRF 24101/175
G-BMRG 24102/179
G-BMRH 24266/210
G-BMRI 24267/211
G-BMRJ 24268/214
G-BPEA 24370/218
G-BPEB 24371/225
G-BPEC 24882/323
G-BPED 25059/363
G-BPEE 25060/364
G-BPEF 24120/174
G-BPEJ 25807/610
G-BPEK 25808/665
G-CPEL 24398/224

Boeing 767-300(ER) *c/n*
G-BNWA 24333/265
G-BNWB 24334/281
G-BNWC 24335/284
G-BNWD 24336/286
G-BNWE 24337/288
G-BNWF 24338/293
G-BNWG 24339/298
G-BNWH 24340/335
G-BNWI 24341/342
G-BNWJ 24342/363
G-BNWK 24343/364
G-BNWL 25203/365
G-BNWM 25204/376
G-BNWN 25444/398
G-BNWO 25442/418
G-BNWP 25443/419
G-BNWR 25732/421
G-BNWS 25826/473
G-BNWT 25828/476
G-BNWU 25829/483
G-BNWV 27140/490
G-BNWW 25831/526
G-BNWX 25832/529
G-BNWY

Boeing 777-200 *c/n*
G-ZZZA 27105/6
G-ZZZB 27106/
G-ZZZC 27107/15
G-ZZZD 27108/17
G-ZZZE 27109/19

Douglas DC-10-30 *c/n*
G-BEBL 46949/179
G-BEBM 46921/214
G-BHDH 47816/316
G-BHDI 47831/327
G-BHDJ 47840/337
G-DCIO 48277/354
G-MULL 47888/291
G-NIUK 46932/158

British Airways is the largest European customer for the Boeing 757, with a total of 43 in service and still more on order.

British Midland Airways (BD/BMA)

History: Formed on 16 February 1949 as Derby Aviation. Flew charters until 18 July 1953 when scheduled services inaugurated from Derby to Jersey with **DH.89A Dragon Rapide**. Fleet later included **Douglas DC-3**, **Miles Marathon** and **Canadair Argonauts** (by October 1961). Name changed to Derby Airways 12 March 1959 then to British Midland Airways 1 October 1964. **Handley Page Herald**, delivered February 1965, supplemented in January 1967 by first **Vickers Viscount**. Expanded domestic network and ventured into inclusive-tour operations with delivery of three **BAC One-Eleven 500**s and first of several **Boeing 707-320**s in early 1970. Airline purchased in 1978 by consortium of directors, concurrent with introduction of **DC-9-10**s. **Fokker F27** and **Shorts 360** added during 1980s. Inaugurated low-fare Heathrow to Glasgow service on 25 October 1982 in competition with British Airways' Shuttle, followed in March 1983 by London-Edinburgh. Launched Manx Airlines with Air UK in November 1982 and took controlling interest in Loganair in September 1983. Started programme of expansion into Europe with services from Heathrow to Amsterdam in 1986, followed by Dublin, Palma, Nice, Brussels and others. Order placed in 1984 for five new **British Aerospace ATP** aircraft to replace F27 and Viscount fleets; entered service on Birmingham-Brussels route 9 May 1988. First **Boeing 737-300** put on London-Edinburgh route 1 December 1987. A 24.5 per cent equity stake, later increased, acquired by SAS in holding company Airlines of Britain, established in March 1987. 737 fleet enlarged with lease of **737-400** and large numbers of **737-500**s. Took delivery of four **Fokker 100**s in 1994, followed by smaller **Fokker 70** in April 1995.

British Midland today: European network of scheduled passenger services from London-Heathrow to 11 European cities, and from Edinburgh and Glasgow to Copenhagen. Domestic points served include Belfast, Birmingham, East Midlands, Edinburgh, Glasgow, Guernsey,

British Midland is the UK's second largest airline. Its once sizeable fleet of DC-9s has been replaced by Fokker 70s and 100s.

Jersey, Leeds Bradford, Liverpool and Teesside. Second-largest operator at Heathrow with over 1,000 movements per week. Code-share and major co-operation with part owner SAS; code-share agreements on specific routes with Air Canada, Alitalia, American Airlines, Austrian Airlines, BWIA, Iberia, Malaysia Airlines, TAP and United Airlines.

Annual revenue: $650 million
Passengers: 4.6 million
Employees: 3,900
Ownership: Owned by Airlines of Britain Holdings, in which SAS has 40 per cent stake

Fleet development: Two Fokker 70s remain on order. DC-9s withdrawn during 1996.

Associate carriers: Wholly-owned subsidiaries Loganair (LC) and Manx Airlines (JE).

Loganair, formed on 1 February 1962, operates all its internal Scottish routes as British Airways Express carrier, following franchise agreement with BA on 11 July 1994. Fleet comprises eight **Shorts 360-100**s, one **Twin Otter** and five **Islanders**.

Manx Airlines, formed 1 November 1982, flies domestic routes from Isle of Man with 11 **BAe ATP**s and two **146-200**s, while **Manx Airlines (Europe)** operates **BAe Jetstream 41** on domestic and European services as British Airways Express carrier, as part of franchise agreement signed 9 January 1995.

British Midland fleet

Boeing 737-300	c/n
G-OBMD	24092/1669
G-OBMH	24460/1831
G-OBMJ	24461/1833
G-OBML	24300/1666
G-OBMP	24963/2193

Boeing 737-400	c/n
G-OBMF	23868/1616
G-OBMG	23870/1647
G-OBMK	25596/2255
G-OBMM	25177/216
G-OBMN	24123/1663
G-OBMO	26280/2239

Boeing 737-500	c/n
G-BVKA	24694/1834
G-BVKB	27268/2592

G-BVKC	24695/1872
G-BVKD	26421/2279
G-BVZE	26422/2412
G-BVZF	25038/1969
G-BVZG	25160/2114
G-BVZH	25166/2129
G-BVZI	25167/2173
G-OBMX	25065/2028
G-OBMY	26419/2186
G-OMBZ	24574/1868

British Aerospace ATP	
G-MANL	2003
G-MAUD	2002

British Aerospace Jetstream 41	c/n
G-MAJA	41032

Douglas DC-9-30	c/n
G-ELDG	47484/648
G-ELDI	47559/672

Fokker 70	c/n
G-BVTE	11538
G-BVTF	11539
G-BVTG	11551

Fokker 100	c/n
G-BVJA	11489
G-BVJB	11488
G-BVJC	11497
G-BVJD	11503

BWIA International (BW/BWA)

ican Airlines on Miami route, and code-share and marketing alliance with British Midland and Air Martinique.

Annual revenue: $225 million
Employees: 2,500
Ownership: divided between Acker Group, together with Caribbean investors (51 per cent), Trinidad & Tobago government (33.5 per cent) and employees (15.5 per cent)

Fleet development: Second **A321** will be delivered in October 1996 on lease from ILFC, with a possible third in spring 1997. Proposed delivery of two/three **A340**s now delayed indefinitely.

Associate carriers: 29.2 per cent stake acquired in inter-island feeder airline **LIAT** (Leeward Island Air Transport) (LI) upon that airline's privatisation on 10 November 1995. LIAT serves 25 points in Leeward and Windward Islands, plus Venezuela from its main base at Antigua's V. C. Bird International Airport. Fleet comprises nine **de Havilland Canada DHC-8-100**s and six **DHC-6**s.

History: Formed 1 January 1980 from merger of BWIA International (British West Indian Airways) and Trinidad and Tobago Air Services. Former's history dates to 27 November 1937 when founded by Lowell Yerex, while TTAS set up in June 1974. Full name of new company Trinidad and Tobago (BWIA International) Airways Corporation. Combined fleet comprised six **Boeing 707-320C**s, four **Douglas DC-9-51**s, and six **HS 748**s. Fleet quickly modernised with first two **TriStar**s, delivered January and August 1980, with two more following in 1981 and 1982. Local route network supplemented with flights to Miami, New York, Toronto, and across Atlantic to London-Heathrow. Five **MD-83**s acquired between 1986 and 1989, with first aircraft in service on Miami route on 14

BWIA's MD-83 fleet is slowly being augmented by Airbus A321s but the acquisition of A340s has been abandoned.

May 1986. Partially privatised in March 1994.

BWIA International today: Wide range of direct flights from three European cities – London, Frankfurt and Zürich – to Caribbean. Regional routes to North America serve Miami, New York and Toronto, and locally to Antigua, Barbados, Grenada, Guyana, Jamaica, St Lucia and St Maarten. Code-share with Amer-

BWIA International fleet

L1011-500 TriStar	c/n	McDonnell Douglas MD-83		
9Y-TGJ	1179	9Y-THN	49390/1269	9Y-THW	49786/1631
9Y-TGN	1191	9Y-THQ	49448/1313	9Y-THX	49789/1642
9Y-THA	1222	9Y-THR	49568/1380		
N314D	1233	9Y-THU	49824/1554		

Note: MD-83 9Y-THV 49632/1603

Canadian Airlines International (CP/CDN)

History: Descended from four predecessor airlines, which amalgamated 27 March 1987: Canadian Pacific Airlines (CP Air), Eastern Provincial Airways, Nordair and Pacific Western Airlines (PWA). Principal partner CP Air formed 31 January 1942. Modern fleet comprised **Boeing 747-200B**, **Douglas DC-10-30** and **737-200**. Pacific Western, formed 1 July 1945, had become Canada's third-largest airline through series of acquisitions, operating large fleet of 737-200 and three **767-200**s at time of merger. Eastern Provincial Airways (EPA) came into being in 1949. Its fleet was made up entirely of Boeing

737-200 aircraft. Nordair, formed in 1957, operated a fleet of 737-200s, **Fairchild FH-227B** and **Lockheed Electra** aircraft. After merger, fleet standardised on 737-200 and DC-10-30, but modernised in subsequent years with addition of **767-300** from April 1988, **747-400** from December 1990, and **Airbus A320-200** from April 1991. In 1989, owner PWA Corporation acquired another Canadian airline, Wardair Canada. Voluntary financial restructuring programme initiated in 1991, which culminated in April 1994 with $246 million equity investment by AMR Corporation, parent company of

American Airlines, and another $200 million investment by Canadian's employees. Prior merger discussions with Air Canada, but no agreement. Cross-border services to United States increased from 10 to 60 daily flights as result of 1995 air services agreement between two countries.

Canadian today: Serves over 150 cities in 18 countries on five continents. Together with its Canadian Partner airlines, flies to 110 points within Canada alone. Intercontinental destinations are Auckland, Bangkok, Beijing, Buenos Aires, Frankfurt, Hong Kong, Kuala

Lumpur, London, Melbourne, Mexico City, Monterrey, Nadi, Nagoya, Paris, Rio de Janeiro, Rome, Santiago de Chile, Sao Paulo, Sydney, Taipei and Tokyo. Plans to add Delhi, Ho Chi Minh City and Manila. Code-share and equity partnership with American Airlines, together with strategic global marketing alliances with Air New Zealand, Alitalia, Japan Airlines, Malaysia Airlines, Mandarin Airlines, Philippine Airlines, Qantas and Varig.

Annual revenue: *$2,300 million*
Passengers: *7.7 million*
Cargo: *115,000 tonnes*
Employees: *16,875*
Ownership: *Principal subsidiary of Canadian Airlines Corporation*

Associate carriers: Local partnership under **Canadian Partner/Canadien Partnaire** title, providing common fares, co-ordinated schedules and one-stop check-in.

Participants include: **Canadian Regional Airlines**, which serves 42 points across Canada and USA with fleet of six **ATR42-300**s, seven **DHC-8-100**s, 16 **DHC-8-300**s, eight **F28-1000**s, and three **Shorts 360**s.

Calm Air International, formed in 1962 and 45 per cent owned by PWA Corporation, operating to 27 communities in northern Manitoba, Northwest Territories and Ontario with two **Saab 340B Plus** and two **Twin Otter**s, and two **Saab 2000**s expected in 1997.

*All **Canadian Partner** airlines wear slight variations on the basic **Canadian International** colour scheme.*

Air Alma, started flying on 22 December 1959 and serves Montreal from Alma, Roberval, Chibougamau and Charlevoix with three **EMB-110**s.

Air Atlantic links 15 destinations throughout the Atlantic provinces, Quebec, Ontario and USA, operating three **BAe 146-200A**s, eight **DHC-8-100**s and five **Jetstream 41**s.

Inter-Canadien provides connections from Ottawa and Toronto to 25 points in Quebec with seven **ATR42-300**s and three

*This **DC-10-30** has been specially decorated with the signatures of **Canadian International** employees.*

F28-1000s. Inter-Canadien has been 100 per cent owned by Canadian Regional Airlines since 27 April 1994. **Canadian North** is new division created to meet special needs of northern regions. A commercial agreement has been signed with **Aklak Air**, an Inuit-owned airline in Northwest Territories.

Canadian Airlines International fleet

Airbus A320-200	c/n	C-FHCP	22024/641	C-GJPW	21713/598	C-GFPW	21294/481	C-FCAU	24087/249
C-FDCA	232	C-GCPM	21716/560	C-GKPW	21819/627	C-GNDC	21728/580	C-FOCA	24575/311
C-FLSI	283	C-GCPN	21717/581	C-GLPW	22086/667	C-GNDU	22877/880	C-FPCA	24306/258
C-FLSS	284	C-GCPO	21718/584	C-GMCP	22864/945	C-GOPW	22160/688	C-FTCA	24307/259
C-FLSU	309	C-GCPP	22255/666	C-GMPW	22087/673	C-GSPW	22618/813	C-FXCA	24574/302
C-FMEQ	302	C-GCPQ	22256/672	C-GNPW	22159/684			C-GLCA	25120/361
C-FMES	305	C-GCPS	22257/756	C-GPPW	22264/753	**Boeing 747-400**	c/n		
C-FNVU	403	C-GCPT	22258/770	C-GQBB	22276/665	C-FBCA	25422/912	**Douglas DC-10-30**	c/n
C-FNVV	404	C-GCPU	22259/771	C-GQPH	22516/759	C-FCRA	24895/837	C-FCRD	47889/229
C-FPWD	231	C-GCPV	22260/784	C-GQCP	22865/960	C-FGHZ	27827/1038	C-FCRE	47868/200
C-FPWE	175	C-GCPX	22341/786	C-GRPW	22266/765	C-GMWW	24883/823	C-GCPC	46540/268
C-GPWG	174	C-GCPY	22342/810	C-GTPW	22807/824			C-GCPD	46541/281
C-GQCA	210	C-GCPZ	22658/861	C-GUPW	22873/898	**Boeing 767-300(ER)**		C-GCPE	46524/295
		C-GEPW	21115/425	C-GVPW	22874/904	C-FCAB	24082/213	C-GCPF	46543/341
Boeing 737-200 Adv		C-GFCP	22659/874	C-GWPW	23283/1109	C-FCAE	24083/215	C-GCPG	48285/352
C-FACP	22072/623	C-GGPW	21639/539			C-FCAF	24084/219	C-GCPH	48288/364
C-FCPM	22761/850	C-GIPW	21712/556	**Boeing 737-200C Adv**		C-FCAG	24085/220	C-GCPI	48296/370
C-FCPN	22762/856	C-GJCP	22728/911	C-GDPA	22056/655	C-FCAJ	24086/248	C-GCPJ	46991/261

Cargolux Airlines (CV/CLX)

The Boeing 747-400F, as flown by Cargolux and others, does not feature the extended upper deck of its passenger-carrying sisters.

1996. Worldwide charter services. Code-share with Lufthansa on Frankfurt and Los Angeles routes, and space exchange with China Airlines on Luxembourg-Taipei route.

Annual revenue: *$310 million*
Cargo: *182,000 tonnes*
Employees: *750*
Shareholders: *Lufthansa (24.53 per cent), Luxair (24.50 per cent), various investment banks (44.69 per cent), private (6.28 per cent)*

History: Founded 4 March 1970 by Luxair, Salen Shipping Group, Loftleidr Icelandic Airlines and private local interests. First flight to Hong Kong in September 1970 using **Canadair CL-44** swing-tail freighter. Five CL-44s followed by **DC-8-61** which marked beginning of jet operations in 1973. **Boeing 747-200F** delivered in 1979, Cargolux becoming first airline in Europe to operate Boeing freighter, and regular flights started to US East Coast and later to US West Coast. DC-8 fleet phased out at end of 1984. Lufthansa acquired 24.5 per cent stake and Luxair increased its share from 10 per cent to 24.53 per cent. Order placed for three **747-400F** freighters, with options for three more. Delivered in November and December 1993.

Cargolux today: Regular all-cargo flights from Luxembourg to Abu Dhabi, Bangkok, Beirut, Colombo, Damascus, Delhi, Detroit, Dubai, Harare, Ho Chi Minh City, Hong Kong, Houston, Istanbul, Johannesburg, Komatsu, Kuala Lumpur, Kuwait, Los Angeles, Mexico City, Moscow, New York, San Francisco, Seattle, Singapore and Taipei. Seattle-Prestwick service added in early

Fleet development: Third 747-400F due for delivery in 1997, two options remaining.

Cargolux fleet

Boeing 747-200F	c/n
LX-ACV	21964/416
LX-BCV	22403/524
LX-DCV	20887/245
LX-ECV	21965/438

Boeing 747-400F	c/n
LX-FCV	25866/1002
LX-GCV	25867/1008

Cathy Pacific Airways (CX/CPA)

History: Founded 24 September 1946 by wartime pilots with one **Douglas C-47 (DC-3)**, initially engaged in cargo charters. Passenger charters soon added and C-47 fleet had grown to six by June 1948 when Cathay reorganised and recapitalised with Butterfield and Swire (renamed John Swire & Sons (HK)) in 1974, acquiring major holding. Minority shareholders have come and gone, but Swire Group still controls airline. Entered period of growth when awarded southern routes out of Hong Kong on 13 May 1949, serving among others Bangkok, Singapore, Saigon and Rangoon. C-47 replaced by two **DC-4**s and **DC-6B**, but major progress initiated only in 1959 with delivery of first of two **L.188A Electra**s 14 April, and take-over of Hong Kong Airways 1 July, giving access to impor-

tant northern routes, especially to Japan. Expansion implemented with acquisition of nine **Convair 880M**. First service 8 April 1962 to Manila and Tokyo. All-jet fleet from 27 February 1967. Introduced first **Boeing 707-320B** into service 3 August 1971, building fleet to 12 over next three years, all acquired from Northwest Airlines. First **TriStar** arrived in Hong Kong on 2 September 1975 and fleet eventually grew to 20. First part of global ambitions realised with service to Bahrain and long-cherished London route, inaugurated 17 July 1980 with **Boeing 747-200B**. Tremendous progress made as 747-200B fleet grew to eight and network expanded. First **747-300** delivered in February 1986, joined in June 1989 by **747-400**. A $9 billion fleet modernisation completed with orders for nine

A330-300s, six A340-300s and 11 Boeing 777s.

Cathay Pacific today: Hong Kong's flag-carrier providing regional/intercontinental services, linking Hong Kong to 44 cities in 27 countries, and another 11 in mainland China through associate Dragonair. Long-haul flights serve Adelaide, Amsterdam, Bahrain, Brisbane, Dubai, Frankfurt, Johannesburg, London, Los Angeles, Manchester, Melbourne, Paris, Perth, Rome, Sydney, Vancouver and Zürich. Third most profitable airline in world. Code-share and joint flights with Air Mauritius and Vietnam Airlines on passenger routes, and with Korean Air and Lufthansa on cargo services.

Annual revenue: *$3,900 million*
Passengers: *9.75 million*
Employees: *14,400*

Cathay Pacific has begun to introduce the Airbus A340, as a Lockheed TriStar replacement, alongside its Boeing 747 fleet.

Shareholding: Swire Pacific (52.4 per cent), China International Trust and Investment Corporation (CITIC) (12.5 per cent), China Travel Service (5.01 per cent), China National Aviation Corporation (CNAC) (5.01 per cent), private (25.08 per cent)

Fleet development: Deliveries of six **A340-300**s will commence in July 1996 and run through to February 1997. Follow-up order for two additional **A330-300**s to be completed in mid-1997. First Boeing 777 to be delivered in May 1996; remaining 10 aircraft (three 777-200 and seven 777-300) to join fleet between 1996 and 2000. Phase-out of TriStars in progress.

Associate carriers: *Dragonair* (Hong Kong Dragon Airlines) (KA), founded in April 1985, was acquired by CITIC (38 per cent) and Cathay (30 per cent) in January 1980. Fifteen-year management contract signed, but changed. Provides services to 18 regional destinations, 11 in China, operating

Dragonair currently operates all of Cathay Pacific's routes into mainland China.

seven Airbus **A320**s and three A330s. Acquisition seen as vital strategic move in preparation for Hong Kong's hand-over to China on 30 June 1997.

In May 1994, Cathay rescued ailing cargo carrier **AHK Air**

Hong Kong (LD) by acquiring 75 per cent shareholding. Founded on 4 February 1988, started scheduled cargo services 10 October 1989 between Hong Kong and Europe and Japan with two **Boeing 747-220F**.

Cathay Pacific Airlines fleet

Airbus A330-300	c/n	Boeing 747-200B	c/n	Boeing 747-300	c/n					Boeing 747-400F	c/n
VR-HLA	071	VR-HIA	21966/416	VR-HII	23221/615	VR-HOV	25082/849			VR-HUH	27175/1020
VR-HLB	083	VR-HLB	22149/466	VR-HIJ	23392/634	VR-HOW	25211/873			VR-HUK	27503/1065
VR-HLC	099	VR-HIC	22429/493	VR-HIK	23534/659	VR-HOX	24955/877				
VR-HLD	102	VR-HID	22530/531	VR-HOL	23709/671	VR-HOY	25351/887			Lockheed L.1011	
VR-HLE	109	VR-HIE	22872/566	VR-HOM	23920/690	VR-HOZ	25871/925			TriStar 1	c/n
VR-HLF	113	VR-HIF	23048/582	VR-HON	24215/709	VR-HUA	25872/930			VR-HHK	1118
VR-HLG	118	VR-HKG	21746/385			VR-HUB	25873/937			VR-HHV	1024
VR-HLH	121			Boeing 747-400	c/n	VR-HUD	25874/949			VR-HHX	1054
		Boeing 747-200F	c/n	VR-HOO	23814/705	VR-HUE	27117/970			VR-HHY	1051
Airbus A340-200	c/n	VR-HIH	23120/596	VR-HOP	23815/728	VR-HUF	25869/993			VR-HOB	1037
VR-HMR	063	VR-HVX	24568/776	VR-HOR	24631/771	VR-HUG	25870/1007			VR-HOD	1043
VR-HMS	074	VR-HVY	22306/480	VR-HOS	24850/788	VR-HUI	27230/1033			VR-HOE	1021
VR-HMT	080	VR-HVZ	23864/687	VR-HOT	24851/813	VR-HUJ	27595/1061			VR-HOI	1039
VR-HMU	085			VR-HOU	24925/834						

China Airlines (CI/CAL)

Chiang Kai-Shek International Airport
Taipei, Taiwan

History: Founded 10 December 1959 by retired air force officers with two **PBY-5 Catalina** flying-boats. Initial period devoted to charter work, before introduction of domestic schedule between Taipei and Hualien in October

1962. Fleet by then comprised **DC-3** and **DC-4** aircraft and growing number of **C-46A**s. Regional service between Taipei and Saigon started 1 December 1966 with **Super Constellation**s, and network expanded rapidly

following introduction of **Boeing 727** jet services 1 April 1967. Designated national airline after demise of Civil Air Transport (CAT) 29 May 1968. Period of steady development over next 10 years notable for first trans-

China Airlines

Above: China Airlines has introduced this new scheme to replace its earlier simple red and blue livery.

Left: CAL subsidiary Mandarin Airlines flies a small fleet of MD-11s and 747s.

important city, southern port of Kaohsiung. Code-share agreements with Garuda and Vietnam Airlines; block-space arrangement on specific cargo routes with Cargolux and Martinair, and for passenger flights between Taipei and Tokyo with Japan Asia Airways.

Annual revenue: $1,750 million
Passengers: 5.9 million
Employees: 7,900
Ownership: largely in hands of China Civil Aviation Development Foundation with 82.4 per cent

pacific flight to San Francisco 2 February 1970 with **Boeing 707-320B**, and further enlargement of fleet with **Caravelle**s, **Boeing 747** (from 3 June 1975) and **737**. Latter entered service 1 May 1976 between Taipei and Kaohsiung. **Boeing 767-200** introduced between Taipei and Bangkok 1 January 1983. First of initial batch of four **Airbus A300B4-200**s delivered between July 1982 and July 1983. **727** fleet then transferred to air force. Beginning of expansion into Europe marked by new cargo service to Luxembourg 10 May 1982, followed by passenger service to Amsterdam 12

April 1983. **747-200F** added in 1985. Initiated major five-year re-equipment programme with orders for five **747-400**s, one **747-400F**, four **MD-11**s and three **A300-600R**s. All delivered between 1990 and 1994. Placed order for six **737-800**s plus nine options on 22 December 1995.

China Airlines today: National flag-carrier providing scheduled passenger and cargo services from capital Taipei to concentration of regional points, and extending to Europe, Africa, Australia and United States. Only domestic route is high-frequency shuttle between Taipei and Taiwan's second most

Fleet development: Six **Boeing 737-400**s to be leased for delivery between December 1996 and March 1997, to replace older 737-200 on domestic routes. First delivery of six 737-800s scheduled for 1998. Plans to add 38 new aircraft over next seven years, bringing fleet to 67 aircraft, after sale of 14 older types. Types will be capacity mix of 150-, 250- and 300- to 350-seat aircraft. Letter of intent signed for four **Boeing 777**s.

Associate carriers: Wholly-owned subsidiary **Mandarin Airlines** (AE) serves Auckland, Brisbane, Sydney and Vancouver with fleet of a single **Boeing 747-400**, three **747SP**s and one **MD-11**.

Also has 19 per cent shareholding in **Far Eastern Air Transport** (**FAT**) (EF), formed 5 June 1957. Operates strong domestic network and regional charters with fleet of two **757**s, eight 737s and six **MD-82**s.

China Airlines fleet

Airbus A300B4-200	c/n						
B-190	193	B-1804	536	B-1876	23913/1579	B-1886	22446/519	B-163	24311/869
B-192	197	B-1806	666	B-1878	24197/1581	B-1888	22447/556	B-164	24312/954
B-194	221	B-1814	578				
B-196	232	N88881	743	**Boeing 747SP**	c/n	**Boeing 747-200F**	c/n	**McDonnell Douglas**
B-1810	179	**Airbus A320-200**		B-1862	21300/304	B-160	24308/752	**MD-11**	c/n
B-1812	171	3B-RGY	376	B-1880	22298/445	B-1864	21454/322	B-150	48468/518
		3B-RGZ	386	N4508H	22547/534	B-1894	22299/462	B-151	48469/519
Airbus A300-600R	c/n			N4522V	22805/564			B-152	48470/546
B-1800	529	**Boeing 737-200 Adv**				**Boeing 747-400**	c/n	B-153	48471/558
B-1802	533	B-182	23796/1420	**Boeing 747-200B**	c/n	B-161	24309/766
				B-1866	21843/386	B-162	24310/778

Condor (DE/CFG)

Rhein-Main Airport
Frankfurt, Germany

History: Founded 21 December 1955 as Deutsche Flugdienst and started charter operations 28 March 1956 with two **Vickers Viking 1B**s. Flights largely served

resorts in Spain, Italy, Greece and Canary Islands. Expanded with **Convair 240** acquired from KLM in December 1957 and more Vikings. Slump in charter

market led to take-over by Deutsche Lufthansa in early 1960 and change of name to Condor Flugdienst on 25 October 1961. Used two Lufthansa

The Boeing 737-300 is now the smallest type in Condor's fleet. In September 1996 it contracted to launch the 757-300, which can seat up to 289 passengers

L.1649A Starliners until 1962 and then built fleet around four **Viscount**s transferred from parent company. Steady expansion facilitated from 1965 with **Boeing 727-100**, **F27-400** and **707-320B** for long-haul charter. All-jet fleet on 1 December 1968, increased again in January 1969 with three Lufthansa **737-100**s. In April 1971 became first charter airline to operate **Boeing 747**. **727-200** added to fleet between March 1973 and December 1975. Placed order for two **DC-10-30**s on 15 June 1978, which replaced two 747s from November 1979. Two **A300B4-200**s and three **A310-200**s added in 1980s. **DC-8-73** was operated from summer 1985. Operations expanded and Airbuses replaced by large fleet of **757-200** and **767-300** twins.

Condor today: Inclusive-tour operations to more than 50 destinations in 34 countries. In addition to short-haul flights to Mediterranean basin, undertakes growing number of long-haul services from Frankfurt, Cologne/Bonn and Hannover to Central America and Caribbean, East Africa and the Far East.

Annual revenue: $1,250 million
Passengers: 5.7 million
Employees: 2,065
Ownership: Wholly-owned by Deutsche Lufthansa

Fleet development: Became launch customer for the **Boeing 757-300** at the 1996 Farnborough air show, with an order for 12 and further options for 12.

Condor fleet

Boeing 737-300	c/n	D-ABNI	25437/422	D-ABUB	26987/466
D-ABWA	23833/1439	D-ABNK	25438/428	D-ABUC	26992/470
D-ABWB	23834/1454	D-ABNL	25439/437	D-ABUD	26983/471
D-AGEC	23972/1537	D-ABNM	25440/443	D-ABUE	26984/518
D-AGED	24269/1628	D-ABNN	25441/446	D-ABUF	26985/537
		D-ABNO	25901/464	D-ABUH	26986/553
Boeing 757-200	c/n	D-ABNP	26433/521	D-ABUI	26988/562
D-ABNA	24737/267	D-ABNR	26434/532		
D-ABNB	24738/274	D-ABNS	26435/537	Douglas DC-10-30	c/n
D-ABNC	24747/275	D-ABNT	26436/587	D-ADJO	47928/192
D-ABND	24748/285	D-ABNX	24838/302	D-ADLO	46917/211
D-ABNE	24749/295			D-ADPO	46595/299
D-ABNF	25140/382	Boeing 767-300(ER)	c/n	D-ADQO	46596/301
D-ABNH	25436/419	D-ABUA	26991/455	D-ADSO	48252/342

Continental Airlines (CO/COA)

Houston Intercontinental
Houston, Texas, USA

History: Started operation 15 July 1934 when **Lockheed Vega** of Varney Speed Lines flew from El Paso to Albuquerque and Pueblo. Moved to Denver after acquiring Denver-Pueblo route from Wyoming Air Service. Changed name to Continental Airlines 1 July 1937, simultaneously with introduction of three **Lockheed L.12 'Baby Electras'**. On 22 July 1944 received first of 14 **Douglas C-47**s (**DC-3**) and network soon encompassed Denver, Kansas City, Oklahoma City, San Antonio, El Paso and all points in between. Ordered five **Convair 240**s 17 August 1946, introduced into service 15 December 1948. In early 1950s fleet upgraded with **Convair 340**

and **DC-6** equipment. In 1955 absorbed routes of Pioneer Air Lines and began transition to major carrier status. Ordered four **Boeing 707**s, 15 **Viscounts** and five **DC-6B**s. First jet service inaugurated 8 June 1959. Other new aircraft introduced included **DC-9-10**, **Boeing 720B** and **727-100**. Formed Air Micronesia in 1967 to provide service to and within US Trust Territory of Pacific. **DC-10** became flagship during 1970s. Texas Air, parent of Texas International Airlines, steadily bought into Continental and two airlines merged under Continental name 31 October 1982. Enlarged carrier operated 112 aircraft, made up of mixed

Continental has disposed of the bulk of its 747s but currently has outstanding orders with Boeing for 767-300ERs and 777s.

Continental Airlines

Continental operates a mix of Boeing 737-100/-200/-300 and -500 aircraft (the latter is seen here).

fleet of **727**s, **DC-9**s and **DC-10**s. Faced enormous financial difficulties and next decade marked by three periods in Chapter 11 bankruptcy protection and as many reorganisations. Acquired 11 more **DC-10-30**s, 10 **Boeing 737-300**s and six **A300B4-200**s nevertheless, grounding older **727-100** and **DC-9-14** fleet. Took over low-cost airline People Express in 1980, together with its affiliates Frontier Airlines and Britt Airways. Initiated feeder network under Continental Express label. Order placed same year for 50 **737-300**s, followed in October 1990 by 25 **757-200**s. Order for **Airbus A330/340** later cancelled.

$450 million cash injected by Air Canada and Air Partners, in exchange for 27.5 per cent stakes. Loss-making CA Lite, low-fare, operation, dismantled in 1994/95.

Continental today: Sixth-largest US airline, serving more than 90 cities within USA, together with 56 international destinations in Canada, Central and South America, Europe, Far East, Australia and New Zealand. Main hubs at Houston, Cleveland, Denver and New York/Newark, with other significant activity at Boston, Los Angeles, New Orleans and New York-LaGuardia. Principal Pacific hubs maintained at Honolulu and Guam. Comprehensive marketing agreement including code-sharing with Air Canada, which has 19.6 per cent holding, Alitalia and America

West. Joint marketing with SAS for flights to Scandinavia.

Annual revenue: *$5,800 million*
Passengers: *42.3 million*
Cargo: *220,000 tonnes*
Employees: *43,000*

Fleet development: 12 **Boeing 767-300ER**s and five **777**s deferred to 1998 at earliest.
Associate carriers: Has 17.7 per cent stake in America West. Large feeder network through *Continental Express* (CO) subsidiary, established in August 1990 through merging Bar Harbor Airlines, Britt Airways and Rocky Mountain Airways. Fleet of 38 **ATR42-300**s, three **ATR72-210**s, 32 **EMB-120RT Brasilia**s, as well as 12 **Beech 1900D**s, with 13 more on order. Order placed for eight **ATR42-500**s in March 1996. Announced massive order for 25 **EMBRAER EMB-145** jets with 175 options at 1996 Farnborough air show.
Continental Micronesia (CS), owned jointly with United Micronesia Development Assn, flies from Guam's Ab Won Pat Airport to destinations within US Trust Territory of Pacific, and to Honolulu and points in Japan, with 10 **Advanced 727-200**s and five **DC-10-30**s. Established in 1966 and formerly known as Air Micronesia.

Continental Airlines fleet

Boeing 727-200		N70755	21366/1274	N24213	19030/113	N61304	23355/1131	N47332	23570/1263
Advanced	**c/n**	N10756	21042/1106	N44214	19031/118	N63305	23356/1133	N69333	23571/1276
N18401	21264/1225	N14760	21118/1167	N77215	19032/119	N17306	23357/1141	N14334	23572/1296
N17407	21270/1231	N16761	21119/1175			N14307	23358/1142	N14335	23573/1298
N10408	21661/1394	N99763	20772/982	**Boeing 737-200**	**c/n**	N14308	23359/1144	N14336	23574/1328
N10409	21662/1421	N88770	20839/1031	N12230	19884/79	N17309	23360/1147	N14337	23575/1333
N17410	21663/1438	N17773	21045/1133	N12231	19885/91	N16310	23361/1150	N59338	23576/1338
N34415	22167/1752	N15774	21242/1196	N16232	19886/101	N69311	23362/1152	N16339	23577/1340
N14416	22168/1770	N17779	20634/917	N14233	19887/109	N60312	23363/1153	N39340	23578/1358
N27417	21854/1532	N77780	20635/918	N13234	19888/112	N12313	23364/1158	N14341	23579/1368
N17418	21855/1535	N15781	20636/919	N12235	19758/16	N71314	23365/1159	N14342	23580/1373
N66734	20663/1073	N27783	20638/926	N10236	19937/148	N34315	23366/1174	N39343	23581/1376
N69735	20664/1079	N16784	20639/927	N14239	19920/100	N17316	23367/1180	N17344	23582/1383
N69736	20665/1149	N33785	20640/935	N14241	20070/124	N17317	23368/1181	N17345	23583/1385
N93738	20666/1151	N14788	20642/944	N10242	20071/131	N12318	23369/1188	N14346	23584/1396
N69741	22250/1684	N59792	20646/967	N73243	20072/136	N12319	23370/1190	N14347	23585/1404
N69742	22251/1687	N45793	20647/968	N11244	20073/142	N14320	23371/1191	N69348	23586/1411
N79743	22252/1697			N14245	20074/170	N17321	23372/1192	N12349	23587/1413
N79744	22253/1702	**Boeing 737-100**	**c/n**	N14246	20129/154	N12322	23373/1202	N18350	23588/1448
N79745	22448/1740	N16201	19018/9	N10248	20344/229	N10323	23374/1204	N69351	23589/1466
N79746	22449/1756	N16203	19020/11	N10251	20361/209	N14324	23375/1207	N70352	23590/1468
N79748	22450/1760	N33202	19019/10	N17252	20362/216	N14325	23455/1228	N70353	23591/1472
N79749	22451/1767	N77204	19021/15	N15255	21069/415	N17326	23456/1230	N76352	23592/1476
N79750	22452/1772	N14206	19023/23			N12327	23457/1238	N76355	23593/1478
N73751	21247/1217	N59207	19024/26	**Boeing 737-300**	**c/n**	N17328	23458/1244	N17356	23942/1522
N76752	21248/1218	N14209	19026/35	N16301	23352/1119	N17329	23459/1247	N19375	23841/1518
N76753	21249/1219	N14211	19028/98	N59302	23353/1129	N70330	23460/1253	N14385	23943/1558
N79754	21363/1258	N14212	19029/108	N77303	23354/1130	N13331	23569/1258	N73380	26309/2674

46

N14381	26310/2680
N19382	26311/2681
N14383	26312/2693
N14384	26313/2704
N73385	26314/2707
N17386	26321/2764

DC-10-30s are now in service with both Continental and Continental Micronesia.

Boeing 737-500 c/n

N14601	27314/2566
N69602	27315/2571
N69603	27316/2573
N14604	27317/2576
N14605	27316/2582
N58606	27319/2590
N16607	27320/2596
N33608	27321/2597
N14609	27322/2607
N27610	27323/2616
N18611	27324/2621
N11612	27325/2630
N14613	27326/2633
N17614	27327/2634
N37615	27328/2640
N52611	27329/2641
N16617	27330/2648
N16618	27331/2652
N17619	27332/2659
N17620	27333/2660
N19621	27334/2661
N18622	27526/2669
N19623	27527/2672
N13634	27528/2675
N46625	27529/2683
N32626	27530/2868
N17627	27531/2700
N14628	27532/2712
N14629	27533/2725
N59630	27534/2726
N62631	27535/2728
N16632	27900/2736
N24633	27901/2743
N19634	26319/2748

Boeing 757-200 c/n

N58101	27291/614
N14102	27292/619
N33103	27293/623
N17104	27294/629
N17105	27295/632

N14106	27296/637
N14107	27297/641
N21108	27298/645
N12109	27299/648
N13310	27300/650
N57111	27301/652
N18112	27302/653
N13113	27555/668
N12114	27556/682
N14115	27557/687

Boeing 747-200B c/n

N78019	20527/179
N33021	20520/190

Douglas DC-9-32

N19504	47638/730
N33506	47765/900
N12507	47788/901
N12508	47797/913
N27509	47798/914
N12510	47799/918
N13512	48111/923
N18513	48112/926
N12514	48113/930
N16521	47521/629
N27522	47524/632
N69523	47520/635
N14524	47539/637
N15525	47531/638
N17531	45847/394
N12532	45791/349
N17533	47281/427
N14534	47110/167
N17535	47111/182
N43537	47112/199
N12538	47218/312
N12539	45792/372
N17541	45793/381
N70542	47535/610
N17543	45789/217
N18544	47219/325

N58545	47094/149	N16802	49222/1139	N18835	49439/1318
N10556	47423/581	N69803	49229/1140	N35836	49441/1322
N17557	47424/582	N16804	49246/1146	N57837	49582/1411
N18563	47487/553	N33805	49249/1149	N34838	49634/1419
N14564	47490/560	N16806	49260/1150	N14839	49635/1420
		N16807	49261/1153	N14840	49580/1369
Douglas DC-10-10 c/n		N16808	49262/1159	N15841	49581/1384
N68041	46900/34	N13809	49263/1163	N83870	48056/1012
N68042	46901/40	N14810	49264/1171	N14871	48022/1079
N68043	46902/41	N12811	49265/1189	N83872	49120/1071
N68044	46903/43	N17812	49250/1186	N83873	49121/1072
N68046	47800/92	N16813	48066/1019	N92874	49122/1073
N68047	47801/98	N14814	49112/1068	N93875	49125/1074
		N16815	49113/1069	N98876	49444/1323
Douglas DC-10-30		N14816	49370/1206	N85877	49450/1324
N68060	47850/331	N33817	49371/1207	N938MC	49525/1340
N12061	47851/334	N14818	49478/1293	N14879	49526/1342
N14062	47863/94	N38819	49479/1297	N14880	48044/967
N14063	47864/121	N15820	49480/1298	N13881	48045/970
N12064	47862/88	N72821	49481/1308	N37882	48027/973
N68065	46590/266	N72822	49482/1309	N16883	48073/1018
N13066	46591/287	N76823	49483/1314	N16884	48074/1026
N13067	47866/149	N72824	49484/1315	N16885	48062/1015
N15069	46584/293	N72825	49485/1316	N14886	48063/1020
N87070	48292/368	N69826	49486/1317	N16887	49116/1061
N83071	48293/371	N77827	49487/1335	N35888	49117/1063
N19072	46576/73	N71828	49488/1350	N14889	49118/1065
N76073	46940/141	N72829	49489/1351	N14890	49114/1066
N138AA	46911/189	N72830	49490/1352	N13891	49102/1076
		N14831	49491/1360	N16892	49391/1270
McDonnell Douglas MD-82 c/n		N35832	49492/1361	N16893	49392/1272
N10801	49127/1082	N18833	49493/1364	N16894	49393/1279
		N10834	49494/1368	N16895	49394/1285

Croatia Airlines (OU/CTN)

Zagreb (Pleso) Airport
Zagreb, Croatia

History: Established on 7 August 1989 as private company under name of Zagreb Airlines (ZAGAL), operating air taxi and express parcel flights. Changed name to Croatia Airlines 23 July 1990, followed by independence of former Yugoslav republic and its designation as national flag-carrier. Began operations 4 May 1991, initially providing domestic and charter flights to Germany and Switzerland with fleet of two **MD-82**s. Closure of Zagreb Airport in September forced move of operating base to Maribor, Slovenia, and then to Graz in Austria. Returned MD-82 fleet to Adria Airways 4 October 1992 and restarted in April 1993 with two **Boeing 737-200**s, adding third in June. Acquired activities of Anic Airways, which has been

Croatia Airlines' Boeing 737-230s are all ex-Lufthansa aircraft and replaced the MD-82s which were returned to Slovenia in 1992.

Croatia Airlines

flying domestic/regional services to Vienna and Zürich with one **ATR42-300** since 1992, but these ceased in November 1993.

Croatia Airlines today: National carrier providing mix of scheduled domestic and European services, migrant worker flights and charters. Scheduled services link Croatia's capital Zagreb with Amsterdam, Berlin, Brussels, Copenhagen, Dublin, Frankfurt, Istanbul, London, Manchester, Moscow, Munich, Paris, Prague, Rome, Skopje, Stockholm, Stuttgart, Tirana, Vienna, Warsaw and Zurich, and internally with Brac, Dubrovnik, Losinj, Pula, Rijeka, Split and Zadar. Commercial agreement with Air France on Paris-Split route.

Annual revenue: $85 million
Passengers: 0.8 million
Employees: 580
Major shareholders: INA Oil (27.1 per cent), Zagreb Airport (14.2 per cent) and Croatian Privatisation Fund (9.5 per cent)

Croatia Airlines fleet

AI(R) ATR42-300	c/n	Boeing 737-200 Advanced			
9A-CTS	312	9A-CTA	22119/714		
9A-CTT	317	9A-CTB	22116/701	9A-CTD	22140/793
9A-CTU	394	9A-CTC	22118/704	9A-CTE	22634/840

Czech Airlines (OK/CSA)

Prague-Ruzyne Airport,
Prague, Czech Republic

Czech Airlines still operates under the CSA moniker inherited from previous days.

Name changed to Czech Airlines (Ceské Aerolinie) 26 March 1995, after break-up of Czechoslovak Federation 1 January 1993.

Czech Airlines today: National carrier serving most European cities, together with points in Middle and Far East, North Africa and North America Marketing alliances including code-share, joint services or block-space agreements with Air France, Austrian Airlines, Iberia, KLM, LOT, Lufthansa, Luxair, Tarom and THY.

History: Founded 29 July 1923 as CSA (Ceskoslovenské Státni Aerolinie) and operated first scheduled flight with **Aero A-14** 29 October between Prague and Bratislava. First CSA international service inaugurated in 1930 to Zagreb using **Fokker F-VIIb/3m**. After World War II, CSA and rival CLS amalgamated and reformed as Ceskoslovenské Aerolinie (CSA), using **Ju 52/3, Ju 325, Ju 290, Noordvyn Norseman** and **Siebel C103**. Most of pre-war network reintroduced and extended to Cairo in 1948. Realignment with Soviet Union forced severe curtailment with only new services Berlin/Schonefeld in 1952 and Moscow in 1955. Fleet developed with Soviet aircraft, including **Il-12** in 1949, six licence-built **Avia 14-32**s (**Il-14P**) in 1957 and **Tu-104A**, put on Prague-Moscow service 9 December 1957. Long-haul services to Conakry, Rangoon and Jakarta introduced in 1960 with delivery of **Il-18**. Transatlantic service to Havana, Cuba, via Shannon, opened 3 February 1962 initially with **Bristol**

Britannias. Three **Tu-124** jets joined fleet in late 1964. From 1969, **Il-62** began to take over most long-haul routes and opened Prague-Montreal-New York service 4 May 1970. Other aircraft to join fleet were **Tu-134A** in November 1971 and **Yak-40** for domestic routes in November 1974. **Il-62M** introduced in 1979. Fleet modernised with **Tu-154** in 1988 and two **Airbus A310-200** in 1991. Following year notable for delivery of four **ATR72-200**s aircraft and first of five **737-300**s in June.

Annual revenue: $260 million
Passengers: 1.25 million
Cargo: 8,000 tonnes
Employees: 3,870.
Ownership: After short-lived equity holding by Air France between 1992 and 1994, ownership now divided between Czech State through Fund of National Property (49 per cent), Konsolidacni Bank (19.1 per cent), European Bank for Reconstruction and Development (EBRD) (19.1 per cent) and Czech insurance companies

Czech Airlines fleet

AI(R) ATR42-300	c/n	Airbus A310-300	c/n	OK-XGE	26543/2339
OK-TFE	084	OK-WAA	564		
OK-TFF	087	OK-WAB	567	**Tupolev Tu-134A**	c/n
				OK-HFL	7349913
AI(R) ATR42-400	c/n	**Boeing 737-400**	c/n	OK-HFM	7360142
OK-AFE	487	OK-WGF	24903/1978	OK-IFN	8360282
OK-AFF	491	OK-WGG	24693/1972		
				Tupolev Tu-154M	c/n
AI(R) ATR72-200	c/n	**Boeing 737-500**	c/n	OK-TCD	792
OK-XFA	285	OK-XGA	26539/2300	OK-UCE	804
OK-XFB	297	OK-XGB	26540/2317	OK-UCF	807
OK-XFC	299	OK-XGC	26541/2319	OK-VCG	838
OK-XFD	303	OK-XGD	26542/2337		

Cubana (CU/CUB)

Jose Marti International Airport
Havana, Cuba

History: Founded 8 October 1929 as Compania Nacional Cubana de Aviacion Curtiss and started operations 30 October 1930 with **Curtiss Robins** and **Ford Tri-Motors**. Curtiss name dropped when bought by Pan American Airways 6 May 1932. Pan Am shareholding reduced to 52 per cent 31 December 1945 and name shortened to Cubana de Aviacion. Expansion accelerated, first with transatlantic service to Madrid, inaugurated in 1948 with **DC-4**, followed by New York, Port-au-Prince and Mexico City in 1953, for which three **L.049 Constellation**s acquired. Pan Am holding finally bought out completely 23 July 1954. **L.1049E Super Constellation**s introduced in November 1954, supplemented by newer **L.1049G** from March 1956. Three **Viscount**s put into service 25 May 1956, and two **Bristol Britannia**s on 22 December 1958. Airline nationalised in May 1959 following Castro's revolution and re-equipped with **Il-14** (1961), **Il-18** (1966), **An-24** (1967) and **An-26** in 1975. No services possible to USA because of political isolation. Fleet joined by **Il-62M** in May 1977, and from December 1980 by **Yak-40** and **Tu-154B. Tu-154M** deliveries began in February 1986. Four **Yak-42**s delivered in 1990/91, replacing last three **Il-18**s, which were converted to freighters.

Cubana today: Wholly government-owned national carrier responsible for international flag services, linking capital Havana with points in Canada, Europe and Central and South America. Also domestic services to all principal towns and cities.

Cubana's F27s, acquired from Aviaco, are Cuba's first Western airliners since the Britannia.

Passengers: *0.9 million*
Employees: *1,100*

Cubana fleet

Antonov An-24V

	c/n
CU-T878	67302410
CU-T880	67302502
CU-T881	67302601

Antonov AN-24RV

	c/n
CU-T923	47309404
CU-T924	47309405
CU-T1260	57310307
CU-T1262	27307610
CU-T1266	57310107
CU-T1267	47309907

Antonov An-26

CU-T1237	7704
CU-T1238	7803
CU-T1239	7907
CU-T1420	6607
CU-T1421	6610
CU-T1422	3805
CU-T1423	3806
CU-T1425	6904
CU-T1426	5603
CU-T1429	7006
CU-T1432	7306
CU-T1434	7701
CU-T1435	7702
CU-T1436	7406

Antonov An-26B

	c/n
CU-T1240	11210
CU-T1241	11301
CU-T1401	
CU-T1402	12605
CU-T1404	12906
CU-T1405	13501
CU-T1407	14306

Fokker F27-600 Friendship

	c/n
CU-T1286	10332
CU-T1287	10343
CU-T1288	10347
CU-T1289	10348
CU-T1290	10352
CU-T1291	10353
CU-T1292	10421
CU-T1293	10429

Ilyushin Il-62M

	c/n
CU-T1208	3726739
CU-T1209	1828132
CU-T1215	1828243
CU-T1216	3829748
CU-T1217	3933232
CU-T1218	2035657
CU-T1225	3139845
CU-T1252	2343341
CU-T1259	3445111
CU-T1280	3749648
CU-T1282	2052436
CU-T1283	4053823

Ilyushin Il-76MD

	c/n
CU-T1258	0043454615
CU-T1271	0053459767

Tupolev Tu-154B-2

	c/n
CU-T1222	447
CU-T1224	493
CU-T1253	576
CU-T1256	599

Tupolev Tu-154M

	c/n
CU-T1264	720
CU-T1265	751
CU-T1275	777
CU-T1276	719

Yakovlev Yak-40

	c/n
CU-T1203	9641450
CU-T1232	9011060
CU-T1440	9631249
CU-T1441	
CU-T1442	9641445
CU-T1444	

Yakovlev Yak-42D

	c/n
CU-T1277	4520423016238
CU-T1278	4520423016269
CU-T1279	4520424914057

Cyprus Airlines (CY/CYP)

Larnaca International Airport
Cyprus

History: Set up 24 September 1947 as joint venture between Cyprus government (22 per cent), British European Airways (44 per cent) and local interests. First service by BEA 6 October from Nicosia to Athens. Own operations started in April 1948 with three **DC-3**s, increased to six by 1951. London service introduced in 1952 with BEA **Airspeed Ambassador**s. Uncertain political situation forced cancellation of **Viscount** order and BEA took over all services from 28 January 1958. Signed contract for two **Hawker Siddeley Trident 2E**s 26 March 1969 allowing route expansion to more European cities, beginning 1 November. Lost Nicosia base and fleet (one leased **BAC One-Eleven** and three Tridents) when Turkey invaded island in July 1974. Limited operations restarted from Larnaca 8 February 1975 with variety of leased aircraft,

Cyprus Airways

Airbus A320s form the bulk of Cyprus Airways' short-haul fleet on its European network.

Salonika, Salzburg, Tel Aviv, Vienna and Zurich. Some destinations also served from Paphos.

Annual revenue: $280 million
Passengers: 1.3 million
Cargo: 15,000 tonnes
Employees: 1,900
Major shareholder: Cyprus government with 80.5 per cent

but bought two **One-Eleven 500**s in 1976, followed by third in October 1978, and three **Boeing 707-120B**s in 1979. Services resumed to all European and Middle Eastern destinations. Initial orders placed for two **Airbus A310-200**s in 1981 and four **A320**s 17 January 1984, plus four options, since taken up. First A310 entered service in March 1984 London-Larnaca route. New A320 touched down at Larnaca 19 May 1989. Established Eurocypria Airlines in 1992 to obtain greater share of charter business into Cyprus.
   Cyprus Airways today: Scheduled passenger services

within Europe and to Middle East, linking Larnaca with Amman, Amsterdam, Athens, Bahrain, Beirut, Berlin, Birmingham, Brussels, Cairo, Damascus, Dubai, Frankfurt, Geneva, Hamburg, Heraklion, Jeddah, Kuwait, Linz, London, Manchester, Munich, Paris, Rhodes, Riyadh, Rome,

Associate companies: *Eurocypria Airlines* (UI), founded as wholly-owned subsidiary to serve charter market into Cyprus. Operated first flight 14 March 1992 with A320 leased from parent company. Main flights from United Kingdom, Ireland, Denmark, Finland and Germany with three A320-200s.

Cyprus Airways fleet

Airbus A310-200	c/n	Airbus A320-200	c/n		
5B-DAQ	300	5B-DAT	028	5B-DBC	295
5B-DAR	309	5B-DAU	035	5B-DBD	316
5B-DAS	352	5B-DAV	037	**BAC One Eleven-500**	**c/n**
5B-DAX	486	5B-DAW	038	5B-DAG	257
		5B-DBA	180	5B-DAH	258
		5B-DBB	256	5B-DAJ	261

Delta Air Lines (DL/DAL)

Hartfield Atlanta International Airport
Atlanta, Georgia, USA

History: Formed 30 May 1924 as Huff Daland Dusters. Reorganised as Delta Air Service 15 November 1928, and 1 June 1929 began passenger service between Dallas and Jackson. Failed to win air mail contract in 1930, but had better luck few years later, opening mail route with **Stinson T 3** June 1934 from Fort Worth to Charleston. **DC-3** replaced **DC-2** in December

1940, remaining in service until October 1960. Name changed to Delta Air Lines 18 December 1945. Opened first non-stop service between Chicago and Miami 1 April 1946 with **DC-4**. **DC-6** added to fleet in December 1948 and **Convair 340** (later **440**) in March 1953. Merger with Chicago & Southern Air Lines 1 May 1953, added 5,590 miles (9000 km) of domestic and Caribbean routes.

Inaugurated **DC-7** service in April 1954. New York and Washington DC routes opened 1 February 1956. Bypassed turboprop era and went straight for new jets, introducing **DC-8** 18 September 1959, **Convair 880** 15 May 1960, and 29 November 1965 presented world premiere of **DC-9** on Atlanta-Memphis-Kansas City round trip. In 1966 **L.100 Hercules** freighter succeeded **Curtiss C-46**, used on cargo flights since 1957. All-jet fleet after retirement of Convair 440 25 April 1970. **Boeing 747** delivered in 1970, **DC-10-30** in 1972 and **L.1011 TriStar** in 1974. Acquired New York-based Northeast Airlines and its extensive eastern seaboard route network on 1 August 1972. International growth started 30 April 1978 with Atlanta-London Gatwick

Like all the major US airlines, Delta operates a large fleet of Boeing 767s. This is a -200 variant.

route, flown with **TriStar 500**. Frankfurt followed 17 June 1979, Paris 1 April 1985, and first service to Tokyo inaugurated 2 March 1987. One month later acquired Los Angeles-based Western Air Lines, giving Delta access to US West Coast and completing its national network. First **MD-11** delivered 21 December 1990 and entered service 5 February 1991. Purchased 10 TriStars and several routes following demise of Eastern Air Lines. Fleet modernisation accelerated with orders for **767** and **757** to replace large number of **737-200** and **727-200**, and 23 January 1986 with huge order for 80 new **MD-88**s. Acquisition of Pan American's assets and North Atlantic routes in 1991 propelled airline to dominance on European routes. First **MD90-30** delivered spring 1995.

Delta today: World's third-largest airline with network serving 197 cities in 26 countries, together with an extensive domestic feeder network under Delta Connection banner. Main hubs operated at Atlanta, Cincinnati, Dallas/Ft Worth, Salt Lake City, Los Angeles, Orlando, New York, and Frankfurt. Intercontinental destinations are Amsterdam, Athens, Barcelona, Berlin, Bombay, Brussels, Budapest, Bucharest, Copenhagen, Dublin, Frankfurt, Helsinki, Istanbul, Lisbon, London, Madrid, Munich, Nagoya, Paris, Prague, Rome, Seoul, St Petersburg, Shannon, Stuttgart, Tokyo, Vienna, Warsaw and Zürich. Vast domestic network and flights to Canada, Mexico and Caribbean. Code-share

Delta was the launch customer for the IAE V2525-powered McDonnell Douglas MD90-30.

agreements with Aer Lingus, Aeroflot, Aeromexico, All Nippon Airways, Austrian Airlines, Finnair, Korean Air, Malév, SABENA, TAP, Varig, Vietnam Airlines and Virgin Atlantic.

Annual revenue: $12,200 million
Passengers: 88.9 million
Cargo: 500,000 tonnes
Employees: 59,700
Major shareholders: Sanford C. Bernstein, Capital Group and Fidelity Management Trust

Fleet development: Outstanding orders include 30 **737**s, four **757-200**s, five **767-300ER**s, four **MD-11**s and 20 **MD-90**s. Options held on further 78 737s, 36 757s, seven 767ERs, 22 MD-11s and 87 MD-90s.
Associate carriers: Cross-equity holdings with Swissair (4.5 per cent by Delta/4.6 per cent by Swissair) and Singapore

Airlines (2.7 per cent by Delta/5.0 per cent by Swissair) in Global Quality Alliance. Feeder network operated by local airlines under **Delta Connection** banner none owned by Delta, comprising:
Atlantic Southeast Airlines (EV), started operations 27 June 1979 and feeds Delta at Atlanta from 39 cities and Dallas/Ft Worth from 26 cities, using fleet of eight **ATR72-210**s, 60 **Brasilia**s and 11 **EMB-110**s.
Business Express (HQ) in Chapter 11 bankruptcy reorganisation since January 1996, hubs at New York and Boston with reduced fleet of 32 **Saab 340**s.
Comair (OH), Delta Connection carrier since 1 September 1984, operates into Cincinnati and Orlando from 76 markets with 30 **Canadair Regional Jet**s (15 more to be delivered).
Skywest Airlines (OO), incorporated 2 March 1972, feeds Delta at Salt Lake City and Los Angeles, using large fleet of 19 **Metro III**s, 33 **EMB-120**s and eight **Canadair Regional Jet**s.

Delta Air Lines fleet

Boeing 727-200							
Advanced		N292WA	22110/1613	N414DA	21256/1212	N479DA	20756/1028	N503DA	21305/1268
	c/n	N293WA	22111/1615	N415DA	21257/1214	N480DA	20860/1038	N504DA	21306/1270
N2807W	20579/886	N294WA	22112/1618	N416DA	21258/1223	N481DA	20861/1041	N505DA	21307/1272
N2809W	20581/890	N295WA	22532/1730	N417DA	21259/1224	N482DA	20862/1042	N506DA	21308/1292
N2810W	20648/895	N296WA	22533/1736	N418DA	21271/1242	N483DA	20863/1053	N507DA	21309/1294
N2811W	20649/896	N297WA	22534/1738	N419DA	21272/1243	N484DA	20864/1060	N508DA	21310/1298
N2812W	20868/1024	N400DA	21104/1157	N420DA	21273/1244	N485DA	20865/1065	N509DA	21311/1300
N2813W	20869/1025	N401DA	21145/1159	N421DA	21274/1245	N489DA	21019/1097	N510DA	21312/1330
N2814W	20870/1032	N402DA	21146/1161	N466DA	20743/971	N490DA	21020/1102	N511DA	21313/1347
N2815W	20871/1039	N403DA	21147/1162	N467DA	20744/972	N491DA	21060/1115	N512DA	21314/1358
N2816W	20872/1040	N404DA	21148/1163	N468DA	20745/980	N492DA	21061/1116	N513DA	21315/1360
N2817W	20873/1043	N405DA	21149/1164	N469DA	20746/981	N493DA	21062/1127	N514DA	21430/1374
N2819W	21057/1135	N406DA	21150/1165	N470DA	20747/987	N494DA	21074/1138	N515DA	21431/1376
N2820W	21058/1136	N407DA	21151/1166	N471DA	20748/988	N495DA	21075/1139	N516DA	21432/1381
N2821W	21059/1137	N408DA	21152/1182	N472DA	20749/990	N496DA	21076/1140	N517DA	21433/1384
N2829W	21481/1338	N409DA	21153/1183	N474DA	20751/1000	N497DA	21077/1147	N518DA	21469/1389
N282WA	21484/1362	N410DA	21222/1205	N475DA	20752/1001	N498DA	21142/1155	N519DA	21470/1400
N283WA	21485/1364	N411DA	21223/1207	N476DA	20753/1012	N499DA	21143/1156	N520DA	21471/1411
N290WA	22108/1587	N412DA	21232/1208	N477DA	20754/1013	N501DA	21303/1262	N521DA	21472/1413
N291WA	22109/1589	N413DA	21233/1211	N478DA	20755/1014	N502DA	21304/1264	N522DA	21582/1422

Delta Air Lines

Delta operates 13 120-seat Boeing 737-347s.

N606DL	22813/49
N607DL	22814/61
N608DA	22815/64
N609DL	22816/65
N610DL	22817/66
N611DL	22818/71
N612DL	22819/73
N613DL	22820/84
N614DL	22821/85
N615DL	22822/87
N616DL	22823/91
N617DL	22907/92
N618DL	22908/95
N619DL	22909/101
N620DL	22910/111
N621DL	22911/112
N622DL	22912/113
N623DL	22913/118
N624DL	22914/120
N625DL	22915/126
N626DL	22916/128
N627DL	22917/129
N628DL	22918/133
N629DL	22919/134
N630DL	22920/135
N631DL	23612/138
N632DL	23613/154
N633DL	23614/157
N634DL	23615/158
N635DL	23762/159
N636DL	23763/164
N637DL	23760/171
N638DL	23761/177
N639DL	23993/198
N640DL	23994/201
N641DL	23995/202
N642DL	23996/205
N643DL	23997/206
N644DL	23998/207
N645DL	24216/216
N646DL	24217/217
N647DL	24218/222
N648DL	24372/223
N649DL	24389/229
N650DL	24390/230
N651DL	24391/238
N652DL	24392/239
N653DL	24393/261
N654DL	24394/264
N655DL	24395/265
N656DL	24396/266
N657DL	24419/286
N658DL	24420/287
N659DL	24421/293
N660DL	24422/294

N661DN	24972/335
N662DN	24991/342
N663DN	24992/343
N664DN	25012/347
N665DN	25013/349
N666DN	25034/354
N667DN	25035/355
N668DN	25141/376
N669DN	25142/377
N670DN	25331/415
N671DN	25332/416
N672DL	25977/429
N673DL	25978/430
N674DL	25979/439
N675DL	25980/448
N676DL	25981/455
N677DL	25982/466
N678DL	25983/465
N679DA	26955/500
N680DA	26956/502
N681DA	26957/516
N682DA	26958/518
N683DA	27103/533
N684DA	27104/535
N685DA	27588/677
N686DA	27589/689

Boeing 767-200 *c/n*

N101DA	22213/6
N102DA	22214/12
N103DA	22215/17
N104DA	22216/26
N105DA	22217/27
N106DA	22218/31
N107DL	22219/37
N108DL	22220/38
N109DL	22221/53
N110DL	22222/56
N111DN	22223/74
N112DL	22224/76
N113DA	22225/77
N114DL	22226/78
N115DA	22227/83

Boeing 767-300 *c/n*

N116DL	23275/136
N117DL	23276/151
N118DL	23277/152
N119DL	23278/153
N120DL	23279/154
N121DE	23435/162
N122DN	23436/163
N123DN	23437/188
N124DE	23438/189
N125DL	24075/200
N126DL	24076/201
N127DL	24077/203
N128DL	24078/207
N129DL	24079/209
N130DL	24080/216
N131DN	24852/320
N132DN	24981/345
N133DN	24982/348
N134DL	25123/353
N135DL	25145/356
N136DL	25146/374
N137DL	25306/392
N138DL	25409/410

Skywest, a Delta Connection carrier, is an important Canadair Regional Jet customer.

N139DL	25984/427
N140LL	25988/499
N1402A	25989/506

Boeing 767-300(ER) *c/n*

N171DN	24759/304
N172DN	24775/312
N173DN	24800/313
N174DN	24802/317
N175DN	24803/318
N176DN	25061/341
N177DN	25122/346
N178DN	25143/349
N179DN	25144/350
N180DN	25985/428
N181DN	25986/446
N182DN	25987/461
N183DN	27110/492
N184DN	27111/496
N185DN	27961/576
N186DA	27962/585

Lockheed L.1011 TriStar 1 *c/n*

N712DA	1088
N714DA	1090
N715DA	1092
N716DA	1095
N717DA	1096
N718DA	1097
N719DA	1135
N720DA	1136
N721DA	1139
N722DA	1147
N723DA	1150
N725DA	1162
N727DA	1167
N728DA	1173
N729DA	1180
N730DA	1199
N173D	1200
N1732D	1213
N733DS	1224
N1734D	1225
N735D	1226
N782DL	1006
N783DL	1009
N784DA	1038
N786DL	1123
N787DL	1126
N789DL	1142
N790DL	1143

Lockheed L.1011 TriStar 200

N724DA	1151

Lockheed L.1011 TriStar 250

N763DY	1227
N737D	1228
N1738D	1234
N1739D	1237
N740DA	1244
N741DA	1245

Lockheed L.1011 TriStar 500

N751DA	1166
N752DA	1172
N753DA	1189
N754DL	1181
N755DL	1184
N756DR	1185

N523DA	21583/1423
N524DA	21584/1478
N525DA	21585/1479
N526DA	21586/1488
N527DA	21587/1492
N528DA	21702/1522
N529DA	21703/1550
N531DA	21814/1556
N532DA	22045/1602
N533DA	22046/1604
N534DA	22047/1606
N535DA	22048/1608
N536DA	22049/1610
N537DA	22073/1624
N538DA	22076/1656
N539DA	22385/1667
N540DA	22386/1669
N541DA	22387/1672
N542DA	22391/1705
N543DA	22392/1707
N544DA	22493/1741
N545DA	22494/1749
N546DA	22677/1785
N830WA	21482/1341
N831L	21826/1509
N831WA	21483/1353
N8873Z	21291/1239
N8875Z	21293/1241
N8889Z	21858/1542
N8890Z	21859/1544
N8891Z	21860/1546

Boeing 737-200 Adv

N235WA	22859/890
N236WA	23184/1061
N237WA	23185/1065
N238WA	23186/1066
N239WA	23187/1010
N242WA	23516/1257
N243WA	23517/1261
N244WA	23518/1265
N245WA	23519/1299
N301DL	23073/991
N302DL	23074/993
N303DL	23075/994
N304DL	23076/995
N305DL	23077/996
N306DL	23078/1000
N307DL	23079/1003
N308DL	23080/1004
N309DL	23081/1005
N310DA	23082/1006
N311DL	23083/1008
N312DL	23084/1009
N313DL	23085/1011
N314DA	23086/1012
N315DL	23087/1013
N316DL	23088/1018
N317DL	23089/1019
N318DL	23090/1020
N319DL	23091/1021

N320DL	23092/1023
N321DL	23093/1024
N322DL	23094/1026
N323DL	23095/1027
N324DL	23096/1028
N325DL	23097/1029
N326DL	23098/1031
N327DL	23099/1035
N328DL	23100/1038
N329DL	23101/1041
N330DL	23102/1045
N331DL	23103/1051
N332DL	23104/1062
N334DL	23105/1068
N367DL	21774/563
N369DL	21776/577
N373DL	23520/1329
N374DL	23521/1342
N375DL	23602/1347
N376DL	23603/1361
N377DL	23604/1369
N378DL	23605/1371
N379DL	23606/1379
N380DL	23607/1387
N381DL	23608/1399
N382DL	23609/1403

Boeing 737-300 *c/n*

N2310	23596/1269
N302WA	23182/1106
N303WA	23183/1108
N304WA	23345/1170
N305WA	23346/1172
N306WA	23347/1173
N307WA	23440/1218
N308WA	23441/1220
N309WA	23442/1239
N311WA	23597/1287
N312WA	23598/1289
N313WA	23599/1324

Boeing 757-200

N601DL	22808/37
N602DL	22809/39
N603DL	22810/41
N604DL	22811/43
N605DL	22812/46

N759DA	1176	N905DL	49536/1348	
N760DH	1194	N906DE	53415/2027	
N761DA	1208	N906DL	49537/1355	
N762DA	1210	N907DE	53416/2029	
N763DL	1197	N907DL	49538/1365	
N764DA	1202	N908DE	53417/2032	
N765DA	1206	N908DL	49539/1366	
N766DA	1207	N909DE	53418/2033	
N767DA	1209	N909DL	49540/1395	
N768DL	1216	N910DE	53419/2036	
N769DL	1218	N910DL	49541/1406	
		N911DE	49967/2037	

Delta's fleet of 265-seat MD-11s is all powered by PW4460 turbofans.

McDonnell Douglas MD-11

N801DE	48472/480	N911DL	49542/1433	
N802DE	48473/481	N912DE	49997/2038	
N803DE	48474/485	N912DL	49543/1434	
N804DE	48475/489	N913DE	49956/2039	
N805DE	48476/510	N913DL	49544/1443	
N806DE	48477/511	N914DE	49957/2049	
N807DE	48478/514	N914DL	49545/1444	
N808DE	48479/536	N915DE	53420/2050	
N809DE	48480/538	N915DL	49546/1447	
N810DE	48565/542	N916DE	53421/2051	
N811DE	48566/543	N916DL	49591/1448	
		N917DE	49958/2054	

McDonnell Douglas MD-88

Reg	Line	Reg	Line
N900DE	53372/1970	N917DL	49573/1469
N901DE	53378/1980	N918DE	49959/2055
N901DL	49532/1338	N918DL	49583/1470
N902DE	53329/1983	N919DE	53422/2058
N902DL	49533/1341	N919DL	49584/1471
N903DE	53380/1986	N920DE	53423/2059
N903DL	49534/1344	N920DL	49644/1473
N904DE	53409/1990	N921DL	49645/1480
N904DL	49535/1347	N922DL	49646/1481
N905DE	53410/1992	N923DL	49705/1491
		N924DL	49711/1492
		N925DL	49712/1500
		N926DL	49713/1523
		N927DA	49714/1524

N928DL	49715/1530	N962DL	49981/1725
N929DL	49716/1531	N963DL	49982/1726
N931DL	49718/1533	N964DL	49983/1743
N932DL	49719/1570	N965DL	49984/1748
N933DL	49720/1571	N966DL	53115/1795
N934DL	49721/1574	N967DL	53116/1796
N935DL	49722/1575	N968DL	53161/1808
N936DL	49723/1576	N969DL	53172/1810
N937DL	49810/1588	N970DL	53173/1811
N938DL	49811/1590	N971DL	53214/1823
N939DL	49812/1593	N972DL	53215/1824
N940DL	49813/1599	N973DL	53241/1832
N941DL	49814/1602	N974DL	53242/1833
N942DL	49815/1605	N975DL	53243/1834
N943DL	49816/1608	N976DL	53257/1845
N944DL	49817/1612	N977DL	53258/1848
N945DL	49818/1613	N978DL	53259/1849
N946DL	49819/1629	N979DL	53266/1859
N947DL	49878/1664	N980DL	53267/1860
N948DL	49879/1666	N981DL	53268/1861
N949DL	49880/1676	N982DL	53273/1870
N950DL	49881/1677	N983DL	53274/1873
N951DL	49882/1679	N984DL	53311/1912
N952DL	49883/1683	N985DL	53312/1914
N953DL	49884/1685	N986DL	53313/1924
N954DL	49885/1689	N987DL	53338/1926
N955DL	49886/1691		
N956DL	49887/1699		
N957DL	49976/1700		
N958DL	49977/1701		
N959DL	49978/1701		
N960DL	49979/1711		
N961DL	49980/1712		

N988DL	53339/1928		
N989DL	53341/1936		
N990DL	53342/1939		
N991DL	53343/1941		
N992DL	53344/1943		
N993DL	53345/1950		
N994DL	53346/1952		
N995DL	53362/1955		
N996DL	53363/1958		
N997DL	53364/1961		
N998DL	53370/1963		
N999DN	53371/1965		

McDonnell Douglas MD-90-30

N901DA	53381/2100
N902DA	53382/2094
N903DA	53383/2095
N904DA	53384/2096
N905DA	53385/2097
N906DA	53386/2099
N907DA	53387/2115
N908DA	53388/2117
N909DA	53389/2122
N910DA	53390/2123
N911DA	53391/2126

DHL Worldwide Express (ER/DHL)

North Kentucky IAP
Cincinnati, USA

History: Founded in 1969 to shuttle cargo manifests and bills of lading between San Francisco and Hawaii. Subsequently developed worldwide express delivery service, using existing airline capacity. Started own airline operations in 1983, providing overnight deliveries and scheduled cargo services across US as DHL Airways, and as DHL Air Cargo within Hawaiian islands. Initial fleet headed by **Boeing 727-100C, Lockheed L.188CF Electra** and **Douglas C-118A (DC-6A)**. Middle East hub established at Bahrain in 1988 and supplemented by new hub in Dubai. Opened European freight hub in Brussels in July 1985, and in May 1986 purchased European Air Transport. Brussels facility doubled in size with acquisition of Federal Express's hub in 1993. Bought five **Douglas DC-8-73CFs** from Air Canada in 1993, to replace previously wet-leased aircraft.

DHL today: Express door-to-door shipments from priority documents to heavy freight, distributed from 19 hubs and serving 220 worldwide gateways. Own services within US, but using other scheduled airlines and contract carriers to meet overseas commitments. Direct service planned from Cincinnati to Montreal, together

The Boeing 727 is still the most important element in the DHL fleet and all have been hushkitted to meet 'Stage Three' standards.

with own transpacific operations. Main US hub at Cincinnati, Ohio, with another 12 regional distribution centres. In conjunction with joint-venture partner, Sinotrans, serves 26 cities in China.

DHL Worldwide Express

Annual revenue: $620 million
Employees: 6,400
Major shareholders: Japan Airlines (25 per cent), Lufthansa (25 per cent), Nissho Iwai (7.5 per cent)

Associate carriers: Japan Airlines and Lufthansa through equity holding. Has itself 3.2 per cent stake in Air Afrique.
Wholly-owned **European Air Transport** (EAT) (QY) provides scheduled distribution services to more than 20 European points with fleet of six **727-100F**s, six **727-200F**s, nine **Convair 580**s and three **Fairchild Metro II**s. Bahrain-based subsidiary **SNAS Aviation**, formerly DHL Aviation

Services, operates four **Fairchild Metro III**s and Convair 580, flying throughout Middle East.

Ameriflight of Burbank operates 10 **SA227AT Expediter**s under contract.

DHL Worldwide Express fleet

Boeing 727-100C	c/n	Boeing 727-200	c/n	N622DH	20896/1051
N701DH	19011/387	N720DH	19544/562	N623DH	20895/1049
N702DH	19793/519	N721DH	19545/564	N624DH	20709/950
N703DH	19010/382	N722DH	19861/682		
N705DH	19191/386	N724DH	19862/685	Douglas DC-8-73F	c/n
N706DH	19192/388	N726DH	20409/845	N801DH	46033/431
N707DH	18321/122	N727DH	20204/778	N802DH	46076/451
N708DH	18275/101			N803DH	46123/508
N709DH	19968/660	Boeing 727-200 Advanced		N804DH	46124/511
N712DH	19401/419	N729DH	22080/1598	N805DH	46125/515
N715DH	19618/461	N740DH	21930/1508	N815UP	46002/394
N717DH	19389/343	N741DH	21931/1531	N816UP	45990/375
		N742DH	21290/1238		

Egyptair (MS/MSR)

Cairo International Airport
Heliopolis, Cairo, Egypt

This Airbus artist's impression shows the new scheme that Egyptair soon hopes to adopt.

History: Founded 7 June 1932 as Misr Airwork and began operations in July 1933 between Cairo and Mersa Matruh with fleet of **de Havilland DH.89A Dragon Rapide**s. All services suspended at outbreak of World War II. Operations resumed in 1945. Fleet rebuilt with second-hand aircraft, including **Avro Anson XIX**s, **Beech C-45**s (**D-18S**), **DC-3**s and, between 1948 and 1954, 10 **Vickers Viking 1B**s. Five **SE.161 Languedoc**s also bought from Air France in 1950. In 1949, airline taken over by Egyptian state and renamed Misrair. Purchase of **Viscount**s from 1955 enabled expansion to London and Karachi. Introduction of first of eight **Comet 4C** jets on 16 July 1960. In January 1961 joined with Syrian Airways under title of United Arab Airlines (UAA) as result of new political links between Egypt and Syria. Accord short-lived and Misrair pulled out, but retained name until change to Egyptair October

1971. Retained **DC-6B**s taken over in merger and added more, but fleet changed to Soviet aircraft after Egypt's political realignment, with exception of order for three **707-320C**s. Aircraft acquired included **An-24V** and **Il-18D**. These, together with three **Il-62**s and eight **Tu-154**s added in 1972/73, were returned when relations between two countries cooled. Order placed for eight **737-200**s in 1976. First of eight **A300B4-200**s delivered in 1980, followed by first **767-200ER** in July 1984, and two **747-300 Combi**s in June 1988. Cairo-Paris-New York service inaugurated in 1985. New decade marked with further fleet upgrade, resulting in delivery of nine **A300-600R**s from May 1990 and seven **A320-200**s from May 1991. Order placed in 1995 for **Boeing 777** and **A340-200**.
Egyptair today: National flag-carrier providing scheduled international links from Cairo to Abidjan, Abu Dhabi, Accra, Aden,

Amman, Asmara, Athens, Bahrain, Bangkok, Barcelona, Beirut, Bombay, Brussels, Budapest, Copenhagen, Damascus, Dar-es-Salaam, Dhahran, Doha, Dubai, Düsseldorf, Entebbe, Frankfurt, Geneva, Helsinki, Istanbul, Jeddah, Johannesburg, Kano, Karachi, Khartoum, Kuwait, Lagos, Larnaca, London, Los Angeles, Madrid, Manila, Milan, Moscow, Munich, Muscat, Nairobi, New York, Osaka, Paris, Ras al Khaimah, Rome, Sana'a, Sharjah, Stockholm, Sydney, Tokyo, Tunis, Vienna and Zürich. Domestic network to 11 destinations, including all major tourist attractions. Joint services with Philippine Airlines and Kuwait Airways.

Annual revenue: $565 million
Passengers: 3.3 million
Cargo: 43,500 tonnes
Employees: 13,000
Wholly-owned by Egyptian government

Fleet development: Three A340-200s and three ordered 777s due for delivery in late 1996/97. Two further options held on A340.
Associate carriers: *Shorouk Air* (7Q), formed jointly with Kuwait Airways in 1991, operated charter services with A320 fleet, but embarked on overambitious expansion and ceased flying.

Egyptair fleet

Airbus A300B4-200	c/n		SU-GAV	579	SU-GBF		351	SU-AYO	21227/466	Boeing 747-300	c/n
SU-BCB	116		SU-GAW	581	SU-GBG		366	SU-		SU-GAL	24161/704
SU-BCC	150		SU-GAX	601						SU-GAM	24162/707
SU-BDG	200		SU-GAY	607	Airbus A340-300	c/n		Boeing 737-500	c/n		
SU-DAR	145		SU-GAZ	616	A40-LE		103	SU-GBH	25084/2019	Boeing 767-200(ER)	
SU-DAS	175							SU-GBI	25307/2135	SU-GAH	23178/97
			Airbus A320-200	c/n	Boeing 707-320C			SU-GBJ	25352/2169	SU-GAI	23179/98
Airbus A300-600R	c/n		SU-GBA	165	SU-AVX	20760/865		SU-GBK	26052/2276	SU-GAJ	23180/99
SU-GAR	557		SU-GBB	166				SU-GBL	26051/2282		
SU-GAS	561		SU-GBC	178	Boeing 737-200					Boeing 767-300(ER)	
SU-GAT	572		SU-GBD	194	Advanced					SU-GAO	24541/275
SU-GAU	575		SU-GBE	198	SU-AYL	21195/457				SU-GAP	24542/282

EL AL Israel Airlines (LY/ELY)

Ben Gurion International
Tel Aviv, Israel

History: Formed 15 November 1948 as national flag-carrier of newly established state. Operations began in August 1949 with **DC-4** service from Tel Aviv to Rome and Paris, extended a year later to London. Four **Lockheed L.049 Constellation**s delivered in 1950 to facilitate expansion to New York, via Europe, and also to Nairobi and Johannesburg. Acquired four **Bristol Britannia**s which set new speed record on London-New York sector of Tel Aviv-New York route 22 December 1957. In January 1961 commenced change to all-Boeing fleet with **707-420**, inaugurating non-stop Tel Aviv-New York service 15 June. Service initiated to Montreal 28 March 1970, and **747-200B** put New York on service 8 June 1970. Operation suffered badly from spate of hijackings and terrorist action in late 1960s and 1970s, and from effect of 1973 war, but expanded once more before four-month strike plunged airline into further difficulties and technical receivership 5 December 1983, situation which persisted until 1995. Aircraft added in 1980s included two **737-200**s from September 1980, four **757-200**s from November 1987 and four **767-200**s from July 1983. Order placed in 1989 for two **747-400**s, delivered in spring 1994, primarily to permit expansion to Far East.

EL AL today: Israeli flag-carrier providing connection between Tel Aviv and all major European cities, and extending to North America, Africa and Far East. serving nearly 50 cities in 31 countries. Destinations outside Europe are Atlanta, Bangkok, Beijing, Bombay, Boston, Cairo, Chicago, Dallas/ Ft Worth, Delhi, Hong Kong, Los Angeles, Miami, Montreal, Nairobi, New York-JFK, New York-Newark and Orlando. High-frequency domestic services are flown between Tel Aviv and Red Sea resort of Eilat, and to Ovda.

Annual revenue: $1,035 million
Passengers: 2.4 million
Cargo: 195,000 tonnes
Employees: 3,400
Ownership: Wholly government-owned, but plans for flotation of 51 per cent stake at Tel Aviv Stock Exchange have been postponed

EL AL took delivery of its first 737-200 in 1980 and both aircraft delivered remain in service.

Associate carriers: *Sun d'Or International Airlines* (ERO), part-owned with Teshet Ltd, provides charter flights from Europe and North America, using EL AL aircraft as required.

Has 24.9 per cent stake in **North American Airlines** (XG), established in April 1989, which provides connections at Chicago, New York and Los Angeles with two **757-200ER**s and one **MD-83**.

EL AL Israel Airlines fleet

Boeing 737-200 Advanced		Boeing 747-200F	c/n	Boeing 757-200(ER)	c/n
4X-ABN	22856/910	4X-AXK	22151/478	4X-EBS	24884/325
4X-ABO	22857/919	4X-AXL	22150/476	4X-EBT	25036/356
				4X-EBU	26053/529
Boeing 747-100F	c/n	Boeing 747-400	c/n	4X-EBV	26054/547
4X-AXZ	19735/64	4X-ELA	26055/1027		
		4X-ELB	26056/1032	Boeing 767-200	c/n
Boeing 747-200B	c/n	4X-ELC	27915/1062	4X-EAA	22972/62
4X-AXA	20135/140			4X-EAB	22973/68
4X-AXB	20274/164	Boeing 757-200	c/n		
4X-AXC	20704/212	4X-EBL	23917/152	Boeing 767-200(ER)	c/n
4X-AXD	21190/272	4X-EBM	23918/156	4X-EAC	22974/86
4X-AXF	21594/327	4X-EBR	24254/185	4X-EAD	22975/89
4X-AXH	22254/418				
4X-AXQ	20841/233				

Emery Worldwide (EB/EWW)

James M. Cox International
Dayton, Ohio, USA

Emery operates re-engined, CFM56-powered DC-8-73Fs plus regular JT3D-powered DC-8Fs.

Services to bring DC-8 fleet to 30 aircraft.

Emery Worldwide today: Cargo schedules and charter flights to more than 125 airports in United States, Canada, Caribbean and Puerto Rico, including dedicated network for US postal service. Services to 89 countries, including Japan, Pacific Rim, Europe, Middle East, Australia, New Zealand and South America. Principal domestic hub at Dayton. International hub operated at Brussels. Signed exclusive agreement with World Airways to use its cargo capacity charters between New York and Paris.

History: Emery Air Freight, formed in April 1946, started its own airline in 1978 following deregulation of air cargo business. Initial fleet of Emery Worldwide Airlines comprised two **DC-8-63CFs**, then added large fleet of **727-100/-200s** and 10 additional **DC-8-63CFs** plus five **DC-8-73CFs**. Door-to-door parcel service and priority mail within US from its 'superhub' at

Cox International soon supplemented by direct flights to Australia, Hong Kong, Japan and Europe. Distribution hubs established at Manchester and Maastricht, later replaced by Brussels. Acquired competitor Purolator Courier after being itself purchased by Consolidated Freightways 6 April 1989. In 1991, acquired 17 more stretched DC-8s from Flagship Express

Annual revenue: *$1,800 million*
Employees: *6,700*
Ownership: *Wholly-owned subsidiary of Consolidated Freightways*

Emery Worldwide fleet

Boeing 727-100	c/n					Douglas DC-8-63F	c/n		
N1928	19386/321	N424EX	20042/626	N7365U	19908/653	N8177U	45983/350		
N1975	18431/32	N426EX	19089/250	N7638U	19911/668	N796AL	46054/453	N870SJ	46039/448
N1978	18434/50	N427EX	19090/277	N7639U	19912/670	N797AL	46163/556		
N1982	18438/65	N428EX	19097/307	N7640U	19913/672	N865F	46088/464	Douglas DC-8-73F	c/n
N1983	18439/67	N429EX	19100/324	N7642U	19915/681	N906R	46087/454	N105WP	46095/497
N1990	18446/123	N432EX	19867/514	N7643U	2037/701	N921R	46145/548	N2674U	46062/486
N210NE	18903/147	N433EX	19868/529	N7644U	20038/716	N929R	45901/293	N791FT	46045/441
N329QS	19038/285	N435EX	19288/389	N7645U	20039/720	N950R	45903/286	N792FT	46046/444
N355QS	19257/385	N436EX	19289/403			N951R	46092/505	N795FT	46103/483
N356QS	19258/397	N526PC	20370/821	Douglas DC-8F-54	c/n	N957R	46137/527	N796FT	46104/488
N357QS	19259/408	N527PC	19665/476	N991CF	45081/235	N959R	46143/547	N870TV	46086/478
N359QS	19007/269	N528PC	19597/524	N992CF	45884/340	N964R	46000/386	N961R	46133/534
N721JE	18843/170					N950R			
		Boeing 727-200	c/n	Douglas DC-8-62F	c/n	Douglas DC-8-71F	c/n	Douglas DC-9-15F	c/n
		N3109E	20241/726	N990CF	46068/463	N500MH	45812/277	N561PC	47014/141
Boeing 727-100C	c/n	N311NE	19703/684	N993CF	46028/461	N8076U	45941/317	N566PC	45828/242
N413EX	19206/294	N312NE	20193/755	N994CF	45956/376	N8079U	45047/341	N567PC	47153/185
N414EX	18899/256	N313NE	19702/680	N995CF	46024/428	N8084U	45974/368	N568PC	47086/219
N416EX	19287/383	N314NE	19495/664	N996CF	46162/555	N8085U	45975/369		
N417EX	19290/417	N315NE	20190/738	N997CF	46154/554	N8087U	45977/373		
N421EX	19099/322	N316NE	19475/511	N998CF	46139/537	N811AL	46099/507		

Emirates Airline (EK/UAE)

Dubai International Airport
Dubai, United Arab Emirates

History: Established in May 1985 by Dubai Emirate in competition with national carrier Gulf Air to provide capacity to match growth of Dubai. Initial fleet two **Boeing 727-200s** provided by Dubai Air Wing. Also wet-leased **Airbus A300** and **737** from PIA. Operations started 25 October

1985. First destinations Bombay, Delhi and Karachi. European destination (Frankfurt and London-Gatwick) in schedule from 1 July 1987 with **Airbus A310-300**. Eastern sector opened with flights to Bangkok, Manila and Singapore from June 1990. Four **A300-600Rs** ordered to replace

leased A300-600, and A310 fleet increased. 727 phased out in 1995. Fleet modernisation and expansion completed with order for seven **Boeing 777s**. First revenue service in April 1996.

Emirates today: Wholly-owned by Dubai government. Flies scheduled services to 38

In mid-1996 Emirates introduced its brand-new Boeing 777s on a range of routes from Dubai. Seven 777s are on firm order.

destinations from home base of Dubai. In addition to regional network, serves Bangkok, Bombay, Colombo, Comores, Delhi, Dhaka, Frankfurt, Ho Chi Min City, Hong Kong, Istanbul, Jakarta, Johannesburg, Karachi, Larnaca, London-Heathrow, London-Gatwick, Male, Manila, Manchester, Nairobi, Nice, Paris, Rome, Singapore and Zürich. Code-share with United Airlines.

Annual revenue: $600 million
Passengers: 2.0 million
Employees: 3,600

Fleet development: Five of original order of seven 777-200s due for delivery between September 1996 and September 1997. Options held on seven extended-range 'B' Model 777s pencilled in for delivery from May 1998 to June 2000.

Associate carrier: *Emirates Sky Cargo* has been operated as separate entity since airline's foundation. Joint Amsterdam-Dubai-Singapore cargo service in conjunction with KLM. Own cargo schedule to Hong Kong and Moscow.

Emirates Airline fleet

Airbus A300-600R	c/n	Airbus A310-300	c/n		
A6-EKC	505	A6-EKA	432	A6-EKL	667
A6-EKD	558	A6-EKB	436	A6-EKN	573
A6-EKE	563	A6-EKG	545	A6-EKP	695
A6-EKF	608	A6-EKH	600	**Boeing 777-200**	**c/n**
A6-EKM	701	A6-EKI	588	A6-EMD	27247/30
A6-EKO	747	A6-EKJ	597	A6-EME	27248/33
		A6-EKK	658		

Estonian Air (OV/ELL)

Ylemiste Airport
Tallinn, Estonia

History: Founded 1 December 1991 as joint-stock company following redeclaration of Estonian independence. Inherited fleet and resources from predecessor Estonian territory, local division of Aeroflot. Included number of **Tupolev Tu-134A**s and **Yakovlev Yak-40**s, both refurbished with new seats and more leg room by November 1994. Direct flights established between capital Tallinn and several European and Commonwealth of Independent States (CIS) cities. Lease deal signed with ILFC 2 June 1994 for two new **Boeing 737-500**s, delivered in June and October 1995. Tupolevs put up for sale.

Estonian Air today: National flag-carrier providing direct flights from Tallinn to Amsterdam, Copenhagen, Frankfurt, Hamburg, Helsinki, Kiev, London Gatwick, Minsk, Munich, Moscow, St Petersburg and Vilnius. No domestic services.

Annual revenue: $30 million
Passengers: 0.18 million
Employees: 480
Ownership: Privatised in summer 1996. Danish airline Maersk Air together with local company Baltic Cesco acquiring 66

Estonian Air's first, newly-delivered, Boeing 737-5Q8 entered service on the airline's Tallinn to Amsterdam route on 12 July 1995. Both of its 737-500s are operated on lease from US lessors ILFC.

per cent. The Estonian State retains a 34 per cent share

Fleet development: Third 737-500 to be leased in late 1996. Six Tu-134As for sale.

Estonian Air fleet

Boeing 737-500	c/n	ES-AAK	60977	Yakovlev Yak-40	c/n
ES-ABC	26324/2735	ES-AAL	62350	ES-AAR	9510439
ES-ABD	26323/2770	ES-AAM	60380	ES-AAS	9632049
		ES-AAN	60560	ES-AAT	9511639
Tupolev Tu-134A	**c/n**			ES-AAU	9411333a
ES-AAE	48395	**Tupolev Tu-134A-3**	**c/n**		
ES-AAH	35270	ES-AAG	49907		
ES-AAI	60350	ES-AAP	38020		

Ethiopian Airlines (ET/ETH)

Bole International Airport,
Addis Ababa, Ethiopia

Ethiopian airlines has three 186-seat Boeing 767-260(ER)s in service, which replaced 707s.

Abidjan, Abu Dhabi, Accra, Asmara, Athens, Bamako, Bangkok, Beijing, Bombay, Brazzaville, Bujunbura, Cairo, Dakar, Dar-es-Salaam, Delhi, Djibouti, Dubai, Durban, Frankfurt, Harare, Jeddah, Johannesburg, Kampala, Karachi, Khartoum, Kigali, Kilimanjaro, Kinshasa, Lagos, Lilongwe, Lomé, London, Luanda, Muscat, Nairobi, N'Djamena, Niamey, Riyadh, Rome and Sana'a. Extensive domestic network serves over 40 communities. Block-space agreement with Air-India between Bombay and Beijing, and commercial agreement with Nigeria Airways.

History: Founded 30 December 1945 by Emperor Haille Selassie I, and began operations 8 April 1946 with fleet of five **Douglas C-47**s (**DC-3**). Initial routes linked Addis Ababa with Assab, Aden, Asmara, Djibouti, Cairo, Khartoum and Nairobi. Service to Bombay opened in 1947, but withdrawn in February 1953. Two **Convair 340**s acquired in 1950 and third in 1955, followed by two **DC-6B**s which were used to open service to Frankfurt in June 1958. Order placed in July 1960 for two **Boeing 720B**s, delivered in November 1962, and used to inaugurate Addis Ababa-Athens-Madrid service in 1963. Third new 720B bought in 1965, and three ex-Continental Airlines aircraft placed into service in 1973/74. Two new **707-320C**s delivered in April and May 1968. Pioneered flights between Africa and China with direct service to Beijing in 1973. Military coup and subsequent abolishment of monarchy in 1975 affected operations for time. Chose **Boeing 727-200** in 1979, resisting pressure from Marxist government to buy **Tu-154**, and in 1984 acquired three **767-200**s. Five **Twin Otter**s bought in March

1985. Two **ATR42-300**s and two **737-200**s added in March 1988. Two **L.100 Hercules** leased from Ministry of Transport for freight work. Fleet further upgraded with delivery of four **757-200**s from August 1990, including first **757-200F** freighters outside US. Seccessionist war with Eritrean rebels posed many problems, including damage to aircraft and hijackings, but network extended 3 June 1992 to Bangkok, and later to Johannesburg.

Ethiopian Airlines today: National flag-carrier operating scheduled services from capital Addis Ababa to destinations in Europe, Africa and Middle and Far East. Points served are

Annual revenue: $255 million
Passengers: 0.75 million
Cargo: 32,000 tonnes
Employees: 3,260
Ownership: Wholly-owned by Ethiopian government

Fleet development: Five Fokker 50s were on order for delivery between June and December 1996, but will not now be delivered.

Ethiopian Airlines fleet

AI(R) ATR42-300	c/n	Boeing 757-200PF	c/n	DHC-6 Twin Otter 300	
ET-AJC	071	ET-AJS	24845/300	ET-AIM	815
ET-AJD	076			ET-AIN	816
		Boeing 767-200(ER)	c/n	ET-AIT	820
Boeing 737-200 Advanced		ET-AIE	23106/90	ET-AIX	835
ET-AJB	23915/1583	ET-AIF	23107/93		
		ET-AIZ	23916/187	Lockheed L.100-30	
Boeing 757-200	c/n			Hercules	c/n
ET-AJX	25014/348	DHC-5A Buffalo	c/n	ET-AJK	5022
ET-AKC	25353/408	ET-AHJ	102A	ET-AKG	5306
ET-AKE	26057/444				
ET-AKF	26058/496				

Eurowings (EW/EWG)

Dortmund and Nuremberg Airports
Germany

History: Formed 1 January 1994 from merger of NFD Luftverkehrs AG of Nuremberg and RFG Regionalflug of Dortmund. RFG founded in 1976 as charter and air-taxi operator and moved into scheduled services in April 1979. First **ATR42-300** delivered in February 1987. NFD started operations as air taxi in

1975, but expanded rapidly into domestic and international services out of Nuremberg, Munich, Bremen and Hannover with fleet of **Metro III** and **Do 228** aircraft. First ATR42-300 delivered in September 1986, followed by larger **ATR72** in March 1991. **BAe 146-200QT** used on night cargo services from 1988. In

1989, Air Europe parent company ILG acquired 49 per cent stake in NFD in quest to become pan-European operator. Following collapse of ILG in 1991, RFG's principal shareholder Dr Albrecht Knauf purchased majority of NFD's shares, leading to merger under name of Eurowings. In October 1995 developed co-operation with Air France and KLM, covering routes between Germany and France and Netherlands, respectively. Marketing agreement signed with Northwest Airlines 1 February 1996.

Eurowings today: Domestic and cross-border European flights from hubs at Dortmund, Nuremberg, Berlin, Paris and Amsterdam. Destinations served include Bayreuth, Brussels, Dresden, Düsseldorf, Frankfurt, Hamburg, Hannover, Hof, Jersey, Krakow, Leipzig, London, Lyon, Munich, Münster/Osnabrück, Newcastle, Nice, Olbia, Paderborn/Lippstadt, Prague, Stuttgart, Sylt, Vienna, Warsaw, Wroclaw and Zürich. Serves six routes from Amsterdam for KLM, and eight for Air France centred on Paris. Marketing and code-share agreements with Air France for flights to Paris and with KLM Royal Dutch Airlines and Northwest Airlines for flights to Amsterdam and onward to US.

Annual revenue: *$200 million*
Passengers: *1.8 million*
Employees: *1,030*
Ownership: *Privately-owned by Dr Albrecht Knauf (93.66 per cent) and Reinhart Santner (6.25 per cent)*

Fleet development: One more **146-300** due in August

1996. Acquisition of 10 jet aircraft, to replace similar number of turboprops, under evaluation. **Avro RJ85** most likely choice.

Eurowings operates a large fleet of ATR turboprops (like this ATR72) and BAe 146 jets on its wide-ranging European network.

Eurowings fleet

AI(R) ATR42-300	c/n				
D-BAAA	011	D-BHHH	173	D-AEWK	446
D-BBBB	055	D-BJJJ	278		
D-BCCC	080			**BAe 146-200**	c/n
D-BCRM	038	**AI(R) ATR72-200**	c/n	D-ACFA	E2200
D-BCRN	053	D-ANFA	224	D-AJET	E2201
D-BCRO	122	D-ANFB	229		
D-BCRP	158	D-ANFC	237	**BAe 146-200QT**	c/n
D-BCRQ	233	D-ANFD	256	D-ADEI	E2086
D-BCRR	255	D-ANFE	294	D-ANTJ	E2100
D-BCRS	287	D-ANFF	292		
D-BCRT	289			**BAe 146-300**	c/n
D-BDDD	110	**AI(R) ATR72-210**	c/n	D-AEWA	E3163
D-BEEE	121	D-AEWG	347		
D-BFFF	130	D-AEWH	359		
D-BGGG	148	D-AEWI	404		

Eva Airways (BR/EVA)

Chiang Kai-Shek International Airport
Taipei, Taiwan

History: Established by Evergreen Corp. in March 1989 and began international passenger and cargo services 1 July 1991, using leased **767-200ERs**. On 6 October 1989 placed orders with Boeing for eight **747-400s** and four **767-300ERs**, and for four **MD-11s** with McDonnell Douglas, later augmented with follow-up contracts. Launched first longhaul service to Vienna 11 November 1991, and transpacific flights to Los Angeles in December 1992 with 747-400. Route system expanded steadily to reach 24 cities in 1995, including three cargo routes to New York, Los Angeles and San Francisco. First MD-11 joined fleet in August 1994, and first **MD-11F**

EVA Air successfully challenged China Airlines' Taiwanese 'monopoly' and is now a major force in the Far Eastern market.

freighter in spring 1995. Signed letter of intent for **Boeing 777** in June 1995. First European freighter service to Amsterdam flown in October 1995, and route to Panama inaugurated 13 December via Los Angeles.

Eva Air today: Passenger and cargo services from Taipei to Amsterdam, Anchorage, Bangkok, Brisbane, Denpasar/Bali, Dubai, Fukuoka, Ho Chi Minh City, Hong Kong, Honolulu, Jakarta, Kuala Lumpur, London, Los Angeles, Macau, Male, Manila, Melbourne, New York-JFK/Newark, Panama, Penang, San Francisco, Seattle, Singapore, Surabaya, Sydney and Vienna. Plans to add Chicago and Wash-

Eva Airways

Great China Airlines is an associate airline of Eva Airways, serving the domestic market.

Taipei, Kaohsiung, Hualien, Kinmen, Makung, Taitung and Tsuxiang; and 25 per cent of **Great China Airlines** (IF), serving Chiyi, Kaohsiung, Kinmen, Makung, Pintung, Taichung, Tainan and Taipei, with 12 **DHC-8-300**s and one **DHC-8-100**s. Six **DHC-8-400B**s and three **MD90-30**s order.

ington in US and Brussels in Europe. Domestic service between Taipei and Kaohsiung, and other destinations via associates. Major marketing and codeshare agreements with Ansett Australia, ANA and Garuda.

Annual revenue: $1,050 million
Passengers: 3.1 million
Cargo: 233,000 tonnes
Employees: 5,000
Major shareholders: Evergreen Marine Corporation (43 per cent), Evergreen International (22 per cent) and EVA Air employees (29 per cent)

Fleet development: Six **MD90-30**s order for delivery from October 1996; one for EVA Air, other five for Makung Airlines. Letter of intent for four **Boeing 777 Combi**s.

Associate carriers: Holds 42 per cent of **Makung Airlines** (B7), which operates one **757-200**, five **BAe 146-300**s and two **HS 748**s on services linking

Intends to acquire 30 per cent stake in **Taiwan Airlines** (WG), and plans to set up airline operation in Panama to facilitate expansion into South America.

Eva Airways fleet

Boeing 747-400	c/n	Boeing 747-400 Combi		N602EV	25117/370
B-16401	27062/942	N408EV	28092/		
B-16402	27063/947	N409EV	28093/	**McDonnell Douglas**	
B-16461	27154/994			**MD-11**	c/n
B-16462	27173/998	**Boeing 767-200**	c/n	B-16101	48542/570
B-16463	27174/1004	B-16621	27192/524	B-16102	48543/572
B-16465	26062/1016	B-16622	27193/527	N103EV	48415/576
N403EV	27141/976	B-16623	27194/532		
N405EV	27142/982	B-16625	27195/535	**McDonnell Douglas**	
N406EV	27898/1051			**MD-11F**	c/n
N407EV	27899/1053	**Boeing 767-300(ER)**	c/n	B-16106	48545/587
		B-16603	26063/434	B-16107	48546/589
		B-16605	26064/438	N105EV	48544/580
		B-16688	25221/384		
		N601EV	25076/366		

Evergreen International (EZ/EIA)

Marana Air Park
Arizona, USA

Evergreen is an important US internal carrier which also maintains sizeable overseas cargo and express freight services.

History: Established 28 November 1975 when Evergreen Helicopters acquired supplemental type certificate of Johnson Flying Service, founded 1924. Initial operations focused on passenger charters, flown with five ex-Lufthansa **Boeing 727-100**s and **Douglas DC-8-50**, but emphasis changed to cargo charters using **Lockheed L.188AF** and **DC-8-32**

freighters. Three **DC-9-32F**s, two **DC-8-33**s and five **Convair 580**s added for military and other long-term contracts in late 1976. Scheduled cargo services inaugurated in autumn 1978 between East and East Coasts, expanded 1 June 1979 with New York-Atlanta and New York-Houston routes, and passenger service between Philadelphia and

Freeport, Bahamas. Order placed for two **747-200F**s, put into service in 1985, with three more added during 1990. **DC-8-63CF** acquired and later re-engined to **DC-8-73** standard to meet noise regulations. Network extended 16 November 1981 to Cozumel, Cancun and Merida in Mexico.

Over following years, fleet grew to almost 40 aircraft, used for passenger and cargo charters, military contract work, and subservices for major international passenger airlines and freight forwarders. Scheduled cargo routes served Atlanta, Chicago, Dallas/Ft Worth, San Francisco, Seattle and Los Angeles.

Evergreen today: Contract cargo services and customised charters across world, with frequent flights to Africa, Australia, China, India, Japan, Middle East, Southeast Asia, Europe and South America. Regular ports of call include Beijing, Brussels, Hong Kong, Khabarovsk, Paris, Petropavlovsk, Seoul, Shanghai, Taipei and Tokyo. Scheduled authority for cargo services between US and Hong Kong and mainland China.

Annual revenue: $270 million
Employees: 450
Ownership: Wholly-owned by Delford M. Smith family through Evergreen International Aviation

Evergreen International fleet

Boeing 727-7100	c/n	Boeing 747-100SR	c/n	Douglas DC-8-62F	c/n
N725EV	19112/299	N477EV	20784/231	N817EV	46022/417
N728EV	18794/99	N478EV	21033/254		
N742EV	19410/369			**Douglas DC-9-15F**	**c/n**
N745EV	19283/502	**Boeing 747-200B**	**c/n**	N915F	47061/207
		N482EV	20713/219	N916F	47044/165
Boeing 747-100F	**c/n**	N485EV	20712/218		
N472EV	20320/98			**Douglas DC-9-30F**	**c/n**
N473EV	19657/37	**Boeing 747-200 Combi**		N932F	47355/452
N474EV	19637/4	N470EV	20653/237	N933F	47191/280
N479EV	19898/94	N471EV	20651/209	N935F	47220/296
N480EV	20348/106			N940F	47414/536
N481EV	19896/72			N944F	47194/324
				N945F	47279/337

FedEx (FM/FDX)

Memphis International Airport
Memphis, Tennessee, USA

History: Founded by Frederick W. Smith in 1972 and began overnight express package delivery service 17 April 1973, flying converted **Dassault Falcon**s to 25 cities from Little Rock, Arkansas. Falcon fleet grew to 32. After 1977 deregulation of US air cargo business seven **Boeing 727-100C**s purchased from United Airlines, followed in March 1980 by **DC-10-30**, acquired from Continental. Four **737-200QC**s also operated for short period. Discussions held with British Airways to use an all-cargo Concorde, and with Airship Industries to utilise large airship for transport of small packages in US. Both plans abandoned. International expansion in 1984 to Europe and Asia, backed up by first schedule to Brussels in July 1985, and to Tokyo in 1988. Acquired first **Cessna Caravan I Cargomaster/Super Cargomaster** in early 1985, to be operated by variety of contract carriers throughout United States. Expansion accelerated with acquisition of Flying Tiger Line in 1989 and integration of that airline's 21-country route network and fleet. Flying Tigers, incorporated 25 June 1945, was at time of takeover world's largest cargo airline. Fleet enlarged and modernised with first of 15 **MD-11F**s in May 1991, and delivery of 13 converted ex-Lufthansa **A310-200F**s from July 1994. Became launch customer for **Airbus A300-600F** with order for 25, plus 25 options, first delivered in April 1994.

FedEx today: World's largest express transportation company providing scheduled and charter services in the US

and to 210 countries. Operations are centred on its 'superhub' at Memphis, regional sorting centres at Newark, Fort Worth, Indianapolis and Oakland, and metroplexes in Chicago and Los Angeles. Major international facilities at Anchorage, Paris, London, Frankfurt, Tokyo and, since September 1995, at Subic Bay in Philippines, from where it launched AsiaOne, first intra-Asia overnight delivery service linking 11 principal cities.

Annual revenue: $9,400 million
Annual shipments: 750 million
Employees: 119,760

Fleet development: Deliveries outstanding include 21 **A300-600F**s, 14 **A310-200**s and 13 **Caravan I**s. Will acquire 12

FedEx is unique in operating a large fleet of dedicated Airbus A300 and A310 freighters.

MD-11s from American Airlines between 1996 and 1999, with options on seven between 2000 and 2002. Will introduce 60+ DC-10s in upgraded **MD-10** standard with new two-crew cockpit. Five **747-200F**s to be sub-leased to Lufthansa from 1998 to 2008, as part of A310 deal.

Associate carriers: US turboprop fleet contracted out to: **Baron Aviation, Corporate Air, CSA Air, Empire Airlines, Era Aviation, Mountain Air Cargo, Westair** and **Wiggins Airways**.

Connecting services to 10 European countries flown by TNT.

FedEx fleet

Airbus A300-600F		N655FE	742	N661FE	760
N650FE	726	N656FE	745	N662FE	762
N651FE	728	N657FE	748	N663FE	766
N652FE	735	N658FE	752	N664FE	768
N635FE	736	N659FE	757		
N654FE	738	N660FE	759		

FedEx

FedEx operates a massive fleet of Cessna Model 208 Caravan Is.

N285FE	22622/1792
N286FE	22623/1803
N287FE	21849/1527
N288FE	21850/1536
N461FE	22548/1734
N462FE	22550/1739
N463FE	22551/1744
N464FE	21288/1234
N465FE	21289/1235
N466FE	21292/1240
N467FE	21449/1306
N468FE	21452/1312
N469FE	21581/1437
N477FE	21394/1281
N478FE	21395/1283
N479FE	21461/1337
N480FE	21462/1342
N481FE	21463/1353
N482FE	21464/1355
N483FE	21465/1363
N484FE	21466/1372
N485FE	21488/1388
N486FE	21489/1390
N487FE	21490/1396
N488FE	21491/1402
N489FE	21492/1440
N490FE	21493/1442
N491FE	21529/1444
N492FE	21530/1446
N493FE	21531/1450
N494FE	21532/1453
N495FE	21669/1484
N496FE	21670/1486
N497FE	20866/1067
N498FE	20867/1068
N499FE	21018/1095

Boeing 747-200F

N636FE	21764/394
N638FE	21841/396
N639FE	21650/354
N640FE	20826/242
N641FE	20827/266

Douglas DC-10-10

N68049	47803/139
N68050	47804/142
N68051	47805/145
N68052	47806/148
N68053	47807/173
N68054	47808/177
N68055	47809/191
N68056	47810/194
N68057	48264/379
N68058	46705/33
N68059	46907/78
N10060	46970/269
N40061	46973/272

Douglas DC-10-30F

N301FE	46800/96
N302FE	46801/103
N303FE	46802/110
N304FE	46992/257

FedEx is eager to acquire additional MD-11F freighters.

N305FE	47870/339
N306FE	48287/409
N307FE	48291/412
N308FE	48297/416
N309FE	48298/419
N310FE	48299/422
N311FE	46871/219
N312FE	48300/433
N313FE	48311/440
N314FE	48312/442
N315FE	48313/443
N316FE	48314/444
N317FE	46835/278
N318FE	46837/282
N319FE	47820/317
N320FE	47835/326
N321FE	47836/330
N322FE	47908/215

Fokker F27-500

N705FE	10367
N706FE	10385
N707FE	10371
N708FE	10372
N709FE	10375
N710FE	10380
N711FE	10383
N712FE	10613
N713FE	10615
N714FE	10461
N715FE	10468
N716FE	10471
N717FE	10455
N718FE	10470
N719FE	10467
N720FE	10464
N721FE	10460
N722FE	10472
N723FE	10682
N724FE	10677
N725FE	10658
N726FE	10683
N727FE	10661
N728FE	10657

Fokker F27-600

N701FE	10419
N702FE	10350
N703FE	10420
N729FE	10385
N730FE	10386
N741FE	10387
N742FE	10349
HB-ISJ	10329
OY-CCL	10450

McDonnell Douglas MD-11F

N601FE	48401/447
N602FE	48402/448
N603FE	48459/470
N604FE	48460/497
N605FE	48514/515
N606FE	48602/549
N607FE	48547/517
N608FE	48548/521
N609FE	48549/545
N610FE	48603/551
N611FE	48604/553
N612FE	48605/555
N614FE	48528/507
N616FE	48747/594
N617FE	48748/595
N	48420/451

Airbus A310-200F

N401FE	191
N402FE	201
N403FE	230
N405FE	233
N406FE	237
N407FE	254
N408FE	257
N409FE	273
N410FE	356
N411FE	359
N412FE	360
N413FE	397
N414FE	400
N415FE	349
N416FE	288
N417FE	333
N418FE	343
N419FE	345
N420FE	339
N421FE	342
N422FE	346
N423FE	281

Boeing 727-100F

N101FE	19197/410
N102FE	19193/392
N103FE	19199/414
N104FE	19198/413
N105FE	19194/394
N106FE	19201/421
N107FE	19202/424
N112FE	19890/630
N113FE	19894/647
N114FE	19527/460
N115FE	19814/600
N116FE	19298/335
N117FE	19299/344
N118FE	19300/346
N119FE	19301/352
N120FE	19356/356
N124FE	19360/371
N127FE	19719/478
N128FE	19720/482
N133FE	19851/510
N134FE	19852/517
N135FE	19853/522
N136FE	19855/632
N143FE	19136/314
N144FE	19137/316
N145FE	19109/271
N146FE	19110/283
N147FE	19080/270
N148FE	19086/353
N149FE	19087/359
N150FE	19141/370
N151FE	19147/472
N152FE	18285/172
N154FE	18287/190

N155FE	18288/192
N156FE	18289/194
N166FE	18863/227
N167FE	18864/231
N168FE	18865/232
N169FE	18866/241
N181FE	18868/248
N184FE	18870/258
N185FE	18871/259
N186FE	18872/261
N187FE	19079/268
N188FE	19081/275
N189FE	19082/279
N190FE	19083/281
N191FE	19084/337
N193FE	19142/440
N194FE	19143/446
N195FE	19144/450
N196FE	19145/451
N198FE	19154/512
N199FE	19509/459
N502FE	18271/82
N503FE	18273/91
N504FE	18274/96
N505FE	18276/103
N507FE	18278/113
N508FE	18279/121
N509FE	18280/129
N510FE	18282/149
N511FE	18283/155

Boeing 727-200 Advanced

N201FE	
N203FE	22924/1818
N204FE	22925/1819
N205FE	22926/1820
N206FE	22927/1821
N207FE	22928/1822
N208FE	22929/1823
N209FE	22930/1824
N210FE	22931/1825
N211FE	22932/1826
N212FE	22933/1827
N213FE	22934/1828
N215FE	22935/1829
	22936/1830

N216FE	22937/1831
N217FE	22938/1832
N218FE	21101/1150
N219FE	21102/1152
N220FE	20934/1074
N221FE	20932/1069
N222FE	20933/1071
N223FE	20935/1076
N233FE	21327/1249
N234FE	21328/1251
N235FE	21329/1254
N236FE	21330/1260
N237FE	21331/1266
N240FE	20978/1083
N241FE	20979/1098
N242FE	21178/1237
N243FE	21480/1352
N244FE	21647/1436
N245FE	22016/1566
N246FE	22068/1660
N254FE	20936/1078
N257FE	22939/1112
N258FE	20940/1120
N262FE	21624/1468
N263FE	21625/1470
N264FE	21626/1472
N265FE	21671/1523
N266FE	21672/1538
N267FE	21673/1541
N268FE	21674/1543
N269FE	21675/1555
N270FE	22035/1578
N271FE	22036/1596
N272FE	22037/1600
N273FE	22038/1612
N274FE	22039/1614
N275FE	22040/1626
N276FE	22041/1628
N277FE	22042/1630
N278FE	22345/1699
N279FE	22346/1704
N280FE	22347/1708
N281FE	22348/1714
N282FE	22349/1722
N283FE	22350/1745
N284FE	22621/1791

Finnair (AY/FIN)

History: Founded 1 November 1923 as Aero OY and began operations 20 March 1924 from Helsinki across Gulf of Finland to Tallinn using **Junkers F 13** float-plane. **Junkers G 24W** joined fleet in June 1926 and **Ju 52/3m** in June 1932. Following construction of airports at Turku and Helsinki, flew last seaplane service December 1936. Two **DH.89A Rapide**s acquired for domestic services inaugurated on 1 May 1937. Domestic flights re-established 13 August 1945, and Helsinki-Stockholm route 1 November 1947. New fleet comprised eight **C-47**s (**DC-3**). First of three **Convair 340**s went into service 19 April 1953, followed by five **Convair 440**s. Marketing name of Finnair in 1953, made official 25 June 1968. Convairs replaced by three **Caravelle IA**s – which entered into service 1 April 1960. Acquired eight **Super Caravelle 10B3**s between 1964/1967, and first of two **DC-8-62CF**s arrived in 8 February 1969, opening transatlantic service to New York 15 May. Fleet further expanded during 1970s with eight **DC-9-15**s, 12 **DC-9-51**s and two **DC-10-30**s. In 1981 **DC-9-41** went into service, followed in April 1983 by **MD-82**. Helsinki-Tokyo route inaugurated same month. Next came introduction of four **MD-87**s from 1987, two **A300B4-200**s in December 1986 and first of four **MD-11**s in December 1990.

Finnair today: International network serving 49 scheduled and charter destinations, with emphasis on Europe where airline flies to 30 cities. Transatlantic routes operated to New York, Miami, San Francisco and Toronto, complementing Far Eastern services to Beijing, Bangkok, Singapore, Osaka and Tokyo. Beijing, Osaka and Tokyo served non-stop across Siberia. Dense, 21-point domestic net-work, flown in conjunction with associates Finnaviation and Karair. Code-share agreement with Transwede on Stockholm to London route, and partnership with Lufthansa, to be reassessed in light of Lufthansa/SAS tie-up. Marketing alliances with Air Canada, Air China, Austrian Airlines, Braathens SAFE, Maersk Air and Delta Air Lines.

Annual revenue: $1,350 million
Passengers: 5.5 million
Cargo: 57.600 tonne
Employees: 7,500
Major shareholders: government of Finland with 60.7 per cent and Neste with 7.0 percent.

Finnair has long been associated with McDonnell Douglas aircraft and has been a steady customer for many years. This is one of 12 DC-9-51s still in use.

Associate carriers: Wholly-owned **Finnaviation** (FA), formed 1950 as Lentohuolto OY. Operates five **Saab 340A**s and two **340B**s schedules to 17 domestic points and to neighbouring Stockholm, Petrozavodsk and Tallinn. **Karair** (KR), also wholly-owned, connects Helsinki with 14 domestic points, and to Stockholm and Tallinn on behalf of Finnair. Fleet comprises six **ATR72-201**s and one **DHC-6-300**.

Finnair fleet

Airbus A300B4-200	c/n	Douglas DC-9-51	c/n	McDonnell Douglas MD-82/83	c/n	McDonnell Douglas MD-87	c/n
OH-LAA	299	OH-LYN	47694/805	OH-LMG	49625/1503	OH-LMA	49403/1404
OH-LAB	302	OH-LYO	47695/806	OH-LMH	53245/1978	OH-LMB	49404/1430
		OH-LYP	47796/806	OH-LMN	49150/1087	OH-LMC	49406/1525
Douglas DC-9-41	c/n	OH-LYR	47736/827	OH-LMO	49151/1088		
OH-LNE	47605/724	OH-LYS	47737/829	OH-LMP	49152/1089	McDonnell Douglas MD-11	c/n
OH-LNF	47614/747	OH-LYT	47738/830	OH-LMR	49284/1209	OH-LGA	48449/455
		OH-LYU	47771/883	OH-LMS	49252/1169	OH-LGB	48450/479
Douglas DC-10-30	c/n	OH-LYV	47772/890	OH-LMT	49877/1594	OH-LGC	48512/529
OH-LHA	47956/181	OH-LYW	47773/891	OH-LMU	49741/1630	OH-LGD	48513/564
OH-LHB	47957/201	OH-LYX	48134/980	OH-LMV	49904/1680		
OH-LHD	47865/135	OH-LYY	48135/987	OH-LMW	49905/1767		
		OH-LYZ	48136/993	OH-LMX	49906/1786		
				OH-LMY	53244/1901		
				OH-LMZ	53246/1918		
				OH-	49401/1357		
				OH-	49708/1561		

Garuda Indonesia (GA/GIA)

History: Founded 28 December 1949, one day after Indonesia's independence. Formally incorporated on 31 March 1950, jointly with KLM. Started domestic operations with fleet of 22 **DC-3**s and eight **Catalina** flying-boats, joined in September and October by eight new **Convair 240**s. From October 1953 14 **de Havil-** land **Heron**s followed by eight **Convair 340**s. Three **Lockheed L.188C Electra**s entered service 19 May 1961 on new route to Hong Kong. Three **Convair 990A**s

Garuda Indonesia

Garuda's DC-10-30s are now giving way in the fleet to more modern MD-11s. Note the non-standard colour scheme on the A300 in the background.

Annual revenue: $2,100 million
Passengers: 6.3 million
Cargo: 160,00 tonnes
Employees: 14,600

added between September 1963 and January 1964, opening first European route 28 September 1963, serving Amsterdam, Frankfurt and Rome via Singapore, Bangkok and Bombay. Eight **Fokker F27 Friendship**s delivered in 1969 together with first of 25 **DC-9-32**s. Also owned and leased several **DC-8-33** and **DC-8-55** jets. Initial order for three **F28-1000**s, first delivered 19 August 1971, increased to 60 by 1981. Leased **DC-10-30** (acquired 1974), replaced by six own aircraft by 1979. Orders placed in March 1980 for four **Boeing 747-200B**s and six **A300B4-200**s. Initiated massive increase in fleet with lease of eight **737-300**s, between 1989 and 1991, several **A300-600R**s and orders for six **MD-11**s, increased to nine, nine **A330-300**s and 12 **Fokker 100**s. Another 16 **737-300**s and six **747-400**s ordered in 1992.

Garuda today: Government-owned national carrier linking Jakarta, and main tourist resort of Bali, with many regional points and further afield to Europe, Middle East, Australia, New Zealand and United States. Destinations are Abu Dhabi, Amsterdam, Auckland, Bangkok, Beijing, Brisbane, Cairns, Darwin,

Dhahran, Frankfurt, Fukuoka, Guangzhou, Ho Chi Minh City, Hong Kong, Honolulu, Jeddah, Kuala Lumpur, London-Gatwick, Los Angeles, Manila, Melbourne, Nagoya, Osaka, Paris, Riyadh, Rome, Seoul, Singapore, Sydney, Taipei, Tokyo and Zürich. Extensive network of routes across Indonesia operated in conjunction with Merpati Nusantara. Code-share, joint services or pool agreements on specific routes with Aeroflot, China Airlines, Eva Air, Iberia, JAL, KLM, Korean Air, Malaysia Airlines and Saudia.

Merpati Nusantara is Garuda's vital domestic arm and undertakes a wide range of passenger and cargo services.

Fleet development: Order placed for six A330-300s, due in 1996 and 1997. Three options also held. Six more 747-400s on order, expected to be delivered between 1997 and 2000, plus nine additional **737-400**s in same timeframe. Three **McDonnell Douglas MD-11ER**s on order for delivery of one aircraft in December 1996, plus two in 1997.

Associate carriers: Wholly-owned *Merpati Nusantara Airlines* (MZ) began services in January 1964 and provides domestic route network to more than 130 destinations, with fleet comprising nine **DHC-6-300**s, 11 **IPTN 212-200 Aviocar**s, 20 **IPTN CN-235**s with another 16 on order, 13 **F27-500**s, 30 **F28**s, 10 **Fokker 100**s with two more on order, one **Boeing 707-320C** and two **L.100-30 Hercules**.

Garuda Indonesia fleet

Airbus A300B4-200	c/n	PK-GAM	625	PK-GWH	24700/1924	PK-GSB	22247/459	PK-GIC	46964/239
PK-GAA	159	PK-GAN	630	PK-GWI	24701/1957	PK-GSC	22248/461	PK-GID	46951/246
PK-GAC	164	PK-GAO	633	PK-GWJ	24702/1994	PK-GSD	22249/468	PK-GIE	46685/284
PK-GAD	165	PK-GAP	657	**Boeing 737-400**	c/n	PK-GSE	22768/561	PK-GIF	46686/286
PK-GAE	166	PK-GAQ	659	PK-GWK	25713/2531	PK-GSF	22769/562		
PK-GAF	167	PK-GAR	664	PK-GWL	25714/2535			**McDonnell Douglas**	
PK-GAG	168	PK-GAS	668	PK-GWM	25715/2537	**Boeing 747-400**	c/n	**MD-11**	c/n
PK-GAH	213	PK-GAT	677	PK-GWN	25716/2540	PK-GSG	25704/1011	PK-GIG	48502/520
PK-GAI	214	**Boeing 737-300**		PK-GWO	25717/2546	PK-GSH	25705/1029	PK-GII	48503/528
PK-GAJ	215	PK-GWA	24403/1706	PK-GWP	25718/2548	PK-GSI	24956/917	PK-GIJ	48504/548
		PK-GWD	24470/1765	PK-GWQ	25719/2549			EI-CDI	48499/486
Airbus A300-600	c/n	PK-GWE	24492/1808			**Douglas DC-10-30**	c/n	EI-CDJ	48500/493
PK-GAK	611	PK-GWF	24698/1846	**Boeing 747-200B**	c/n	PK-GIA	46918/223	EI-CDK	48501/513
PK-GAL	613	PK-GWG	24699/1886	PK-GSA	22246/452	PK-GIB	46918/226		

Gulf Air (GF/GFA)

History: Formed as Gulf Aviation on 24 March 1950 and began charter operations over local network on 5 July 1950. BOAC purchased 22 per cent stake in 1951. **De Havilland Dove** fleet acquired same year, remaining only type in service until May 1956 when replaced by **Heron**. Operated total of five **DC-3**s between 1958 and 1972. Kuwait **Vickers Viscount**s, **DC-6B** and **Trident**s used until introduction of own **F27-400**s in 1967 and **BAC One-Eleven** jets in 1970. Light aviation division operated from Abu Dhabi with small **BN Islander** and **Shorts Skyvan**s. Started service from Gulf States to London in April 1970, using **VC 10** chartered from BOAC, later replaced by its own. Name changed to Gulf Air for marketing purposes from early 1993. On 1 April 1974 Gulf Air became designated carrier for Bahrain, Qatar, Oman and UAE. Contract signed 10 December 1974 for two **Lockheed TriStar**s, with options for more, introduced 1 April 1976. One-Elevens replaced with **737-200** a year later, permitting expansion throughout Gulf. First **Boeing 767-300ER**s purchased in 1988, permitting introduction of routes to Africa. Further 767-300s and first **A320-200** acquired in May 1992. **757-200PF** acquired in December 1993. Routes established in early 1990s to Singapore, Sydney, Johannesburg and Tokyo, and in 1994 to New York, its first to the Americas, flown with newly-delivered **A340-300**. Placed order for six **A330-300**s 15 November 1995.

Gulf Air today: Flag-carrier for four Gulf states providing links with 60 cities in Middle East, Europe, Africa, Asia Pacific and US. Cargo-only flights to Brussels and Lahore. Code-share and joint operations with Alitalia, Air-India, AirLanka, Air Seychelles, American Airlines, Cyprus Airways and Saudia.

Annual revenue: $1,200 million
Passengers: 5.0 million
Cargo: 170,000 tonnes
Employees: 6,400

Gulf Air introduced its 124-seat A320-212s from May 1992 onwards to replace its less economical Boeing 737-200s.

Owned in equal proportions by Bahrain, Oman, Qatar and Abu Dhabi

Fleet development: One A340-300 due in 1996, but delivery of four A320-200s expected to be deferred by up to three years. Delivery of six Airbus A330-300s ordered to begin in 1998. Order for six **Boeing 777**s cancelled.

Gulf Air fleet

Airbus A320-200	c/n	Airbus A340-300	c/n		
A40-EA	313	A40-LA	036	A40-GN	24985/340
A40-EB	325	A40-LB	039	A40-GO	25241/389
A40-EC	345	A40-LC	040	A40-GP	25269/390
A40-ED	375	A40-LD	103	A40-GR	25254/406
A40-EE	419			A40-GS	26236/436
A40-EF	421	**Boeing 767-300(ER)**	c/n	A40-GT	26238/440
A40-EG	438	A40-GH	24484/260	A40-GU	26233/501
A40-EH	445	A40-GI	24485/264	A40-GV	26235/502
A40-EI	459	A40-GJ	24495/267	A40-GW	27254/522
A40-EJ	466	A40-GK	24496/270	A40-GX	27255/525
A40-EK	481	A40-GL	24983/334	A40-GY	26234/538
A40-EL	497	A40-GM	24984/339	A40-GZ	26237/544

Hapag-Lloyd (HF/HLF)

History: Founded 20 June 1972 as subsidiary of Hapag-Lloyd shipping group and began charter and inclusive-tour operations 30 March 1973. Fleet of three ex-All Nippon Airways **Boeing 727-100**s, increased to eight by 1977. In April 1977 took over Munich-based charter airline Bavaria-Germanair, but had to wait until January 1979 for authority for full merger. Two **Airbus A300B4**s taken over, and fleet further upgraded with nine **Advanced Boeing 727-200**s, and more **Airbus A300B4-200**s.

From January 1988, older fleet replaced entirely with four new **Airbus A310-200**s, four **A310-300**s, and mix of **Boeing 737-400** and **737-500** models.

Hapag-Lloyd today: Inclusive-tour holiday charter flights to Central and Eastern Europe, Mediterranean Basin and West Africa, operated from Bremen, Düsseldorf, Frankfurt, Hamburg, Hannover, Munich and Stuttgart.

Annual revenue: $665 million
Passengers: 4.1 million
Employees: 1,600
Ownership: Wholly-owned subsidiary of Hapag-Lloyd AG

Fleet development: Total of 16 new-generation **Boeing 737-800**s order for delivery in 1998.

Hapag Lloyd relies heavily on the Boeing 737-400, as seen here, and 737-500 to operate its medium-range charters. Long-haul routes are the responsibility of the A310.

Hapag Lloyd fleet

Airbus A310-200		D-AHLL	24127/1707
D-AHLV	430	D-AHLM	27102/2394
D-AHLW	427	D-AHLO	24128/1715
D-AHLX	487	D-AHLP	24129/1783
D-AHLZ	468	D-AHLQ	24130/1827
		D-AHLR	24901/1854
Airbus A310-300		D-AHLS	27074/2281
D-AHLA	520	D-AHLT	27830/2670
D-AHLB	528	D-AHLU	27831/2677
D-AHLC	620		
D-APOM	448	**Boeing 737-500**	
		D-AHLD	24926/1966
Boeing 737-400		D-AHLE	24776/1848
D-AHLG	26316/2711	D-AHLF	24927/1968
D-AHLJ	24125/1687	D-AHLI	25037/2022
D-AHLK	24126/1697	D-AHLN	25062/2044

HeavyLift (NP/HLA)

London-Stansted Airport
Stansted, Essex, UK

HeavyLift is the sole operator of the Shorts Belfast, an invaluable outsize cargo carrier.

HeavyLift today: Specialist operations in carriage of outsize and bulky freight anywhere in world.

Annual revenue: $110 million
Employees: 150
Wholly-owned by Trafalgar House

Fleet development: Acquisition of two **A300B4-200**s for conversion to cargo planned for introduction in early 1997.
Associate carriers: Joint-venture with Russian company **VolgaDnepr** provides leased Antonov and Ilyushin transports.

History: Formed 31 October 1978 as TAC HeavyLift and began worldwide cargo charter operations in March 1980 following civil certification of Royal Air Force **Shorts Belfast**. Renamed HeavyLift Cargo Airlines 1 September 1980. Apart from *ad hoc* charters, contract work developed for aerospace industry. **Canadair CL-44J** entered service in July 1989, joined by two leased **L.100-30 Hercule**s for work in Africa and Far East, and two leased **Boeing 707-320C**s. Own 707-320C delivered in 1990. Joint venture with VolgaDnepr, aviation enterprise of Aviation Industrial Complex at Ulyanovsk in Russia, gives access to fleet of 150-tonne capacity **Antonov An-124** (the world's largest freighter), **Ilyushin Il-76** and **Antonov An-12** transports.

HeavyLift fleet

Antonov An-12	c/n	RA-82044	9773054155109	Lockheed L.100-30	
LZ-BAC	343708	RA-82045	9773052255113	**Hercules**	c/n
LZ-BAE	402001	RA-82046	9773052255117	PK-PLR	4889
LZ-BAF	402408	RA-82047	9773053259121	PK-PLU	4824
				PK-PLW	4828

Antonov An-124-100		Ilyushin Il-76TD	c/n		
Ruslan	c/n	RA-76401	1023412399	**Shorts SC.5 Belfast**	c/n
RA-82042	9773054055093	RA-76758	0073474203	G-BEPS	SH.1822
RA-82043	9773054155101			G-HLFT	SH.1819

Iberia (IB/IBE)

Madrid-Barajas Airport
Madrid, Spain

History: Founded 28 June 1927 and began flying 14 December between Madrid and Barcelona using **Rohrbach Roland** trimotor. Merged with two other airlines, CETA and UAE, to form CLASSA 31 December 1928, before airline reformed after end of Spanish Civil War as Iberia-Lineas Aereas de Espana. **DC-3** re-established post-war services to Las Palmas in March 1946. Madrid-London route opened 3 May 1946 and 22 September **DC-4** inaugurated South American routes. Service to Havana and Mexico City opened 15 March 1950. New York reached 4 August 1954 with **L.1049E**, later **L.1049G Super Constellation**s. **Convair 440** introduced on European routes in February 1961, replaced by **Caravelle VIR**, from May 1962. First jet operations

Iberia has selected the Airbus A340-300 as the replacement for its DC-10-30s, while A321s will replace Boeing 727s.

with delivery of three **DC-8-52** July 1961. First **DC-9** delivered in June 1967, followed in September by **Fokker F27**. Caravelle replaced by early 1972 soon after acquisition of **Boeing 727-200**. Long-haul fleet modernisation begun with **DC-8-63** in August 1968, and continued with **747** on 22 October 1970, **DC-10-30** in March 1973 and **A300B4-200** which entered service on 29 March 1981. Embarked on spree of equity alliances with major South American carriers including: Aerolineas Argentinas (1990), Chile's Ladeco (1991) and VIASA. Developed Caribbean and Central American hub at Miami. In December 1995 European Commission approved $690 million government aid package under condition that Iberia sell substantial part of its holdings in Latin America. An extra $330 million may be granted in 1997. First **A340** delivered March 1996.

Iberia today: National flag-carrier providing scheduled domestic and international services to all continents, serving 68 destinations in 53 countries. Network particularly strong in Latin America.

Code-sharing agreements on specific routes with Air Canada, Air Mauritanie, Air Seychelles, Austrian Airlines, Balkan, British Midland, Carnival Airlines, Czech Airlines, Dominicana, Finnair,

Right: Aviaco is a long-established Spanish carrier which now undertakes schedules services for Iberia.

Garuda, Lufthansa, Kuwait Airways, LOT, Malév, MEA, Royal Air Maroc and Tarom.

Annual revenue: $3,270 million
Passengers: 13.8 million
Cargo: 200,000 tonnes
Employees: 23,500
Owned 99.9 per cent by government through holding company Teneo

Fleet development: Two more A340-300s to be delivered in September 1996, remaining five over five years to 2001. Eight **A321**s also signed for.

Associate carriers: Subsidiaries **Binter Canarias** (NT) and **Binter Mediterraneo** (AX), owned 99.99 per cent, serve Canaries, mainland and Balearics, with fleet of six **ATR72-200**s, four **DC-9-32**s and 10 **CN.235**s.

Virtually wholly-owned **Viva Air** (FV), initially founded 24 February 1988 as joint-venture with Lufthansa, provides short-haul charter services from Palma de Mallorca with eight **737-300**s.

Also holds 32.93 per cent stake in local airline **Aviaco** (AO), founded 18 February 1948, which operates schedules for Iberia to 29 Spanish destinations and to Paris and London-Stansted. Fleet 14 McDonnell Douglas DC-9-32s, three **DC-9-34**s, three **DC-9-34F**s and 13 **MD-88**s.

Comprehensive marketing agreements with Aerolineas Argentinas (AR) in which it presently has 83.55 per cent holding but expects to relinquish, Ladeco (UC) (38.07 per cent holding) and VIASA (VA) (45 per cent holding).

Iberia fleet

Airbus A300B4-200	c/n	EC-FLP	266	EC-CFI	20819/1018	Douglas DC-9-30	c/n	EC-EXF	49832/1703
EC-DLG	135	EC-FLQ	274	EC-CFK	20821/1035	EC-BIM	47088/180	EC-EXG	49833/1706
EC-DLH	136	EC-FML	203	EC-CID	20974/1077	EC-CTR	47702/819	EC-EXM	49835/1717
EC-DNQ	156	EC-FMN	312	EC-CIE	20975/1080	EC-CTT	47706/821	EC-EXN	49836/1721
EC-DNR	170	EC-FNR	323	EC-DCC	21609/1369	EC-DGB	48103/925	EC-EXR	49834/1714
		EC-FQY	356	EC-DCD	21610/1380			EC-EXT	49837/1730
Airbus A320-200	c/n			EC-DCE	21611/1382	**Douglas DC-10-30**	c/n	EC-EYB	49838/1733
EC-FAS	134	**Airbus A340-300**	c/n	EC-DDV	21778/1490	EC-CBO	46926/99	EC-EYX	49839/1739
EC-FBQ	136	EC-154	125	EC-DDX	21779/1498	EC-CBP	46927/100	EC-EYY	49840/1745
EC-FBS	146			EC-DDY	21780/1499	EC-CEZ	47980/150	EC-EYZ	49841/1751
EC-FCB	143	**Boeing 727-200**		EC-DDZ	21781/1501	EC-CLB	47981/186	EC-EZA	49842/1763
EC-FDA	176	**Advanced**	c/n			EC-CSJ	46922/221	EC-EZS	49843/1771
EC-FDB	173	EC-CBA	20595/905	**Boeing 757-200**	c/n	EC-DEA	47982/279	EC-FEY	53208/1865
EC-FEO	177	EC-CBF	20600/912	EC-FTR	26239/553	EC-DHZ	47834/324	EC-FEZ	53207/1862
EC_FGH	223	EC-CBG	20601/913	EC-FXU	26240/561			EC-FFA	53209/1867
EC-FGR	224	EC-CBM	20607/943	EC-FXV	26241/572	**McDonnell Douglas**		EC-FFH	53211/1874
EC-FGU	199	EC-CFA	20811/1003	EC-FYJ	26242/593	**MD-87**	c/n	EC-FFI	53210/1871
EC-FGV	207	EC-CFB	20812/1004	EC-FYK	26243/603	EC-EUC	49829/1678	EC-FHD	53212/1877
EC-FIA	240	EC-CFC	20813/1005	EC-FYL	26244/616	EC-EUD	49828/1676	EC-FHK	53213/1879
EC-FIC	241	EC-CFE	20815/1007	EC-FYM	26245/617	EC-EUE	49827/1654		
EC-FKD	264	EC-CFF	20816/1008	EC-FYN	26246/620	EC-EUL	49830/1684		
EC-FKH	246	EC-CFH	20817/1009			EC-EVB	49831/1688		

Icelandair (FI/ICE)

Despite its relatively small fleet and geographic isolation, Icelandair maintains an impressive route network to the rest of Europe and the USA.

History: Formed 3 June 1937 as Flugfelag Akureyrar and began operations 4 May 1938 with single **Waco YKS** floatplane. Reorganised in 1940 as Flugfelag Islands and moved to Reykjavik. Started scheduled service to Prestwick and Copenhagen with **Liberator**s and **DC-3** 27 May 1946, then to London 3 May 1949 flown with **DC-4**. Adopted name of Icelandair and in February 1952 took over domestic network from Loftleidr, formed 10 March 1944. **Vickers Viscount** entered service Reykjavik-Copenhagen service 3 May 1957. Fleet upgraded in 1965 with first of five **F27-200**s. First **Boeing 727-100** jet introduced 24 June 1967. Decision made in June 1973 to merge Icelandair and Loftleidr under Flugleidr holding company, with effect from 6 October 1973. Three **Douglas DC-8-63**s acquired in 1970. After merger, continued to use old names for a time with Loftleidr Icelandic concentrating on transatlantic flights from Iceland and Luxemburg, and Icelandair maintaining European and domestic network. **DC-10-30CF** delivered in January 1979 but operated for short time only. In 1988 moved international flights from Reykjavik to Keflavik, and initiated $335 million fleet renewal programme, completed in May 1992 with delivery of fourth **Fokker 50**. Fleet then comprised three **757-200**s, five **737-400**s and four Fokker 50s.

Icelandair today: National flag-carrier serving 22 international destinations with direct flights, and links 15 European cities to its four US points – New York, Baltimore/Washington, Orlando and Ft Lauderdale. Also operates extensive domestic network and flights to Narsarsuaq in Greenland and Tórshavn in Faroes. Co-operation with SAS flights to Scandinavia. Code-share agreement with SAS for some services between Iceland and Scandinavia, and with Faroe Islands-based Atlantic Airways flying one BAe 146-200.

Annual revenue: $220 million
Passengers: 1.1 million
Cargo: 15,600 tonnes
Employees: 1,275
Major shareholders: Burdaras (34 per cent), employees (13 per cent) and Lifeyrissjodur Verzlunarmanna (6.2 per cent)

Fleet development: Plans to replace Boeing 757 and 737 fleet with single aircraft type between 2000 and 2005.

Icelandair fleet

Boeing 737-400		Boeing 757-200		Fokker 50	
TF-FIA	24352/1705	TF-FIH	24739/273	TF-FIR	20243
TF-FIB	24353/1721	TF-FII	24760/281	TF-FIS	20244
TF-FIC	24804/1851	TF-FIJ	25085/368	TF-FIT	20250
TF-FID	25063/2032			TF-FIU	20251

Indian Airlines (IC/IAC)

History: Established as state corporation 1 August 1953. Initial operations with **DC-3**, but new de Havilland Herons introduced in 1955. Night mail services begun 5 November 1955 with **DC-4**. Modernisation initiated 10 October 1957, with first of eight **Vickers Viscount**s. Fleet supplemented from May 1961 with **Fokker F27-100**, and in February 1964, first jet – **Caravelle VIN** – entered service. Domestic network grew with introduction of more aircraft, including large fleet of locally-built **HAL 748**s (Hawker Siddeley HS 748s) from December 1967 and **Boeing** 737-200s on trunk routes from January 1971. On 1 December 1976 became one of the few airlines to operate wide-bodies with delivery of **Airbus A300B2**, eventually totalling eight aircraft, plus two **A300B4-200**s. Order placed 15 March 1986 for 19 **A320-200**, later increased to 31. First delivery took place 27 June 1989 and type entered service 2 July on main Bombay-Delhi route. Airbus order replaced one for 12 **Boeing 757-200**s not taken up. Last A320 delivered in December 1994. Phase-out of older Boeing 737-200s started in 1995.

Indian Airlines today: Serves 70 cities from main hubs at Delhi, Bombay, Calcutta and Madras. In addition to operating one of world's densest and most extensive domestic network, also flies regionally to Bangkok, Colombo, Dhaka, Fujairah, Karachi, Kuwait, Kuala Lumpur, Malé, Muscat, Ras al Khaimah, Sharjah, Singapore and Yangon.

Annual revenue: $575 million
Passengers: 8.0 million
Cargo: 75,000 tonnes
Employees: 22,100
Ownership: Wholly-owned by Indian government

Indian Airways is currently suffering a shortage of pilots for its A320s and is working with Airbus to remedy this situation and respond to a burgeoning domestic travel market.

Fleet development: 737-200 being phased out gradually, but no decision yet made on replacement. 737s being transferred in interim to newly set up regional division under name of **Allied Services**. Airbus A300 also needs imminent replacing.

Indian Airlines fleet

Airbus A300B2-100	c/n	Airbus A320-200	c/n						
VT-EDW	036	VT-EPB	045	VT-EPO		080	VT-ESH	469	VT-EGI	22285/798
VT-EDX	038	EC-EPC	046	VT-EPP		089	VT-ESI	486	VT-EGJ	22286/799
VT-EDY	059	VT-EPD	047	VT-EPQ		090	VT-ESJ	490	VT-EGM	22473/747
VT-EDZ	060	VT-EPE	048	VT-EPR		095	VT-ESK	492	VT-EHE	22860/899
VT-EFV	088	VT-EPF	049	VT-EPS		096	VT-ESL	499	VT-EHF	22861/902
VT-EFW	111	VT-EPG	050	VT-ESA		097			VT-EHG	22862/903
VT-EFX	113	VT-EPH	051	VT-ESB		396	**Boeing 737-200**		VT-EHH	22863/907
VT-ELW	026	VT-EPI	056	VT-ESC		398	**Advanced**	c/n		
		VT-EPJ	057	VT-ESD		416	VT-EGD	22280/671	**Boeing 737-200C**	
Airbus A300B4-200	c/n	VT-EPK	058	VT-ESE		423	VT-EGE	22281/679	**Advanced**	c/n
VT-EHC	181	VT-EPL	074	VT-ESF		431	VT-EGF	22282/681	VT-EGM	22473/747
VT-EHD	182	VT-EPM	075	VT-ESG		432	VT-EGG	22283/689		
						451	VT-EGH	22284/739		

Iran Air (IR/IRA)

History: Founded 24 February 1962 as Iran National Airlines Corporation as successor to two privately-owned carriers, Iranian Airways and Persian Air Services (PAS). Iran Air added to its fleet of **DC-6B**, **DC-3** and **Viscount**s taken over, and 4 July 1965 first of four **Boeing 727-100**s entered service on European routes. 727s flown to London from 3 July 1966. **Advanced 727-200**s added to fleet in 1974 and 1975. Two **707-320C**s delivered in early 1970 followed by three **737-200QC**s, gradually replacing DC-3 and DC-6 fleet. Tehran-New York service inaugurated May 1975 with **Boeing 707-320C**, replaced from 1 May 1976 by **747SP**. Six **Airbus A300B2-200**s, ordered in May 1978, arrived in Tehran from March 1980, but this was last new aircraft to be delivered for 10 years. After Islamic Revolution in 1979, airline hit hard by eight-year war with Iraq and political isolation, compounded by US sanctions. In 1990/91, acquired six **Fokker 100**s, but plans to purchase seven **A300-600R**s delayed by US sanctions until 1994.

US sanctions hit the delivery of Iran Air's Airbus A300-600Rs and the airline is now examining the Tu-154M as a replacement for its ageing Boeing 727s and 737s.

Iran Air today: National flag-carrier providing scheduled services in Middle East, to Asian CIS republics, and to Europe and Far East. Twenty-point domestic route system is also operated. International destinations are Abu Dhabi, Almaty, Amsterdam, Ashkabad, Athens, Bahrain, Baku, Beijing, Bombay, Damascus, Doha, Dubai, Hamburg, Kuwait, Frankfurt, Geneva, Istanbul, Jeddah, Karachi, Kuala Lumpur, Larnaca, London, Madrid, Muscat, Moscow, Paris, Rome, Sharjah, Tashkent, Tokyo and Vienna. Joint service with Malaysia Airlines on Tehran-Kuala Lumpur route.

Annual revenue: *$390 million*
Passengers: *5.4 million*
Cargo: *35,000 tonnes*
Employees: *11,850*
Wholly-owned by Iranian government through Ministry of Roads

Associate carriers: *Iran Air Tours* (IRB), established in 1992 as joint venture with Tajik Air, for tourist charter flights with leased fleet of four **Tu-154M**s.

Iran Air fleet

Airbus A300B2-200	c/n	Boeing 727-100	c/n	Boeing 737-200C Adv		Boeing 747-100	c/n	Fokker 100	c/n
EP-IBR	061	EP-IRB	19172/323	EP-IRF	20498/283	EP-IAM	21759/381	EP-IDA	11292
EP-IBS	080	EP-IRC	19816/505	EP-IRH	20500/286			EP-IDB	11299
EP-IBT	185			EP-IRI	20740/321	Boeing 747-200B	c/n	EP-IDC	11276
EP-IBV	187	Boeing 727-200 Adv				EP-IAG	21217/291	EP-IDD	11294
EP-IBZ	226	EP-IRP	20945/1048	Boeing 747SP	c/n	EP-IAH	21218/300	EP-IDF	11298
		EP-IRR	20946/1052	EP-IAA	20998/275			EP-IDG	11302
Airbus A300-600R	c/n	EP-IRS	20947/1070	EP-IAB	20999/278	Boeing 747-200F	c/n		
EP-IBA	723	EP-IRT	21078/1114	EP-IAC	21093/307	EP-ICA	21487/319		
EP-IBB	727	EP-IRU	21079/1131	EP-IAD	21758/371	EP-ICC	21514/343		

Japan Airlines (JL/JAL)

Narita International and Haneda Airports
Tokyo, Japan

Japan Airlines operates the world's largest Boeing 747 fleet with over 80 in current service.

Amsterdam, Atlanta, Auckland, Bangkok, Beijing, Brisbane, Cairns, Chicago, Christchurch, Denpasar, Frankfurt, Guam, Ho Chi Minh City, Hong Kong, Honolulu, Jakarta, Khabarovsk, Kona, Kuala Lumpur, London, Los Angeles, Madrid, Manila, Mexico City, Milan, Moscow, New York, Paris, Pusan, Rome, Saipan, San Francisco, Sao Paulo, Seoul, Shanghai, Singapore, Sydney, Vancouver and Zurich. Joint operation or codeshare with Aeromexico, Air France, Air New Zealand, DHL, KLM, Lufthansa, Thai and Varig.

History: Founded as private company 1 August 1951 and began operations from Tokyo to Osaka 25 October 1951 with **Douglas DC-4** and three **Martin 2-0-2**s. Acquired seven DC-4s in 1952 followed by five **DC-6B**s. Transpacific service to San Francisco, via Wake Island and Honolulu, inaugurated 17 January 1954 with DC-6B, taken over by **DC-7C** June 1959. Joint service with Air France to Paris over North Pole started in April 1960, using Air France **Boeing 707**. **DC-8-33** delivered 12 August 1960. London added in September 1962 with **Convair 880M**, and New York in 1966 with **DC-8-53**. Tokyo-Moscow link established in April 1967, first with Aeroflot **Tu-114D**, later **Il-62**, and then its own **DC-8-62**. Fleet boosted with **727-100** in July 1965. Widebodies introduced 1 June

1970 when first **747-100** entered service, followed by **DC-10-40** from July 1976. Ordered fleet of **767-200/-300**s with first delivery taking place in 1985, and four **747-300**s, from September 1986. Lost sole rights to international routes in April 1986 in change of government policy, but also given greater access to domestic market. First **747-400** delivered in January 1990, followed by **MD-11** in November 1993. First **Boeing 777-200** entered service in April 1996 between Tokyo and Kagoshima.

Japan Airlines today: Global passenger and cargo network serving 62 cities in 26 countries and territories. Also 21 local points giving JAL 27 per cent share of domestic traffic. Cargo-only flights to Anchorage and Fairbanks in Alaska. International destinations include

In JAL service the MD-11 has been dubbed the 'J-Bird'. The airline's relatively small fleet of 10 MD-11s wil soon be joined by 10 Boeing 777s.

Annual revenue: $10 billion
Passengers: 26.5 million
Cargo: 755,000 tonnes
Employees: 20,500
Major shareholders: Tokyo Marine and Fire Insurance (2.9 per cent), Industrial Bank of Japan (2.8 per cent), Fukoku Mutual Life Insurance (2.8 per cent), Nippon Dantai Insurance (2.7 per cent), Nippon Life Insurance (2.5 per cent) and Dowa Fire and Marine Insurance (2.5 per cent)

Associate carriers: *Japan Asia Airways* (EG), founded 8 August 1975 and 90.5 per cent owned, flies to Hong Kong, Taipei and Kaohsiung from hubs at Nagoya, Okinawa, Osaka and Tokyo. Also operates Tokyo to Taipei cargo schedule. Fleet comprises one **747-100**, two **747-200**s, one **747-300** and four **DC-10-40**s.
Japan Air Charter (JAC) (JZ), 82 per cent owned, utilises four **747**s and four **DC-10-40**s on schedules from Tokyo, Osaka, Sapporo, Fukuoka, Sendai and Nagasaki to Honolulu, Hawaii.

Japan Airlines fleet

Boeing 737-400 c/n

Reg	c/n
JA8991	27916/2718
JA8992	27917/2729

Boeing 747-100 c/n

Reg	c/n
JA8115	20531/197
JA8116	20532/199
JA8142	22066/426
JA8143	22067/427
JA8164	23150/601
JA8170	23390/636
JA8176	23637/655

Boeing 747-200B c/n

Reg	c/n	Reg	c/n
JA8104	19823/116	JA8150	22479/496
JA8105	19824/112	JA8154	22745/547
JA8106	19825/137	JA8161	22990/579
JA8108	20333/166	JA8162	22991/581
JA8110	20504/181	JA8169	23389/635
JA8111	20505/182		
JA8113	20529/192		
JA8114	20530/196		
JA8122	20924/235		
JA8125	21030/251		
JA8127	21031/255		
JA8130	21679/376		
JA8131	21680/380		
JA8140	22064/407		
JA8141	22065/411		
JA8149	22478/489		

Boeing 747-200F c/n

Reg	c/n
JA8123	21034/243
JA8132	21681/382
JA8144	22063/432
JA8160	21744/392
JA8165	21743/384
JA8171	23391/654
JA8180	23641/684
JA8193	21940/457

Boeing 747-300 c/n

Reg	c/n
JA8163	23149/599
JA8166	23151/607
JA8173	23482/640
JA8177	23638/658
JA8178	23639/664
JA8179	23640/668
JA8183	23967/692
JA8184	23968/693
JA8185	23969/691
JA8186	24018/694
JA8187	24019/695
N212JL	23067/588
N213JL	23068/589

Boeing 747-400 c/n

Reg	c/n	Reg	c/n
JA8071	24423/758	JA8911	26356/1026
JA8072	24424/760	JA8912	27099/1031
JA8073	24425/767	JA8913	27827/1038
JA8074	24426/768	JA8914	27828/1039
JA8075	24427/780		
JA8076	24777/797		
JA8077	24784/798		
JA8078	24870/821		
JA8079	24885/824		
JA8080	24886/825		
JA8081	25064/851		
JA8082	25212/871		
JA8083	25213/844		
JA8084	25214/879		
JA8086	25308/885		
JA8087	26346/897		
JA8088	26341/902		
JA8089	26342/905		
JA8090	26347/907		
JA8901	26343/918		
JA8902	26344/929		
JA8903	26345/935		
JA8904	26348/941		
JA8905	26349/948		
JA8906	26350/961		
JA8907	26351/963		
JA8908	26352/978		
JA8909	26353/980		
JA8910	26355/1024		

Boeing 767-200 c/n

Reg	c/n
JA8232	23213/118
JA8233	23214/122

Boeing 767-300 c/n

Reg	c/n
JA8234	23216/148
JA8235	23217/150
JA8236	23215/132
JA8253	23645/174
JA8264	23965/186
JA8265	23961/192
JA8266	23966/191
JA8267	23962/193
JA8268	23963/224
JA8269	23964/225
JA8299	24498/277
JA8364	24782/327
JA8365	24783/329
JA8397	27311/547
JA8398	27312/548
JA8399	27313/554
JA8975	27658/581

Boeing 777-200 c/n

Reg	c/n
JA8981	27364/23

Douglas DC-10-40 c/n

Reg	c/n
JA8530	46920/212
JA8533	46661/224
JA8535	46662/230
JA8536	46966/262
JA8538	46974/274
JA8540	47823/306
JA8541	47824/308
JA8542	47825/310
JA8543	47826/313
JA8545	47853/343
JA8546	47855/349
JA8547	47856/366
JA8548	47857/367
JA8549	48301/381

McDonnell Douglas MD-11 c/n

Reg	c/n
JA8580	48571/552
JA8581	48572/556
JA8582	48573/559
JA8583	48574/566
JA8584	48575/568
JA8585	48576/574
JA8586	48577/583
JA8587	48578/588

KLM Royal Dutch Airlines (KL/KLM)

Schiphol Airport
Amsterdam

History: Incorporated 7 October 1919 as Koninklijke Luchtvaart Maatschappij voor Nederland en Kolonien. First service 17 May 1920 from Croydon to Amsterdam with **de Havilland DH.16**. Opened intercontinental flight to Batavia (today's Jakarta) in then Netherlands East Indies 1 October 1924 with **Fokker F.VII**. Fleet developed with more Fokker designs, and in 1934 with introduction of modern **Douglas DC-2**, followed in June 1937 by **DC-3**. First transatlantic flight from Amsterdam to Curaçao 15 December 1934, flown with **Fokker XVIII**. In 1938, **Lockheed L.14 Super Electra**s and four-engined **DC-5** ordered for delivery in 1940. Services to East Indies resumed on 10 November 1945 and gradually reintroduced European network with fleet of 19 **C-54**s (**DC-4**) and 30 **C-47**s (DC-3). Reopening of domestic services in September 1945, followed by schedule to New York 21 May 1946 and to Japan, over Polar route, 11 November 1958. Over next 10 years, early post-war aircraft succeeded by **DC-6**, **DC-7C**, **Constellation**s and **Super Constellation**s for long-haul routes, and **Convair 240/340**, and **Viscount** turboprops for European sectors. **L.188C Electra** entered service in 1959. Jet age opened by **DC-8** in March 1960, augmented with **DC-9-32** for short-haul flights in 1966. Introduction of **Boeing 747-200B** in February 1971, progressing through to **747-200 Combi** in November 1975 and **747-400** in June 1989. In July 1989 took step towards establishing global airline system through acquisition of 20 per cent stake in Northwest Airlines,

The Boeing 767-306(ER) is a recent addition to the KLM fleet. The first arrived in July 1995.

further consolidated in January 1993 when both granted immunity from US anti-trust legislation. From September 1993 all transatlantic services now joint flights.

KLM today: National flag-carrier serving 148 cities in 82 countries in Europe, North, Central and South America, Africa, Middle and Far East, and Australia. Commercial agreements, including code-shares with Air Excel, Atlas Air (Cargo), Austrian

KLM Royal Dutch Airlines

KLM operates 94-seat Fokker 100s but smaller Saab 340s, Fokker 50s and Fokker 70s are the responsibility of KLM Cityhopper.

Airlines, Cyprus Airways, Eurowings, Garuda, Japan Airlines, Jet Airways, Nippon Cargo Airlines and Tyrolean Airways.

Annual revenue: *$5,250 million*
Passengers: *11.7 million*
Cargo: *565,000 tonnes*
Employees: *26,030*
Major shareholder: *State of Netherlands (38.2 per cent of shares)*

Fleet development: Five more **767-300(ER)s** to be leased

from ILFC to bring total fleet to 10. Also four 747-400s due for delivery October 1996, May and August 1997 and January 1998. One **MD-11** leased to VASP until November 1998, and 10th MD-11 due for delivery in April 1997.

Associate carriers: Major strategic equity alliances with

Northwest Airlines (NW) and Air UK (UK), holding 25 and 45 per cent of shares respectively.

KLM Cityhopper (HN), formed in April 1991 through merger of NLM CityHopper and Netherlines, provides European services from Amsterdam, Eindhoven and Rotterdam with fleet of 10 **Fokker 50**s, two **F28-4000**s, four **Fokker 70**s and 11 **Saab 340B**s.

Other shareholdings are maintained in: **Martinair** (50 per cent) and **Transavia Airlines** (80 per cent), which maintains scheduled leisure routes to Spain and inclusive-tour charters with 11 **737-300**s and four **757-200**s, and has eight **737-800**s order for delivery from 1998.

ALM Antillean Airlines (40 per cent), which operates four **MD-82**s and two **DHC-8-300**s on scheduled network in Netherlands Antilles.

KLM Era Helicopters, supporting North Sea oil and gas business from bases in Netherlands and UK with **Sikorsky S-61N** and **S-76** helicopters.

KLM Royal Dutch Airlines fleet

Boeing 737-300	c/n	Boeing 737-400	c/n	Boeing 747-300 Combi		Boeing 747-400 Combi		Fokker 100	c/n
PH-BDA	23537/1275	PH-BDR	24514/1768	PH-BUH	21110/271	PH-BFC	23982/735	PH-KLC	11268
PH-BDB	23538/1288	PH-BDS	24529/1770	PH-BUI	21111/276	PH-BFD	24001/737	PH-KLD	11269
PH-BDC	23539/1295	PH-BDT	24530/1772	PH-BUK	21549/336	PH-BFE	24201/763	PH-KLE	11270
PH-BDD	23540/1303	PH-BDU	24857/1902	PH-BUL	21550/344	PH-BFF	24202/770	PH-KLG	11271
PH-BDE	23541/1309	PH-BDW	24858/1903	PH-BUM	21659/369	PH-BFH	24518/783	PH-KLH	11272
PH-BDG	23542/1317	PH-BDY	24959/1949	PH-BUN	21660/309	PH-BFI	25086/850	PH-KLI	11273
PH-BDH	23543/1325	PH-BDZ	25355/2132	PH-BUU	23056/587	PH-BFK	25087/854		
PH-BDI	23544/1335	PH-BTA	25412/2161	PH-BUV	23137/600	PH-BFM	26373/896	**McDonnell Douglas**	
PH-BDK	23545/1343	PH-BTB	25423/2184	PH-BUW	23508/657	PH-BFO	25413/938	**MD-11**	c/n
PH-BDL	23546/1349	PH-BTC	25424/2200	N1309E	22380/539	PH-BFP	26374/992	PH-KCA	48555/557
PH-BDN	24261/1640	PH-BTF	27232/2591			PH-BFR	27202/1014	PH-KCB	48556/561
PH-BDO	24262/1642	PH-BTG	27233/2601	**Boeing 747-400**	c/n			PH-KCC	48557/569
PH-BDP	24404/1681			PH-BFA	23999/725	**Boeing 767-300(ER)**	c/n	PH-KCE	48559/575
PH-BTD	27420/2406	**Boeing 747-300**	c/n	PH-BFB	24000/732	PH-BZA	27957/587	PH-KCF	48560/579
PH-BTE	27421/2438	PH-BUO	21848/397	PH-BFG	24517/782	PH-BZB	27958/589	PH-KCG	48561/588
		PH-BUP	22376/474	PH-BFL	25356/888	PH-BZC	26263/592	PH-KCH	48562/596
		PH-BUR	22379/491	PH-BFN	26372/969	PH-BZD	27610/		
						PH-BZE	28098/		

Korean Air (KE/KAL)

Kimpo International Airport
Seoul, South Korea

History: Founded in June 1962 when government took control of Korean National Airlines, which had started operations in 1947. Opened regional routes from Seoul and Pusan. **F27-200**s supplemented **DC-3** on domestic flights. Hanjin Group asked to take over struggling carrier 1 March 1969 and its then fleet of one **DC-9-32**, two F27-200s, two **FH-227B**s, one DC-3 and one **DC-4**. Services to Taipei and

Hong Kong reactivated and transpacific freight line opened 26 April 1971 with **Boeing 720B**. Seoul-Tokyo-Honolulu-Los Angeles passenger service introduced 19 April 1972. Infrastructure developments and modernisation added **Boeing 727-100** (July 1972), and **747**, (May 1973). Network extended to more regional points, Middle East and, in 1975, to Europe with service to Paris. New York passenger service

opened 29 March 1979. All-cargo routes developed to Paris, Singapore, Amsterdam, Frankfurt and Zürich. Fleet enhanced with **DC-10-30** (February 1975), and **A300B4-200** (November 1975). Signed largest aircraft deal in its history 7 February 1979 for 18 **747-200B**s and **747-300**s, and later introduced two **747SP**s 8 February 1981. Entry into Africa 25 August 1981 with service to Tripoli. Ordered five **MD-11**s in

Korean Airlines

Korean Airlines has garnered a large fleet of Airbus A300s since its first was delivered in 1975. It now also has orders for the A330.

February 1987, two **A300-600s** 11 March 1988 and 10 **747-400s** 14 April 1989. First of 12 **Fokker 100s** delivered in April 1992, replacing **F28-4000s**. Signed contract for eight **Boeing 777s** 16 December 1993.

Korean Air today: Privately-owned flag-carrier, and one of fastest-growing and most successful in world. Serves more than 70 cities in 32 countries, together with dense domestic network including high-frequency shuttle between Seoul and major port of Pusan. Joint freighter services specific routes with Lufthansa, Malaysia Airlines and Philippine Airlines. Block-space agreement and code-share with Saudia and Vietnam Airlines.

Annual revenue: $3,790 million
Passengers: 20.5 million
Cargo: 750,000 tonnes
Employees: 16,500
Wholly-owned by Hanjin Group

Fleet development: Orders for delivery up to June 1999 include 10 **747-400s**, four 747-400Fs, four **777-200** and eight **777-300s**, seven **A330-300s**, and one **MD-83**. Three DC-10-30 and three 727-200s to be sold during 1996. Plans to spend $14 billion on 50 new aircraft.

Korean Airlines fleet

Airbus A300-600	c/n
HL7280	361
HL7281	365
HL7287	358
HL7290	388
HL7291	417

Airbus A300-600R	c/n
HL7239	627
HL7240	631
HL7241	662
HL7242	685
HL7243	692
HL7244	722
HL7245	731
HL7288	477
HL7289	479
HL7292	543
HL7293	554
HL7294	560
HL7295	582
HL7297	609
HL7298	614
HL7299	717
HL7580	756
HL7581	762

Airbus A300B4-100	c/n
HL7218	014
HL7219	016
HL7220	018
HL7221	024
HL7223	028
HL7224	030
HL7238	031
HL7246	081

Airbus A300F4-200	c/n
HL7278	277
HL7279	292

Boeing 727-200 Adv	
HL7354	21455/1316
HL7356	21456/1318
HL7357	21474/1378

Boeing 747SP	c/n
HL7456	22483/501
HL7457	22484/507

Boeing 747-200B	c/n
HL7443	21772/363
HL7453	21938/436
HL7463	20770/213
HL7464	20771/215

Boeing 747-200C	c/n
HL7471	20652/211

Boeing 747-200F	c/n
HL7401	22245/458
HL7441	20373/168
HL7451	22480/448
HL7452	22481/454
HL7454	22482/484
HL7458	22485/513
HL7459	22486/520
HI7474	22169/472
HL7475	24195/718
HL7476	24196/720

Boeing 747-300	c/n
HL7468	22487/605
HL7469	22489/611
HL7470	24194/713

Boeing 747-400	c/n
HL7477	24198/729
HL7478	24199/739
HL7479	24200/748
HL7480	24619/793
HL7481	24621/830
HL7482	25205/853
HL7483	25275/874
HL7484	26392/893
HL7485	26395/922
HL7486	23396/951
HL7487	26393/958
HL7488	26394/986
HL7489	27072/1013
HL7490	27177/1019
HL7491	27341/1037
HL7492	26397/1055
HL7493	26398/1057
HL7494	27662/1067
HL7495	28096/1073

Douglas DC-10-30	c/n
HL7315	46934/160
HL7316	46912/188
HL7317	46915/199

Fokker 100	c/n
HL7206	11378
HL7207	11387
HL7208	11388
HL7210	11432
HL7211	11438
HL7212	11439
HL7213	11476
HL7214	11504
	11513
HL7215	11519
HL7216	11522
HL7217	11523

McDonnell Douglas MD-11	c/n
HL7371	48407/456
HL7372	48408/457
HL7373	48409/490
HL7374	48410/495
HL7375	48523/516

McDonnell Douglas MD-82/83	c/n
HL7203	53147/2069
HL7204	53148/2072
HL7225	53467/2102
HL7236	53468/2114
HL7237	53469/2116
HL7272	49373/1201
HL7273	49374/1208
HL7275	49416/1271
HL7276	49417/1278
HL7282	49418/1394
HL7283	49419/1403

Kuwait Airways (KU/KAC)

Kuwait International Airport
Safat, Kuwait

History: Founded in March 1954 as Kuwait National Airways Company and began operations with one **DC-3** between Kuwait and Iraq. Two more **DC-3s** acquired and network widened across Middle East, but fierce competition from other airlines in region resulted in bail-out by Kuwaiti government, which took 50 per cent stake and renamed company Kuwait Airways Corporation. Fleet supplemented with various leased aircraft, following signing of five-year management contract with BOAC in 1958. All shares purchased by government in May 1962. Leased **Comet 4C** entered service in June 1962, replaced from March 1966 by three **Trident 1Es**. One **DC-4** and three **DC-6s** also added with take-over of Trans Arabian Airways in April 1964. Routes expanded to London, Paris, Frankfurt and Rome. First **Boeing 707-320C** arrived in November 1968 and by early 1978 eight were in use. First **747-200B** entered service on Kuwait-London route 19 July 1979 and type also put on new services to Manila and New York

Kuwait Airways

in late 1980. Four **727-200**s joined fleet from September 1980, and most 707s replaced by five **Airbus A310-200** and three **A300C4-620**s between 1983 and 1984. Three **Boeing 767-200ER**s delivered in March 1986. On 2 August 1990, Iraqi troops invaded Kuwait. Most of fleet flown to Baghdad, and five destroyed in air attacks. By mid-1992, airline back in business with five **Airbus A310-300**s (leased), joined within two years by three **A320-200**s, three more A310-300s and five **A300-600R**s, all ordered new from Airbus Industrie. In 1995, fleet further modernised with acquisition of four **Airbus A340-300**s and two **Boeing 747-400**s.

Kuwait Airways today: National flag-carrier operating

international passenger and cargo services from Kuwait to Abu Dhabi, Amsterdam, Athens, Bahrain, Bangkok, Beirut, Bombay, Cairo, Casablanca, Chicago, Colombo, Copenhagen, Damascus, Delhi, Dhahran, Dhaka, Doha, Dubai, Frankfurt, Geneva, Istanbul, Jakarta, Jeddah, Karachi, Kuala Lumpur, Lahore,

Larnaca, London, Madrid, Malaga, Manila, Munich, Muscat, New York, Paris, Rome, Sharjah, Shiraz, Singapore, Tehran and Trivandrum. Code-share with Iberia between Madrid and Kuwait, and joint service with Philippine Airlines to Manila.

Annual revenue: $500 million
Passengers: 1.8 million
Cargo: 85,000 tonnes
Employees: 5,800
Wholly-owned by Kuwaiti government

Fleet development: One more 747-400 to be delivered. Options held on one A300-600R, two **A321**s and four A340s.

Kuwait Airways fleet

Airbus A310-300	c/n	Airbus A320-200	c/n	Boeing 747-200B	c/n
9K-ALA	647	9K-AKA	181	9K-ADB	21542/335
9K-ALB	649	9K-AKB	182	9K-ADD	22740/553
9K-ALC	663	9K-AKC	195		
				Boeing 747-400	c/n
Airbus A300-600R	c/n	Airbus A340-300	c/n	9K-ADE	27338/1046
9K-AMA	673	9K-ANA	089	9K-ADF	27663/
9K-AMB	694	9K-ANB	090		
9K-AMC	699	9K-ANC	101		
9K-AMD	719	9K-AND	104		
9K-AME	721				

LAN Chile (LA/LAN)

Arturo Merino Benitez International Airport
Santiago de Chile

History: Established 5 March 1929 as Linea Aéropostal Santiago-Arica. Name changed to Linea Aerea Nacional (LAN) 12 July 1932. Domestic network expanded and strengthened in 1941 with delivery of **Lockheed 10A Electra**s. First cross-border flight opened to Buenos Aires in October 1946 with **DC-3**. Fleet modernisation continued, first

with **Martin 2-0-2**s bought in November 1947, followed by small **de Havilland Dove**s for local routes. New international services added to Lima and La Paz in 1953, and introduction of **DC-6B** two years later permitted first non-stop flights to Arica, Antofagasta and Punta Arenas. Expansion to USA in 1958 with service to Miami, via Lima and

Panama City. First jet, **Caravelle VIR**, joined fleet in 1964. Service opened to Easter Island 3 August 1967 and extended to Tahiti with **DC-8** in 1968. **Boeing 707**, **727** and **HS748** added before end of 1960s plus first transatlantic service to Madrid, Paris and Frankfurt. Modernisation continued with addition of **737-200** and **DC-10-30**, latter replaced in 1986 by **767-200ER**. **747-100** leased in 1988 for new service to Los Angeles. Name changed to Linea Aerea Nacional Chile SA in July 1985 and airline partially privatised through Corfo, with SAS acquiring minority stake, since sold. Subsequent capital injection enabled acquisition of **BAe 146-200**. LAN Chile fully privatised 26 May 1994.

LAN Chile has been a Boeing 767 operator since 1986 and these aircraft have served as the airline's primary long-haul type over the following years.

LAN Chile today: Privately-owned national airline. Serves 15 cities in 12 countries, in addition to 15 domestic points and Easter Island. International destinations are Buenos Aires, Caracas, Frankfurt, La Paz, Lima, Los Angeles, Madrid, Mexico City, Montevideo, New York, Papeete, Rio de Janeiro, Sao Paulo and Santa Cruz de la Sierra.

Annual revenue: $410 million
Passengers: 1.2 million
Cargo: 60,000 tonnes
Employees: 2,700
Ownership: Shares distributed among Cueto Group (38.5 per cent), Pinera Group (33.1 per cent), Hirmas Group (19.0 per cent) and Eblen Group (8.1 per cent)

Associate carriers: On 23 August 1995, acquired 56.91 per cent of shares of Chile's second airline *Ladeco Airlines* (UC). Complaint against this move by Spanish airline Iberia, which holds 35 per cent, was rejected by Supreme Court. Ladeco flies domestic and regional routes with two **Boeing 757-200s**, eight **Boeing 737-200s**, two **737-300s**, four **BAC One Elevens** and one **Airbus A320**.
Fast Air Carrier SA (UD), wholly-owned since May 1994, operates cargo services using one **Boeing 707-320C** and five **McDonnell Douglas DC-8-71Fs**.

LAN Chile fleet

Boeing 737-200 Advanced	c/n		
CC-CDE	22744/923	CC-CJW	22397/737
CC-CDG	23024/965	**Boeing 767-200(ER)**	**c/n**
CC-CEA	22743/909	CC-CDH	24716/297
CC-CEE	22407/698	CC-CDJ	24762/307
CC-CEI	20219/208		
CC-CHR	21792/628	**Boeing 767-300(ER)**	**c/n**
CC-CHS	21802/670	CC-CDM	26261/575

CC-CDP	27597/602
CC-CEU	25403/409
CC-CEY	24947/351
British Aerospace	
146-200A	**c/n**
CC-CEJ	E2059
CC-CEN	E2064

Lauda Air (NG/LDA)

Vienna International Airport
Vienna, Austria

History: Founded in April 1979 by Niki Lauda and began charter operations 24 May 1979 with two **Fokker F27s**. In summer 1985 replaced F27s with two **BAC One Eleven-500s** and began association with tour operator ITAS. ITAS took 49 per cent stake in airline, remainder held by Niki Lauda. Two **737-300s** added to fleet and long-haul flights to Bangkok, Sydney and Hong Kong started in 1988 with first of two **767-300ERs**. Quoted on Vienna stock exchange in June 1990. Schedules between Vienna and London-Gatwick inaugurated in December 1990 and further European destinations added from January 1993 following alliance with Lufthansa. Equity stake taken by German carrier, increased to 39.7 per cent in 1994. Two more 767-300ERs delivered in August/December 1992. Two **737-400s** also added, as were seven **Canadair 100ER Regional Jets** in 1994/95, put on growing number of European flights from both Vienna and Salzburg. Scheduled services started 26 March 1995 out of Milan-Malpensa to six European cities for Lufthansa.
Lauda Air today: Long-haul scheduled services from Vienna to Bangkok, Phuket, Hong Kong, Singapore, Sydney and Melbourne, and in conjunction with Lufthansa to Miami via Munich. Also large charter programme from Vienna and Milan to European destinations and to Cuba, Dominican Republic, Mexico,

Sri Lanka and Maldives. Joint Lauda Air/Lufthansa services from Vienna to Barcelona, Brussels, Düsseldorf, Frankfurt, Lisbon, London/Gatwick, Madrid, Manchester, Munich and Paris/Orly. Flights from Salzburg to Berlin-Tegel, Brussels, Frankfurt, London and Paris. Code-sharing with part-owner Lufthansa to 15 European cities.

Annual revenue: $200 million
Passengers: 0.9 million
Employees: 950
Major shareholders: Lauda Air GesmbH (39.71 per cent) and Lufthansa (39.71 per cent)

Lauda Air was the first operator of the extended-range Canadair Regional Jet 100ER.

Fleet development: Four **Boeing 777-200Bs** on order for planned delivery between September 1997 and 2000. Two new-generation **737-800s** due to join fleet in 1998.
Associate carriers: *Lauda Air SpA*, founded at beginning of 1993, flying charters from Milan to Caribbean with a **767-300ER**.
In 1994, *Lauda Air Executive* entered into executive travel market with **Learjet 60** and **Cessna Citation II**.

Lauda Air fleet

Boeing 737-300	c/n	Boeing 767-300ER	c/n	Canadair 100ER	
OE-ILF	(23601/1254)	OE-LAS	(27908/591)	**Regional Jet**	**c/n**
OE-ILG	(24081/1515)	OE-LAT	(25273/393)	OE-LRA	(7032)
		OE-LAU	(23765/165)	OE-LRD	(7033)
Boeing 737-400	**c/n**	OE-LAW	(26417/448)	OE-LRD	(7052)
OE-LNH	(25147/2043)	OE-LAX	(27095/467)	OE-LRE	(7059)
OE-LNI	(27094/2439)			OE-LRF	(7061)
				OE-LRG	(7063)

Lithuanian Airlines (TE/LIL)

Vilnius Airport, Vilnius
Lithuania

Lithuanian Airlines is looking to acquire additional Western aircraft to replace Soviet-era jets.

Stockholm and Warsaw, and coastal city of Palanga with Frankfurt and Moscow. Charters to Casablanca, Damascus and Tel Aviv.

Marketing agreement with **Air Lithuania**, serving small local network based on Kaunas and Palanga with five **Yak-40**s.

History: Established in August 1991, days before Lithuania's independence from USSR. Based on former local directorate of Aeroflot and inherited fleet of 12 **Yakovlev Yak-42**s, seven **Tupolev Tu-134A**s, four **Antonov An-24**s and three **An-26** freighters. First scheduled flight in December 1991 between Vilnius and Frankfurt, with leased **Boeing 737-200**. Two more delivered in June and September 1995. Four **Yak-42D**s refurbished with 108-seat interior. European network developed gradually and service to London-Gatwick inau-

gurated 23 August 1992.

Lithuanian Airlines today: Government-owned flag-carrier linking capital Vilnius with Amsterdam, Berlin, Copenhagen, Dubai, Frankfurt, Istanbul, Kiev, Larnaca, London, Moscow, Rome,

Passengers: 0.25 million
Cargo: 4,300 tonnes
Employees: 1,000

Fleet development: Aims to replace ex-Soviet equipment, starting with Tu-134A, with more Western aircraft.

Lithuanian Airlines fleet

Boeing 737-200 Advanced		Tupolev Tu-134A-3	c/n	Yakovlev Yak-42D	c/n
LY-BSD	22701/886	LY-ABE	60076	LY-AAS	4520421811395
LY-BSG	22793/892	LY-ABF	60172	LY-AAU	4520424711397
LY-GPA	22453/748			LY-AAV	4520424711399
		Yakovlev Yak-42	c/n	LY-AAW	4520423811417
Tupolev Tu-134A	c/n	LY-AAM	4520423606235	LY-AAX	4520424811431
LY-ABD	60054	LY-AAN	4520423606235		

LOT Polish Airlines (LO/LOT)

Warsaw-Okęcie Airport
Warsaw, Poland

History: Established 1 January 1929. Developed existing domestic route structure with fleet of **Junkers F 13**, **Fokker F.VIIa** and **F.VIIb-3m**, and other locally produced aircraft. Opened service to Bucharest 1 April 1930, later extended southwards to Athens and Beirut, and northwards as far as Helsinki. Modern **Douglas DC-2** and **Lockheed L.10A Electra**s entered service

in 1935 and 1936 respectively, followed by **Junkers Ju 52/3m**. **L.14 Super Electra** added to fleet in 1938. Invasion of Poland 1 September 1939, leading to World War II, forced suspension of all flights. Twenty-one of 26 aircraft in service managed to escape, but never returned. Those in Poland were destroyed. **Lisunov Li-2**, **Polikarpov Po-2** and nine **DC-3**s acquired, post-

war, and domestic service reactivated 1 April 1945, with international routes reintroduced from 11 May. Five **SNCASE SE.161 Languedoc**s took over thesel flights from July 1947. First Soviet aircraft, **Ilyushin Il-12B**, entered service 24 April 1949, and Warsaw-Moscow opened in 1955 with newer **Il-14**. Western aircraft bought – **Convair 240**s in 1957 and **Vickers Viscount**s in 1962 – but fleet dominated by Soviet equipment. **Ilyushin Il-18** enabled introduction of new routes to Africa and Middle East, in May 1961. **Antonov An-24**s scheduled from April 1966 and jet era begun with delivery of first of five **Tupolev Tu-134**s 5 November 1968. Transatlantic service to Montreal and New York followed 16 April 1973 with **Il-62**. Late 1980s marked by

The Boeing 737-300 and 737-500 replaced the Tu-154 and Tu-134, respectively, in LOT service.

gradual process of changing from Soviet to Western equipment, first with acquisition of **Boeing 767-200ER** in 1989, then **ATR72-200** from August 1991, **737-500** in December 1992 and **737-400** in April 1993. Became joint-stock company in 1992 as transitional step towards privatisation and outside investment. Neither yet implemented, but privatisation is on course for end of 1996, with government retaining 51 per cent majority stake. Some 20 per cent will be sold to employees.

LOT today: Government-owned national airline offering scheduled international passenger and cargo services to 46 cities in 33 countries. Domestic flights from Warsaw to five major cities. International destinations include Amsterdam, Athens, Bangkok, Beijing, Berlin, Brussels, Budapest, Cairo, Chicago, Cologne, Copenhagen, Damascus, Dubai, Düsseldorf, Frankfurt, Geneva, Hamburg,

Helsinki, Istanbul, Kiev, Larnaca, London, Lvov, Lyon, Madrid, Milan, Minsk, Moscow, New York-JFK, New York-Newark, Nice, Oslo, Paris, Prague, Riga, Rome, Sofia, Stockholm, St Petersburg, Tallinn, Tel Aviv, Thessaloniki, Vienna, Vilnius, Zagreb and Zürich. Code-share or block-space agreement with Austrian Airlines, Czech Airlines and Iberia. Joint venture with Air France on routes between France and Poland.

Annual revenue: $320 million
Passengers: 1.6 million
Cargo: 15,500 tonnes
Employees: 4,000

Fleet development: One ATR72-200 and 737-400 due in 1996. Additional **767-300ER** and two 737-400 for delivery in 1997. Regional jet to replace ATR72 under consideration as is **Boeing 777** for expansion of long-haul routes after 2000.

LOT Polish Airlines fleet

AI(R) ATR72-200	c/n	Boeing 737-400	c/n		
SP-LFA	246	SP-LLA	27131/2458	SP-LKE	27130/2448
SP-LFB	265	SP-LLB	27156/2492	SP-LKF	27368/2603
SP-LFC	272	SP-LLC	27157/2502		
SP-LFD	279	SP-LLD	27256/2589	**Boeing 767-200(ER)**	c/n
SP-LFE	328			SP-LOA	24733/261
SP-LFF	402	**Boeing 737-500**	c/n	SP-LOB	24734/266
SP-LFG	411	SP-LKA	27416/2389		
		SP-LKB	27417/2392	**Boeing 767-300(ER)**	c/n
		SP-LKC	27418/2397	SP-LPA	24865/322
		SP-LKD	27419/2401	SP-LPB	27902/577

LTU International Airways (LT/LTU) Rhein-Ruhr AP Düsseldorf

History: Founded in Frankfurt 20 October 1955 as Lufttransport-Union, initially operating five **Vickers Viking**s on *ad hoc* charters starting in spring 1956. Airline acquired by Duisburg architect Kurt Conle, who soon became sole owner. Charter crisis in early 1960s almost caused bankruptcy, but move to booming Rhein-Ruhr area proved inspirational. First jet aircraft, **Caravelle III**, added in 1965, followed by more Caravelles and four **F28-1000**s. First German charter airline to have all-jet fleet (1969). First **Lockheed L1011-100 TriStar** delivered in 1973. Fleet eventually reached 10 – last left fleet in 1996. Passenger base broadened with setting up in 1983 of Lufttransport Süd in Munich. Next major step acquisition of **Boeing 757-200** from 1984, and four **767-300ER**s from 1988. Established Spanish associate LTE International Airways in April 1987. Order placed in 1989 for four **MD-11**s, with deliveries completed between 1991 and 1993, supplemented with contract for five **Airbus A330-300**s. First Airbus joined fleet in December 1994.

LTU today: Scheduled European and international leisure flights, plus charters. Scheduled

The MD-11 partners the A330-300 on LTU's worldwide holiday charter network.

destinations include Abu Dhabi, Acapulco, Alicante, Almeria, Antalya, Arrecife, Bangkok, Barbados, Cancun, Cape Town, Cayo Largo, Colombo, Curaçao, Daytona, Denpasar/Bali, Durban, Faro, Fort Myers, Fuerteventura, Funchal, Havana, Holguin, Ibiza, Jerba, Larnaca, Las Palmas, Los Angeles, Malaga, Malé, Miami, Monastir, Montego Bay, Orlando, Palma de Mallorca, Phuket, Puerto Plata, Punta Cana, Salzburg, San José, Santo Domingo, Santa Cruz, Tampa, Tenerife, Varadero and Windhoek. Operates out of

Berlin, Düsseldorf, Frankfurt, Hamburg, Hannover, Cologne/Bonn, Leipzig, Münster/Osnabrück, Nuremberg and Munich.

Annual revenue: $2,700 million
Passengers: 6.4 million
Employees: 2,600
Ownership: divided between Conle & Co. oHG (60.6 per cent), Westdeutsche Landesbank (34.3 per cent) and Erwin Walter Gräber (5.1 per cent)

Fleet development: One 767-300ER yet to be delivered.

Associate carriers: Wholly-owned charter division **LTU Süd International Airways** (**LTS**), based in Munich. Set up in December 1983 as Lufttransport

LTU International Airways

Süd and started flying in 1984. Scheduled and charter flights with seven 757-200s and four 767-300ERs.

LTE International Airways (XO), now also wholly-owned, started flying from its base at Palma de Mallorca 1 November 1987 and also operates out of Gran Canaria and Tenerife in Canary Islands, serving Austria, Finland, Germany, Italy, Norway and Switzerland. Fleet comprises three 757-200s leased from LTU.

LTU International Airways fleet

Airbus A330-300	c/n	D-AMUU	22688/115	Boeing 767-300(ER)	c/n
D-AERF	082	D-AMUV	23928/146	D-AMUN	24259/268
D-AERG	072	D-AMUW	23929/153	D-AMUP	25531/423
D-AERH	087	D-AMUX	23983/161	D-AMUR	24257/251
D-AERJ	095	D-AMUY	24176/173	D-AMUS	24258/255
D-AERK	120	D-AMUZ	22497/228		
D-AERQ	127	EC-EFX	23118/36	**McDonnell Douglas**	
		EC-EGH	23119/51	**MD-11**	c/n
Boeing 757-200	c/n	EC-ENQ	23651/116	D-AERB	48484/484
D-AMUK	22689/117			D-AERW	48485/502
D-AMUM	24451/227			D-AERX	48486/509
D-AMUQ	26278/671			D-AERZ	48538/533

Lufthansa (LH/DLH)

Rhein-Main Airport
Frankfurt, Germany

Lufthansa is one of the few airlines which operate the Boeing 747-400 alongside the rival A340.

History: Founded 6 January 1953 as Luftag, following liquidation of old Luft Hansa in 1951, which had been formed January 1926. In years prior to World War II was one of world's leading airlines, pioneering routes to Far East and across North and South Atlantic. After outbreak of war in 1939 was able to maintain only services to neutral countries, but all flying suspended following Germany's defeat in 1945. On 6 August 1954, readopted Lufthansa name and set about re-establishing its pre-war network. Operations started 15 May 1955 to points in Europe and 8 June to New York with **L.1049G Super Constellation**s. South Atlantic routes resumed in August 1956. Early fleet also

included **Convair 340**, **Vickers Viking** and **Douglas DC-3**. First **L.1649A Starliner** undertook its first service 28 February 1958. In same year placed order for four **Boeing 707-430**s which inaugurated jet services from Frankfurt to New York in March 1960. **Boeing 720B** bought to back up 707, and Far East route extended beyond Bangkok to Hong Kong and Tokyo 23 January 1961. Lagos and Johannesburg added in 1962. Put first **Boeing 727** into service in 1964, and in May introduced polar route to Tokyo. Ordered 21 **Boeing 737-100**s in February 1965, introduced in 1968. Inaugural **747-100** flight 26 April 1970 marked beginning of widebody era. First service to South America opened March

1971. Four **DC-10-30**s purchsed in September 1970. Signed in May 1973 for three **A300B2-200**s, delivered February 1976. Launch customer, with Swissair, for **A310-200**, with an order for 25 aircraft signed April 1979. First delivery 29 March 1983. Fleet-modernisation programme for 1990s initiated 29 June 1985 with order for 15 **A320**s and seven **A300-600**s, with 25 and seven options respectively. Ten **737-300**s ordered few days later. All delivered between 1987 and 1992. Fleet enhanced with acquisition of **Airbus A321**, **A340**, **A319**, and **Boeing 747-400**.

Lufthansa today: Privately-owned national carrier operating scheduled passenger and cargo services to 227 destinations in 88 countries across world. In addition to almost total coverage of European cities, long-haul flights extend to Africa, Middle East, Asia/Pacific and North, Central and South America. Transatlantic flights serve Atlanta, Bogotá, Boston, Buenos Aires, Caracas, Chicago, Dallas, La Paz, Lima, Los Angeles, Mexico City, Miami, New York, Quito, Recife, Rio de Janeiro, San Francisco, Santiago de Chile, Sao Paulo, plus others in major alliance with United Airlines. Signed wide-ranging co-operation agreement 11 May 1995 SAS, put into effect 1 February 1996 with code-share flights between Germany and

Lufthansa Express was set up to offer low cost flights around Lufthansa's European network.

Scandinavia, and with SAA, Finnair, Thai and ModiLuft. Also operates code-share/block-space flights on routes with Adria , Air Dolomiti, Canadian, Cargolux, Czech Airlines, JAL, Korean Air, Lauda Air, LOT and Varig.

Annual revenue: *$13,500 million*
Passengers: *40.7 million*
Cargo/mail: *1.575 million tonnes*
Employees: *57,700*
German government remains largest shareholder with 35.7 per cent

Fleet development: Delivery of 11 more **A321-100**s and 20 **A319**s began in July 1996 and scheduled for completion by November 1998. Two more 747-400s, one A340-300 and three 737-300s also being added from 1997.

Associate carriers: *Lufthansa CityLine* (CL), formed 1 October 1974 as DLT and renamed in March 1992, prior to becoming wholly-owned subsidiary 1 January 1993. Provides extensive European and domestic services from/between German cities Fleet comprises 10 **Avro RJ85**s (plus five on order), 20

The Avro Regional Jet beat stiff competition from Fokker to win a 1994 order from Lufthansa.

Canadair Regional Jets (with eight on order), five **DHC-8-300**s and 15 **Fokker 50**s. Aircraft on order will be delivered by end of 1996, and by May 1997 will return DHC-8-300s to manufacturer and transfer its Fokker 50 fleet and routes to contract partner **Contact Air** (3T) of Stuttgart.

Other wholly-owned subsidiaries are *Lufthansa Cargo* FX), operating 10 **747-200F**s (five

more from FedEx for delivery in 1997), five **DC-8-73CF**s and two 737s, and **Condor Flugdienst** (DE).

Equity holdings in Cargolux (24.53 per cent), DHL (25 per cent), Lauda Air (39.71 per cent), Luxair (13.0 per cent), and Turkish holiday airline *Sunexpress* (XQ) (40 per cent), with fleet of three **737-300**s and two **737-400**s.

Lufthansa Cargo India (40 per cent) set up in joint venture with Hinduja Group, to be based at Delhi. Operations due to start in late 1996 with two **727-200F**s.

Lufthansa fleet

Airbus A300-600R	c/n								
D-AIAH	380	D-AIPL	094	D-AIRL	505	D-ABHF	22134/777	D-ABXH	23528/1290
D-AIAI	391	D-AIPM	104	D-AIRM	518	D-ABHH	22135/781	D-ABXI	23529/1293
D-AIAK	401	D-AIPP	110	D-AIRN	560	D-ABHM	22138/790	D-ABXK	23530/1297
D-AIAL	405	D-AIPR	111	D-AIRO	563	D-ABHN	22139/791	D-ABXL	23531/1307
D-AIAM	408	D-AIPS	116	D-AIRP	564	D-ABMA	23153/1075	D-ABXM	23871/1433
D-AIAN	411	D-AIPT	117	D-AIRR	567	D-ABMB	23154/1078	D-ABXN	23872/1447
D-AIAP	414	D-AIPU	135			D-ABMC	23155/1079	D-ABXO	23873/1489
D-AIAR	546	D-AIPW	137	**Airbus A340-200**	c/n	D-ABMD	23156/1082	D-ABXP	23874/1495
D-AIAS	553	D-AIPX	147	D-AIBA	008	D-ABME	23157/1085	D-ABXR	23875/1500
D-AIAT	618	D-AIPY	161	D-AIBC	011	D-ABMF	23158/1089	D-ABXS	24280/1656
D-AIAU	623	D-AIPZ	162	D-AIBD	018			D-ANXT	24281/1664
		D-AIQA	172	D-AIBE	019	**Boeing 737-300**	c/n	D-ABU	24282/1671
Airbus A310-300	c/n	D-AIQB	200	D-AIBF	006	D-ABEA	24565/1818	D-ABXW	24561/1785
D-AIDA	434	D-AIQC	201	D-AIBH	021	D-ABEB	25148/2077	D-ABXX	24562/1787
D-AIDB	484	D-AIQD	202			D-ABEC	25149/2081	D-ABXY	24563/1801
D-AIDC	485	D-AIQE	209	**Airbus A340-300**	c/n	D-ABED	25215/2082	D-ABXZ	24564/1807
D-AIDD	488	D-AIQF	216	D-AIGA	020	D-ABEE	25216/2084		
D-AIDE	522	D-AIQH	217	D-AIGB	024	D-ABEF	25217/2094	**Boeing 737-300QC**	c/n
D-AIDF	524	D-AIQK	218	D-AIGC	027	D-ABEH	25242/2102	D-ABWC	23835/1465
D-AIDH	527	D-AIQL	267	D-AIGD	028	D-ABEI	25359/2158	D-ABWD	23836/1508
D-AIDI	523	D-AIQM	268	D-AIGF	035	D-ABEK	25414/2164	D-ABWE	23837/1514
D-AIDK	526	D-AIQN	269	D-AIGH	052	D-ABEL	25415/2175	D-ABWF	24283/1677
D-AIDL	547	D-AIQP	346	D-AIGI	053	D-ABEM	25416/2182	D-ABXA	23522/1246
D-AIDM	595	D-AIQR	382	D-AIGK	056	D-ABEN	26426/2196	D-ABXB	23523/1271
D-AIDN	599	D-AIQS	401			D-ABEO	26429/2207	D-ABXC	23524/1272
				Boeing 737-200		D-ABEP	26430/2216		
Airbus A320-200	c/n	**Airbus A321-100**	c/n	**Advanced**	c/n	D-ABER	26431/2242	**Boeing 737-400**	c/n
D-AIPA	069	D-AIRA	458	D-ABFA	22114/657	D-ABES	26432/2247	D-ABKA	27000/2311
D-AIPB	070	D-AIRB	468	D-ABFB	22113/649	D-ABET	27903/2682	D-ABKB	27001/2316
D-AIPC	071	D-AIRC	473	D-ABFP	22123/726	D-ABEU	27904/2691	D-ABKC	27002/2323
D-AIPD	072	D-AIRD	474	D-ABFR	22124/727	D-ABEW	27905/2705	D-ABKD	27003/2328
D-AIPE	078	D-AIRE	484	D-ABFU	22126/735	D-ABWH	24284/1685	D-ABKF	27004/2344
D-AIPF	083	D-AIRF	493	D-ABFW	22127/745	D-ABXD	23525/1278	D-ABKK	27005/2359
D-AIPH	086	D-AIRH	412	D-ABFX	22128/752	D-ABXE	23526/1682	D-ABKL	27007/2367

Additional c/n column entries:
D-AIPK	093	D-AIRK	502	D-ABHC	22133/772	D-ABXF	23527/1285

79

Lufthansa

Boeing 737-500	c/n								
D-ABIA	24815/1933	D-ABIO	24939/2031	D-ABJC	25272/2118	D-ABYR	21643/352	D-ABTH	25047/856
D-ABIB	24816/1958	D-ABIP	24940/2034	D-ABJD	25309/2122	D-ABYX	22670/550	D-ABVA	23816/723
D-ABIC	24817/1967	D-ABIR	24941/2034	D-ABJE	25310/2126	D-ABZD	23407/639	D-ABVB	23817/700
D-ABID	24818/1974	D-ABIS	24942/2048	D-ABJF	25311/2128	D-ABZH	23622/665	D-ABVC	24288/757
D-ABIE	24819/1979	D-ABIT	24943/2049	D-ABJH	25357/2141			D-ABVD	24740/786
D-ABIF	24820/1985	D-ABIU	24944/2051	D-ABJI	25358/2151	Boeing 747-400	c/n	D-ABVE	24741/787
D-ABIH	24821/1993	D-ABIW	24945/2063			D-ABTA	24285/747	D-ABVF	24761/796
D-ABII	24822/1997	D-ABIX	24946/2070	Boeing 747-200B	c/n	D-ABTB	24286/749	D-ABVH	25045/845
D-ABIK	24823/2000	D-ABIY	25243/2086	D-ABYJ	21220/294	D-ABTC	24287/754	D-ABVK	25046/847
D-ABIL	24824/2006	D-ABIZ	25244/2098	D-ABYM	21588/342	D-ABTD	24715/785	D-ABVL	26425/898
D-ABIM	24937/2011	D-ABJA	25270/2116	D-ABYP	21590/348	D-ABTE	24966/846	D-ABVN	26427/915
		D-ABIN	24938/2023	D-ABJB	25271/2117	D-ABYQ	21591/350	D-ABTF	24967/848

Luxair (LG/LGI)

Luxair's Fokker 50s took over from F27s in 1989 and partner Luxair Commuter's EMB-120s.

Europe. Partnership, including code-share flights, with minority shareholder Lufthansa.

Annual revenue: *$235 million*
Passengers: *0.7 million*
Employees: *1,235*
Ownership: *State owns 23.1 per cent of shares, Lufthansa 13.0 per cent, Luxair Group 13.2 per cent, Compagnie Luxembourgeoise de Télédiffusion 12.1 per cent and local banks the remainder*

History: Founded in early 1948 as Luxembourg Airlines. Started flying 2 February 1948 with **DC-3** routes from Luxembourg to Frankfurt, Paris and Zürich, but all services suspended in 1950. Reorganised in 1961 as Luxair-Société Luxembourgeoise de Navigation Aérienne and began operations with **Fokker F27-100** on Luxembourg-Paris route 2 April 1962, followed by Brussels, Frankfurt and Zürich when own F27s added in May 1963, April 1965, October 1967, and single **Vickers Viscount** in April 1966. Agreement with Trek Airways of South Africa, under which **L.1649A Starliner** was operated in Luxair colours and registrations on low-fare flights to Johannesburg, as means by Trek to circumvent any hostility by

certain African countries towards South Africa. Luxair operated connecting flight from Luxembourg to London in its own right. Starliner replaced by **707-320** from 30 May 1969. In 1970 participated in establishment of Cargolux. Jet aircraft in shape of **Caravelle VIR** joined fleet 7 March 1970, followed by two ex-Austrian aircraft in spring 1972. **Boeing 737-200** arrived in December 1977 and April 1978. Scheduled services network extended within Europe, augmented by charters. **Airbus A300B4-200** used for short period from 19 December 1984. Lufthansa acquired 13 per cent stake in April 1992.

Luxair today: National flag-carrier providing scheduled and charter services entirely within

Associate carriers: Has 24.50 per cent shareholding in Cargolux (CV). Wholly-owned subsidiary, **Luxair Commuter,** operates three EMB-120ERs on thinner routes for parent.

Luxair fleet

Boeing 737-500	c/n
LX-LGO	26438/2413
LX-LGP	26439/2444
LX-LGR	27424/2720
LX-LGS	27425/2730

Fokker 50	c/n
LX-LGB	20221
LX-LGC	20168
LX-LGD	20171
LX-LGE	20180

Malaysia Airlines (MH/MAS)

History: Founded as Malayan Airways in 1937 by Imperial Airways and two prominent shipping companies. Services inaugurated 9 June 1947 with three **Airspeed Consul**s. Consuls replaced by six **DC-3**s and international routes developed from November 1947, initially serving Batavia (Jakarta), Palembang, Medan and Saigon. Leased

aircraft operated on new Hong Kong route and others from 1958, including **DC-4, Viscount, Lockheed Super Constellation, Bristol Britannia** and, from 1962, **de Havilland Comet IV.** Federation of Malaysia established 1 April 1965. Renamed Malaysian Airways in November 1963, concurrent with arrival of five **Fokker F27**s. After operating

as Malaysia-Singapore Airlines (MSA) under joint control of both governments between 1966 and 1971, partnership dissolved and Malaysian Airlines System (MAS) created as national carrier 3 April 1971. Inherited fleet of seven **Boeing 737-200**s, nine F27s and three **Britten-Norman Islander**s. Network then served 34 domestic and six regional destinations.

In 1995 Malaysia selected the A330-300, but in 1996 ordered 15 Boeing 777s and more 747-400s.

Long-haul routes developed to Europe, Australia, Japan and Middle East, using **DC-10-30** and **747-200B** aircraft acquired in 1976 and 1982 respectively. Three **Airbus A300B4-200s** added between 1979 and 1981 for regional routes. Name again changed in October 1987, to Malaysia Airlines. Expansion of domestic fleet with **Boeing 737-400/500** and **Fokker 50**, and new **Boeing 747-400** for international flights boosted fleet to 64 aircraft between 1989-94. Considerable financial problems turned around by acquisition of controlling stake for $700 million by Malaysian Helicopter Services in June 1994 and subsequent restructuring. Leased **McDonnell Douglas MD-11s** in June 1994 and **A330-300** in March 1995.

Malaysia Airlines today: Privately-owned national carrier serving 76 international destinations, except CIS, together with 36 domestic points. Network focuses heavily on Asia and Pacific Rim, but also reaches Adelaide, Amman, Amsterdam, Auckland, Beijing, Beirut, Brisbane, Brussels, Buenos Aires, Cairns, Canberra, Cape Town, Christchurch, Darwin, Dubai, Dublin, Frankfurt, Hobart, Istanbul, Jeddah, Johannesburg, London, Los Angeles, Madrid, Mauritius, Munich, Melbourne, Mexico

City, Paris, Perth, Rome, San Francisco, Sydney, Tehran, Tokyo, Vienna and Zürich. Code-share alliances with Ansett, British Midland and Virgin Atlantic, and marketing agreements with Cathay Pacific and Singapore Airlines.

Annual revenue: $1,950 million
Passengers: 14.3 million
Cargo: 250,000 tonnes
Employees: 19,600
Major shareholders: DCB Merchant Nominees (MHS) (32 per cent), Kumpulan Wang Amanah Pencen (11.6 per cent), Brunei Investment Agency (10.0 per cent), Pemegang Amanah Raya Malaysia (9.8 per cent) and Employee Provident Fund Board (5.6 per cent). Malaysian government retains special share to ensure control of major policies

Fleet development: Placed $4 billion order with Boeing in January 1996 for 25 aircraft,

including 10 747-400s and 15 **777-200/300s**, with options on additional three 747-400s and two 777s. Deliveries to start in early 1997 and run through to 1999. One more 747-400 and two 737-400s to be delivered from previous orders.

Associate carriers: Through its parent company has 40 per cent stake in **Royal Air Cambodge** (VJ), operating from Phnom Penh with two **ATR72-200s** and two **737-400s**; 18 per cent in local airline **Pelangi Air** (9P), operating four **Do 228s** and four **Fokker 50s**, soon to be supplanted by **DHC-8-200/300**; 49 per cent in **Air Maldives** (L6), which uses two Do 228s on flights within Maldives and is expanding internationally with an **A300B4** leased from Malaysia Airlines; 20 per cent in US carrier World Airways (WO) and 44 per cent in Dutch Schreiner Aviation Group.

Malaysia Airlines fleet

Airbus A330-300	c/n	9M-MMG	26467/2378	9M-MQE	26462/2542	Boeing 747-300	c/n	Douglas DC-10-30	
9M-MKA	067	9M-MMH	27084/2391	9M-MQF	26463/2560	9M-MHK	23600/650	9M-MAS	46955/228
9M-MKB	068	9M-MMI	27096/2393	9M-MQG	27190/2568			9M-MAV	48283/350
9M-MKC	069	9M-MMJ	27097/2399	9M-MQH	27352/2624	Boeing 747-400	c/n		
9M-MKD	073	9M-MMK	27083/2403	9M-MQI	27353/2632	9M-MHL	24315/738	Fokker 50	c/n
9M-MKE	077	9M-MML	27085/2407	9M-MQJ	27383/2657	9M-MHM	24405/745	9M-MGA	20150
9M-MKF	100	9M-MMM	27166/2410	9M-MQK	27384/2673	9M-MHN	24836/808	9M-MGB	20156
9M-MKG	107	9M-MMN	27167/2419	9M-MQL	27191/2676	9M-MHQ	25126/858	9M-MGC	20161
9M-MKH	110	9M-MMO	27086/2426	9M-MQM	27306/2685	9M-MPA	27042/932	9M-MGD	20164
9M-MKI	121	9M-MMP	27168/2435			9M-MPB	25699/965	9M-MGE	20166
9M-MKJ	122	9M-MMQ	27087/2441	Boeing 737-500	c/n	9M-MPC	25700/974	9M-MGF	20167
9M-MKZ	096	9M-MMR	26468/2445	9M-MFA	26445/2327	9M-MPD	25701/997	9M-MGG	20170
		9M-MMS	27169/2450	9M-MMB	26446/2358	9M-MPE	25702/999	9M-MGI	20175
Boeing 737-300F	c/n	9M-MMT	27170/2462	9M-MMC	26448/2484	9M-MPF	27043/1017		
9M-MZA	27125/2415	9M-MMU	26447/2479	9M-MFD	26450/2503	9M-MPG	25703/1025	McDonnell Douglas	
9M-MZB	27347/2615	9M-MMV	26449/2491	9M-MFE	26454/2511	9M-MPH	27044/1041	MD-11/MD-11CF	c/n
		9M-MMW	27451/2496	9M-MFF	26456/2527			N271WA	48518/525
Boeing 737-400	c/n	9M-MMX	26452/2501	9M-MFG	27354/2637	DHC-6 Twin Otter 300		N272WA	48437/506
9M-MMA	26443/2272	9M-MMY	26455/2507	9M-MFH	27355/2646	9M-MDJ	791	N273WA	48519/539
9M-MMB	26444/2308	9M-MMZ	26457/2521	9M-MFI	27356/2654	9M-MDK	792	N275WA	48631/579
9M-MMC	26453/2332	9M-MQA	26458/2525			9M-MDL	802	N276WA	48632/582
9M-MMD	26464/2340	9M-MQB	26459/2530	Boeing 747-200F	c/n	9M-MDM	804		
9M-MME	26465/2362	9M-MQC	26460/2533	9M-MHI	22304/502	9M-MDN	844		
9M-MMF	26466/2372	9M-MQD	26461/2536	9M-MHJ	22442/526	9M-MDO	629		

Malév Hungarian (MA/MAH)

Malév was the first Eastern Bloc airline to adopt Western aircraft, in the shape of the Boeing 737.

Dubai, Düsseldorf, Frankfurt, Hamburg, Helsinki, Istanbul, Kiev, Larnaca, Leipzig, London, Madrid, Milan, Moscow, Munich, New York, Paris, Prague, Rome, St Petersburg, Sofia, Stockholm, Stuttgart, Tel Aviv, Thessalonika, Tirana, Trieste, Varna, Venice, Vienna, Vilnius, Warsaw and Zürich. Code-share flights and joint services with Air France, Alitalia, Austrian Airlines, Delta Air Lines and Iberia.

History: Founded 26 April 1946 as joint Hungarian/Soviet airline under name of Maszovlét. Began flying with 11 **Lisunov Li-2**s and six **Polikarpov Po-2**s from Budapest to Debrecen and Szombathely. Network quickly extended and cross-border route opened to Bucharest 2 May 1948, followed by Prague, Warsaw, Venice, Belgrade and Tirana. Soviet interest reverted to Hungarian state 25 November 1954, when Malév established as successor. Domestic services cut back from 1957 and discontinued altogether in 1969. First of 10 **Ilyushin Il-14**s (including five built by VEB in East Germany) delivered 10 April 1957, enabling introduction of further European services including, from 7 April 1957, Budapest-Moscow. This route taken over by **Il-18** turbo-props from 25 May 1960. During 1960s, several routes added to Western Europe, serving among others London, Frankfurt, Paris and Rome. Il-14 phased out by time of **Tupolev Tu-134** induction into service 1 April 1969. Improved **Tu-134A** came in June 1971, followed by **Tu-154** in September 1973, and **Tu-154B** and **Tu-154M**. Gradual move towards West, starting in 1988

with **Boeing 737** and accelerating after acquisition of 30 per cent stake by Alitalia in September 1993. First long-haul route inaugurated with **767-200** same year to New York, via Rome, replaced by direct flights 29 May 1994. **Fokker 70**s delivered from 20 December 1995, at which time most Soviet aircraft withdrawn.

Malév today: National flag-carrier serving predominantly European route system, with limited extensions to Middle East and North America. Destinations served include Amsterdam, Athens, Barcelona, Beirut, Berlin, Brussels, Bucharest, Cairo, Cologne/Bonn, Copenhagen, Damascus, Dresden,

Annual revenue: $300 million
Passengers: 1.4 million
Cargo: 8,000 tonnes
Employees: 3,600
Shareholders: include Hungarian government with 63.9 per cent, Alitalia 30 per cent and Simest five per cent. Plans by government privatisation agency AVP to sell another 10-30 per cent into private sector

Fleet development: One further Fokker 70 order may not be delivered. Remaining Soviet aircraft to be withdrawn within next two years.

Malév Hungarian Airlines fleet

Boeing 737-200 Advanced		Boeing 737-400	c/n	Tupolev Tu-134A-3	
HA-LEA	21735/528	HA-LEN	26069/2352	HA-LBP	63560
HA-LEB	22090/664	HA-LEO	26071/2361	HA-LPR	63580
HA-LEC	22979/950				
HA-LEI	22803/906	**Boeing 767-200(ER)**	c/n	**Tupolev Tu-154B-2**	c/n
HA-LEK	23404/1176	HA-LHA	27048/475	HA-LCM	325
HA-LEM	22804/908	HA-LHB	27049/482	HA-LCN	326
				HA-LCO	473
Boeing 737-300	c/n	**Fokker 70**	c/n	HA-LCP	474
HA-LED	24909/2021	HA-LMA	11564	HA-LCR	543
HA-LEF	24914/2054	HA-LMB	11565	HA-LCU	531
HA-LEG	24916/2066	HA-LMC	11569	HA-LCV	544
HA-LEJ	26303/2635				

Martinair Holland (MA/MAH)

History: Founded 24 May 1958 by Martin Schröder as Martin's Luchtvervoermaatschappij (Martin's Air Charter), with a single **de Havilland Dove**. Charter work soon added, together with **Vickers Viking**, **de Havilland Heron** and two **DC-3**s. Entered inclusive-tour business and period of expansion from 1964 with

acquisition of Fairways Rotterdam, and changed ownership when KLM took 25 per cent stake. As result, **Convair 340** and **DC-7C** taken over from KLM, as well as first jet, **DC-8-33**, in November 1967, enabling long-haul passenger/cargo flights. Short-haul fleet upgraded with **DC-9-34RC** which entered service 1 August 1968.

DC-10-30CF entered service 30 November 1973, followed by a second in November 1975. Name changed to Martinair Holland in 1974. Fleet grew again in 1981 with three **MD-82**s and first **A310-200** in March 1984. Regular transatlantic passenger services added from Amsterdam to Baltimore, Detroit,

Los Angeles, Miami, Minneapolis, New York, San Francisco, Seattle and Toronto. First **MD-11 Combi** delivered in December 1994. Last DC-10 and A310 retired in 1995.

Martinair today: Scheduled international passenger services and inclusive-tour flights from Amsterdam to Bangkok, Banjul, Bridgetown, Cancun, Denver, Grenada, Holguin, Isla Margarita, Los Angeles, Miami, Montego Bay, New York, Oakland, Orlando, Phuket, Puerto Plata, Puerto Vallarta, Punta Cana, Santo Domingo, Seattle, Tampa, Toronto, Varadero, and many Mediterranean resorts. Cargo flights to all continents. Space-purchase agreement with China Airlines on Amsterdam-Taipei route.

Annual revenue: $600 million
Passengers: 1.9 million
Employees: 2,145
Shareholders: KLM (50 per cent) and Nedlloyd (50 per cent)

The three 747 freighters in service with Martinair today were acquired in 1987, 1988 and 1991. All are powered by General Electric CF6 engines and the Combi aircraft can accommodate up to 516 passengers.

Martinair fleet

Boeing 747-200 Combi		PH-MCH	24429/294	Dornier 228-200	c/n
PH-MCE	23652/669	PH-MCI	25312/400	PH-MNZ	8206
PH-MCF	24134/712	PH-MCL	26469/415		
		PH-MCM	26470/416	**McDonnell Douglas**	
Boeing 747-200F	c/n	PH-MCV	27619/595	**MD-11CF**	c/n
PH-MCN	25266/878			PH-MCP	48616/577
		Cessna 650 Citation IV		PH-MCR	48617/583
Boeing 767-300(ER)	c/n	PH-MEX	0217	PH-MCS	48618/584
PH-MCG	24428/279	PH-MFX	0240	PH-MCT	48629/586

Mexicana (MX/AMX)

Benito Juarez International Airport
Mexico City, Mexico

History: Founded as Compania de Transportes Aerea 21 July 1921, but officially incorporated under name of Compania Mexicana de Aviacion, known as Mexicana, 20 August 1924. Scheduled Mexico City-Tampico service inaugurated 15 April 1928 with **Fairchild 71**, before five **Ford Trimotor**s added. Control passed to Pan American Airways, which purchased entire stock 2 January 1929. Opened mail service to Texasand added major trunk route between Mexico City and Los Angeles September 1934, using **Lockheed L.10A Electra**. Fleet modernised with **Boeing 247D** in 1936, **Douglas DC-2** in 1937, and **DC-3** 1938. After war, **DC-4** introduced on 6 June 1946, followed by **DC-6** in 1952. **Fairchild C-82** joined DC-6 cargo flights.On 15 October 1958, **DC-7C** opened Chicago route, and first jet, **de Havilland Comet IVC**, put on Los Angeles service 4 July 1960. Period of financial difficulties and decline followed until Mexicana became wholly Mexican-owned January 1968. Fleet of **Boeing 727-100** and 'hot-and-high' **727-200** with JATO-assisted take-off added, accompanied by restructuring programme. New route to Dallas

opened 13 December 1971 and services to USA expanded considerably, following authorisation April 1978 for 13 additional points. High-capacity **DC-10-15** added to fleet in 1981. Reprivatised 15 September 1989 with sale of shares worth $140 million. Opened first South American route January 1992 to Caracas, and 6 April to Bogotá. Delivery of first **A320-200** in December 1991 and first of 10 **Fokker 100**s in December 1992.

Mexicana today: High-frequency domestic services and regional links to USA and Latin American countries. In addition to almost 40 domestic points, regional flights serve Baltimore, Bogotá, Caracas, Chicago, Dallas/

Mexicana's striking tail designs differ in style and colour from aircraft to aircraft.

Ft Worth, Denver, Guatemala City, Havana, Los Angeles, Miami, New York, Philadelphia, San Antonio, San Jose, San Juan, San Francisco, Seattle and Tampa. Close co-operation, with part-owner Aeromexico.

Annual revenue: $925 million
Passengers: 7.2 million
Cargo: 45,000 tonnes
Employees: 7,500
Major shareholders: Aeromexico and Mexican government . Currently being restructured under CINTRA holding company

Mexicana

Fleet development: Eight more Airbus A320-200s to be delivered between 1996 and 1998, bringing total fleet to 20 aircraft.

Associate carriers: Founded in 1975 **Aerocaribe** (QA) was acquired by Mexicana 23 August 1990. **Aerocozumel** (AZ) – also wholly-owned – began operations 20 November 1978. Both provide closely-integrated feeder services to major Mexican hubs from destinations in Yucatan Peninsula. Aerocaribe flies two **Douglas DC-9-10**s and six **Fairchild F27/FH-227B**s, while Aerocozumel operates a single **Fokker F27**.

Mexicana fleet

Airbus A320-200		XA-HOV	21637/1429	XA-MXC	22663/1778
F-OHMA	368	XA-HOX	21638/1457	XA-MXD	22664/1780
F-OHMD	433	XA-IEU	21836/1497	XA-MXI	21346/1675
F-OHME	252	XA-MEB	21837/1545	XA-MXJ	21600/1679
F-OHMF	259	XA-MEC	21838/1547		
F-OHMG	260	XA-MED	22156/1607	**Fokker 100**	
F-OHMH	261	XA-MEE	22157/1619	XA-SGE	11382
F-OHMI	275	XA-MEF	22158/1642	XA-SGF	11384
F-OHMJ	276	XA-MEH	22409/1676	XA-SHI	11309
F-OHMK	296	XA-MEI	22410/1678	XA-SHJ	11319
F-OHML	320	XA-MEJ	22411/1696	XA-TCG	11374
F-OHMM	321	XA-MEK	22412/1720	XA-TCH	11375
F-OHMN	353	XA-MEL	22413/1728	PH-JXW	11390
		XA-MER	22425/1698	PH-KXJ	11400
Boeing 727-200 Advanced		XA-MEZ	22676/1754	PH-KXR	11410
XA-HOH	21577/1379	XA-MXA	22661/1757	PH-LXG	11420
XA-HON	21617/1416	XA-MXB	22662/1776		

Middle East Airlines (ME/MEA)

Beirut International Airport
Beirut, Lebanon

MEA retired the last of its Boeing 720s in early 1996 and its 707s will soon be withdrawn also. This will leave three 747-200Bs partnering an all-Airbus fleet.

History: Founded 31 May 1945 with BOAC assistance, and three **DH.89A Rapides**. First flight Beirut-Nicosia 30 November. Flights to Lydda and Haifa discontinued in 1948 due to Palestine crisis. Agreement with Pan American September 1949, added three **DC-3**s plus management and technical expertise in exchange for shareholding. Route network extended to several points in Middle East under Pan Am's guidance, but agreement cancelled in 1955, with BOAC taking 49 per cent stake. **Vickers Viscount** introduced in October 1955, followed by new Beirut-Athens-Rome link 24 November. Three **Avro York**s leased in June 1957 for cargo work. Delivery of first of four **de Havilland Comet IVB**s 15 December 1960. Association with BOAC terminated 16 August 1961. On 7 June 1963 merged with Air Liban which gave Air France 30 per cent holding. New full title now Middle East Airlines Airliban.

Types operated in subsequent years included **Caravelle**s (April 1963), **Boeing 720B**s (January 1966), **Vickers VC 10** (March 1967) and **707-320C**s from November 1967. Services interrupted by Six-Day War in June 1967, and on night of 28/29 December 1968 Israeli commando unit destroyed 13 aircraft at Beirut Airport, including MEA 707, two Comets, two Caravelles, VC 10 and Viscount. With much-reduced fleet operations restarted few days later. **Convair 990A** acquired from American Airlines, entering service 24 June 1969, followed by 16 Boeing 720Bs in October 1970. Assets of Lebanese International Airways taken over in 1969. **747-200B** entered service in June 1975 on Beirut-London service. Another attack Beirut airport 27 June 1976 forced its closure. MEA transferred operations to Paris and satellite stations in Gulf and North Africa, and did not fully return until February 1977. 1980s brought more difficulties

in region leading to yet another temporary closure of airport and damage to MEA aircraft. Fleet modernisation hampered by lack of funds and many aircraft also leased out over subsequent years. First intercontinental route inaugurated 1 March 1983 from Beirut to New York, via Paris. Political situation now stabilised enabling acquisition of two new **Airbus A310-300**s in 1993 and 1994.

MEA today: National flag-carrier providing scheduled international passenger and cargo services from Beirut to Abidjan, Abu Dhabi, Accra, Amman, Athens, Bahrain, Berlin, Brussels, Cairo, Colombo, Copenhagen, Dhahran, Doha, Dubai, Frankfurt, Geneva, Jeddah, Kano, Khartoum, Kuwait, Lagos, Larnaca, London, Madrid, Milan, Nice, Paris-Orly, Riyadh, Rome, Singapore, Sydney and Zürich. Code-share and joint flights with Air France, AirLanka, Iberia and Nigeria Airways.

Annual revenue: *$265 million*
Passengers: *0.8 million*
Cargo: *16,500 tonnes*
Employees: *4,250*
Major shareholders: *Intra Investment (62.5 per cent), comprising Lebanese government, Bank of Lebanon and Kuwaiti government, and Air France (28 per cent)*

Fleet development: Capital injection imminent for replacement of ageing and inappropriate fleet of hush-kitted Boeing 707-320C with five smaller aircraft, either **Boeing 737-800** or **Airbus A320-200**. Phase out of 707 could begin in spring 1997 and will be completed within two years.

Middle East Airlines fleet

Airbus A310-200	c/n	Boeing 707-320C	c/n	OD-AHF	20170/795
PH-AGC	248	OD-AFD	20259/822		
PH-AGE	283	OD-AFE	20260/823	Boeing 747-200B	c/n
PH-AGF	297	OD-AGU	19966/743	N202AE	21097/262
		OD-AGV	19967/745	N203AE	21098/263
Airbus A310-300	c/n	OD-AHC	19589/701	N204AE	21090/264
F-OHLH	447	OD-AHD	19515/608		
F-OHLI	481	OD-AHE	19516/612		

Monarch Airlines (ZB/MON)

Luton International Airport,
Luton, UK

History: Founded by Cosmos Tours 1 June 1967 and started flying 5 April 1968 with two **Bristol Britannia**s on inclusive tours to Mediterranean resorts. By end of year Britannia fleet increased to six, and first of four **Boeing 720B** jets entered service on 13 December 1971. Two **BAC One-Eleven 500**s added in summer 1975. Britannias retired at end of same year. 720B fleet changed for bigger **707**, itself replaced by 1983 with arrival of **757-200**. Monarch first charter airline and third operator of new Boeing twin-jet. First of number of **737-200**s arrived in 1981 forming basis of new short-haul fleet, augmented from March 1986 with **737-300**. Added scheduled leisure routes to IT flights from 5 July 1986. Announced order for **Airbus A300-600R** with high-density seating 2 November 1988, which arrived in March and April 1990. Plans in 1991 to acquire two **767-300ER**s shelved, but fleet expanded with **A320-200**s.

Monarch Airlines today: Extensive charters and inclusive-tour packages for all leading tour operators, including sister company Cosmos, from Luton, London-Gatwick, Stansted, Manchester Birmingham, Leeds Bradford and Glasgow to Europe and Mediterranean Basin, as

Monarch took delivery of its first A320-212 in February 1993. All are configured with 180 seats.

well as long-haul flights to destinations in United States, Bahamas, Mexico, Brazil, Kenya, Malaysia and Thailand. Additionally has scheduled leisure routes which link Luton with Spanish resorts of Alicante, Mahon (Menorca), Malaga, Palma de Mallorca and Tenerife in Canary Islands.

Annual revenue: $535 million
Passengers 4.6 million
Employees: 2,100
Ownership: Wholly-owned by tour operator Globus Gateway

Monarch Airlines fleet

Airbus A300-600R	c/n	G-MPCD	379	G-MONB	22780/15
G-MAJS	604	G-OZBA	422	G-MONC	22781/18
G-MONR	540	G-OZBB	389	G-MOND	22960/19
G-MONS	556			G-MONE	23293/56
G-OJMR	605	Boeing 737-300	c/n	G-MONJ	24104/170
		G-MONH	26385/1357	G-MONK	24105/172
Airbus A320-200	c/n	G-MONP	24028/1599		
G-MONW	391			Douglas DC-10-30	c/n
G-MONX	392	Boeing 757-200	c/n	G-DMON	48266/348
G-MONY	279	G-DAJB	23770/125		
G-MONZ	446	G-MCKE	4368/213		

Nigeria Airways (WT/NGA)

Murtala Muhammed Airport
Lagos, Nigeria

History: Founded as WAAC (Nigeria) 23 August 1958 to succeed West African Airways Corporation, which had served Gold Coast (now Ghana), Nigeria, Sierra Leone and Gambia since 1946. Initial shareholding divided between Nigerian government, Elder Dempster Line and BOAC, but entire stock purchased by government 1 May 1959, prior to independence 1 October 1960. Began operations over former network, including Lagos-London route, using marketing name of Nigeria Airways, officially adopted 22 January 1971. Mixed fleet of **de Havilland Dove**s and **Heron**s, and **Douglas DC-3**, gradually replaced by five **Fokker F27-200**s in 1963, doubled in number in 1969, with long-haul routes flown by variety of aircraft leased from BOAC. Network expanded throughout Africa. Civil war in Biafra brought chaos to Nigeria and airline's progress halted until 1970. Reconstruction programme by new federal military government brought new routes and

Nigeria Airways

Six 737-2F9s, delivered between 1973 and 1983, form the backbone of Nigeria Airway's fleet.

national flag-carrier operating reduced services from Lagos to Abidjan, Accra, Banjul, Beirut, Conakry, Cotonou, Douala, Jeddah, Kinshasa, Libreville, Lome and London. Some flights also operate out of Kano. Domestic flights link Abuja, Calabar, Enugu, Jos, Kaduna, Kano, Lagos, Maiduguri, Makurdi, Port Harcourt, Sokoto and Yola. Plans for Lagos-Johannesburg link. Commercial agreements with Cameroon Airlines and Ethiopian Airlines, and discussions with Ghana Airways for possible joint operation to New York.

new aircraft – 10 **F28-1000/2000**s delivered from October 1972, two **Boeing 707-320C**s in August 1971, two **737-200**s in January 1973, two **DC-10-30**s from September 1976 and three **727-200**s from August 1977. Progress did not continue at same level, and two decades that followed were punctuated by long periods of instability and political interference, frequent management changes and technical deficiencies. This resulted in intermittent grounding of much of fleet, in spite of acquisition of six more 737-200s, and four **Airbus A310-200**s in December 1984. Airline also suffered from heavy competition

from independent airlines, following withdrawal of monopoly on domestic routes in 1988. Plans to set up Air Nigeria to take over long-haul routes, plus search for an airline equity partner, came to nothing, and long-haul and regional network drastically reduced. Latest restructuring initiated in September 1995.
Nigeria Airways today: Wholly government-owned

Annual passengers: 0.65 million
Cargo: 4,500 tonnes
Employees: 4,400

Nigeria Airways fleet

Airbus A310-200	c/n	Boeing 737-200 Adv	c/n		
5N-AUE	270	5N-ANC	20671/312	5N-ANZ	22774/895
5N-AUF	285	5N-AND	20672/313	5N-AUB	22986/925
5N-AUG	329	5N-ANW	22771/866	**Douglas DC-10-30**	c/n
5N-AUH	340	5N-ANY	22773/892	5N-ANN	46957/231

Northwest Airlines (NW/NWA)
Minneapolis-St Paul IAP
Minneapolis, Minnesota, USA

History: Established as Northwest Airways 1 September 1926. Started operations 1 October 1926 with mail service between Minneapolis/St Paul and Chicago. First passenger carried on 5 July 1927. Chartered fleet replaced with own **Stinson Detroiter**, **Ford Trimotor**s, **Hamilton Metalplane**s and **Travelair 6000A**s. **Lockheed Orion**s added in 1931. International route to Winnipeg started in February 1928 and transcontinental penetration achieved 3 December 1933, linking Great

Lakes to Pacific with route to Seattle. More cities in Lakes area served with **Sikorsky S-38** flying-boats. Name changed to Northwest Airlines 16 April 1934. First airline to introduce **Lockheed L.10A Electra** in 1934, followed by **L.14-H Zephyr** in 1937 and **DC-3** in April 1939. Post-war commercial operations restarted in September 1946 with **DC-4** service to New York, and Detroit. New Great Circle route from Twin Cities to Tokyo, Seoul, Shanghai and Manila, introduced 15 July 1947, gave

rise to title of Northwest Orient Airlines, which remained in use until 1985. New aircraft purchases included **Martin 2-0-2**s (in service April 1947), **Boeing 377 Stratocruiser**s (June 1949), **Douglas DC-6B**s (September 1953), **Lockheed L.1049G Super Constellation**s (February 1955) and **DC-7C**s (April 1957). Turboprop service initiated 25 July 1959 with first **Lockheed L.188 Electra**s, followed by first **DC-8** jet in July 1960. Both operations short-lived, as re-equipment programme switched to large numbers of **Boeing 720B** and **707-320B** models. Domestic jet operations commenced in November 1964 with first of 85 **Boeing 727-100/-200**s. **Boeing 747** Minneapolis/St Paul-New York route inaugurated 22 June 1970. Long-haul fleet supplemented with 22 **DC-10-30**s

Northwest, then Northwest Orient, was an important early US customer for the A320. Its first example was delivered in 1989.

Northwest Airlines operates a number of 747-200F (SCD)s under the Northwest Cargo banner.

following year. Routes extended to Europe in 1979. London added 2 June 1980 from Twin Cities, followed by Boston-London. Placed largest aircraft order in its history in 1985 via $2 billion contract for 10 new **747-400**s, three 747-200Bs and 10 **757-200**s, followed by another order for up to 100 **Airbus A320-200**s in 1986. Other significant events in 1980s included setting up of Northwest Airlink system in 1984, and take-over of Republic Airlines 12 August 1986, adding vast domestic route structure and large numbers of **DC-9**s. Rapid expansion, recession and competitive pressure plunged Northwest into sharp decline which persisted for several years. In 1989, alliance forged with KLM, later developed through equity participation into major strategic partnership, providing global access to both airlines. Reorganised in 1985 under NWA holding company, but became privately-owned in 1989 in $3.65 billion transaction by group of investors.

Northwest today: Fourth-largest airline in world, serving more than 240 cities in 22 countries from main hubs at Detroit, Minneapolis/St Paul, Memphis and Tokyo-Narita. Apart from extensive domestic network to 104 cities in 45 US states, and frequent connections to Canada, Mexico and Caribbean, operates transpacific services to Bangkok, Beijing, Bombay, Delhi, Fukuoka, Guam, Hong Kong, Manila, Nagoya, Osaka, Saipan, Seoul, Shanghai, Singapore, Taipei and Tokyo. Amsterdam, Frankfurt, London-Gatwick and Paris-CDG served in Europe. Bombay and Delhi served from January 1997. Wide-ranging transatlantic equity alliance with KLM Royal Dutch Airlines considered one of most advanced partnerships in airline industry. Marketing agreements with Asiana, Aloha, Alaska Airlines, Eurowings (code-share) and Pacific Island Aviation.

Annual revenue: $9,085 million
Passengers: 45.8 million
Cargo: 760,000 tonnes
Employees: 47,000
Major shareholders: employees 27.0 per cent, KLM Royal Dutch Airlines 18.8 per cent, Alfred Checchi 11.0 per cent, Gary Wilson 11.0 per cent

Fleet development: Outstanding orders total 77, including four 747-400s, due 1996 and 1997; 37 **757-200**s, for delivery by 1998; 16 **A330-300**s, deferred to 2004/2005; and 20 A320-200s, of which 10 will be delivered in 1998 and further 10 in 1999. Some older 727s and DC-9s are being hushkitted.

Associate carriers: Several local airlines operating under **Northwest Airlink** banner, serving 200 communities in 44 states.

These are: **Express Airlines** (II), founded in February 1985, serves 52 cities in 22 states from Memphis and Minneapolis with 25 **Saab 340A**s, 11 **Saab 340B**s and 22 **BAe Jetstream 31**s;

Business Express (HQ), also Delta Connection partner, at present in Chapter 11 but operating with 35 Saab 340s;

Horizon Air (QX), part of Alaska Air Group, operating fleet of **DHC-8-100**s, **Do 328**s, **Metro III**s and **F28-1000**s from Seattle;

Mesaba Airlines (XJ), signed first code-share with Northwest in 1984. Provides feeder services to Northwest's Detroit and Minneapolis hubs from 62 cities in 16 states and two Canadian provinces with 25 **DHC-8-100**s and 26 **Metro III**s. Signed agreement to acquire 50 **Saab 340**s (30 **340BPlus** and 20 **340A**) within next three years.

Mesaba Airlines operates as part of the Northwest Airlink network with DHC-8-100s.

Northwest Airlines fleet

Airbus A320-200	c/n								
N301US	031	N309US	118	N318US	206	N327NW	297	N336NW	355
N302US	032	N310NW	121	N319US	208	N328NW	298	N337NW	358
N303US	034	N311US	125	N320US	213	N329NW	306	N338NW	360
N304US	040	N312US	152	N321US	262	N330NW	307	N339NW	367
N305US	041	N313US	153	N322US	263	N331NW	318	N340NW	372
N306US	060	N314US	160	N323US	272	N332NW	319	N341NW	380
N307US	106	N315US	171	N324US	273	N333NW	329	N342NW	381
N308US	107	N316US	192	N325US	281	N334NW	339	N343NW	387
		N317US	197	N326US	282	N335NW	340	N344NW	388

Northwest Airlines

Reg	c/n
N345NW	399
N346NW	400
N347NW	408
N348NW	410
N349NW	417
N350NA	418

Boeing 727-200 Adv c/n

Reg	c/n	Reg	c/n
N201US	22154/1645	N8878Z	21451/1310
N202US	22155/1648		
N203US	22543/1700		
N204US	22544/1703		
N275US	21154/1168		
N276US	21155/1169		
N283US	21322/1265		
N284US	21323/1284		
N285US	21324/1286		
N286US	21325/1288		
N287US	21375/1290		
N288US	21376/1293		
N289US	21377/1295		
N290US	21378/1279		
N291US	21379/1299		
N292US	21503/1317		
N293US	21504/1319		
N294US	21505/1391		
N295US	21506/1392		
N296US	21788/1495		
N297US	21789/1496		
N298US	22152/1599		
N299US	22153/1601		
N712RC	22020/1592		
N715RC	22019/1584		
N716RC	22021/1617		
N718RC	22344/1654		
N719RC	22490/1721		
N720RC	22491/1726		
N721RC	22492/1729		
N721RW	21200/1202		
N722RW	21201/1220		
N725RW	21502/1339		
N727RW	21656/1455		
N728RW	21741/1491		
N729RW	21742/1514		
N742RW	21952/1693		
N801EA	22432/1658		
N802EA	22433/1668		
N815EA	22552/1773		
N816EA	22553/1775		
N817EA	22554/1781		
N818EA	22555/1783		
N820EA	22557/1795		
N8877Z	21450/1308		

Boeing 747-100 c/n

Reg	c/n
N601US	19778/27
N603US	19780/45
N608US	19785/75

Boeing 747-200B c/n

Reg	c/n
N611US	20356/88
N612US	20357/135
N613US	20358/141
N614US	20359/163
N615US	20360/165
N622US	21704/357
N623US	21705/374
N624US	21706/377
N625US	21707/378
N626US	21708/379
N627US	21709/412
N628US	22389/442
N631US	23111/594
N632US	23112/595
N633US	21991/437
N634US	22234/465
N635US	21682/375
N636US	23547/642
N637US	23548/644
N638US	23549/651

Boeing 747-200F c/n

Reg	c/n
N616US	21120/258
N617US	21121/261
N618US	21122/269
N619US	21321/308
N629US	22388/444
N630US	21668/400
N639US	23887/680
N640US	23888/682

Boeing 747-400 c/n

Reg	c/n
N661US	23719/696
N662US	23720/708
N663US	23818/715
N664US	23819/721
N665US	23820/726
N666US	23821/742
N667US	24222/799
N668US	24223/800
N669US	24224/803
N670US	24225/804

Boeing 757-200 c/n

Reg	c/n
N501US	23190/53

The bulk of Northwest's 747 fleet are 747-251B models, but the airline is gradually introducing more modern 747-451s.

Reg	c/n
N502US	23191/55
N503US	23192/59
N504US	23193/60
N505US	23194/62
N506US	23195/67
N507US	23196/68
N508US	23197/69
N509US	23198/70
N511US	23199/73
N512US	23200/82
N513US	23201/83
N514US	23202/86
N515US	23203/88
N516US	23204/104
N517US	23205/105
N518US	23206/107
N519US	23207/108
N520US	23208/109
N521US	23209/110
N522US	23616/119
N523US	23617/121
N524US	23618/122
N525US	23619/124
N526US	23620/131
N527US	23842/136
N528US	23843/137
N529US	23844/140
N530US	23845/188
N531US	23846/190
N532US	24263/192
N533US	24264/194
N534US	24265/196
N535US	26479/693
N536US	26480/695
N537US	26484/697

Douglas DC-9-14/15 c/n

Reg	c/n
N3310L	45705/53
N3312L	45707/70
N8903E	45744/31
N8905E	45746/38
N8906E	45747/40
N8907E	45748/47
N8908E	45749/50
N8909E	45770/57
N8911E	45825/67
N8912E	45829/68
N8913E	45830/75
N8914E	45831/76
N8915E	45832/84
N91S	47063/111
N92S	47064/120
N930RC	45729/16
N9348	45787/127
N93S	47078/146

Reg	c/n
N948L	47049/42
N94S	47204/245
N95S	47205/250
N96S	47206/328

Douglas DC-9-31/32

Reg	c/n
N1308T	47315/433
N1309T	47316/439
N1332U	47404/554
N1334U	47280/597
N1798U	47369/529
N1799U	47370/551
N3322L	47031/187
N3991C	47175/298
N601NW	47038/136
N602NW	47046/168
N603NW	47101/195
N604NW	47222/299
N605NW	47223/300
N606NW	47225/317
N607NW	47232/428
N608NW	47233/429
N609NW	47234/435
N610NW	47432/525
N611NW	47435/540
N612NW	47436/541
N8920E	45835/95
N8921E	45836/96
N8923E	45838/104
N8925E	45840/117
N8926E	45863/124
N8928E	45865/137
N8929E	45866/138
N8932E	47141/227
N8933E	47142/232
N8934E	47143/238
N8938E	47161/249
N8944E	47167/266
N8945E	47181/267
N8950E	47186/276
N8957E	47215/313
N8960E	45869/331
N8978E	47327/391
N8979E	47328/392
N8986E	47402/482
N89S	47042/486
N908H	47517/583
N90S	47244/498
N911RW	47149/202
N912RW	47150/284
N913RW	47171/473
N914RW	47362/492
N915RW	47139/169
N916RW	47144/239
N917RW	47145/247
N918RW	47158/248
N919RW	47162/255
N920RW	47163/256
N921RW	47164/259
N922RW	47182/271
N923RW	47183/272
N924RW	47185/275
N925US	47472/596
N926NW	47425/589
N926RC	47473/598
N927RC	47469/590
N9330	47138/318
N9331	47263/320
N9332	47264/329
N9333	47246/292
N9334	47247/342
N9335	47337/415
N9336	47338/416
N9337	47346/464
N9338	47347/478
N9339	47382/479
N9340	47389/489
N9341	47390/490
N9342	47391/491
N9343	47439/501
N9344	47440/502
N9346	47376/517
N940N	47572/708
N941N	47450/535
N942N	47459/549
N943N	47647/773
N945N	47664/775
N949N	47566/691
N952N	47073/161
N953N	47083/177
N955N	47160/241
N956N	47252/294
N957N	47253/295
N958N	47254/301
N959N	47255/310
N960N	47256/326
N961N	47405/487
N962N	47406/499
N963N	47415/511
N964N	47416/512
N965N	47417/518
N966N	47573/694
N982US	47590/264
N983US	47282/446
N984US	47383/538
N985US	47479/605
N986US	47480/607
N987US	47458/646
N994Z	47097/193

Douglas DC-9-41 c/n

Reg	c/n
N750NW	47114/218
N751NW	47115/261
N752NW	47116/308
N753NW	47117/319
N754NW	47178/323
N755NW	47179/335
N756NW	47180/354
N758NW	47286/359
N759NW	47287/364
N760NW	47288/369
N762NW	47395/555
N763NW	47396/557

Douglas DC-9-51 c/n

Reg	c/n
N401EA	47682/788
N600TR	47783/899
N760NC	47708/813
N761NC	47709/814
N762NC	47710/818
N763NC	47716/832
N764NC	47717/833
N765NC	47718/834
N766NC	47739/852
N767NC	47724/853
N768NC	47729/864
N769NC	47757/877
N770NC	47758/880
N771NC	47769/881
N772NC	47774/884
N773NC	47775/888
N774NC	47776/889
N775NC	47785/904
N776NC	47786/905
N777NC	47787/912
N778NC	48100/927
N779NC	48101/931
N780NC	48102/932

In common with many of the other US majors, Northwest still maintains a sizeable fleet of Boeing 727-200s. It is also the world's largest DC-9 operator.

N781NC	48121/935	N221NW	46579/132	**Douglas DC-10-40** *c/n*	N152US	46761/124	**McDonnell Douglas**	
N782NC	48107/936	N223NW	46580/183	N133JC	46752/53	N153US	46762/126	**MD-82**	*c/n*
N783NC	48108/937	N224NW	46581/184	N141US	46750/28	N154US	46763/128	N301RC	48054/996
N784NC	48109/939	N225NW	46582/187	N144JC	46753/66	N155US	46764/130	N302RC	48055/1007
N785NC	48110/945	N226NW	46583/292	N145US	46754/79	N156US	46765/143	N307RC	48086/1029
N786NC	48148/984	N227NW	46969/241	N146US	46755/97	N157US	46766/151	N309RC	48088/1037
N787NC	48149/990	N229NW	46551/60	N147US	46756/102	N158US	46767/161	N311RC	48089/1038
		N230NW	46552/71	N148US	46757/108	N159US	46768/164	N313RC	48091/1041
Douglas DC-10-30 *c/n*		N232NW	46961/236	N149US	46758/111	N160US	46769/168	N314RC	49110/1062
N211NW	48868/171	N233NW	46640/240	N150US	46759/113	N161US	46770/175	N931MC	48057/1023
N220NW	46577/114			N151US	46760/120	N162US	46771/180		

Olympic Airways (OA/OAL)

Athens International Airport
Helliniki, Greece

History: Founded by shipping magnate Aristotle Onassis 6 April 1957 out of remains of former national carrier, Technical and Aeronautical Exploitation Company (TAE). Began operations with fleet of 14 **DC-3**s and one **DC-4**, soon supplemented by three **DC-6B**s which opened new route to Rome, Paris and London 2 May 1957. **Comet 4B** jet services introduced 18 May 1960. North Atlantic service to New York added 1 June 1966 with delivery of three **Boeing 707-320B**s. Five **727-200**, five **720B**, and **NAMC YS-11A**s added for domestic services. Started non-stop New York service with **Boeing 747-200B** in June 1973. Bought by Greek government 1 January 1975. Announced purchase of four **737-200**s and six **Airbus A300B4-200**s, first delivered 23 June 1976 and 5 February 1979 respectively. First **737-400** delivered in June 1991, followed by two **A300-600R**s in June 1992 and October 1993. Domestic monopoly ended January 1993. Airline in final year of draconian reorganisation imposed in 1994 as condition of EU acceptance of state aid to return airline to profitability for first time since 1978; included discontinuation of Chicago service in June 1994 and Tokyo service in November 1994.

Olympic Airways today: National flag-carrier providing scheduled passenger and cargo services from Athens to most European capital cities and to destinations in Middle and Far East, Africa and North America. Long-haul routes serve New York, Boston, Chicago, Montreal, Toronto, Nairobi, Johannesburg, Bangkok, Singapore and Sydney. Domestic route network serves 36 points, most flown by Olympic Aviation. Block-space

agreement with Saudia on Jeddah and Riyadh routes, and marketing alliances with Cyprus Airways and VASP.

Annual revenue: $930 million
Passengers: 5.8 million
Cargo: 65,000 tonnes
Employees: 9,800
Wholly government-owned

Fleet Development: Reorganising around nucleus of Boeing 737-400. Decision on long-haul replacement for 747-200B to be made in 1997.
Associate carriers: *Olympic Aviation* (7U), set up

Olympic Airways now has seven 737-400s in service. More will replace older 737-200s and 727s.

in 1971 to provide helicopter and agricultural flying services. Fleet now built around 50-seat **ATR42** (four in service) and 70-seat **ATR72** (seven), supplemented by five **Shorts 330** and seven **Dornier Do 228**s. Since 1 January 1992, operationally independent.
Macedonian Airlines (M7) was formed in 1992 as subsidiary, providing charter services with Olympic Airways aircraft as and when required.

Olympic Airways fleet

Airbus A300B4-100	c/n	Boeing 727-200 Advanced		Boeing 737-400	c/n
SX-BED	058	SX-CBG	20918/1093	SX-BKA	25313/2109
SX-BEE	103	SX-CBH	20790/1021	SX-BKB	25314/2124
SX-BEF	105	SX-CBI	20791/1022	SX-BKC	25361/2130
SX-BEG	148			SX-BKD	25362/2142
SX-BEH	184	Boeing 737-200 Advanced		SX-BKE	25417/2160
SX-BEI	189	SX-BCA	21224/463	SX-BKF	25430/2174
		SX-BCB	21225/464	SX-BKG	27149/2471
Airbus A300-600R	c/n	SX-BCC	21301/474		
SX-BEL	696	SX-BCD	21302/475	Boeing 747-200B	c/n
		SX-BCE	22300/674	SX-OAB	20825/223
Boeing 727-200	c/n	SX-BCF	22301/683	SX-OAC	21683/387
SX-CBC	20005/687	SX-BCG	22338/691	SX-OAD	21684/391
SX-CBD	20006/688	SX-BCH	22339/692	SX-OAE	21935/399
		SX-BCI	22343/695		
		SX-BXK	22400/766		
		SX-BCL	22401/780		

89

Pakistan International (PK/PIA)

Quaid-e-Azam Airport
Karachi, Pakistan

Pakistan International Airway's six A310-300s, the extended range wingletted version, are an important part of the PIA fleet.

Ashkhabad, Athens, Baku, Bangkok, Beijing, Cairo, Colombo, Copenhagen, Dhaka, Frankfurt, Istanbul, Jakarta, Kathmandu, Kuala Lumpur, London, Male, Manchester, Manila, Moscow, Nairobi, New York, Paris, Rome, Singapore, Tashkent, Tokyo, Toronto and Zürich. Revenue share with AirLanka on routes through Colombo.

History: Established 1954 and started operations 10 May 1954 with **Lockheed L.1049G Super Constellation**s. Service introduced between West and East Pakistan (now Bangladesh). First international route opened from Karachi to London via Cairo and Rome 1 February 1955. Pakistan International Airlines Corporation created 10 March 1955 through merging PIA and Orient Airways. Placed order for two **L.1049H**s and three **Vickers Viscounts**, replacing **Convair 240**. **Boeing 707-320B** introduced on London route in 1959. Early 1960s notable for addition of five **Fokker F27**s, three **Boeing 720B**s and opening of New York service. **Trident 1E** added to fleet in summer 1966. Two **DC-10-30**s took over long-haul routes in 1974. Fleet increased with more DC-10-30s, followed by two leased **747-200B**s in April 1976. Four **A300B4-200**s introduced in 1980. Five **737-300**s delivered in May and June 1985. **DHC-6** acquired to serve Muzaffarabad and Rawalakot. **Airbus A310-300** introduced in 1991.

PIA today: Flag-carrier serving 52 international destinations in 43 countries, together with 36 domestic points. In addition to connecting Pakistan with all Middle Eastern cities, longer-haul flights operated to Almaty, Amsterdam,

Annual revenue: $745 million
Passengers: 5.5 million
Cargo: 127,000 tonnes
Employees: 20,405

Pakistan International fleet

Airbus A300B4-200	c/n	Boeing 737-300	c/n	Fokker F27-200	
AP-BAX	096	AP-BCA	23294/1114	**Friendship**	c/n
AP-BAY	098	AP-BCB	23295/1116	AP-ALN	10164
AP-BAZ	099	AP-BCC	23296/1121	AP-ATU	10278
AP-BBA	114	AP-BCD	23297/1122	AP-AUR	10307
AP-BBM	064	AP-BCE	23298/1123	AP-AXB	10288
AP-BBV	144	AP-BCF	23299/1235	AP-BAL	10243
AP-BCJ	268			AP-BAO	10230
AP-BEL	269	**Boeing 747-200B**	c/n	AP-BCT	10289
AP-BEY	146	AP-AYV	20928/239	AP-BCZ	10305
		AP-AYW	21035/256	AP-BDB	10292
Airbus A310-300	c/n	AP-BCL	20929/247	AP-BDP	10170
AP-BDZ	585	AP-BCM	20802/226	AP-BDQ	10253
AP-BEB	587	AP-BCN	20801/225	AP-BDR	10134
AP-BEC	590	AP-BCO	20927/244	AP-BDS	10133
AP-BEG	653				
AP-BEQ	656	**Boeing 747-200B Combi**		**Fokker F27-400**	
AP-BEU	691	AP-BAK	21825/383	**Friendship**	c/n
		AP-BAT	22077/429	AP-ALW	10187
Boeing 707-320C	c/n				
AP-AXG	20488/849	**DHC-6 Twin Otter 300** c/n			
AP-BBK	19576/719	AP-BCG	726		
		AP-BCH	768		

Philippine Airlines (PR/PAL)

Ninoy Aquino International Airport
Pasay City, Metro Manila, Philippines

History: Founded 25 February 1941 as Philippine Air Lines (PAL). Operations started 15 March with two **Beech 18**s and one **Beech 17 Staggerwing**. Outbreak of Pacific War 8 December 1941 cut short PAL's progress and flying only resumed 14 February 1946 on local routes, using **DC-3** and **Beech C-45** (Model 18) equipment. International expansion with **DC-4** began 31 July to Oakland on US West Coast, followed within

weeks with connections to Hong Kong, Shanghai, Taipei and Bangkok. Fleet grew to 35 DC-3s and seven DC-4s, and order placed for two **DC-6**s. Route to Madrid inaugurated 3 May 1947, extended 29 May 1948 to London. By 1948, PAL had absorbed only other scheduled airlines, Far Eastern Air Transport Inc. and Commercial Air Lines. In March 1949 started DC-4 'coach' service from Manila to Hong Kong and Tokyo. First **DC-6B** delivered 23

July 1952, followed by **Convair 340** in April 1953 and first turboprop, **Vickers Viscount**, 22 May 1957. Lack of finance to buy jet equipment forced suspension of all international flights in March 1954, except for Hong Kong service. Domestic stations increased to 45. **Fokker F27**s bought in 1960 for local routes. US West Coast flights resumed 20 June 1962 using newly-acquired **DC-8** jets. Government holding reduced to 49 per cent

90

September 1964 and cash injection from private sector enabled acquisition of **DC-8F** freighter and **BAC One-Eleven**s, which went into service to Hong Kong and Taipei 1 May 1966. First of 15 **HS 748** replacements for DC-3 put into service in November 1967. Progress steady until operations taken over by Philippine air force after declaration of martial law in September 1972. PAL designated sole Philippine flag-carrier 10 March 1973. Long-haul routes served with **DC-8-63** and later **DC-10-30**, but expansion hampered by lack of cash and airline sold back to government. Major step forward initiated with orders for two **Airbus A300B4**s and three **Boeing 747-200B**s, first delivered in November and December 1979. Ten **Fokker 50**s bought for local routes in 1989/90. Partially privatised in 1992 and fleet modernisation initiated with an order for four **A340-200**s. Two **747-400**s delivered in winter 1993.

Philippine Airlines today: National flag-carrier linking Manila with 34 cities in 23 countries, together with more than 40 domestic points. International destinations include Abu Dhabi, Al Ain, Bahrain, Bandar Seri Begawan, Bangkok, Brisbane, Dhahran, Doha, Dubai, Frankfurt, Fukuoka, Ho Chi Minh City, Hong Kong, Jakarta, Jeddah, Kaohsiung, Kota Kinabalu, Kuala Lumpur, Kuwait, London, Los Angeles, Melbourne, Muscat, Osaka, Paris, Port Moresby, Riyadh, San Francisco, Seoul, Singapore, Sydney, Taipei, Tokyo and Xiamen. Joint services on specific routes with Air Niugini, Bouraq Indonesia, Egyptair, Korean Air and Kuwait Airways. Code-

share with Trans World. Plans to add Shanghai plus more destinations in Japan.

Annual revenue: $1,020 million
Passengers: 6.9 million
Cargo: 140,000 tonnes
Employees: 14,125
Shareholders: PR Holdings (67 per cent – 51 per cent owned by chairman Lucio Tan), and Philippine government (33 per cent)

From 1989, Fokker 50s replaced Shorts 360s and BAC One-Elevens on domestic services.

Fleet development: Four Airbus A340-200s to be delivered by end of 1996. Large order placed in December 1995 for four **A340-300**s, eight **A330-300**s, 12 **A320-200**s and eight Boeing 747-400s, deliveries scheduled from mid-1997.

Philippine Airlines fleet

Airbus A300B4-100	c/n	RP-C4007	25996/2488	Boeing 747-200B Combi	
RP-C3001	063	EI-BZE	24464/1753	EI-BTS	22381/500
RP-C3002	069	EI-BZF	24465/1755		
		EI-BZH	24546/1811	Boeing 747-400	c/n
Airbus A300B4-200	c/n	EI-BZI	24547/1813	N751PR	27261/1005
RP-C3003	125	EI-BZJ	24677/1837	N752PR	27262/1012
RP-C3004	203	EI-BZK	24678/1853	N753PR	27828/1039
RP-C3005	219	EI-BZL	24680/1927		
RP-C3006	222	EI-BZM	24681/1929	Fokker 50	c/n
EI-CEB	240	EI-BZN	24770/1941	PH-PRA	20128
F-OHPA	234			PH-PRB	20138
F-OHPB	235	Boeing 747-200B	c/n	PH-PRC	20146
F-OHPC	304	RP-C5746	21943/475	PH-PRD	20147
F-OHPD	305	EI-BZA	22496/540	PH-PRE	20151
		N207AE	21516/326	PH-PRF	20152
Airbus A300C4-200	c/n	N208AE	21517/368	PH-PRG	20155
EI-BZB	083	N741PR	21832/421	PH-PRH	20200
		N742PR	21833/423	PH-PRI	20201
Boeing 737-300	c/n	N743PR	21834/425	PH-PRJ	20212
RP-C4005	24060/1519	N744PR	22382/498		
RP-C4006	24059/1517				

QANTAS Airways (QF/QFA)

Sydney (Kingsford Smith) Airport
Mascot, New South Wales, Australia

History: Founded 16 November 1920 as Queensland and Northern Territory Aerial Services with **Avro 504K** and **Bristol Fighter**. First scheduled flight 2 November 1922 from Charleville to Cloncurry, via Longreach. Built own **DH.50** fleet, established flying schools at Brisbane and Longreach and commenced Flying Doctor Service. Qantas Empire Airways (QEA) formed 18 January 1934 jointly with Imperial Airways (later BOAC) to operate Brisbane-

Singapore sector of England-Australia Empire air service. First mail service inaugurated 10 December 1934 and flown mostly with **DH.86**, replaced 5 July 1938 by through service with new **Short S.23 Empire** flying-boat. Passengers carried on route for first time 17 April 1935.

Services to England were interrupted during World War II. Australia-England service suspended in 1942, but resumed again in July 1943, rerouted from

Ceylon to Perth. Original route via Singapore recommenced 4 October 1945. Own 'Kangaroo Route' through to London opened 1 December 1947. Rapid post-war expansion, both regionally and to Hong Kong, Thailand and South Africa, with **DC-4**, **Short Sandringham** flying-boats and four new **Lockheed L.749 Constellation**, ordered in October 1946. First **L.1049C** delivered 15 April 1954 and operated inaugural Southern Cross service to San

QANTAS Airways

Annual Group revenue: $5,350 million
Passengers: 16.05 million
Cargo: 287,000 tonnes
Employees: 28,950

Francisco one month later. Service extended 14 January 1958 to New York and London – world's first round-the-world service. **Lockheed Electra** and **Boeing 707-138** introduced in 1959, but replaced in 1968 when delivery of 21 larger **707-338Cs** completed. Name changed to Qantas Airways Ltd 1 August 1967, and order placed for four **Boeing 747-200Bs** in October. First 747 service 17 September 1971 to Singapore. Transition to all-747 fleet completed by 1979. Two **747SPs** added in 1981 and initial **747-300** in November 1984. In October 1985, **767-200ER** introduced on thinner local routes, and 16 August 1989 first **747-400** set new world record flying London-Sydney route non-stop in 20 hours 8 minutes. Purchased Australian Airlines in September 1992, merging two operations in October 1993 under single brand name of Qantas Australian Airline. In March 1993, British Airways purchased 25 per cent stake in Qantas and 75 per cent government holding floated on

Until the introduction of the Boeing 767 in 1985, QANTAS had operated an all-747 fleet.

Australian Stock Exchange 31 July 1995.

Qantas Airways today: Operates domestic and international services to 92 destinations in 24 countries. Asia/Pacific destinations include Auckland, Bangkok, Beijing, Christchurch, Denpasar, Fukuoka, Ho Chi Minh City, Hong Kong, Honiara, Honolulu, Jakarta, Kuala Lumpur, Los Angeles, Mt Hagen, Manila, Nadi, Nagoya, Noumea, Osaka, Papeete, Port Moresby, Sapporo, Seoul, Singapore, Taipei (flown by Australia-Asia Airlines), Tokyo and Wellington. Destinations in North America are Boston, Chicago, Los Angeles, New York, San Francisco, Toronto, Vancouver and Washington DC, all except Los Angeles flown on code-share agreement with American Airlines. Frankfurt, Rome and London served in Europe. African points are Harare and Johannesburg.

Fleet development: One **737-400** order for delivery in November 1996, together with one more **767-300ERs** due in August 1996. Options held for 19 747-400s, one 737-400 and two 767-300ERs.

Associate carriers: Holds 19.9 per cent stake in Air New Zealand and 17.5 per cent in Fijian carrier Air Pacific, and major marketing alliances with British Airways and associates, Canadian Airlines International, American Airlines and USAir. Taiwan flights operated by subsidiary **Australia-Asia Airlines** with 747SP. Domestic cargo flown by **Australian air Express** (AaE), joint venture company formed in August 1992 with Australia Post.

Also operates number of wholly-owned regional airlines. **Airlink**, based at Brisbane, serves southeastern Queensland area. Established Western Australia network centred on Perth 14 November 1994. Fleet made up of four **BAe 146-100**, three **146-200** and two **146-300** models.

Eastern Australia Airlines, based in Sydney, operates to 15 points along East Coast of Queensland and New South Wales, and to Lord Howe Island,

QANTAS Airways fleet

Airbus A300B4-200 c/n		Boeing 737-400 c/n		Boeing 747-200B c/n		VH-OJH	(24806/807)	VH-EAQ	(23896/183)
VH-TAA	(134)	VH-TJE	(24430/1820)	VH-EBQ	(22145/410)	VH-OJI	(24887/826)	VH-E	
VH-TAC	(157)	VH-TJF	(24431/1863)	VH-EBR	(22614/464)	VH-OJJ	(24974/835)		
VH-TAD	(196)	VH-TJG	(24432/1879)	VH-EBS	(22616/543)	VH-OJK	(25067/857)	**Boeing 767-300ER c/n**	
VH-TAE	(218)	VH-TJH	(24433/1881)	VH-ECB	(21977/409)	VH-OJL	(25151/865)	VH-OGA	(24146/231)
		VH-TJI	(24434/1912)	VH-ECC	(22615/483)	VH-OJM	(25245/875)	VH-OGB	(24316/242)
Boeing 737-300 c/n		VH-TJJ	(24435/1959)			VH-OJN	(25315/883)	VH-OGC	(24317/246)
VH-TAF	(23477/1225)	VH-TJK	(24436/1998)	**Boeing 747-300 c/n**		VH-OJO	(25544/894)	VH-OGD	(24407/247)
VH-TAG	(23478/1251)	VH-TJL	(24437/2162)	VH-EBT	(23222/602)	VH-OJP	(25545/916)	VH-OGE	(24531/278)
VH-TAH	(23479/1259)	VH-TJM	(24438/2171)	VH-EBU	(23223/606)	VH-OJQ	(25546/924)	VH-OGF	(24853/319)
VH-TAI	(23483/1264)	VH-TJN	(24439/2265)	VH-EBV	(23224/610)	VH-OJR	(25547/936)	VH-OGG	(24929/343)
VH-TAJ	(23484/1270)	VH-TJO	(24440/2324)	VH-EBW	(23408/638)			VH-OGH	(24930/344)
VH-TAK	(23485/1277)	VH-TJP	(24441/2363)	VH-EBX	(23688/662)	**Boeing 747SP c/n**		VH-OGI	(25246/387)
VH-TAU	(23486/1286)	VH-TJQ	(24442/2371)	VH-EBY	(23823/678)	VH-EAA	(22495/505)	VH-OGJ	(25274/396)
VH-TAV	(23487/1306)	VH-TJR	(24443/2398)			VH-EAB	(22672/537)	VH-OGK	(25316/397)
VH-TAW	(23488/1352)	VH-TJS	(24444/2454)	**Boeing 747-400 c/n**				VH-OGL	(25363/402)
VH-TAX	(23489/1356)	VH-TJT	(24445/2539)	VH-OJA	(24354/731)	**Boeing 767-200ER c/n**		VH-OGM	(25575/451)
VH-TAY	(23490/1390)	VH-TJU	(24446/2569)	VH-OJB	(24373/746)	VH-EAJ	(23304/119)	VH-OGN	(25576/549)
VH-TAZ	(23491/1391)	VH-TJW	(26961/2517)	VH-OJC	(24406/757)	VH-EAK	(23305/120)	VH-OGO	(25577/550)
VH-TJA	(24295/1649)	VH-TJX	(28150/)	VH-OJD	(24481/764)	VH-EAL	(23306/125)		
VH-TJB	(24296/1653)			VH-OJE	(24482/765)	VH-EAM	(23309/129)		
VH-TJC	(24297/1740)			VH-OJF	(24483/781)	VH-EAN	(23402/133)		
VH-TJD	(24298/1761)			VH-OJG	(24779/801)	VH-EAO	(23403/137)		

with fleet of six **DHC-8-100**s, one **DHC-8-200** and four **BAe Jetstream 31**s.

Southern Australia Airlines flies three **DHC-8-100**s and two **Cessna 404 Titan**s on network from Melbourne and Mildura, and **Sunstate Airlines** operates four **DHC-8-100**s, six **Shorts 360**s and five **DHC-6-300**s within Queensland from Brisbane.

QANTAS acquired its first 747-300 in 1984 and now operates six, all configured for 396 seats.

Reno Air (QQ/ROA)

Cannon International Airport
Reno, Nevada, USA

History: Incorporated in June 1990 and started commercial flight operations 1 July 1992, offering full service schedule to West Coast markets through Reno, with single leased **MD-82**. Initial north-south route structure incorporated Los Angeles, Ontario, Portland, San Diego, San Francisco and Seattle. Expansion continued with establishment in June 1993 of second hub at San Jose, California, replacing American Airlines in several markets. Chicago service eventually introduced. Fleet grown to five MD-80s by end of 1992 and to 17 MD-80s by January 1994. Two leased **MD-90**s delivered in March 1996.

Reno Air today: Frequent full-service scheduled operations from Pacific northwest to southern California centred on Reno and San Jose hubs. Destinations are Chicago-O'Hare, Colorado Springs, Las Vegas, Los Angeles, Ontario, Orange County, Phoenix, Portland, San Diego, Seattle, South Lake Tahoe and Tucson. Marketing alliance with American Airlines.

Annual revenue: $195 million
Passengers: 3.4 million
Employees: 1,500

This Reno Air MD-90 has gained an additional 'Orange County Flyer' logo to mark the Nevada-based airline's services to California.

Reno Air fleet

McDonnell Douglas MD-82/83	c/n			McDonnell Douglas MD-87	c/n
N821RA	49931/1754	N841RA	49421/1263	N751RA	49779/1670
N822RA	49932/1756	N842RA	49604/1456	N752RA	49780/1674
N823RA	49889/1761	N843RA	49615/1543	N753RA	49587/1541
N824RA	53017/1797	N871RA	49788/1637	N754RA	49641/1617
N832RA	53044/1776	N872RA	49793/1656		
N833RA	53045/1777	N873RA	53093/2066	**McDonnell Douglas**	
N834RA	53124/1991	N875RA	53182/2068	**MD90-30**	c/n
N836RA	53046/1794	N876RA	53183/2071	N901RA	53489/
N840RA	49424/1284	N878RA	53184/2088	N902RA	53490/
		N879RA	53185/2090		
		N880RA	53186/2092		

Royal Air Maroc (AT/RAM)

Mohammed V International Airport
Casablanca, Morocco

History: Established 8 June 1953 through amalgamation of Société Air Atlas and Air Maroc, formed by private investors in 1947. New company known as Compagnie Cherifienne de Transports Aeriens (CGTA), operating a fleet of two **DC-4**s (a third added

later that year), five **DC-3**s, four **Curtiss C-46A**s and six **S.O.30P Bretagne**s. In addition to domestic routes, served Algiers and destinations in France. Briefly under control of French Line steamship company, until majority 55 per cent transferred to government

28 June 1957, following independence. Airline renamed Royal Air Maroc and designated national flag-carrier of new Kingdom of Morocco. Prior to replacing DC-4 with four **L.049 Constellation**s, leased from Air France 1958, ordered three **Caravelle III**s and

Royal Air Maroc

Two 46-seat ATR42-300s remain in the Royal Air Maroc fleet. They replaced F27s on domestic services from Casablanca.

Bamako, Cairo, Conakry, Dakar, Damascus, Dhahran, Jeddah, Kuwait, Las Palmas de Gran Canarias, Libreville, Malabo, Montreal, New York, Nouak-chott, Oran, Rio de Janeiro, Riyadh and Tunis. Joint flights with Air France, Iberia and Tunisair.

began Casablanca-Paris jet service 20 May 1960. Network extended southwards to Bamako, Mali in July 1961. European network extended to Germany, Spain and Italy. Royal Air Inter set up as subsidiary in early 1970 to take over domestic opera-tions. Began flying 2 April with two **Fokker F27-600s**. In same year RAM took delivery of first of four **Boeing 727-200s**. **707-320B** leased from Air France 31 March 1975, pending delivery of its own aircraft, which were used to open transatlantic service to New York and to Middle East. Fleet reinforced in 1978 with **747-200B** and in 1986 with two **757-200s**. Further modernisation put in place between 1989 and 1993 with acquisition of three **ATR42-300s** for domestic routes, and **Boeing 737-400** and **-500** models for European services. Entered into wide-ranging co-operation with Air France in October 1993, including lease of **Boeing 747-400**.

Royal Air Maroc today: National flag-carrier providing scheduled passenger and cargo services from Casablanca to 50 destinations in 31 countries, with another 13 points served within Morocco, including the busy Casablanca-Marrakech and Agadir routes. In addition to strong European network, also serves Abidjan, Abu Dhabi, Algiers,

Annual revenue: $490 million
Passengers: 2.2 million
Cargo: 25,000 tonnes
Employees: 5,360
Ownership: Moroccan government remains as major shareholder with 92.7 per cent

Fleet development: 10 outstanding 737-400 orders have been deferred for two years.

Royal Air Maroc fleet

AI(R) ATR42-300	c/n	Boeing 737-200C Adv	c/n	CN-RMW	25364/2166
CN-CDU	134	CN-RMM	23049/951	CN-RMY	26525/2209
CN-CDV	137	CN-RMN	23050/975	CN-RNB	26527/2472
				CN-RNG	27679/2734
Boeing 727-200 Advanced		**Boeing 737-400**	c/n		
CN-RMO	21297/1236	CN-RMF	24807/1880	**Boeing 747-200B Combi**	
CN-RMP	21298/1246	CN-RMG	24808/1888	CN-RME	21615/338
CN-RMQ	21299/1247	CN-RMX	26526/2219		
CN-RMR	22377/1633	CN-RNA	26531/2453	**Boeing 747-400**	c/n
		CN-RNC	26529/2584	CN-RGA	25629/956
Boeing 737-200 Advanced		CN-RND	26530/2588		
CN-RMI	21214/449	CN-RNF	27678/2733	**Boeing 757-200**	c/n
CN-RMJ	21215/452			CN-RMT	23686/103
CN-RMK	21216/456	**Boeing 737-500**	c/n	CN-RMZ	23687/106
CN-RML	22767/851	CN-RMV	25317/2157		

Royal Jordanian Airlines (RJ/RJA) Queen Alia Airport
Amman, Jordan

History: Established by Royal Decree 8 December 1963 as Alia, so named after King's daughter, meaning 'high and exalted one'. Started operations 15 December 1963 with one **DC-7** and two **Handley Page Heralds**. First external services to Beirut, Cairo and Kuwait followed in July 1965 by Rome with first of three **Caravelle 10R** jets. Growth curtailed by June 1967 war when two DC-7s were destroyed, and by subsequent Israeli occupation of West Bank. Stock purchased by government in March 1968. Major step taken in 1971 with introduction of two **Boeing 707-320Cs**, but opera-tions frequently disrupted by

uneasy political climate and another war in October 1973. Three-year technical and man-agement assistance provided by PIA. Routes and fleet expanded with addition of two **Boeing 720Bs** in 1972, three **727-200s** in 1974 and two **747-200Bs** in 1977, latter used to open service to New York. Four years later first of eight **L1011-500 TriStars** entered service, supplemented between 1987 and 1990 by six **Airbus A310-300s** on European routes. Name changed from Alia to Royal Jordanian Airlines in December 1986. **A320-200s**, acquired in 1990, enabled conver-sion of **707** to freighters and gradual replacement of 727 fleet.

Royal Jordanian today: National flag-carrier operating international passenger and cargo services from capital Amman to destinations in Middle East, Europe, Southeast Asia, North Africa and North America. In addition to Middle East network and domestic Amman-Aqaba route, serves Amsterdam, Ankara, Athens, Bangkok, Berlin, Brussels, Cairo, Calcutta, Casablanca, Colombo, Frankfurt, Geneva, Istanbul, Jakarta, Karachi, Kuala Lumpur, Larnaca, London, Madrid, Montreal, New York, Paris, Rome, Singapore, Toronto, Tunis and Vienna. Osaka to be added to network in 1996. Maintains joint service

Royal Jordanian ordered six A340s, but their delivery coincided with the outbreak of the Gulf War in 1990, and three were cancelled as a result.

with Malaysia Airlines on Amman-Kuala Lumpur route.

Annual revenue: *$400 million*
Passengers: *1.25 million*
Cargo: *55,000 tonnes*
Employees: *4,970*
Ownership: *Wholly-owned by Jordanian government, but privatisation seen as best solution to reverse increasing losses. Now expected to start with commercialisation, leading to partial privatisation by 1998*

Fleet development: Letter of intent signed for five **Airbus A340**s, but **Boeing 777** and **McDonnell Douglas MD-11** also considered for future replacement of TriStars.

Associate carriers: Wholly-owned subsidiary **Arab Wings**, established in 1975 to provide executive charter services throughout region. Operates two **Rockwell 75A Sabreliner** jets and **Cessna 340A**.

New subsidiary **Royal Wings** formed 1 January 1996 to provide first direct service between Jordan and Israel, following signing of bilateral agreement in October 1995. In addition to Amman-Tel Aviv, will fly to Aqaba, and eventually to Beirut and Cairo. Operates a single **DHC-8-300**.

Royal Jordanian Airlines fleet

Airbus A310-200	c/n	F-OGYB	088	Boeing 727-200 Advanced	
7T-VJF	306	F-OGYC	569	JY-AFU	22269/1701
				JY-AFV	22270/1709
Airbus A310-300	c/n	Boeing 707-320C	c/n		
F-ODVF	445	JY-AJK	18948/495	Lockheed L.1011	
F-ODVG	490	JY-AJM	19590/654	TriStar 500	c/n
F-ODVH	491	JY-AJN	20720/874	JY-AGA	1217
F-ODVI	531	JY-AJO	20723/879	JY-AGB	1219
				JY-AGC	1220
Airbus A320-200	c/n			JY-AGD	1229
F-OGYA	087			JY-AGE	1238

Ryanair (RY/RYR)

Dublin Airport
Dublin, Ireland

History: Founded in May 1985 and began operations with service between Waterford and London-Gatwick. Initial fleet comprised single **EMB-110P1 Bandeirante**, but quickly supplemented with two **HS 748** and first **BAC One-Eleven**, which became standard equipment. Operations transferred to Luton Airport and further Irish points added to network. Three **ATR42-200**s added in 1988/89 and more ordered, then cancelled. Services between Ireland and UK grew rapidly, forcing radical restructuring in February 1991. Fleet standardised on **Boeing 737-200** and routes cut from 18 to nine. Significant portion of flights transferred to London-Stansted from 29 April 1991.

Ryanair today: Leading Irish independent airline offering low-fare no-frills service between Irish Republic and UK, with hubs at Dublin, Cork and London-Stansted. Services link Dublin to Birmingham, Glasgow, Liverpool, London-Gatwick/Stansted, Luton, Manchester and Prestwick.

Stansted also served from Cork and Knock. Scheduled expansion into Europe planned for 1996, charters already operated.

Annual revenue: *$125 million*
Passengers: *2.3 million*
Employees: *620*
Major shareholders: *Declan Ryan and Cathal Ryan. In July 1996 20 per cent stake (valued at £11.2 million) sold to US consortium headed by David Binderman through Irish company Air LP*

Associate carrier: Set up in 1995 **Ryanair UK** to provide London-Stansted/Prestwick

Ryanair operates a fleet of Boeing 737-200s on low-cost services from Ireland to the UK.

service and plans to enter the UK-Europe market during 1996. Operates single Boeing 737-200.

Ryanair fleet

Boeing 737-200			
Advanced	c/n	EI-CJH	22057/621
EI-CJC	22640/867	EI-CJI	22875/917
EI-CJD	22966/946	EI-CKP	22296/668
EI-CJE	22639/863	EI-CKQ	22906/888
EI-CJF	22967/953	EI-CKR	22025/647
EI-CJG	22058/629	EI-CKS	22023/636

SABENA (SN/SAB)

SABENA operates a mixed fleet of Boeing 737-200/-300/-400/-500s in parallel with subsidiary Sobelair.

shareholding and took over operation of newly-delivered **A340**, but alliance not success and ended prior to Swissair acquiring 49.5 per cent holding in 1995.

SABENA today: National flag-carrier linking Brussels with 81 destinations in 47 countries, with strong emphasis on Europe and West Africa. Outside Europe and Africa serves only Atlanta, Boston, Chicago and Tokyo in Japan. Block-space agreements with Air France and Delta Air Lines.

Annual Group revenue: $1,850 million
Passengers: 4.3 million
Cargo: 90,000 tonnes
Employees: 9,500
Shareholding: divided between government and Swissair with 49.5 per cent and Swissair with 49.5 per cent, with an option to increase this to controlling interest in 2000, if permitted

Associate carriers: Swissair, through equity partnership.

Wholly-owned subsidiary **Sobelair** (S3), founded 30 July 1946, undertakes *ad hoc* and charter services with fleet of three **737-200s**, one **737-300**, three **737-400s**, and one **767-300**. Is taking 40 per cent stake in **TEA of Switzerland**.

Has 79 per cent shareholding in regional airline **Delta Air Transport** (**DAT**), founded 1967, which links Brussels and Antwerp with 23 European cities. Fleet comprises eight **BAe 146-200s**, 10 **EMB-120s**, eight **Fokker F28s** and four **Avro RJ85s**, with another 19 order.

History: Founded 23 May 1923 as Société Anonyme Belge d'Exploitation de la Navigation Aérienne, more commonly known as SABENA. Began operations on same day with newspaper and mail flights over Brussels-Ostend-Lympne route, using **de Havilland DH.9**. First passengers carried with **Handley Page W.8e** on Rotterdam-Brussels-Basle route 14 July 1924. Fleet augmented by small numbers of **Junkers F 13, DH.50, Fokker F.II** and locally-built **W.8f**, and from 1929 by **Fokker F.VIIIb-3m**. The first Brussels-Leopoldville service inaugurated 23 February 1935. Main fleet comprised progressively **Fokker F.VIIIa** (1931) and **Junkers Ju 52/3m** (1938), while **Savoia-Marchetti S.73** (1936) and **S.83** (1938) introduced on routes between Belgium and Africa. **DC-3** acquired in 1939 for growing European network. When war came to Belgium 10 May 1940, most of fleet managed to escape, although several were later shot down or seized when under military orders. Operations shifted to Africa in support of Allied war effort. At end of war, fleet comprised eight **Lockheed L.14 Super Electra**s and **L.18 Lodestar**s, four **Ju 52/3m**s and one DC-3. Congo link re-established 8 July 1945. European services restored from December 1945 with DC-3s, **DC-4** (first introduced in January 1946) and three **DC-6**s delivered in summer 1947. Transatlantic link to New York opened 4 June 1947 and DC-6 also put on Johannesburg service. **Convair 240** entered service in March 1949, followed by **440** and **DC-7C** in 1956. Jets came in January 1960 with **Boeing 707-370**s, then **Caravelle VIR** in February 1961 and **727-100** in April 1967. First **Boeing 747** service Brussels-New York 8 January 1971. Fleet modernised with **737-200 Advanced**, first delivered in April 1974, while addition of flights to Toronto, Lomé, Cotonou and Niamey in 1987 coincided with arrival of **Airbus A310-300**. Newer **737-300** added in August 1987, followed by **737-500** in September 1991. In April 1992 Air France bought 37.5 per cent

SABENA Belgian World Airways fleet

Airbus A310-200	c/n	Airbus A340-300	c/n	OO-SDO	21177/433	OO-SYA	24355/1709	OO-SYJ	26537/2296
OO-SCA	303	F-GNID	047			OO-SYB	24356/1711	OO-SYK	26358/2298
OO-SCB	313	F-GNIE	051	**Boeing 737-200C Adv**					
OO-SCI	331			OO-SDJ	20915/401	**Boeing 737-400**	c/n	**Boeing 747-200B Combi**	
		Boeing 737-200 Adv		OO-SDK	20916/403	OO-SYC	25226/2104	F-GCBB	22272/463
Airbus A310-300	c/n	OO-SDA	20907/351	OO-SDP	21139/437	OO-SYD	25247/2106		
OO-SCC	437	OO-SDD	20910/358	OO-SDR	21738/576	OO-SYF	25248/2120	**Boeing 747-300 Combi**	
		OO-SDE	20911/360					OO-SGC	23439/646
Airbus A340-200	c/n	OO-SDF	20912/365	**Boeing 737-300**	c/n	**Boeing 737-500**	c/n	OO-SGD	24837/810
F-GNIB	014	OO-SDG	21135/418	OO-SDV	23771/1430	OO-SYE	25218/2111		
F-GNIC	022	OO-SDL	21136/420	OO-SDW	23772/1432	OO-SYG	25249/2145	**Douglas DC-10-30**	c/n
		OO-SDM	21137/421	OO-SDX	23773/1441	OO-SYH	25418/2163	OO-SLG	47926/170
		OO-SDN	21176/431	OO-SDY	23774/1443	OO-SYI	25419/2165	OO-SLH	47927/190

SAS (SK/SAS)

History: Founded 1 August 1946 when consortium agreement signed by Det Danske Luftfartselskab (Denmark), Det Norske Luftfartselskap (Norway), and AB Aerotransport and Svensk Interkontinental Lufttrafik AB (Sweden). Individual constituent companies' histories went back as far as 1918. First flight in SAS colours operated 17 September 1946 serving New York with **Douglas DC-4**. SAS operations initially split into OSAS (Overseas SAS) and ESAS (European SAS), but combined 8 February 1951 into single entity. Network extended to South America in November 1946 (Montevideo and later Buenos Aires), eastwards in 1949 (Bangkok), and to Nairobi three years later. Fleet included 12 **DC-6**s (ordered in 1946), nine DC-4s, 26 **DC-3**s, six **Saab Scandia**s, two **Shorts Sandringham**s and two float-equipped Junkers **Ju52/3m**s. In November 1954 inaugurated scheduled service over North Pole to US West Coast. Fourteen **DC-7C 'Seven Seas'** and 11 **Convair 440**s ordered in next stage of modernisation. DC-7C put into service 8 September 1956. **DC-8-33** jets, ordered 20 December 1955, entered service to New York and Los Angeles in 1960, followed by polar short-cut to Tokyo, first introduced in 1957. Participated in establishment of Thai Airways in 1959. Added 12 **Caravelle**s delivered between 1959 and 1966. 1967 notable for introduction of ultra-long-range **DC-8-62** and short-haul **DC-9-21/-32** models. Ten-year KSSU co-operation agreement signed in February 1970 between KLM, SAS, Swissair and UTA of France, to standardise specifications on new aircraft, including **Boeing 747-200B** put on New York route in 1971 and **Douglas DC-10-30** added in October 1974. Sixteen **DC-9-41**s acquired in largest-ever single order, signed in January 1973 for $106 million. Fleet eventually totalled 40 of type. DC-10-30 was replaced by **Boeing 767**

Two SAS MD-80s adopted this special scheme during 1996 – one blue, one red. Many airlines claim such schemes boost traffic.

from 1989, and DC-9 fleet by large numbers of **MD-80** from mid-1980s. Domestic subsidiary ***Linjeflyg*** integrated into SAS 1 January 1993, together with its **Fokker F28**s and **737-500**s. Period of losses, and collapse in November 1993 of attempt to merge with Austrian Airlines, KLM and Swissair into mega-carrier under Alcazar Project, led to major restructuring, including divestment of investments in Continental Airlines and LAN Chile. 1995 co-operation agreement with Lufthansa given go-ahead by European Commission in January 1996.

SAS today: Tri-national Scandinavian flag-carrier operating domestic and international services from three hubs at Copenhagen, Oslo and Stockholm. Network encompasses more than 100 destinations in 34 countries, with long-haul flights serving Bangkok, Beijing, Chicago, Delhi, Hong Kong, New York-Newark, Osaka, Rio de Janeiro, São Paulo, Seattle, Singapore and Tokyo. New services to be inaugurated in 1996 to Houston, New York-JFK, San Francisco and Washington, DC. Major strategic alliance with Lufthansa. Code-share or connecting flights

The Fokker 50s of Scandanavian Commuter feed the primary international services of SAS.

with Air New Zealand, British Midland, Continental Airlines, Icelandair, Qantas, Thai International and Varig. Joint flights and code-shares with European Quality Alliance partners Austrian Airlines and Swissair.

Annual Group revenue: $5,365 million
Passengers: 19.0 million
Cargo: 130,000 tonnes
Employees: 20,900
Shareholding: divided between AB Aerotransport, Sweden (42.8 per cent), Det Danske Luftfartselskab, Denmark (28.6 per cent) and Det Norske Luftfartselskap, Norway (28.6 per cent), all three being owned 50 per cent by their respective governments

Fleet development: Total of 35 **Boeing 737-600**s ordered in March 1995 for delivery between 1998 and 2000. Six more ordered in October 1995. Hushkitting of remaining DC-9 fleet to be completed by January 1997. Initiating study into its fleet requirements by 2000. Needs 10-20 long-range aircraft with 250-300 seats, five with 180-200 seats, and up to 50

SAS Scandanavian Airlines System

SAS inherited its F28 fleet from domestic airline Linjeflyg, which was absorbed in 1993.

regional jets, between 2000 and 2015. If Boeing 767 is retained, could add some **Boeing 777** or **McDonnell Douglas MD-11 Combi**s, while an all-Airbus re-equipment would involve **A330-200, A340-300** and **A321**. Deliveries to start in 1999. Eight **MD90-30**s on order, first deliveries in mid 1996.

Associate carriers: Has 40 per cent stake in Airlines of Britain, parent of **British Midland** and one-third share in **Greenlandair (Grönlandsfly)** (GL), founded 7 November 1960. Provides domestic services and charters within Greenland, using four **DHC-7**s and two **DHC-6-300**s, together with 20 helicopters. Also owns 49 per cent of Spanish holiday airline **Spanair** (JK).

Wholly-owns **SAS Commuter**, founded 24 September 1989, which operates Norlink and Eurolink services inter-Scandinavian, domestic and Northern European routes with fleet of 22 **Fokker 50**s.

SAS Scandanavian Airlines System fleet

Boeing 767-200

Reg	c/n
LN-RCF	26546/
SE-DKP	24727/301
SE-DKY	26545/

Boeing 767-300(ER)

Reg	c/n
LN-RCD	24847/315
LN-RCE	24846/309
LN-RCG	24475/273
LN-RCH	24318/257
LN-RCI	24476/274
LN-RCK	24729/358
LN-RCL	25365/395
OY-KDH	24358/263
OY-KDL	24477/337
OY-KDM	25088/359
OY-KDN	24848/325
OY-KDO	24849/330
SE-DOC	26544/412

Douglas DC-9-41

Reg	c/n
LN-RLA	47599/716
LN-RLH	47748/855
LN-RLN	47630/745
LN-RLP	47778/897
LN-RLS	47623/728
LN-RLT	47626/738
LN-RLX	47513/679
LN-RLZ	47634/756
OY-KGL	47597/713
OY-KGM	47624/733
OY-KGN	47628/740
OY-KGO	47632/748
OY-KGP	47646/755
OY-KGR	47725/831
OY-KGS	47766/886
SE-DAR	47596/714
SE-DAS	47610/725
SE-DAU	47627/739
SE-DAW	47629/744
SE-DAX	47631/743
SE-DBM	47633/752
SE-DDP	47747/839
SE-DDR	47750/870
SE-DDS	47777/896
SE-DDT	47779/898

Fokker F28-1000 Fellowship

Reg	c/n
SE-DGA	11067
SE-DGB	11068
SE-DGC	11069

Fokker F28-4000 Fellowship

Reg	c/n
SE-DGE	11112
SE-DGF	11115
SE-DGG	11116
SE-DGH	11120
SE-DGI	11122
SE-DGK	11123
SE-DGL	11126
SE-DGM	11128
SE-DGN	11130
SE-DGO	11190
SE-DGP	11191
SE-DGR	11204
SE-DGS	11236
SE-DGT	11239
SE-DGU	11241
SE-DGX	11225

McDonnell Douglas MD-81/82/83

Reg	c/n
LN-RLE	49382/1232
LN-RLF	49383/1236
LN-RLG	49423/1283
LN-RLR	49437/1345
LN-RMA	49554/1379
LN-RMD	49555/1402
LN-RMF	49556/1415
LN-RMJ	49912/1659
LN-RML	53002/1835
LN-RMM	53005/1855
LN-RMN	53295/1922
LN-RMO	53315/1947
LN-RMS	53368/2003
LN-RMT	53001/1815
OY-KGT	49380/1225
OY-KGY	49420/1254
OY-KGZ	49381/1231
OY-KHC	49436/1303
OY-KHE	49604/1456
OY-KHG	49613/1519
OY-KHK	49910/1638
OY-KHL	49911/1653
OY-KHM	49914/1693
OY-KHN	53000/1812
OY-KHP	53007/1882
OY-KHR	53275/1896
OY-KHT	53296/1937
OY-KIG	48006/966
OY-KIH	48007/971
OY-KII	48008/981
SE-DFR	49422/1264
SE-DFS	49384/1237
SE-DFT	49385/1244
SE-DFU	49421/1263
SE-DFX	49424/1284
SE-DFY	49438/1353
SE-DIA	49603/1442
SE-DID	49615/1543
SE-DII	49909/1625
SE-DIK	49728/1553
SE-DIL	49913/1665
SE-DIN	49999/1803
SE-DIR	53004/1846
SE-DIS	53006/1869
SE-DIX	49998/1800
SE-DIY	53008/1895
SE-DIZ	53294/1917
SE-DMB	53314/1946
SE-DMD	53347/1979
SE-DME	53366/1999
SE-DMY	48010/992
SE-DMZ	48009/985
SE-DPI	49557/1436

McDonnell Douglas MD-87

Reg	c/n
LN-RMG	49611/1522
LN-RMH	49612/1827
LN-RMK	49610/1705
LN-RMP	53337/1962
LN-RMU	53340/1967
LN-RMX	49585/1457
LN-RMY	49586/1472
OY-KHF	49609/1517
OY-KHI	49614/1556
OY-KHU	53336/1953
OY-KHW	53348/1985
SE-DIB	49605/1501
SE-DIC	49607/1512
SE-DIF	49606/1569
SE-DIH	49608/1572
SE-DIP	53010/1921
SE-DIU	53011/1931
SE-DMA	53009/1916

McDonnell Douglas MD90-30

Reg	c/n
LN-ROA	53459/2141
OY-KIL	53458/2140
SE-DMF	53457/2135

Saudia (SV/SVA)

King Abdul Aziz International Airport
Jeddah, Saudi Arabia

History: Established 27 May 1945 with gift of one **DC-3** presented to King Abdul Aziz by US President Roosevelt. Full name Saudi Arabian Airlines. Started operation under that name 14 March 1947 with Jeddah-Dhahran service, after acquisition of more DC-3 aircraft. First international route opened 10 June to Damascus. Fleet supplemented with first of five **Bristol 170 Freighter**s 28 June 1940 and four **Lockheed Lodestar**s 15 May 1950, but operated little. **Douglas DC-4** placed on trans-Arabian trunk route in June 1952. Intermittent regional services until introduction of pressurised **Convair 340** on Jeddah-Riyadh-Dhahran-Beirut link 23 June 1954. Two **Boeing 720B** jets put on main routes 15 March 1962, and 3 March 1964 two **DC-6**s acquired to provide additional freight capacity. In 1965 expanded network to Karachi and Bombay, followed by link between eastern and western sector of Arab world with service 20 February

Saudia introduced this new blue, yellow and gold scheme in September 1996, replacing the long-lived green and white colours of previous decades.

1967 from Jeddah to Rabat, via Beirut, Tripoli and Tunis. First route to Europe, serving Geneva, Frankfurt and London, inaugurated 1 May 1967. Fleet augmented with three **DC-9-15**s, put on domestic trunk routes 4 March 1967, and first of 16 **Boeing 707-320** which went into service 15 January 1968. Adopted Saudia operating name 1 April 1972. **737-200** put into service 12 days later. Also leased many **DC-8** models for cargo flights. **Lockheed L.1011** added on 15 August 1975, augmented by two leased **747-200B**s 1 June 1977. New Jeddah-New York service opened 3 February 1979, flown jointly with Pan American. Routes also added to Far East. Fleet upgraded with **Airbus A300-600** from 14 May 1984 and **747-300** from 12 July 1985. All schedules suspended between 17 January and 4 March 1991, as Saudi Arabian airports closed during Gulf War. Long-overdue fleet modernisation implemented 26 October 1995, with signing of $6 billion contract for 61 US-built aircraft for delivery

Saudia today: Wholly government-owned flag-carrier operating passenger/cargo services to 52 international and 25 domestic destinations from hubs at Riyadh, Jeddah and Dhahran. Apart from services to cities in Arab world of Middle East, and North and Northeast Africa, has scheduled flights to Amsterdam, Athens, Bangkok, Bombay, Colombo, Dakar, Delhi, Dhaka, Frankfurt, Geneva, Istanbul, Jakarta, Kano, Karachi, Kuala Lumpur, Lahore, Larnaca, London, Madras, Manila, Nairobi, New York, Nice, Paris, Rome, Singapore and Washington, DC. Cargo-only flights serve Brussels, Taipei, Milan and Tokyo. Also

operates Royal fleet. Block-space agreement or revenue-sharing with Cyprus Airways, Garuda Indonesia, KLM, Korean Air and Olympic Airways. Operates Dhahran-Bahrain air bridge jointly with Gulf Air.

Annual revenue: $2,250 million
Passengers: 12.0 million

Cargo: 225,000 tonnes
Employees: 24,825

Fleet development: Deliveries begin in 1997 of 61 aircraft, including 23 **Boeing 777-200**s, five 747-400s, 29 **McDonnell Douglas MD90-30**s and four **MD-11F**s. Last delivery scheduled for 2001.

Saudia fleet

Airbus A300-600	c/n				
HZ-AJA	284	HZ-AGQ	21362/511	HZ-AIS	23270/645
HZ-AJB	294	HZ-AGR	21653/531	HZ-AIT	23271/652
HZ-AJC	301	HZ-AGS	21654/532		
HZ-AJD	307	**Boeing 747SP**	c/n	**Lockheed L.1011**	
HZ-AJE	312	HZ-AIF	22503/529	**TriStar 200**	c/n
HZ-AJF	317			HZ-AHA	1110
HZ-AJG	321	**Boeing 747-100**	c/n	HZ-AHB	1116
HZ-AJH	336	HZ-AIA	22498/512	HZ-AHC	1137
HZ-AJI	341	HZ-AIB	22499/517	HZ-AHD	1144
HZ-AJJ	348	HZ-AIC	22500/522	HZ-AHE	1124
HZ-AJK	351	HZ-AID	22501/525	HZ-AHF	1130
		HZ-AIE	22502/530	HZ-AHG	1148
Boeing 737-200		HZ-AIG	22747/551	HZ-AHH	1149
Advanced	c/n	HZ-AIH	22748/555	HZ-AHI	1160
HZ-AGA	20574/294	HZ-AII	22749/557	HZ-AHJ	1161
HZ-AGB	20575/295	N703CK	19727/54	HZ-AHL	1170
HZ-AGC	20576/297	N704CK	20528/191	HZ-AHM	1171
HZ-AGD	20577/298			HZ-AHN	1175
HZ-AGE	20578/299	**Boeing 747-200F**	c/n	HZ-AHO	1187
HZ-AGF	20882/356	HZ-AIU	24359/724	HZ-AHP	1190
HZ-AGG	20883/366			HZ-AHQ	1192
HZ-AGH	21275/467	**Boeing 747-300**	c/n	HZ-AHR	1214
HZ-AGI	21276/468	HZ-AIK	23262/616		
HZ-AGJ	21277/469	HZ-AIL	23263/619	*Plus:*	
HZ-AGK	21280/471	HZ-AIM	23264/620	fleet of **Gulfstream II, III**	
HZ-AGL	21281/472	HZ-AIN	23265/622	and **IV, Cessna Citation II,**	
HZ-AGM	21282/476	HZ-AIO	23266/624	**Beech A100 King Air** and	
HZ-AGN	21283/477	HZ-AIP	23267/630	de Havilland Canada	
HZ-AGO	21360/485	HZ-AIQ	23268/631	**DHC-6-300 Twin Otter** for	
HZ-AGP	21361/488	HZ-AIR	23269/643	executive flights.	

Singapore Airlines (SQ/SIA)

Changi International Airport
Singapore

History: Incorporated 28 January 1972 as national airline, following restructuring of joint Malaysia-Singapore Airlines (MSA). Started operations 1 October 1972 with fleet of 10 aircraft, including five

Boeing 707-320B/Cs and five **737-100**s, serving 22 cities in 18 countries. Prior to that date, ordered two **747-200B**s, first airline in Southeast Asia to acquire new jumbo jet; it entered

service 1 October 1973. Concluded joint venture with KLM in September 1974 for **DC-8** cargo service between to Amsterdam. Paris and Auckland added to passenger network in 1975 and

Singapore Airlines

Singapore Airlines has seen a bitter battle in recent times between Airbus (A340) and Boeing (747-400) to win orders for new long-haul aircraft from this very important airline.

(2.7 per cent owned, 0.6 per cent held by Swissair) and Delta Air Lines (5.0 per cent stake, 2.7 per cent held by Delta). Joint services with Air Niugini, KLM and Vietnam Airlines.

Annual revenue: *$4,600 million*
Passengers: *10 million*
Cargo: *550,000 tonnes*
Employees: *12,550*
Ownership: *Singapore government holds controlling stake of 54 per cent*

SIA won coveted rights to fly to US in December 1977. Announced selection of **727-200** to replace 707s and 737s on regional routes, with total of six acquired in 1977/78. Massive re-equipment resulted in addition of 10 more **747-200B**s, eight **DC-10-30**s and four more 727-200s. Short-lived supersonic **Concorde** service introduced jointly with BOAC to London 9 December 1977. First passenger service to US (San Francisco and Honolulu) inaugurated in April 1979. Following decade noteworthy for additional record purchases, including eight **747-300 'Big Tops'** and six **Airbus A300**s in 1981, and six 747-300s, four **757-200**s and six **A310**s two years later. $3.3 billion order for 20 **747-400 'Megatops'** announced in 1986, extended by

another 30 in 1990. One year later, signed another contract for 20 **Airbus A340-300**s worth $3.4 million. Announced trilateral 'Global Excellence' alliance, including equity swaps, with Swissair and Delta Air Lines in November 1990.

SIA today: Provides extensive scheduled regional and long-haul passenger services to 75 cities in 42 countries, together with large freight network. Long-haul destinations include Amsterdam, Athens, Berlin, Brussels, Cairo, Copenhagen, Chicago, Dallas/Ft Worth, Dhahran, Dubai, Frankfurt, Istanbul, Johannesburg, London, Los Angeles, Madrid, Manchester, New York, Paris, Rome, San Francisco, Vancouver, Vienna and Zurich. Partnership and equity alliance with Swissair

Fleet development: Over years to 2004, fleet will double to more than 150 aircraft. In June 1994, $10.3 billion order placed for 52 aircraft, comprising 30 **A340-300E**s and 22 747-400 'Megatops', of which 10 A340s and 11 747-400s are on firm contract. Option retained to convert some A340s into **A330**s. Followed up 14 November 1995 with $12.7 billion order for 77 Rolls-Royce Trent-powered **Boeing 777**s for delivery between 1997 and 2004. Of 77 aircraft, 34 are firm order, with remaining 43 on option. Basic **777-200B** will form bulk of purchase, with later delivery likely to include stretched **777-300** and ultra long-range **777-100**. Sixteen aircraft intended for its leasing subsidiary, Singapore Aircraft Leasing Enterprise.

Associate carriers: Wholly-owned *SilkAir* (MI), established in 1975 and until 1992 known as Tradewinds. Five **737-300**s and two **Fokker 70**s operated on regional services to 20 destinations in Malaysia, Indonesia, Philippines, Cambodia, Myanmar, Laos, Vietnam and China, in particular serving burgeoning tourist industry.

Singapore Airlines fleet

Airbus A310-200	c/n			Boeing 747-300	c/n				
9V-STM	367	9V-STS	501	9V-SKA	23026/580	9V-SMF	24066/791	9V-SMY	27217/1023
9V-STN	372	9V-STT	534	9V-SKD	23029/590	9V-SMG	24226/809	9V-SMZ	26549/1030
		9V-STU	548	9V-SKM	23409/637	9V-SMH	24227/831	9V-SPA	26550/1040
Airbus A310-300	**c/n**	9V-STV	570	9V-SKN	23410/653	9V-SMI	24975/838	9V-SPB	26551/1045
		9V-STW	589	9V-SKP	23769/666	9V-SMJ	25068/852	9V-SPC	27070/1049
9V-SJA	123	9V-STY	634	N121KG	23032/603	9V-SMK	25127/859	9V-SPD`	26552/1056
9V-SJB	126	9V-STZ	654	N122KH	23033/609	9V-SML	25128/860	9V-SPE	26554/1069
9V-STA	665			N123KJ	23243/612	9V-SMM	26547/921	9V-SPF	27071/1072
9V-STB	669	**Boeing 747-200B**	**c/n**	N124KK	23244/621	9V-SMN	26548/923	9V-SPG	26562/1074
9V-STC	680	9V-SQP	21941/470	N125KL	23245/626	9V-SMO	27066/940	9V-SPH	26555/1075
9V-STD	684	9V-SQQ	21942/471			9V-SMP	27067/953	9V-SPI	28022/1082
9V-STE	693	9V-SQR	21943/475	**Boeing 747-400**	**c/n**	9V-SMQ	27132/955	9V-SPJ	26556/1084
9V-STF	697	9V-SQS	21944/510	9V-SMA	24061/717	9V-SMR	27133/962		
9V-STO	433			9V-SMB	24062/722	9V-SMS	27134/981	**Boeing 747-400F**	**c/n**
9V-STP	443	**Boeing 747-200F**	**c/n**	9V-SMC	24063/736	9V-SMT	27137/990	9V-SFA	26563/1036
9V-STQ	493	9V-SKQ	24177/710	9V-SMD	24064/255	9V0SMV	27068/1000	9V-SFB	26561/1042
9V-STR	500	9V-SQV	22245/458	9V-SME	24065/761	9V-SMW	27178/1015	9V-SFC	26560/1052
								9V-SFD	26553/1069

South African Airways (SA/SAA)

Jan Smuts Airport
Johannesburg

History: Founded 1 February 1934, taking over assets of Union Airways. Three German **Junkers Ju 52/3m**s added to develop domestic route structure and regional services to Tanganyika and Kenya. Progress interrupted by World War II. Towards end of 1944, civil operations resumed with **Lockheed Lodestar**s and first 'Springbok' service opened between South Africa and UK (Bournemouth) 10 November 1945 with **Avro York**, flown in conjunction with BOAC. Yorks replaced by **DC-4** on Johannesburg-London route, via Nairobi, Khartoum and Castel Benito (Tripoli), in July 1946. By end of 1947, fleet included seven DC-4s, eight **Vickers Viking**s, five **DC-3**s, two **de Havilland DH.104 Dove**s and 19 **Lodestar**s. Three **Lockheed Constellation**s, delivered in 1950, cut flying time between Johannesburg and London to 28 hours, and again to 21 hours with **DC-7B** in 1956. Made aviation history in 1953 as first airline outside UK to operate world's first pure jetliner, **Comet 1** on lease from BOAC. Added 'Wallaby' service 25 November 1957 to Perth in Australia and, after introduction of **Boeing 707** in October 1960, first non-stop schedule between South Africa and Europe with nine-hour flight to Athens. New York route, via Rio de Janeiro, opened 23 February 1969. First **747-200B** entered service in 1971, followed by **747SP** (1976) and by **747-300** (1983), which provided first non-stop flights between Johannesburg and London. Delivery of **Advanced 737-200** and **Airbus A320-200**s started in 1981 and 1991 respectively, for domestic routes. Became division of commercialised state-owned company Transnet 1 April 1990, as first step towards eventual privatisation.

SAA today: National airline wholly-owned by South African government through Transnet. Provides domestic trunk services centred on 'Golden Triangle' route between Johannesburg, Durban and Cape Town, which also serve as main hubs for its regional and intercontinental network. Major marketing alliances with Air Afrique, American Airlines, Lufthansa, Thai International, Ansett Australia and British Midland, involving codeshare and joint services.

Revenue: $1,225 million
Passengers: 4.6 million
Cargo: 66,000 tonnes
Employees: 10,100

Fleet development: 3 November 1995 announced intention to acquire four **Boeing 777-200**s and two **747-400**s, in $960 billion deal. Original 1997 delivery date now under review, along with terms of contract.

Associate carriers: Has 40 per cent holding in *Alliance Airlines* (Y2), set up 20 November 1994 as joint venture, with participation of Uganda Airlines and Air Tanzania (10 per cent each). Remaining shares are

After years of sanctions and embargoes SAA is now free to expand and acquire new aircraft, like its seven Airbus A320-231s.

retained in trust by two governments. Started operations 1 July 1995, flying SAA **Boeing 747SP** between Dar-es-Salaam, Entebbe and London-Heathrow.

SA Express (YB), owned 51 per cent be Thebe Investments, 21 per cent by SA Enterprises (Canada) and 20 per cent by SAA, serves thinner routes with fleet of 12 **DHC-8-300B**s. Founded December 1994 and started flying 24 April 1995.

Privately-owned *Airlink Airline*s, operating as *SA Airlink*, feeds SAA at Johannesburg. Fleet is nine **BAe Jetstream 41**s, two **Do 228-200**s, two **SA226TC Metro II**s.

South African Airways fleet

Airbus A300B2K-3C	c/n	ZS-SIB	22581/796	ZS-São	20556/194
ZS-SDA	032	ZS-SIC	22582/805	ZS-SAP	20557/198
ZS-SDB	037	ZS-SIE	22584/821		
ZS-SDC	039	ZS-SIG	22586/829	**Boeing 747-200F**	c/n
ZS-SDD	040	ZS-SIH	22587/835	ZS-SAR	22170/486
		ZS-SII	22588/836		
Airbus A300B4-200	c/n	ZS-SIJ	22589/843	**Boeing 747-300**	c/n
ZS-SDE	138	ZS-SIK	22590/854	ZS-SAC	23031/598
ZS-SDF	192	ZS-SIL	22591/859	ZS-SAJ	23027/583
ZS-SDH	222	ZS-SIM	22828/881	ZS-SAT	22970/577
				ZS-SAU	22971/578
Airbus A300C4-200	c/n	**Boeing 737-200F**	c/n		
ZS-SDG	212	ZS-SID	22583/809	**Boeing 747-400**	c/n
		ZS-SIF	22585/828	ZS-SAV	24976/827
Airbus A320-200	c/n			ZS-SAW	25152/861
ZS-SHA	243	**Boeing 747SP**	c/n	ZS-SAX	26637/943
ZS-SHB	249	ZS-SPA	21132/280	ZS-SAY	26638/995
ZS-SHC	250	ZS-SPC	21134/288		
ZS-SHD	251	ZS-SPE	21254/298	**Boeing 767-200(ER)**	c/n
ZS-SHE	334	ZS-SPF	21263/301	ZS-SRA	26471/511
ZS-SHF	335				
ZS-SHG	440	**Boeing 747-200B**	c/n	*Plus:* Douglas DC-3, DC-4,
		ZS-SAL	20237/154	**CASA 352L (Junkers**
Boeing 737-200 Advanced		ZS-SAM	20238/158	**Ju 52/3m)** and **Harvard**,
ZS-SIA	22580/787	ZS-SAN	20239/160	for historical flight

101

Southwest Airlines (WN/SAL)

Dallas-Love Field, Dallas Texas, USA

This is one of three 'Shamu' killer-whale lookalikes flown by Southwest Airlines for Sea World.

History: Incorporated as Air Southwest 15 March 1967, but changed name to Southwest Airlines 29 March 1971. After overcoming fierce objections from airlines, and restraining orders, inaugurated high-frequency, low-fare jet service 18 June 1971 with three **Boeing 737-200**s over 'Texas Triangle' linking Dallas, Houston and San Antonio. Airline Deregulation Act in October 1978 provided impetus for further expansion, leading to first service outside Texas with opening of Houston/Hobby-New Orleans route 25 January 1979. Oklahoma City, Tulsa and Albuquerque came next. First **Boeing 737-300** introduced 17 December 1984.

Following year took over Muse Air, another Dallas-based low-fare operator, founded in January 1980 by ex-Southwest president Lamar Muse. By 31 December 1989, Southwest served 29 cities in 14 states with fleet of 46 737-200s and 48 737-300s, achieving major airline status and serving as model for low-cost, low-fare airline operations. Accepted first **737-500** in February 1990 and committed to purchase of total of 62 more 737 models within 1990-95 timeframe. Another huge order placed for 50 new-generation **737-600/700/800** models in 1993. Expanded into Florida 22 January 1996. **Southwest today:** High-

frequency, low-fare jet service between 44 airports in 20 US states. In addition to 10 cities served within Texas, also connects Albuquerque, Baltimore, Boise, Burbank, Chicago-Midway, Cleveland, Columbus, Detroit, Fort Lauderdale, Indianapolis, Kansas City, Las Vegas, Little Rock, Los Angeles, Louisville, Nashville, New Orleans, Oakland, Oklahoma City, Omaha, Ontario, Phoenix, Reno, Sacramento, Salt Lake City, San Diego, San Francisco, San Jose, Seattle, Spokane, St Louis, Tampa, Tucson and Tulsa.

Annual revenue: *$2,875 million*
Passengers: *42.75 million*
Employees: *14,000*

Fleet development: Seventeen 737-300s to be delivered in 1996 and early 1997, to be followed by 50 new-generation 737 models (**737X**), with contract providing for flexibility in mix of -600, -700 and -800 variants. Delivery to be completed by 1999.

Southwest Airlines fleet

Boeing 737-200 Advanced	c/n								
N102SW	23108/1014	N64SW	22062/640	N302SW	22942/1052	N332SW	23696/1545	N362SW	26573/2322
N103SW	23109/1016	N67SW	22356/719	N303SW	22943/1101	N333SW	23697/1547	N363SW	26574/2429
N104SW	23110/1017	N68SW	22357/725	N304SW	22944/1138	N334SW	23938/1549	N364SW	26575/2430
N105SW	23249/1095	N702ML	22054/624	N305SW	22945/1139	N335SW	23939/1553	N365SW	26576/2433
N129SW	22340/678	N71SW	22358/732	N306SW	22946/1148	N336SW	23940/1557	N366SW	26577/2469
N130SW	22699/855	N721WN	22697/817	N307SW	22947/1156	N337SW	23959/1567	N367SW	26578/2470
N20SW	21337/490	N722WN	22698/823	N309SW	22948/1160	N338SW	23960/1571	N368SW	26579/2473
N23SW	21338/494	N73SW	22673/826	N310SW	22949/1161	N339SW	24090/1591	N369SW	26580/2477
N24SW	20925/373	N74SW	22674/827	N311SW	23333/1183	N341SW	24091/1593	N370SW	26597/2497
N26SW	21117/423	N75SW	22675/839	N312SW	23334/1185	N342SW	24133/1682	N371SW	26598/2500
N27SW	21262/470	N80SW	22730/841	N313SW	23335/1201	N343SW	24151/1686	N372SW	26599/2504
N28SW	21339/495	N81SW	22731/864	N314SW	23336/1229	N344SW	24152/1688	N373SW	26581/2509
N29SW	21340/499	N82SW	22732/877	N315SW	23337/1231	N346SW	24153/1690	N374SW	26582/2515
N50SW	21447/508	N83SW	22826/878	N316SW	23338/1232	N347SW	24374/1708	N375SW	26583/2520
N51SW	21448/509	N85SW	22827/882	N318SW	23339/1255	N348SW	24375/1710	N376SW	26584/2570
N52SW	21533/524	N86SW	22903/905	N319SW	23340/1348	N349SW	24408/1734	N378SW	26585/2579
N53SW	21534/526	N87SW	22904/913	N320SW	23341/1350	N350SW	24409/1748	N379SW	26586/2580
N54SW	21535/543	N89SW	22905/918	N321SW	23342/1351	N351SW	24572/1790	N380SW	26587/2610
N55SW	21593/544	N90SW	22963/929	N322SW	23343/1377	N352SW	24888/1942	N382SW	26588/2611
N56SW	21721/553	N91SW	22964/933	N323SW	23344/1378	N353SW	24889/1947	N383SW	26589/2612
N57SW	21722/568	N92SW	22965/942	N324SW	23414/1384	N354SW	25219/2092	N384SW	26590/2613
N59SW	21811/609	N93SW	23053/966	N325SW	23689/1398	N355SW	25250/2103	N385SW	26600/2617
N60SW	21812/611	N94SW	23054/969	N326SW	23690/1400	N356SW	25251/2105	N386SW	26601/2626
N61SW	21970/613	N95SW	23455/970	N327SW	23691/1407	N357SW	26594/2294	N387SW	26602/2627
N62SW	22060/638	N96SW		N328SW	23692/1521	N358SW	26595/2295	N388SW	26591/2628
N63SW	22061/639	**Boeing 737-300**	c/n	N329SW	23693/1525	N359SW	26596/2297	N389SW	26592/2629
		N300SW	22940/1037	N330SW	23694/1529	N360SW	26571/2307	N390SW	26593/2642
		N301SW	22941/1048	N331SW	23695/1536	N361SW	26572/2309	N391SW	27378/2643

N392S	27379/2604		
N394SW	27380/2645		
N395SW	27689/2667		
N396SW	27690/2668		
N397SW	27691/2695		
N398SW	27692/2696		
N399WN	27693/2697		
N600WN	27694/2699	N662SW	23255/1125
N601WN	27695/2702	N663SW	23256/1128
N602SW	27953/2713	N664WN	23495/1206
N603SW	27954/2714	N665WN	23497/1227
N604SW	27955/2715	N667SW	23063/1092
N605SW	27956/2716	N668SW	23060/1069
N606SW	27926/2740	N669SW	23752/1484
N607SW	27927/2741	N670SW	23784/1533
N608SW	27928/2742	N671SW	23785/1535
N609SW	27929/2744	N672SW	23406/1215
N610WN	27696/2745	N673AA	23251/1063
N611SW	27697/2750	N674AA	23252/1094
N612SW	27930/2753	N675AA	23253/1096
N613SW	27931/2754	N676SW	23288/1100
N614SW	28033/2755	N677AA	23289/1182
N615SW	27698/2757	N678AA	23290/1205
N616SW	27699/2758	N679AA	23291/1211
N617SW	27700/2759	N680AA	23505/1318
N618WN	28034/2761	N682SW	23496/1217
N619SW	28035/2762	N683SW	24008/1576
N620SW	28036/2766	N684WN	23941/1520
N621SW	28037/2767	N685SW	23401/1209

Southwest's orange 737s are a beacon in the airline industry showing how to run a succesful and profitable airline.

		Boeing 737-500 c/n			
N686SW	23175/1110	N501SW	24178/1718	N514SW	25153/2078
N687SW	23388/1187	N502SW	24179/1744	N515SW	25154/2080
N688SW	23254/1107	N503SW	24180/1766	N519SW	25318/2121
N689SW	23387/1163	N504SW	24181/1804	N520SW	25319/2134
N690SW	23783/1531	N505SW	24182/1826	N521SW	25320/2136
N691WN	23781/1494	N506SW	24183/1852	N522SW	26564/2202
N692SW	23062/1083	N507SW	24184/1864	N523SW	26565/2204
N693SW	23174/1104	N508SW	24185/1932	N524SW	26566/2224
N694SW	23061/1080	N509SW	24186/1934	N525SW	26567/2283
N695SW	23506/1249	N510SW	24187/1940	N526SW	26568/2285
N696SW	23064/1527	N511SW	24188/2029	N527SW	26569/2287
N697SW	23838/1505	N512SW	24189/2056	N528SW	26570/2292
N698SW	23176/1213	N513SW	24190/2058		
N699SW	23826/1372				

Swissair (SR/SWR)

Zürich Airport
Zürich, Switzerland

History: Established 26 March 1931 through merger of Balair and Ad Astra. Started operations 1 April 1931 with six **Fokker F.VIIb**s. Became first European airline to introduce **Lockheed Orion** inaugural Basle-Zürich-Munich-Vienna service one year later. Fleet modernised first with **DC-2** in 1935, and then **DC-3** in 1936. Eight in service by August 1939 when all scheduled service suspended at outbreak of World War II. Services resumed 30 July 1945 and **DC-4** added in 1947, when Swissair was designated national airline. First scheduled North Atlantic service inaugurated 29 April 1949 to New York, via Shannon and Gander. **Convair 240** joined fleet that same year. Notable achievements in 1950s included introduction of new types, among them **DC-6B** (1951), **DC-7C** and **Convair 440** (1956), first services to South America and Far East, and signing of far-reaching co-operation agreement with SAS in 1958, later to include KLM and UTA in KSSU Consortium. Jet age arrived in 1960 with delivery of

Swissair was an early customer for the A321 and now operates the short-fuselage A319, A320 and stretched A321 alongside A310s.

DC-8 and **Caravelle**, supplemented two years later with first five **Convair 990**, then fastest jetliner in service. All-jet fleet, also including first **DC-9**, from 1969. First **Boeing 747-200B** delivered in 1971, followed by first of six **DC-10-30**s in 1972. Order placed for 10 **DC-9-51**s next year, followed in 1977 with an order for two DC-9-51s and 15 **MD-81**s. Network extended as far as Beijing, Shanghai and Toronto in 1975.

Swissair today: National airline with government entities holding major block of shares totalling 20.5 per cent. Provides extensive scheduled passenger and cargo services to 125 cities in 67 countries on all continents, except Australia. Code-sharing on specific routes with Air Afrique, Air Madagascar, Austrian Airlines, Delta Air Lines, SAS, Singapore Airlines and Ukraine International.

Annual revenue: $4,700 million
Passengers: 8.4 million
Cargo: 285,000 tonnes
Employees: 17,350

Fleet development: Two more **MD-11**s due in March 1997 and one in 1998. Five **Airbus A319-100**s to be delivered between April and November

Swissair

1996, with another three ordered subsequently for delivery in 1997. Fleet also being enlarged and modernised with 18 **Airbus A320-200**s, of which nine remain to be delivered up to May 1997. Two more **A321-200**s to be taken in 1997. Concurrent with delivery of new A320 and A319 twin-jets, McDonnell Douglas MD-81 fleet will be phased out. **Fokker 100** being traded in to Avro in part-exchange for **RJ100** fleet for Crossair.

Associate carriers: Cross-equity holdings with Delta Air Lines (Swissair holds 4.6 per cent/Delta 4.5 per cent) and Singapore Airlines (0.6 per cent each) under Global Quality Alliance put into effect in November 1990. Also has 10 per cent stake in Austrian Airlines. Agreement signed 6 March 1995 for acquisition of 49.5 per cent stake in SABENA.

Crossair (LX), owned 56.1 per cent, is Europe's largest regional airline, serving 76 destinations in 23 European countries from hubs at Basle and Lugano with modern fleet of five **Avro RJ100**s, four **RJ85**s, two **BAe 146-300**s, 15 **Saab 2000**s, four **Saab 340A**s and 15 **340B**s.

Seven RJ100s and 10 Saab 2000s remain to be delivered. Since November 1995 also responsible for holiday charter flights with four **MD-82**s and four **MD-83**s, previously provided independently by **Balair/CTA**, which has been dissolved. Crossair founded in February 1975 as Business Flyers and began scheduled services under the Crossair name 26 April 1979.

Swissair fleet

Airbus A310-300	c/n	HB-IOF	541	HB-IWE	48447/464
HB-IPF	399			HB-IWF	48448/465
HB-IPG	404	**Boeing 747-300**	c/n	HB-IWG	48452/472
HB-IPH	409	HB-IGE	22995/585	HB-IWH	48453/473
HB-IPI	410	HB-IGF	22996/586	HB-IWI	48454/477
HB-IPK	412			HB-IWK	48455/487
HB-IPL	640	**Boeing 747-300 Combi**		HB-IWL	48456/494
HB-IPM	642	HB-IGC	22704/570	HB-IWM	48457/498
HB-IPN	672	HB-IGD	22705/576	HB-IWN	48539/571
		HB-IGG	23751/686		
Airbus A320-200	c/n			**McDonnell Douglas**	
HB-IJA	533	**Fokker 100**	c/n	**MD-81**	c/n
HB-IJB	545	HB-IVC	11251	HB-INA	49100/1025
HB-IJC	548	HB-IVD	11252	HB-INB	49101/1051
HB-IJD	553	HB-IVE	11253	HB-INC	48002/938
HB-IJE	559	HB-IVF	11254	HB-IND	48003/944
HB-IJF	562	HB-IVG	11255	HB-INE	48004/950
HB-IJG	566	HB-IVH	11256	HB-INF	48005/957
HB-IJH	574	HB-IVI	11381	HB-INM	48011/994
HB-IJI	577	HB-IVK	11386	HB-INN	48012/997
				HB-INO	48013/1000
Airbus A321-100	c/n	**McDonnell Douglas**		HB-INP	48014/1013
HB-IOA	517	**MD-11**	c/n	HB-INS	49356/1250
HB-IOB	519	HB-IWA	48443/458	HB-INT	49357/1251
HB-IOC	520	HB-IWB	48444/459	HB-INU	49358/1294
HB-IOD	522	HB-IWC	48445/460	HB-INX	49570/1440
HB-IOE	535	HB-IWD	48446/463	HB-INY	49571/1458

Syrianair (RB/SYR)

Damascus International Airport
Damascus, Syria

Syrianair is now looking to modernise its largely 1970s vintage fleet, such as this 727.

History: Established in October 1961 as government corporation to succeed Syrian Airways, which itself came into being in June 1954 as department of Ministry of Defence. Fleet comprised four **DC-3**s, and a **DC-4**. Domestic flights established, together with regional services to Amman, Baghdad, Beirut, Cairo, Jeddah and Kuwait. The union of Syria and Egypt as the United Arab Republic, also led to merger of Syrian Airways and Misrair to form short-lived United Arab Airlines in January 1961.

New Syrian Arab Airlines began operations in October 1961 with three **DC-6**s, two DC-4s and three DC-3s. Expansion began in summer 1963 to Rome and Munich, extended following year to London and Paris. First of four **Super Caravelle 10B3**s entered service to London in October 1965. All-jet fleet in spring 1976 with acquisition of three **Boeing 727-200**s and two **747SP**s, latter used to open joint service with Jordan to New York in April 1978. Fleet profile quickly altered as result of closer ties with Soviet

Union, with several Soviet types acquired in barter deals, including **Antonov An-26**, **Yakovlev Yak-40** and **Ilyushin Il-76** in mid-to late 1970s, plus six **Tupolev Tu-134B-3**s from 1983 and **Tu-154M**s from 1985. US sanctions imposed in 1986, plus collapse of Soviet Union, put considerable strain on its ageing fleet. Although US softened its line after Syria's participation during Gulf War, financial pressures have prevented fleet renewal to date.

Syrianair today: Wholly-owned national flag-carrier providing Damascus with scheduled connections to 34 cities in Europe, Middle East and Arabic North Africa. Destinations are Abu Dhabi, Algiers, Athens, Bahrain, Beirut, Berlin-Schöne-feld, Bombay, Bucharest, Budapest, Cairo, Delhi, Dhahran,

Doha, Dubai, Frankfurt, Istanbul, Jeddah, Karachi, Khartoum, Kuwait, Larnaca, London, Madrid, Moscow, Munich, Paris, Riyadh, Rome, Sana'a, Sharjah, Sofia, Stockholm, Tehran and Tunis. Main domestic route between Damascus and Aleppo.

Annual passengers: 0.47 million
Cargo: 5,000 tonnes
Employees: 3,565

Syrianair fleet

Boeing 727-200 Advanced		YK-AHB	21175/290	YK-AYB	63994
YK-AGA	21203/1188			YK-AYC	63989
YK-AGB	21204/1194	**Ilyushin Il-76M**	**c/n**	YK-AYD	63990
YK-AGC	21205/1198	YK-ATA	093421613	YK-AYE	66187
YK-AGD	22360/1670	YK-ATB	093421619	YK-AYF	66190
YK-AGE	22361/1716	YK-ATC	0013431911		
YK-AGF	22763/1788	YK-ATD	0013431915	**Tupolev Tu-154M**	**c/n**
				YK-AIA	708
Boeing 747SP	**c/n**	**Tupolev Tu-134B-3**	**c/n**	YK-AIB	709
YK-AHA	21174/284	YK-AYA	63992	YK-AIC	710

TAP Air Portugal (TP/TAP)

Lisbon Airport
Lisbon, Portugal

History: Established by state 14 March 1945 as Transportes Aéreos Portugueses. Start of commercial flights on Lisbon-Madrid route with war-surplus **DC-3** 19 September 1946, followed by 'Imperial Line' to Luanda and Lourenco Marques 31 December. Four **DC-4s** bought from KLM in 1947. Paris added 10 August 1948 and London (Northolt) 27 May 1949. Became limited liability company 1 June 1953 with state retaining majority holding. Also merged with Aero Portuguesa, founded in 1934. First of two **Lockheed L1049G Super Constellations** entered service on African route in 1954. Rio de Janeiro served in conjunction with Panair do Brasil. Introduced first **Caravelle VIRs** in August 1962 on Lisbon-Madrid route. **Boeing 707-320B** and **727-100** entered service 22 December 1965 and in 1967 respectively. 707 used to introduce Lisbon-Johannesburg link. European network further expanded and New York, via Santa Maria in Azores, reached in April 1969. Set up air taxi subsidiary Transportes Aéreos Continentais (TAC) in same year, replaced in 1985 by Linhas Aéreas Regionais (LAR). First two **747-200Bs** delivered in February 1972 and two more ordered. TAP renationalised 15 April three years later. Increasing use made of Portugal's second city Oporto in international route network. Caracas added in 1976. Fleet modernised in 1980s with addition of **Lockheed L1011 TriStars** (from January 1983), **Boeing 737-200** (June 1983) and **-300** (March 1989) and **Airbus A310-300** in October 1988. Air Atlantis charter subsidiary established in June 1985, but reintegrated 30 April 1993. In

TAP Air Portrugal's fleet of six 156-seat A320s partners the airline's A310s and newly-delivered A340s on TAP's route network from Lisbon.

spring 1992 took delivery of four **Airbus A320-200s**, followed in December 1994 by first two **A340-300s**.

Air Portugal today: Wholly government-owned flag-carrier linking Lisbon with 46 destinations in Europe, Africa, Americas and Macau in Far East. Points served include Abidjan, Amsterdam, Athens, Barcelona, Berlin-Tegel, Bissau, Bologna, Brazzaville, Brussels, Caracas, Copenhagen, Curaçao, Dublin, Geneva, Hamburg, Hannover, Harare, Johannesburg, Kinshasa, London, Luanda, Luxembourg, Lyon, Madrid, Macau, Maputo, Milan, Munich, New York, Nice, Oslo, Paris, Recife, Rio de Janeiro, Rome, Sal, Salvador da Bahia, Santo Domingo, São Paulo, São Tomé, Stockholm, Stuttgart, Tel Aviv, Turin, Vienna and Zürich. Also domestic services to all

major points on Portuguese mainland, Madeira and Azores. Code-share alliances or joint services with Air Afrique, British Midland, Delta Air Lines, Portugalia, SABENA and TAAG Angola Airlines.

Annual revenue: $950 million
Passengers: 3.75 million
Cargo: 60,000 tonnes
Employees: 8,800

Fleet development: Remaining Lockheed TriStars for sale.

Associate carriers: Has 25 per cent stake in new airline **Air Macau** (NX), which began operations in November 1995, following opening of new Macau International Airport. Serves mainland China and regional points with three **A321-100s**. One **A320-200** on order.

Active participant in founding of **Air São Tomé e Principe** (GJ) 1 October 1993, providing 40 per cent of capital. Flies within islands and to Libreville, Gabon with single **de Havilland Canada DHC-6 Twin Otter 300**.

TAP Air Portugal fleet

Airbus A310-300	c/n	CS-TNC	234	Boeing 737-200		Boeing 737-300	c/n	CS-TIO	23830/1462
CS-TEH	483	CS-TND	235	**Advanced**	c/n	CS-TIB	24365/1695		
CS-TEI	495	CS-TNE	395	CS-TEM	23043/972	CS-TIC	24366/1699	**Lockheed L.1011**	
CS-TEJ	494	CS-TNF	407	CS-TEN	23044/973	CS-TID	24449/1857	**TriStar 500**	c/n
CS-TEW	541			CS-TEO	23045/978	CS-TIE	24450/1873	CS-TEA	1239
CS-TEX	565	**Airbus A340-300**		CS-TEP	23046/981	CS-TIG	24213/1794	CS-TEC	1241
		CS-TOA	041	CS-TES	22637/848	CS-TIH	24214/1796	CS-TED	1242
Airbus A320-200	c/n	CS-TOB	044			CS-TIK	25161/2226	CS-TEE	1243
CS-TNA	185	CS-TOC	079	**Boeing 737-200C Adv**		CS-TIL	25162/2241		
CS-TNB	191	CS-TOD	091	CS-TEQ	23051/1002	CS-TIN	23827/1444		

Tarom Romanian (RO/ROT)

Otopeni International Airport
Bucharest, Romania

Tarom acquired the A310-300 to replace its Soviet-era Ilyushin Il-62Ms, the remaining examples of which are now up for sale.

History: Founded 8 August 1945 as Transporturi Aeriene Romana Sovietica under joint ownership of Romania and Soviet Union. Began domestic operations 1 February 1946 with 16 **Lisunov Li-2**s, some **Ju 52/3m**s, and three **Lockheed L.14**s. Routes to Budapest, Prague and Warsaw opened in 1947, and domestic network expanded to 12 points by October 1949. Soviet shares purchased by Romania in autumn 1954 and airline renamed Transporturile Aeriene Romane (Tarom). Network extended with arrival of new **Ilyushin Il-14**, first to Moscow, then Berlin, Copenhagen, Brussels, Vienna, Sofia, Athens, and important Bucharest-Vienna-Zurich-Paris route 28 July 1960. **Il-18** entered service in 1962, total of 12 delivered by October 1966. First of 30 **Antonov An-24**s arrived in 1966, joined in 1975 by single **An-26**. Order for six **BAC One-Eleven 400**s 28 February 1968. Three **Boeing 707-320C**s and three **Il-62**s ordered in 1973, and confirmed 26 April 1974 with Bucharest-Peking (Beijing) service, followed in June by transatlantic link to New York. Charter subsidiary Linie Aeriene Romani (LAR) created in 1975.

Services developed to Middle East in 1975, and three years later new routes opened to Bangkok and Singapore. Last Soviet type, **Tupolev Tu-154B-1**, acquired in 1977. Five **One-Eleven 500**s ordered in April 1975 and first Romanian-built **ROMBAC One-Eleven** went into service 28 January 1983. **Airbus A310-300** acquired in December 1992 followed by **737-300** in

October 1993. Incorporated in present form March 1991 as joint-stock company.

Tarom today: National airline operating international services from Bucharest-Otopeni, and domestic network centred on Bucharest-Baneasa Airport. Serves 33 cities in 20 European countries, plus Abu Dhabi, Amman, Bahrain, Bangkok, Beijing, Beirut, Cairo, Calcutta, Chicago, Damascus, Delhi, Dubai, Karachi, Kuwait, Malé, New York and Tel Aviv. Code-share and joint services with Air France, Austrian Airlines, Iberia and THY.

Annual revenue: $182 million
Passengers: 1.25 million
Cargo: 6,500 tonnes
Employees: 3,345

Tarom Romanian Airlines fleet

Airbus A310-300	c/n	BAC One-Eleven 500	c/n	Ilyushin Il-18V	c/n
YR-LCA	636	YR-BCI	252	YR-IMF	184007105
YR-LCB	644	YR-BCJ	253	YR-IMG	184007301
		YR-BCK	254		
Antonov An-24RV	c/n	YR-BCL	255	**RomBac One-Eleven**	
YR-AMK	09705	YR-BCM	256	**561RC**	c/n
YR-AMY	09809	YR-BCN	266	YR-BRA	401
YR-BMA	10105			YR-BRB	402
YR-BMB	10106	**Boeing 707-320C**	c/n	YR-BRC	403
YR-BMC	10201	YR-ABA	20803/878	YR-BRD	404
YR-BME	10310	YR-ABC	20805/884	YR-BRF	406
YR-BMF	10404			YR-BRG	407
YR-BMG	10405	**Boeing 737-300**	c/n		
YR-BMH	10407	YR-BGA	27179/2524	**Tupolev Tu-154B-1/B-2**	
YR-BMI	10408	YR-BGB	27180/2529	YR-TPB	161
YR-BML	10805	YR-BGC	27181/2662	YR-TPD	224
YR-BMM	10807	YR-BGD	27182/2663	YR-TPF	239
YR-BMN	10808	YR-BGE	27395/2671	YR-TPG	262
YR-BMO	10710			YR-TPI	342
		Ilyushin Il-18D	c/n	YR-TPK	415
		YR-IMJ	186009102	YR-TPL	428
		YR-IML	187009903		

Thai International (TG/THA)

Don Muang International Airport
Bangkok, Thailand

History: Founded 24 August 1959 as joint venture between Thailand's domestic carrier Thai Airways Company and SAS, with Scandinavian airline initially providing capital of Baht 2 million for 30 per cent stake. SAS also provided operational, management and marketing expertise. Operations began 1 May 1960 with two leased **DC-6B**s from Bangkok to nine points within Southeast Asia. DC-6 quickly replaced and **Convair 990A** (May 1962), **Caravelle III** (January 1964), **DC-9** (February 1969) and **DC-8** (April 1970) added. Standardised into all-DC-8 operation, initially using **DC-8-33**, then longer range **DC-8-62**, and finally **DC-8-63**. Intercontinental services launched in 1971 with flights to Australia, followed by Copenhagen 3 June 1972. London and Frankfurt routes opened 3 November 1973. Two leased **DC-10-30**s entered service March 1974 prior to purchasing its own aircraft. SAS holding and influence gradually reduced, and airline became wholly state-owned 1 April 1977. First **Airbus A300B4-200** introduced on regional routes 1 November 1977, joined later by **A300-600R**, and in 1979 by **Boeing 747**. North America added to network 3 March 1980, with DC-10 service from Bangkok to Los Angeles, via Seattle. Growth accelerated 1 April 1988 as result of merger with Thai Airways Company, receiving sole responsibility for domestic and international flights. Authority granted by Cabinet 25 June 1991 to list shares on Stock Exchange of Thailand to obtain additional funds. First two **MD-11**s delivered in 1991 and latest aircraft to join fleet was **Airbus A330-300** in December 1994 and **Boeing 777-200** in April 1996.

Thai International today: Operates to 51 international points in 36 countries across four continents from its home base at Bangkok's Don Muang Airport. Operates from Bangkok to 20 Thai towns. In addition to its extensive 32-point network in Asia/Pacific region, flies long-haul routes to Athens, Amsterdam, Brussels, Copenhagen, Dubai, Frankfurt, Istanbul, London-Heathrow, Los Angeles, Madrid, Muscat, Paris, Rome, Stockholm and Zürich. Major marketing alliances with Air New Zealand, Ansett Australia, Lufthansa, Japan Airlines, SAS and United Airlines.

Annual revenue: $2,525 million
Passengers: 11.4 million
Cargo: 340,000 tonnes
Employees: 21,540

Fleet development: Placed order for 21 new aircraft in early 1996, comprising five additional A300-600Rs, four A330s (-300 or -200 variants), six **777-300**s, two more **747-400**s, three **737-300**s

Having added the A330 to its fleet in 1994, Thai's major equipment order in 1996 added Boeing 777s to more Airbuses.

and one **737-400**. Six 777-200s from original order due for delivery between October 1996 and December 1997. Three 747-400s remain scheduled for December 1996 and August and October 1997. Long-term planning calls for reduction of types in fleet from 14 to six. A300B4/C4, A310-200, 747-300 and DC-10-30ER to be sold, together with four **BAe 146-300**s and four **ATR42/72**s.

Thai International fleet

Airbus A300B4-100	c/n
HS-THN	071
HS-THP	084
HS-THR	085

Airbus A300B4-200	c/n
HS-THT	141
HS-THW	149
HS-THX	249
HS-THY	265

Airbus A300-600	c/n
HS-TAA	368
HS-TAB	371
HS-TAC	377
HS-TAD	384
HS-TAE	395
HS-TAF	398

Airbus A300-600R	c/n
HS-TAG	464
HS-TAH	518
HS-TAK	566
HS-TAL	569
HS-TAM	577
HS-TAN	628
HS-TAO	629
HS-TAP	635
HS-TAR	681
HS-TAS	705

Airbus A310-300	c/n
HS-TIA	415
HS-TIB	424

Airbus A330-300	c/n
HS-TEA	050
HS-TEB	060
HS-TEC	062
HS-TED	064
HS-TEE	065
HS-TEF	066
HS-TEG	112
HS-TEH	122

AI(R) ATR42-300	c/n
HS-TRK	190
HS-TRL	206

AI(R) ATR72-200	c/n
HS-TRA	164
HS-TRB	167

Boeing 737-400	c/n
HS-TDA	24830/1899
HS-TDB	24831/1922
HS-TDC	25321/2113
HS-TDD	26611/2318
HS-TDE	26612/2330
HS-TDF	26613/2338
HS-TDG	26614/2481

Boeing 747-300	c/n
HS-TGD	23721/681
HS-TGE	23722/688

Boeing 747-400	c/n
HS-TGH	24458/769
HS-TGJ	24459/777
HS-TGK	24993/833
HS-TGL	25366/890
HS-TGM	27093/945
HS-TGN	26615/950
HS-TGO	26609/1001
HS-TGP	26610/1047
HS-TGR	27723/1091

Boeing 777-200	c/n
HS-TJA	27726/
HS-TJB	27727/

British Aerospace 146-300	c/n
HS-TBJ	E3191
HS-TBK	E3185
HS-TBL	E3181
HS-TBM	E3206
HS-TBO	E3189

Douglas DC-10-30ER	c/n
HS-TMA	48267/434
HS-TMB	48290/435
HS-TMC	48319/438

McDonnell Douglas MD-11	c/n
HS-TMD	48416/466
HS-TME	48417/467
HS-TMF	48418/501
HS-TMG	48451/505

Trans World Airlines (TW/TWA)

TWA's new colours and corporate logo have appeared on relatively few aircraft to date.

History: Founded 1 October 1930 as Transcontinental and Western Air (TWA) through merger of Transcontinental Air Transport and Western Air Express. Fleet included **Fokker F-X, F-XA, F-XIV, F-XXXII, Ford Trimotor** and others, soon followed by **Lockheed Vega**. Introduced transcontinental service 25 October 1930, linking Los Angeles and New York. Joined with Douglas Aircraft Company in November 1932 to formulate **DC-1**, the beginning of famous Douglas Commercial series. First of 32 improved **DC-2**s entered service on 18 May 1934 and another TWA (and Pan Am) initiative led to **Boeing 307** which went into service 8 July 1940. One year before, controlling interest purchased by Howard Hughes. Most of fleet put under control of Military Air Transport Command during World War II. Order for 40 **Lockheed L.049 Constellation**s also diverted to USAAF, but services started in 1946 with non-stop Los Angeles-New York flight. Expansion initiated 5 February 1946 with service from New York to Paris via Gander and Shannon. Cairo, Madrid, Bombay and London followed. Renamed as Trans World Airlines 17 May 1950.

Twelve **Martin 2-0-2**s put on domestic routes in September 1950 supplemented by first of 41 pressurised **Model 4-0-4** in October 1951. **L.1049 Super Constellation** service between Los Angeles and New York 10 September 1952, and followed from March 1955 by improved **L.1049G** and in October 1957 by **L.1649A Starliner**. Made early entry into jet age with **Boeing 707-120B** in March 1959 and **707-320B** years later, joined for short period by fast but uneconomical **Convair 880**. Re-equipment for shorter stages focused on mix of **727**s, which entered service 1 June 1964, and **DC-9** in February 1966. Became first all-jet US airline in April 1967 with retirement of last Super Constellation, and then to introduce **747** on US trunk routes inaugurating 'jumbo' flights 25 February 1970. 747 joined by 38 **L.1011 TriStar**s delivered between May 1972 and May 1982. Ordered 10 **Boeing 767-200**s in December 1979 for delivery starting in November 1982. Used on transatlantic routes from 1 February 1985 under new ETOPS (Extended Twin-engined OPerationS) rules. Overseas flights expanded in April 1984 with flights to Amsterdam, Brussels, Munich, Kuwait

and Zurich. Took over St Louis-based Ozark Airlines 30 September 1986, only four days after having itself been bought by investor Carl Icahn. Enlarged operations in part responsible for subsequent financial problems resulting in controversial sale of profitable London-Heathrow routes in May 1991 and period in Chapter 11 bankruptcy protection. Emerged from Chapter 11 in August 1995 revitalised, after substantial restructuring.

TWA today: Operates extensive network of scheduled passenger flights, which, together with Trans World Express feeder partner Trans World States Airlines, serve more than 110 destinations in United States and Caribbean, from hubs at St Louis and New York. Transatlantic services to Europe and Middle East operate out of New York and serve Athens, Barcelona, Cairo, Frankfurt, London-Gatwick, Madrid, Lisbon, Paris, Riyadh, Rome and Tel Aviv. Code-share with Philippine Airlines, but is seeking more substantial strategic alliances with foreign carriers.

Annual revenue: $3,317 million
Passengers: 21.0 million
Cargo: 125,000 tonnes
Employees: 23,000

Fleet development: Placed order with Boeing in February 1996 for 10 **757-200**s and will lease another 10 from ILFC. Three will be delivered in 1996 (first in July) and 12 in 1997, to replace its 14 TriStars, plus two more in 1998 and final three in 1999, to replace some 727s. Delivery of 10 **A330-300**s has been deferred to 1998, but negotiations under way to cancel altogether. Hushkits will be fitted to 28 DC-9-30s and additional **MD-80**s may be acquired to replace the Boeing 727.

Feeder services for the TWA network are flown by TW Express (Trans State Airlines) which currently operates eight (AIR) ATR42s in its fleet.

Associate carrier: *Trans States Airlines* (9N), formed in 1982, signed five-year agreement in October 1984 to feed TWA at St Louis hub under *Trans World Express* banner. 7 November, took over operations at New York hub from TWA's own subsidiary, Trans World Express, which closed down day before. Operates 350 daily flights with fleet of eight **ATR42-300**s, three **ATR72-200**s, 12 **BAe Jetstream 41**s, 33 **Jetstream 31**s and four **EMBRAER EMB-120 Brasilia**s. Another 13 Jetstream 41s remain to be delivered.

A single Trans World Airlines MD-80 has adopted this reversed 'negative' version of the 'old-style' TWA scheme.

Trans World Airlines (TWA) fleet

	c/n								
Boeing 727-200	*c/n*	N53110	19676/63	N936L	47711/844	N31013	1035	N920TW	49369/1199
N52310	19829/629	N53116	20321/102	N937F	47409/497	N31014	1036	N931TW	49527/1382
N52311	19830/633	N133TW	19957/76	N976Z	47248/257	N41016	1060	N9302B	49528/1383
N52312	19831/636	N134TW	19958/91	N977Z	47249/297	N15017	1063	N9303K	49529/1396
N52313	19832/642			N978Z	47250/309			N9304C	49530/1397
N94314	20047/675	**Boeing 747-200B**	*c/n*	N979Z	47343/460	**Lockheed L.1011**		N9307R	49663/1437
N64315	20048/679	N303TW	20116/112	N980Z	47344/472	**TriStar 50**	*c/n*	N9401W	53137/1872
N64319	20052/709	N305TW	20742/216	N981Z	47345/485	N31019	1066	N9402W	53138/1886
N64320	20053/713	N306TW	20398/152	N982PS	47251/244	N31023	1080	N9403W	53139/1899
N64322	20055/719			N983Z	47411/533			N9404V	53140/1923
N54325	20232/785	**Boeing 767-200(ER)**	*c/n*	N984Z	47412/534	**Lockheed L.1011**		N9405T	53141/1935
N54326	20233/786	N601TW	22564/14	N985Z	47491/599	**TriStar 100**	*c/n*	N9406W	53126/2026
N54327	20234/790	N602TW	22565/21	N986Z	47589/711	N31029	1109	N9407R	49400/1356
N54329	20307/792	N603TW	22566/29	N987Z	47137/258	N31031	1115	N9409F	53121/1971
N54330	20308/795	N604TW	22567/30	N988Z	47134/215	N7036T	1232	N9412W	53187/2118
N54331	20309/796	N605TW	22568/33	N989Z	47135/233			N9413T	53188/2119
N54332	20310/802	N606TW	22569/39	N990Z	47136/243	**McDonnell Douglas**		N9414W	53189/2121
N54333	20460/859	N607TW	22570/63	N991Z	47096/192	**MD-82/83**	*c/n*	N950U	49230/1141
N54334	20461/860	N608TW	22571/64	N992Z	47095/191	N110HM	49787/1636	N951U	49245/1145
N54335	20462/862	N609TW	22572/65	N993Z	47082/181	N901TW	49166/1098	N952U	49266/1238
N54336	20490/863	N610TW	22573/70	N995Z	47027/132	N902TW	49153/1101	N953U	49267/1239
N54337	20491/864	N650TW	23057/81	N996Z	47028/145	N903TW	49154/1102	N954U	49426/1399
		N651TW	23058/101	N997Z	47029/157	N904TW	49156/1104	N955U	49427/1401
Boeing 727-200				N998R	47030/174	N905TW	49157/1105	N956U	49701/1478
Advanced	*c/n*	**Boeing 767-300(ER)**	*c/n*			N906TW	49160/1108	N957U	49702/1479
N54338	20843/1063	N691LF	25137/377	**Douglas DC-9-41**		N907TW	49165/1117	N958U	49703/1489
N64339	20844/1065	EI-CAL	24952/357	N933L	47617/762	N908TW	49169/1118	N959U	49704/1490
N54340	20845/1066	EI-CAM	24953/405	N934L	47618/764	N909TW	49170/1119	EI-BWD	49575/1414
N54341	21628/1454			N935L	47603/720	N911TW	49182/1128	EI-CIW	49785/1628
N54342	21629/1456	**Douglas DC-9-15**	*c/n*			N912TW	49183/1129		
N24343	21630/1458	N490SA	45798/59	**Douglas DC-9-51**		N913TW	49184/1131		
N54344	21631/1460	N491SA	45799/69	N405EA	47688/799	N914TW	49185/1132	*TWA's familiar*	
N54345	21632/1462	N969Z	47001/94	N406EA	47686/800	N915TW	49186/1133	*'old-style' red and*	
N64346	21633/1464	N970Z	45772/30	N408EA	47693/804	N916TW	49187/1134	*white livery is still*	
N64347	21634/1466	N971Z	45773/39	N409EA	47728/858	N917TW	49366/1196	*predominant among*	
N54348	21967/1563	N973Z	47033/147	N410EA	47731/860	N918TW	49367/1197	*the huge St Louis-*	
N54349	21968/1565	N975Z	47035/178	N411EA	47732/861	N919TW	49368/1198	*based fleet.*	
N54350	21969/1567			N412EA	47733/862				
N54351	21983/1569	**Douglas DC-9-30**	*c/n*	N414EA	47746/864				
N54352	21984/1574	N920L	47734/868	N415EA	47749/865				
N54353	21985/1576	N921L	47107/236	N416EA	47751/866				
N54354	21986/1580	N922L	47108/251	N417EA	47753/867				
N84355	21987/1582	N923L	47109/252	N418EA	47676/785				
N84357	21989/1590	N924L	47324/469						
		N925L	47357/476	**Lockheed L.1011**					
Boeing 747-100	*c/n*	N926L	47172/263	**TriStar 1**					
N93104	19670/20	N927L	48123/934	N11003	1015				
N93105	19671/21	N928L	48124/954	N11004	1016				
N93107	19673/35	N929L	47174/286	N11005	1017				
N93108	19674/38	N931L	47173/273	N11006	1018				
N93109	19675/43	N932L	47669/776	N31008	1028				

Tunisair (TU/TAR)

Eight Airbus A320-211s currently wear the springing antelope symbol of Tunisair.

France (which has 5.6 per cent stake) on routes between Tunisia and France; scheduled co-ordination with Gulf Air for routes eastwards, and with Royal Air Maroc for connections to New York. Plans for joint marketing with RAM for routes to Eastern Europe.

History: Founded in 1948 as Société Tunisienne de l'Air by government, Air France and private interests. Began operations in 1949 over local routes, with three **DC-3**s and two **DC-4**s. Expansion inaugurated with routes to Casablanca, Ghadames and Tripoli also in 1949, and to Sebha deep in Sahara year later. Received authority at end of 1953 to serve Paris, via Marseilles and Nice in collaboration with Air France. Tunisian government acquired majority holding following independence in 1955. Geneva and Frankfurt added to network in 1961, together with one **Caravelle III**, with two more purchased in 1964/65. More European routes opened and network extended eastwards to Cairo, Damascus and Kuwait. Rapid growth in tourist traffic met with four **Boeing 727-200**s. Six more 727-200s bought between 1976 and 1978 and first **737-200** arrived in October 1979. Last Caravelle phased out 1 November 1977. Single **Airbus A300B4-200** delivered 28 May 1982. Modernisation of fleet effected with arrival of first **A320-200** in October 1990, and four **737-500**s, delivered one per year from 16 April 1992.

Tunisair today: National flag-carrier providing short- to medium-haul routes from capital Tunis to destinations in Europe, Middle East and North and West Africa. Destinations are Abu Dhabi, Algiers, Amman, Amsterdam, Athens, Barcelona, Berlin-Schönefeld, Bordeaux, Cairo, Casablanca, Copenhagen, Dakar, Damascus, Düsseldorf, Frankfurt, Geneva, Hamburg, Istanbul, Jeddah, Lille, Lisbon, London, Lyon, Madrid, Marseilles, Milan, Munich, Nice, Nouakchott, Paris-Orly, Prague, Rome, Strasbourg, Toulouse, Vienna, Warsaw and Zürich. Extensive inclusive-tour charters are flown into principal tourist gateways of Jerba and Monastir. Agreement with Air

Annual revenue: $505 million
Passengers: 2.7 million
Employees: 7,200
Major shareholder: Tunisian government with 45.2 per cent

Associate carrier: *Tuninter* (UG), established 27 July 1991 by Tunisair (40 per cent) and private capital and began operations in March 1992. Utilises two **ATR72-200**s and an **ATR42-300** on domestic routes and services to Palermo and Malta.

Tunisavia (TT), founded 27 April 1974 and jointly owned with Heli-Union of France, provides charter flights with two **DHC-6-300**s and three Aérospatiale helicopters.

Tunisair fleet

Airbus A300B4-200	c/n	Boeing 727-200 Advanced		TS-IOF	22625/776
TS-IMA	188	TS-JHN	20545/877		
		TS-JHQ	20948/1084	**Boeing 737-200C**	
Airbus A320-200	c/n	TS-JHR	21179/1171	**Advanced**	c/n
TS-IMB	119	TS-JHS	21234/1209	TS-IOD	21974/615
TS-IMC	124	TS-JHT	21235/1210		
TS-IMD	205	TS-JHU	21318/1252	**Boeing 737-500**	c/n
TS-IME	123	TS-JHW	21320/1271	TS-IOG	26639/2253
TS-IMF	370			TS-IOH	26640/2474
TS-IMG	390	**Boeing 737-200 Advanced**		TS-IOI	27257/2583
TS-IMH	402	TS-IOC	21973/607	TS-IOJ	27912/2701
TS-IMI	511	TS-IOE	22624/758		

Turkish Airlines (TK/THY)

History: Founded 20 May 1933 as Hava Yollari Devlet Isletmesi Idaresi and began operations with two **Junkers F 13**s, two **Curtiss-Wright King Bird**s and one **ANT-9**, making inaugural flight in August on Istanbul-Eskisehir-Ankara route. Re-equipped over next five years with four **DH.86B Expresses**, four **DH.89A Dragon Rapides**, one **DH.82A Tiger Moth** and one **DH.90 Dragonfly**. Name changed to Devlet Hava Yollari (DHY) in June 1938. Domestic network expanded to 19 points and fleet supplemented at end of World War II by 33 **C-47** (**DC-3**). First international route opened in 1947, linking Ankara to Athens. Major reorganisation of civil aviation structure resulted in replace-ment of state company DHY by new mixed corporation, Turk Hava Yollari Anonim Ortakligi (THY) on 20 February 1956. Shares held by Turkish state (51 per cent) and private interests. At same time, fleet modernised with seven **de Havilland Heron**s and four **Vickers Viscount**s, supplemented by 10 **Fokker F27**s/**Fairchild FH-227B**s from

Turkish Airlines flies the Airbus A310-310, as does its Turkish Cypriot associate Kibris THY.

1 July 1960. **Douglas DC-9-14** and larger **DC-9-32** arrived in August 1967. Fleet increased during 1970s with leased **Boeing 707** and purchase of three **Douglas DC-10-30**s (December 1972), five **Fokker F28**s (January 1973) and four **727-200**s, all delivered in 1974. Plans for expansion to Far East and acquisition of new aircraft postponed until 1983 when delivery accepted of four new **Advanced 727-200**s. First of seven **A310-200**s arrived in May 1985. Further fleet expansion and renewal programme during early 1990s and addition of long-haul flights to New York, Bangkok and Singapore. New aircraft deliveries between 1991 and 1993 included **737-400/-500**, **Avro RJ100** and **A340-300**.

Turkish Airlines today: National airline serving 56 cities, with strong emphasis on its European network which links Istanbul and Ankara with 34 destinations. Points served on other continents include Abu Dhabi, Ashkhabad, Almaty, Amman, Bahrain, Baku, Bangkok, Beirut, Cairo, Damascus, Dubai, Jeddah, Karachi, Kuwait, New York-JFK, Osaka, Riyadh, Singapore, Tashkent, Tehran, Tunis and Tokyo. Dense domestic network encompasses 26 towns and cities. Joint services with Czech Airlines, Balkan and Tarom.

Annual revenue: $920 million
Passengers: 6.9 million
Cargo: 80,000 tonnes
Employees: 8,550
Ownership: State-owned Public Participation Administration owns 99.24 per cent of airline's shares

Fleet development: One A340-300 to be delivered in April 1997, plus one 737-500.

Associate carriers: Has 50 per cent stake in *Kibris Turkish Airlines* (*Kibris Turk Hava Yollari*) (YK), owned jointly with Cyprus Turkish Community Assembly Consolidated Improvement Fund. Founded December 1974 and provides services from Nicosia to Adana, Ankara, Antalya, Istanbul and Izmir in Turkey, and to London, with one **A310-300** and four **727-200**.

Also shares ownership on equal basis with Lufthansa in holiday airline *SunExpress* (XQ), utilising three **737-300**s and two **737-400**s.

Turkish Airlines fleet

Airbus A310-200	c/n				
TC-JCL	338	TC-THL	E1249	TC-JDY	26065/2284
TC-JCM	375	TC-THM	E1252	TC-JDZ	26066/2301
TC-JCN	379			TC-JEA	27143/2457
TC-JCO	386	**AI(R) Avro RJ100**	c/n	TC-JED	25740/2461
TC-JCR	370	TC-THA	E3232	TC-JEE	26290/2482
TC-JCS	389	TC-THB	E3234	TC-JEF	26291/2513
TC-JCU	390	TC-THC	E3236	TC-JEG	25374/2562
		TC-THD	E3237	TC-JEH	26320/2563
Airbus A310-300	c/n	TC-THE	E3238	TC-JEI	26298/2564
TC-JCV	476	TC-THF	E3240	TC-JEJ	25375/2598
TC-JCY	478	TC-THG	E3241	TC-JEK	26299/2602
TC-JCZ	480	TC-THH	E3243	TC-JEL	26300/2604
TC-JDA	496	TC-THM	E3264	TC-JEM	26302/2620
TC-JDB	497	TC-THO	E3265	TC-JEN	25376/2689
TC-JDC	537			TC-JEO	25377/2717
TC-JDD	586	**Boeing 727-200F**	c/n	TC-JEP	25378/2732
		TC-JCA	22992/1804	TC-JER	26073/2375
Airbus A340-300	c/n	TC-JCB	22993/1808	TC-JET	26077/2425
TC-JDJ	023	TC-JCD	22998/1810	TC-JEU	26078/2431
TC-JDK	025			TC-JEV	26085/2468
TC-JDL	057	**Boeing 737-400**	c/n	TC-JEY	26086/2475
TC-JDM	115	TC-JDE	24904/1988	TC-JEZ	26088/2487
		TC-JDF	24917/2071		
(AIR) Avro RJ70R	c/n	TC-JDG	25181/2203	**Boeing 737-500**	c/n
TC-THI	E1229	TC-JDH	25184/2227	TC-JDU	25288/2286
TC-THJ	E1230	TC-JDI	25372/2280	TC-JDV	25289/2288
		TC-JDT	25261/2258		

United Airlines (UA/UAL)

Chicago-O'Hare Airport
Chicago, Illinois, USA

History: Established 1 July 1931 as management company for four airlines – Varney Speed Lines, National Air Transport, Pacific Air Transport and Boeing Air Transport. Individual airline names gradually disappeared. First US all-metal aircraft, **Boeing 247**, entered service 30 March 1933, with total of 30 added to fleet within few weeks. Route network comprised coast-to-coast link from Los Angeles to New York, via San Francisco, Salt Lake City, Chicago, Cleveland and other stops, plus north-south system in Pacific Northwest. Large numbers of **DC-3**s, including 10 **DST** (**Douglas Sleeper Transport**), acquired after putting type into service on Los Angeles-San Francisco route 1 January 1937. In 1942, turned over more than half of fleet of 69 aircraft to control of US Army and served transpacific network and Alaskan supply routes. Order for 15 new **DC-4**s replaced by war-surplus **C-54**, put into service 1 March 1946, and 35 **DC-6** obtained from 27 April 1947. New cities added included Boston, Hartford, Detroit, Milwaukee and Honolulu; Hawaiian route flown with **Boeing 377 Stratocruiser**. Placed orders for

United Airlines

30 **Convair 340**s 20 February 1951 and for 25 **DC-7**s 25 June 1952, introduced into service 16 November 1952 and 1 June 1954 respectively. Biggest merger in US history with Capital Airlines 1 June 1961, made United largest airline in Western world, serving 116 cities with fleet of 267 aircraft. Progressive purchases of jet aircraft, including **DC-8** (1959), **Boeing 720B** (1960), **Caravelle** (1961), **727** (1963), **DC-8F** (1965) and stretched **'Super' DC-8** and **737** (1967), achieving all-jet status in 1969. **Boeing 747** put into service to Hawaii 23 July 1970, followed by **DC-10-10** 14 August 1970. Mexico added to network December 1980, and 1 April 1983 first flight made outside American continent with service to Tokyo, followed by Hong Kong. **767-200** delivered in August 1983. International services strengthened 11 February 1986 with purchase of Pan America's Pacific division, adding 11 cities in Pacific Rim. Europe reached 15 May 1990, linking Chicago and Washington, DC with Frankfurt. Placed largest-ever airline order in spring 1989 for 32 widebody and 370 narrow-body aircraft. Became launch customer for

United Airline's Boeing 777s entered service on the London-Washington DC route in 1995.

Boeing 777, with order for 34 aircraft in October 1990, first of which entered service 7 June 1995. Started round-the-world service in December 1995.

United Airlines today: World's second-largest airline, serving total of 104 domestic and 40 international destinations in 30 countries and three US territories. Main US gateways are Chicago-O'Hare and San Francisco International airports. Major marketing and code-share agreements with Air Canada and Lufthansa; and similar, but less extensive alliances with ALM Antillean Airlines, Aloha, Ansett Australia, British Midland, Cayman Airways, Emirates, Gulfstream International Airlines, Royal Brunei, Thai International and Transbrasil. Low-fare **Shuttle by United** operation serving 11 cities US West Coast with 380 daily departures.

Annual revenue: $14,943 million
Passengers: 75.0 million
Cargo: 525,000 tonnes
Employees: 82,230
Ownership: Major shareholding by

employees with 55 per cent. Wholly-owned subsidiary of UAL Corporation

Fleet development: 55 aircraft remain on firm order, comprising four more **747-400**s, four **757-200**s, 21 **A320-200**s and 24 777s. Also holds total of 292 options, including 135 737s, 39 A320s, 40 747-400s, five 767s and 34 777s.

Associate carriers: Large feeder network throughout United States operated by several regional airlines under **United Express** umbrella.

Includes: **Air Wisconsin** (UA), bought from United by CJT Holdings in December 1993, but continues to feed United hubs at Chicago and Denver, operating 12 **BAe 146-100/-200**s;

Atlantic Coast Airlines (DH), formed 15 December 1989, provides feed into Washington DC from 41 cities in Eastern USA, with 29 **BAe Jetstream 31/32**, and 25 **Jetstream 41**s, with another 11 to be delivered;

Great Lakes Aviation (ZK), founded 25 October 1979 and started flying 12 October 1981, now feeding United with fleet of 30 **Beech 1900C**s, eight **1900D**s and 12 **EMB-120ER**s;

Mountain West (UA), established in 1990 and part of Mesa Air Group, feeds into Albuquerque, Denver, Los Angeles and Phoenix from 71 cities, operating 47 **Beech 1900C/D**s, seven **DHC-8-300**s and 10 **EMB-120RT**s.

Another Mesa Air Group company, **WestAir** (OE), flying since 1972, hubs into Seattle, Portland, San Francisco and Los Angeles from 25 cities in Washington, Oregon and California, with 21 **BAe Jetstream 31**s and 15 **EMB-120RT**s.

United Airlines fleet

Airbus A320-200	c/n			Boeing 727-200 Adv					
N401UA	435	N416UA	479		N7266U	N7251U	21413/1351	N7282U	21560/1405
N402UA	439	N417UA	483	N7251U	21398/1296	N7267U	21414/1354	N7283U	21561/1408
N403UA	442	N418UA	485	N7252U	21399/1303	N7268U	21415/1356	N7284U	21562/1410
N404UA	450	N419UA	487	N7253U	21400/1309	N7269U	21416/1366	N7285U	21563/1418
N405UA	452	N420UA	489	N7254U	21401/1311	N7270U	21417/1368	N7286U	21564/1420
N406UA	454	N421UA	500	N7255U	21402/1313	N7271U	21418/1370	N7287U	21565/1424
N407UA	456	N422UA	503	N7256U	21403/1315	N7272U	21419/1375	N7288U	21566/1428
N408UA	457	N423UA	504	N7257U	21404/1321	N7273U	21420/1377	N7289U	21567/1430
N409UA	462	N424UA	506	N7258U	21405/1323	N7274U	21421/1383	N7290U	21568/1432
N410UA	463	N425UA	508	N7259U	21406/1325	N7275U	21422/1385	N7291U	21569/1441
N411UA	464	N426UA	510	N7260U	21407/1332	N7276U	21423/1387	N7292U	21570/1443
N412UA	465	N427UA	512	N7261U	21408/1334	N7277U	21424/1393	N7293U	21571/1445
N413UA	470	N428UA	523	N7262U	21409/1336	N7278U	21425/1395	N7294U	21572/1447
N414UA	472	N429UA	539	N7263U	21410/1344	N7279U	21557/1397	N7295U	21573/1449
N415UA	475			N7264U	21411/1346	N7280U	21558/1399	N7297U	21892/1500
				N7265U	21412/1348	N7281U	21559/1401	N7298U	21893/1503

Boeing 737-200 Adv

Reg	c/n
N974UA	21597/510
N976UA	21598/512
N977UA	21508/518
N978UA	21509/521
N979UA	21544/523
N980UA	21545/525
N981UA	21546/527
N982UA	21640/536
N983UA	21641/537
N984UA	21642/540
N985UA	21747/555
N986UA	21748/558
N987UA	21749/569
N988UA	21750/574
N989UA	21751/575
N990UA	21980/596
N991UA	21981/601
N992UA	22089/632
N993UA	22383/213
N994UA	22384/718
N995UA	22399/723
N996UA	22456/740
N997UA	22457/757
N998UA	22741/871

Reg	c/n
N7299U	21894/1505
N7441U	21895/1507
N7442U	21896/1511
N7443U	21897/1513
N7444U	21898/1515
N7445U	21899/1517
N7446U	21900/1519
N7447U	21901/1521
N7448U	21902/1524
N7449U	21903/1526
N7450U	21904/1528
N7451U	21905/1530
N7452U	21906/1548
N7453U	21907/1558
N7454U	21908/1560
N7455U	21909/1562
N7456U	21910/1570
N7457U	21911/1572
N7458U	21912/1575
N7459U	21913/1593
N7460U	21914/1597
N7462U	21916/1611
N7463U	21917/1616
N7464U	21918/1625
N7465U	21919/1632
N7466U	21920/1634
N7467U	21921/1639

Boeing 737-200

Reg	c/n
N9001U	19039/6
N9002U	19040/8
N9003U	19041/12
N9004U	19042/14
N9006U	19044/19
N9007U	19045/21
N9008U	19046/22
N9009U	19047/24
N9010U	19048/25
N9011U	19049/27
N9012U	19050/28
N9013U	19051/30
N9015U	19053/34
N9016U	19054/36
N9017U	19055/37
N9018U	19056/42
N9019U	19057/48
N9022U	19060/55
N9023U	19061/58
N9024U	19062/59
N9025U	19063/62
N9027U	19065/65
N9030U	19068/74
N9032U	19070/76
N9038U	19076/99
N9039U	19077/103
N9040U	19078/106
N9045U	19551/117
N9051U	19932/133
N9052U	19933/135
N9053U	19934/137
N9054U	19935/138
N9060U	19941/174
N9061U	19942/175
N9062U	19943/179
N9063U	19944/183
N9065U	19946/186
N9066U	19947/187
N9067U	19948/191
N9068U	19949/197
N9069U	19950/198
N9070U	19951/200
N9071U	19952/201
N9072U	19953/202
N9075U	19956/211

Boeing 737-300   c/n

Reg	c/n
N202UA	24717/1930
N203UA	24718/1937
N301UA	23642/1300
N302UA	23643/1315
N303UA	23644/1322
N304UA	23665/1330
N305UA	23666/1332
N306UA	23667/1334
N307UA	23668/1346
N308UA	23669/1354
N309UA	23670/1364
N310UA	23671/1370
N311UA	23672/1470
N312UA	23673/1479
N313UA	23674/1481
N314UA	23675/1483
N315UA	23947/1485
N316UA	23948/1491
N317UA	23949/1493
N318UA	23950/1504
N319UA	23951/1532
N320UA	23952/1534
N321UA	23953/1546
N322UA	23954/1548
N323UA	23955/1550
N324UA	23956/1564
N325UA	23957/1566
N326UA	23958/1568
N327UA	24147/1570
N328UA	24148/1572
N329UA	24149/1574
N330UA	24191/1588
N331UA	24192/1590
N332UA	24193/1592
N333UA	24228/1594
N334UA	24229/1605
N335UA	24230/1607
N336UA	24240/1609
N337UA	24241/1611
N338UA	24242/1613
N339UA	24243/1615
N340UA	24244/1617
N341UA	24245/1619
N342UA	24246/1632
N343UA	24247/1634
N344UA	24248/1636
N345UA	24249/1638
N346UA	24250/1644
N347UA	24251/1646
N348UA	24252/1648
N349UA	24253/1650
N350UA	24301/1652
N351UA	24319/1668
N352UA	24320/1670
N353UA	24321/1672
N354UA	24360/1692
N355UA	24361/1694
N356UA	24362/1696
N357UA	24378/1704
N358UA	24379/1724
N359UA	24452/1728
N360UA	24453/1730
N361UA	24454/1750
N362UA	24455/1752
N363UA	24532/1754
N364UA	24533/1756
N365UA	24534/1758
N366UA	24535/1760
N367UA	24536/1762
N368UA	24537/1774
N369UA	24538/1776
N370UA	24539/1778
N371UA	24540/1780
N372UA	24637/1782
N373UA	24638/1784
N374UA	24639/1786
N375UA	24640/1798
N376UA	24641/1802
N377UA	24642/1806
N378UA	24653/1810
N379UA	24654/1812
N380UA	24655/1814
N381UA	24656/1816
N382UA	24657/1830
N383UA	24658/1832
N384UA	24659/1836
N385UA	24660/1838
N386UA	24661/1840
N387UA	24662/1862
N388UA	24663/1875
N389UA	24664/1877
N390UA	24665/1889
N391UA	24666/1891
N392UA	24667/1893
N393UA	24668/1905
N394UA	24669/1907
N395UA	24670/1909
N396UA	24671/1913
N397UA	24672/1915
N398UA	24673/1920
N399UA	24674/1928

Boeing 737-500   c/n

Reg	c/n
N901UA	25001/1948
N902UA	25002/1950
N903UA	25003/1952
N904UA	25004/1965
N905UA	25005/1976
N906UA	25006/1981
N907UA	25007/1983
N908UA	25008/1987
N909UA	25009/1999
N910UA	25254/2073
N911UA	25255/2075
N912UA	25290/2096
N913UA	25291/2101
N914UA	25381/2110
N915UA	25382/2119
N916UA	25383/2146
N917UA	25384/2149
N918UA	25385/2152
N919UA	25386/2154
N920UA	25387/2179
N912UA	25388/2181
N922UA	26642/2189
N923UA	26643/2190
N924UA	26645/2212
N925UA	26646/2214
N926UA	26648/2230
N927UA	26648/2246
N928UA	26651/2257
N929UA	26652/2259
N930UA	26655/2274
N931UA	26656/2289
N932UA	26658/2291
N933UA	26659/2293
N934UA	26662/2312
N935UA	26663/2315
N936UA	26667/2325
N937UA	26668/2329
N938UA	26671/2336
N939UA	26672/2343
N940UA	26675/2345
N941UA	22676/2364
N942UA	26679/2365
N943UA	26680/2366
N944UA	26683/2368
N945UA	26684/2388
N946UA	26687/2402
N947UA	26688/2404
N948UA	26691/2408
N949UA	26692/2421
N950UA	26695/2423
N951UA	26696/2440
N952UA	26699/2485
N953UA	26700/2490
N954UA	26739/2494
N955UA	26703/2498
N956UA	26704/2508
N957UA	26707/2512

United's 144-seat A320-232s fill a gap between the airline's Boeing 737s and 727s.

Boeing 747-100   c/n

Reg	c/n
N153UA	20102/59
N154UA	20103/65
N155UA	20104/69
N156UA	20105/77
N157UA	20106/79
N4714U	19876/97
N4716U	19877/99
N4717U	19878/101
N4718U	18879/139
N4719U	19880/145
N4720U	19881/148
N4723U	19882/175
N4724U	19875/89
N4727U	19883/193
N4728U	19925/205
N4729U	19926/206
N4732U	19927/207
N4735U	19928/208

Boeing 747-200B   c/n

Reg	c/n
N151UA	23736/673
N152UA	23737/675
N158UA	21054/260
N159UA	21140/267

Feeder services are flown by the many United Express carriers. This is a Beech 1900D of Mountain West.

United Airlines

N160UA	21237/285	N514UA	24839/305	N560UA	26660/469	**Boeing 767-200(ER)**		**Douglas DC-10-10** *c/n*	
N161UA	21352/310	N515UA	24840/306	N561UA	26661/479	N602UA	21863/3	N1810U	46609/27
N163UA	21353/316	N516UA	24860/307	N562UA	26664/487	N605UA	21866/7	N1811U	46610/32
N164UA	21657/339	N517UA	24861/310	N563UA	26665/488	N606UA	21867/9	N1812U	46611/35
N165UA	21658/341	N518UA	24871/311	N564UA	26666/490	N607UA	21868/10	N1813U	46612/39
		N519UA	24872/312	N565UA	26669/492	N608UA	21869/11	N1814U	46613/42
Boeing 747-400 *c/n*		N520UA	24890/313	N566UA	26670/494	N609UA	21870/13	N1815U	46614/45
N105UA	26473/985	N521UA	24891/319	N567UA	26673/497	N610UA	21871/15	N1816U	46615/76
N106UA	26474/988	N522UA	24931/320	N568UA	26674/498	N611UA	21872/20	N1817U	46616/86
N171UA	24322/733	N523UA	24932/329	N569UA	26677/499			N1823U	46622/144
N172UA	24363/740	N524UA	24977/331	N570UA	26678/501	**Boeing 767-300(ER)**		N1824U	46623/154
N173UA	24380/759	N525UA	24978/338	N571UA	26681/506	N641UA	25091/360	N1825U	46624/155
N174UA	24381/762	N526UA	24994/339	N572UA	26682/508	N642UA	25092/367	N1826U	46625/169
N175UA	24382/806	N527UA	24995/341	N573UA	26685/512	N643UA	25093/368	N1827U	46626/198
N176UA	24383/811	N528UA	25018/346	N574UA	26686/513	N644UA	25094/369	N1828U	46627/205
N177UA	24384/819	N529UA	25019/352	N575UA	26689/515	N645UA	25280/391	N1829U	46628/207
N178UA	24385/820	N530UA	25043/353	N576UA	26690/524	N646UA	25283/420	N1830U	46629/208
N179UA	25158/866	N531UA	25042/361	N577UA	26693/527	N647UA	25284/424	N1831U	46630/209
N180UA	25224/867	N532UA	25072/366	N578UA	26694/531	N648UA	25285/443	N1832U	46631/210
N181UA	25278/881	N533UA	25073/367	N579UA	26697/539	N649UA	25286/444	N1833U	47965/59
N182UA	25279/882	N524UA	25129/372	N580UA	26698/542	N650UA	25287/449	N1834U	47966/64
N183UA	25379/911	N535UA	25130/373	N581UA	26701/543	N651UA	25389/452	N1835U	47967/67
N184UA	25380/913	N536UA	25156/380	N582UA	26702/550	N652UA	25390/457	N1836U	47968/74
N185UA	25395/919	N537UA	25157/381	N583UA	26705/556	N653UA	25391/460	N1837U	47969/80
N186UA	26875/931	N538UA	25222/385	N584UA	26706/559	N654UA	25392/462	N1838U	46632/296
N187UA	26876/939	N539UA	25223/386	N585UA	26709/563	N655UA	25393/468	N1839U	46633/297
N188UA	26877/944	N540UA	25252/393	N586UA	26710/567	N656UA	25394/472	N1841U	46634/298
N189UA	26878/966	N541UA	25253/394	N587UA	26713/570	N657UA	27112/479	N1842U	46635/307
N190UA	26879/973	N542UA	25276/396	N588UA	26717/571	N658UA	27113/480	N1843U	46636/309
N191UA	26880/984	N543UA	25698/401			N659UA	27114/485	N1844U	48260/344
N192UA	26881/989	N544UA	26322/405	**Boeing 767-200** *c/n*		N660UA	27115/494	N1845U	48261/347
		N545UA	25323/406	N601UA	21862/2	N661UA	27158/507	N1846U	48262/351
Boeing 757-200 *c/n*		N546UA	25367/413	N603UA	21864/4	N662UA	27159/513	N1847U	48263/353
N501UA	24622/241	N547UA	25368/414	N604UA	21865/5	N663UA	27160/514	N1849U	46939/203
N502UA	24623/246	N548UA	25396/420	N612UA	21873/41				
N503UA	24624/247	N549UA	25397/421	N613UA	21874/42	**Boeing 777-200** *c/n*		**Douglas DC-10-30**	
N504UA	24625/251	N550UA	25398/426	N614UA	21875/43	N766UA	26917/8	N1852U	47811/302
N505UA	24626/254	N551UA	25399/427	N615UA	21876/45	N767UA	26918/9	N1853U	47812/303
N506UA	24627/263	N552UA	26641/431	N617UA	21877/46	N768UA	26919/11	N1854U	47813/312
N507UA	24743/270	N553UA	25277/434	N618UA	21878/48	N769UA	26921/12	N1855U	47837/328
N508UA	24744/277	N554UA	26644/435	N619UA	21879/49	N770UA	26925/13	N1856U	46975/248
N509UA	24763/284	N555UA	26647/442	N620UA	21880/50	N771UA	26932/3	N1857U	46986/253
N510UA	24780/290	N556UA	26650/447			N772UA	26930/5	N1858U	46987/255
N511UA	24799/291	N557UA	26653/454			N773UA	26929/4	N1859U	47819/314
N512UA	24809/298	N558UA	26654/462			N775UA	26947/22		
N513UA	24810/299	N559UA	26657/467			N777UA	26916/7		

United Parcel Service (5X/UPS)

The 767-300F freighter was first ordered by UPS, opening up a whole new market for Boeing.

History: After brief spell in air-express business (US West Coast between 1929 and 1931), began air operations in 1981, setting up package delivery service from hub at Louisville. Initially using own aircraft, flown under contract by others, set up its own airline 1 February 1988. By then fleet had grown to more than 100 aircraft, including **Boeing 727Fs**, **DC-8-71F/73Fs**, **Fairchild Expediters**, plus first of what eventually will be 70

Boeing 757-200PFs (Package Freighter), delivered from September 1987. Embarked on $400 million re-engining programme of 40 727-100s with Rolls-Royce Tays, to meet new Stage 3 noise regulations. In October 1995, became first airline to operate new **767-300F** freighter.

UPS today: World's largest package delivery service, providing network of scheduled services to more than 200 countries. Offers next day and two-day delivery service to anywhere in world. Major hubs and distribution points include Bergamo,

United Parcel Service (UPS)

UPS is one of many cargo airlines that still appreciate the the stretched, re-engined DC-8-70 series as a freighter.

Cologne, East Midlands, Guadalajara, Hamilton, Hong Kong, Louisville, Mexico City, Montreal, Monterrey, Nuremberg, Porto, Rome, Seoul, Singapore, Taipei, Tokyo-Narita, Vienna and Zaragoza.

Annual revenue: *$1,465 million*
Cargo: *185,000 tonnes*
Employees: *1,830*
Ownership: *Owned by management*

United Parcel Service (UPS) fleet

Boeing 727-100F	c/n			Boeing 757-200PF	c/n	N440UP	25471/636	N748UP	45948/321
N902UP	18898/244	N946UP	19721/490	N401UP	23723/139	N441UP	27386/638	N750UP	45950/354
N903UP	18945/263	N947UP	19722/493	N402UP	23724/141	N442UP	27387/640	N752UP	45952/348
N904UP	18946/274	N948UP	19357/360	N403UP	23725/143	N443UP	27388/642	N755UP	46055/492
N905UP	18947/286	N949UP	19717/468	N404UP	23726/147	N444UP	27389/644	N772UP	46072/477
N906UP	19314/437	N950UP	19718/474	N405UP	23727/149	N445UP	27390/646	N779UP	45979/363
N907UP	19118/379	N951UP	19850/497	N406UP	23728/176	N446UP	27735/649	N783UP	45973/358
N908UP	19114/312	N954UP	19827/527	N407UP	23729/181	N447UP	27736/651	N797UP	45897/313
N909UP	19115/328	OY-UPD	19103/341	N408UP	23730/184	N448UP	27737/654	N798UP	45898/320
N910UP	19117/376	OY-UPJ	19102/336	N409UP	23731/186	N449UP	27738/656		
N911UP	19119/393	OY-UPS	19232/425	N410UP	23732/189	N450UP	25472/659	**Douglas DC-8-73F**	c/n
N912UP	19244/338	OY-UPT	19094/295	N411UP	23851/191	N451UP	27739/675	N801UP	46101/489
N913UP	19245/342			N412UP	23852/193	N452UP	25473/679	N802UP	46100/502
N914UP	19246/423	**Boeing 727-200F**	c/n	N413UP	23853/195	N453UP	25474/683	N803UP	46073/485
N915UP	19533/475	N208UP	21701/1493	N414UP	23854/197	N454UP	25475/687	N804UP	46004/403
N916UP	19808/615	N209UP	21698/1474	N415UP	23855/199	N455UP	25476/691	N805UP	46117/525
N917UP	19310/395	N210UP	21697/1471	N416UP	23903/318			N806UP	46006/413
N918UP	19008/364	N211UP	21700/1489	N417UP	23904/322	**Boeing 767-300F**	c/n	N807UP	46007/422
N919UP	19012/391	N212UP	21392/1305	N418UP	23905/326	N301UP	27239/580	N808UP	46008/423
N920UP	19873/604	N213UP	21341/1253	N419UP	23906/330	N302UP	27240/590	N809UP	46109/493
N921UP	19874/534	N214UP	21342/1256	N420UP	23907/334	N303UP	27241/594	N810UP	46001/395
N922UP	19231/404			N421UP	25281/395	N304UP	27242/598	N811UP	46089/501
N923UP	19229/390	**Boeing 747-100F**	c/n	N422UP	25324/399	N305UP	27243/600	N812UP	46112/520
N924UP	19234/463	N671UP	20323/115	N423UP	25325/403			N813UP	46059/456
N925UP	19230/402	N672UP	20324/119	N424UP	25369/407	**Douglas DC-8-71F**	c/n	N814UP	46090/504
N926UP	19233/458	N673UP	20325/125	N425UP	25370/411	N700UP	45900/316	N815UP	46002/394
N928UP	19091/280	N674UP	20100/46	N426UP	25457/477	N701UP	45938/331	N816UP	45990/375
N929UP	19092/291	N675UP	20390/136	N427UP	25458/481	N702UP	45902/294	N818UP	46108/522
N930UP	19096/305	N676UP	20101/57	N428UP	25459/485	N703UP	45939/351	N819UP	46019/411
N931UP	19858/645	N677UP	20391/143	N429UP	25460/489	N705UP	45949/329	N836UP	45936/344
N932UP	19856/635	N680UP	20923/234	N430UP	25461/493	N706UP	46056/495	N840UP	46140/528
N933UP	19857/641	N681UP	19661/70	N431UP	25462/569	N707UP	45907/288	N851UP	46051/440
N934UP	19135/301	N682UP	20349/110	N432UP	25463/573	N708UP	46048/450	N852UP	46052/442
N935UP	20143/619	N683UP	20353/131	N433UP	25464/577	N709UP	45914/292	N866UP	45966/393
N936UP	19503/420	N688UP	20784/231	N434UP	25465/579	N713UP	46014/400	N867UP	45967/385
N937UP	19302/354	N689UP	21033/254	N435UP	25466/581	N715UP	45915/295	N868UP	45968/389
N938UP	19506/447	N690UP	20348/106	N436UP	25467/625	N718UP	46018/420	N874UP	46074/468
N939UP	19532/469	N691UP	19641/7	N437UP	25468/628	N729UP	46029/425	N880UP	46080/466
N940UP	19826/546			N438UP	25469/631	N730UP	46030/426	N894UP	46094/482
N941UP	19196/407			N439UP	25470/634	N744UP	45944/326		
N942UP	19101/333								

USAir (US/USA)

Greater Pittsburgh Airport, Pennsylvania and Washington-National, USA

History: Founded 5 March 1937 as All American Aviation and began scheduled mail routes with six **Stinson Reliant**s 12 May 1939, linking Philadelphia, Pittsburgh and Huntington, via several intermediate points, totalling 54 communities. Fleet supplemented by small number of **Beech 18**s in 1946 and 11 **DC-3**s following temporary CAB approval for passenger service in late 1948. First passenger flight inaugurated 7 March 1949 and postal services abandoned three months later. Changed name to Allegheny Airlines in 1953. **Martin 2-0-2** fleet acquired for busier routes in 1955. Large numbers of **Convair 340/440** purchased in 1959/60, converted

USAir

USAir's order for Fokker 100s in 1985 was an important early order for the Dutch manufacturers. Deliveries began in 1989.

to turbine power as **Convair 580**s between 1962 and 1968, supplemented thinner routes by 10 **Fairchild F-27**s from October 1965. Route extended to Chicago and Detroit, then further filled in with take-over of Indianapolis-based Lake Central Airlines 14 March 1968. At same time, introduced leased **DC-9-14**, prior to purchasing own **DC-9-31** fleet. Merger with Mohawk Airlines 12 April 1972 extended network north as far as Montreal and Toronto in Canada. Hitherto-small local carrier now in sixth position among US airlines. Withdrew from some smaller communities and transferred services to other companies which began operation under the **Allegheny Commuter** title, later to become **USAir Express**. First such operation started 15 November 1967 over Baltimore-Hagerstown route by Henson Aviation. Deregulation in 1978 provided opportunity to break free from confines of its Local Service Carrier status and network extended to include destinations in Alabama, Arizona, Florida, Louisiana and Texas. As result name changed to USAir 30 October 1979. DC-9 and ex-Mohawk **BAC One-Eleven** fleet gradually replaced by **Boeing 727-100** (May 1978), **727-200** (August 1979) and **737-200**

(November 1983). Launch customer for **Boeing 737-300** in March 1981, and also contracted for 20 **Fokker 100**s in September 1985. Extension to California in 1983 ensured coverage right across country and acquisition of Piedmont Airlines in April 1988 and Pacific Southwest Airlines (PSA) one year later virtually doubled its fleet and operations. Also gave access to first international route – Charlotte to London – used as stepping stone for further international expansion. These routes flown with new **767-200**. Instant growth and almost immediate stagnation of domestic market led to heavy losses until 1995, in spite of $400 million investment by British Airways, now the holder of 22 per cent of voting rights.

USAir today: Fifth-largest passenger airline in USA, providing vast domestic network which, together with its USAir Express regional partners, serves destinations from main hubs at Charlotte, Philadelphia, Pittsburgh and Washington, DC. Also operates international services in North America, Caribbean and to Europe. Destinations are Athens, Cancun, Bermuda, Frankfurt, Grand Cayman, London-Gatwick, London (Canada), Madrid, Munich, Ottawa, Paris, Rome, St Maarten and Toronto. Compre-

hensive marketing agreement, including code-share to 64 US destinations, with equity partner British Airways. Also block-space agreements and code-shares with All Nippon Airways, Northwest Airlines and Qantas, and plans to fly joint services with Air Aruba and TACA.

Associate carriers: *USAir Shuttle* (TB), formerly Trump Shuttle, acquired 10 April 1992. Provides services between Washington and New York-LaGuardia, and from New York to Boston, using one **Boeing 727-100** and 12 **727-200**s.

Regional services under *USAir Express* banner, operated by:

Allegheny Commuter (US), founded in 1941 and owned since 1986, serves 48 cities based on Harrisburg hub. Fleet comprises 36 **DHC-8-100**s, 13 **Beech 1900C**s, two **Shorts 330**s and two **Shorts 360**s;

CCAir (ED), established in 1979, serves 25 cities in 10 states from its Charlotte hub, with fleet of 14 **Jetstream 31**s, four **DHC-8-100**s and nine **Shorts 360**s;

Chautauqua Airlines (US), founded 3 May 1973 and started operations 1 August 1974. Feeds into Indianapolis hub from Eastern Seaboard and Toronto, London and Hamilton in Canada serving 26 destinations with large fleet of 12 **Saab 340**s, 17 **Jetstream 31**s and 10 **Metro III**s;

Commutair (US) feeds into Boston, Indianapolis, New York, Albany and Philadelphia hubs with 30 **Beech 1900D**s. Founded in July 1989;

Paradise Island Airlines (BK) links Miami, Ft Lauderdale and West Palm Beach with Nassau in Bahamas, with four **DHC-7**s;

PSA Airlines (US), previously Jetstream International Airlines and owned since 1988, operates 20 **Do 328**s and has five more on order plus 15 on option;

Piedmont Airlines (PI), founded in 1931 as Henson Aviation, became USAir Express carrier

USAir Express functions as the feeder network for its parent airline. This is a DHC-8-100 of associate Piedmont Airlines.

following Piedmont merger 5 August 1989. Wholly-owned by USAir. Serves 42 destinations from Toronto to Florida and Bahamas with of 43 **DHC-8-100**s and three **DHC-7**s.

USAir Express services also flown by Mesa Air Group members **Liberty Express** (US), **Air Midwest** (ZV) and **Florida Gulf Airlines**. Liberty Express feeds into Pittsburgh from 14 cities with 10 **Beech 1900C/D**s and five **Shorts 360**s. Air Midwest connects 15 cities to Kansas City hub using fleet of 13 **Beech 1900C**. Finally, Florida Gulf Airlines feeds into Boston, New Orleans, Orlando and Tampa from 27 cities, flying 40 **Beech 1900D**s and nine **EMB-120RT**s.

USAir fleet

The 189-seat 757 is second only in size to the 210-seat 767 in USAir's Boeing-dominated fleet.

Boeing 737-200 Advanced	c/n								
N223US	21665/534	N285AU	23132/1044						
N224US	21666/547	N286AU	23133/1049						
N225US	21667/548	N287AU	23134/1050						
N226US	21815/589	N288AU	23135/1054						
N227AU	21816/592	**Boeing 737-300**	**c/n**						
N228US	21817/602	N300AU	23228/1103						
N229US	21818/606	N334US	23231/1164						
N230AU	21975/612	N335US	23232/1169						
N231US	21976/625	N336US	23233/1200						
N232US	22018/651	N337US	23235/1214						
N233US	22273/680	N338US	23234/1208						
N234US	22274/682	N339US	23236/1219	N525AU	23860/1560	N426US	24548/1789		
N235US	22275/687	N340US	23237/1222	N526AU	23861/1584	N427US	24549/1791		
N236US	22352/728	N341US	23510/1248	N527AU	23862/1586	N428US	24550/1793		
N237US	22353/731	N342US	23511/1268	N528AU	24410/1703	N429US	24551/1795		
N238US	22398/733	N346US	23515/1355	N529AU	24411/1713	N430US	24552/1797		
N239US	22354/736	N349US	23552/1382	N530AU	24412/1735	N431US	24553/1799		
N240AU	22355/741	N350US	23553/1406	N531AU	24478/1743	N432US	24554/1817	N613AU	27144/544
N241US	22443/782	N351US	23554/1408	N532AU	24479/1745	N433US	24555/1819	N614AU	27145/546
N242US	22444/800	N352US	23555/1428	N533AU	24515/1767	N434US	24556/1821	N615AU	27146/551
N243US	22445/837	N353US	23556/1435	N534AU	24516/1769	N435US	24557/1835	N616AU	27147/552
N244US	22752/845	N354US	23557/1437	N558AU	23512/1291	N436US	24558/1845	N617AU	27148/564
N245US	22751/857	N355US	23558/1449	N559AU	23513/1327	N437US	24559/1847	N618AU	22210/42
N246US	22753/865	N371US	22950/1001	N560AU	23514/1331	N438US	24560/1849	N619AU	27198/584
N247US	22754/870	N373US	22952/1015	N562AU	23550/1367	N439US	24781/1874	N620AU	27199/586
N248US	22755/873	N374US	22953/1022	N563AU	23551/1380	N440US	24811/1890	N621AU	27200/589
N249US	22756/879	N375US	22954/1030	N573US	23560/1463	N441US	24812/1892	N622AU	27201/605
N251AU	22757/883	N376US	22955/1043	N574US	23739/1469	N442US	24841/1906	N623AU	27244/607
N252AU	22758/889	N383US	22956/1057	N575US	23740/1477	N443US	24842/1908	N624AU	27245/630
N263AU	22795/912	N384US	22957/1127	N576US	23741/1498	N444US	24862/1910	N625VJ	27246/643
N254AU	22796/914	N385US	22958/1137	N577US	23742/1502	N445US	24863/1914	N626AU	27303/647
N255AU	22797/916	N387US	22959/1140	N584US	23743/1510	N446US	24873/1931	N627AU	27805/655
N256AU	22796/924	N389US	23311/1149	N585US	23930/1539	N447US	24874/1936	N628AU	27806/657
N257AU	22799/932	N390US	23312/1162	N586US	23931/1552	N448US	24892/1944	N629AU	27807/662
N259AU	22806/938	N391US	23313/1177	N587US	23932/1554	N449US	24893/1946	N630AU	27808/666
N260AU	22866/940	N392US	23314/1179	N588US	23933/1559	N775AU	24933/1954	N631AU	27809/673
N261AU	22867/961	N393US	23315/1210	N589US	23934/1563	N776AU	24934/1956	N632AU	27810/678
N262AU	22868/963	N394US	23316/1212	N590US	23935/1569	N777AU	24979/1980	N633AU	27811/681
N263AU	22869/964	N395US	23317/1221	N591US	23936/1575	N778AU	24980/1982		
N264AU	22961/984	N396US	23318/1234	N592US	23937/1587	N779AU	24996/1986	**Boeing 767-200(ER)**	c/n
N265AU	22962/987	N397US	23319/1250			N780AU	24997/1990	N645US	23897/173
N266AU	22878/921	N504US	23379/1362	**Boeing 737-400**	c/n	N781AU	25020/1992	N646US	23898/175
N267AU	22879/926	N505US	23380/1366	N404US	23886/1487	N782AU	25021/1995	N647US	23899/182
N268AU	22880/927	N506AU	23381/1394	N405US	23885/1512	N783AU	25022/2010	N648US	23900/190
N269AU	22881/931	N507AU	23382/1410	N406US	23876/1528	N784AU	25023/2020	N649US	23901/197
N270AU	22882/934	N508AU	23383/1425	N407US	23877/1543	N785AU	25024/2026	N650US	23902/217
N271AU	22883/935	N510AU	23385/1440	N408US	23878/1561			N651US	24764/306
N272AU	22884/956	N511AU	23594/1442	N409US	23879/1573	**Boeing 757-200**	c/n	N652US	24765/308
N273AU	22885/966	N512AU	23595/1450	N411US	23880/1596	N600AU	22192/3	N653US	24894/338
N274AU	22886/974	N514AU	23700/1461	N412US	23881/1610	N601AU	22193/4	N654US	25225/375
N275AU	22887/976	N515AU	23701/1464	N413US	23882/1621	N602AU	22196/7	N655US	25257/383
N276AU	22888/979	N516AU	23702/1475	N415US	23883/1631	N603AU	22198/12	N656US	26847/486
N277AU	22889/983	N517AU	23703/1480	N417US	23984/1674	N604AU	22199/17		
N278AU	22890/986	N518AU	23704/1488	N418US	23985/1676	N605AU	22201/21	**Douglas DC-9-31/32** c/n	
N279AU	22891/988	N519AU	23705/1497	N419US	23986/1684	N606AU	22202/22	N912VJ	47020/126
N280AU	22892/990	N520AU	23706/1499	N421US	23988/1714	N607AU	22203/26	N913VJ	45846/112
N281AU	23114/997	N521AU	23856/1501	N422US	23989/1716	N608AU	22204/27	N914VJ	47068/160
N282AU	23115/998	N522AU	23857/1503	N423US	23990/1732	N609AU	22205/28	N916VJ	47023/158
N283AU	23116/999	N523AU	23858/1509	N424US	23991/1746	N610AU	27122/525	N918VJ	48138/1021
N284AU	23131/1039	N524AU	23859/1551	N425US	23992/1764	N611AU	27123/534	N919VJ	48139/1024
						N612AU	27124/540	N920VJ	48140/1027

USAir

Reg	c/n	Reg	c/n	Reg	c/n	Reg	c/n	Reg	c/n
N921VJ	48141/1030	N967VJ	47375/531	N463AU	11061	N852US	11280	N899US	11399
N922VJ	48142/1033	N968VJ	47429/532	N464US	11063	N853US	11281	**McDonnell Douglas**	
N923VJ	48143/1036	N969VJ	47421/558	N465AU	11064	N854US	11282	**MD-81/82**	*c/n*
N924VJ	48144/1039	N970VJ	47050/118	N466US	11075	N855US	11283	N800US	48034/946
N925VJ	48145/1042	N971VJ	47051/131	N467US	11087	N856US	11286	N801US	48037/965
N925VJ	48146/1044	N972VJ	47052/142	N468US	11095	N857US	11289	N802US	48036/963
N927VJ	48154/1046	N973VJ	47099/197	N469US	11096	N858US	11291	N803US	48035/955
N928VJ	48131/940	N974VJ	47130/211			N859US	11293	N804US	48052/974
N929VJ	48118/942	N975VJ	47146/226	**Fokker F28-4000**	*c/n*	N860US	11295	N805US	48053/986
N930VJ	45868/290	N976VJ	48147/1048	N475AU	11222	N861US	11297	N806US	48038/1002
N931VJ	47188/291	N977VJ	48155/1050	N476US	11224	N862US	11300	N807US	48039/1003
N932VJ	47189/303	N978VJ	47371/506	N477AU	11226	N863US	11303	N808US	48040/1006
N933VJ	47216/315	N980VJ	48156/1052	N478US	11227	N864US	11306	N809US	48041/1008
N934VJ	48114/919	N981VJ	48157/1054	N479AU	11228	N865US	11308	N810US	48042/1009
N935VJ	48115/920	N982VJ	48158/1056	N480AU	11229	N866US	11310	N811US	48043/1010
N936VJ	48116/921	N983VJ	48159/1058	N481US	11230	N867US	11312	N812US	48092/1034
N937VJ	48117/922	N984VJ	47201/293	N482US	11231	N868US	11313	N813US	48093/1049
N938VJ	48119/943	N985VJ	47208/307	N483US	11233	N869US	11314	N814US	48094/1053
N939VJ	48120/949	N986VJ	47208/327	N484US	11234	N880US	11331	N815US	48095/1055
N940VJ	47053/107	N987VJ	47210/341	N486US	11239	N881US	11333	N816US	48096/1057
N941VJ	47054/110	N989VJ	47212/368	N487US	11238	N882US	11334	N817US	48097/1059
N942VJ	47057/122	N991VJ	47310/449	N488US	11240	N883US	11337	N818US	48098/1060
N943VJ	47058/123	N993VJ	47332/461	N489US	11149	N884US	11338	N819US	48099/1067
N945VJ	47066/150	N995VJ	47334/493	N490US	11152	N885US	11345	N820US	49119/1070
N946VJ	47026/119	N996VJ	47335/494	N491US	11156	N886US	11346	N821US	49138/1090
N950VJ	47564/681	N997VJ	47336/500	N492US	11159	N887US	11349	N822US	49139/1091
N951VJ	47576/682			N493US	11161	N888AU	11357	N823US	49142/1094
N952VJ	47574/690	**Fokker F28-1000**	*c/n*	N494US	11167	N889US	11358	N824US	49143/1095
N953VJ	47583/697	N452US	11105	N495US	11168	N890US	11365	N825US	49237/1144
N955VJ	47593/705	N454US	11107	N496US	11169	N891US	11366	N826US	48026/960
N956VJ	47588/699	N456US	11035	N497US	11173	N892US	11372	N827US	48049/983
N958VJ	47351/442	N457US	11036	N498US	11181	N893US	11373	N828US	48028/979
N959VJ	47352/453	N458US	11037	N499US	11182	N894US	11379	N829US	49429/1242
N960VJ	47505/586	N459US	11043			N895US	11380	N830US	49443/1291
N962VJ	47507/594	N460AU	11044	**Fokker 100**	*c/n*	N896US	11391		
N963VJ	47508/595	N461AU	11032	N850US	11276	N897US	11392		
N966VJ	47420/556	N462AU	11054	N851US	11278	N898US	11398		

VARIG (RG/VRG)

Galeao International Airport
Rio de Janeiro, Brazil

DC-10-30s still operate alongside next-generation MD-11s on VARIG's international routes. VARIG also flies Boeing 747-300s, with 747-400s now on order.

History: Founded 7 May 1927 as Viação Aérea Rio-Gradense (VARIG). First service operated with **Dornier Wal** 15 July 1927 German influence diminished when Brazil sided with Allies during World War II, and **DH.89A Dragon Rapide** bought to open first international route from Porto Alegre to Montevideo 5 August 1942. Fleet modernised with seven **Lockheed L.10A/E Electra**s from June 1943. During 1946 bought five of eventually large fleet of **DC-3**s, followed by equally large number of **Curtiss** C-46As. Second international route opened to Buenos Aires in 1951. **Convair 240** ordered for domestic routes, while three **Lockheed L.1049G**s delivered for New York service, 2 August 1955. Super Constellations replaced by **Caravelle**s in 1959 and by two **Boeing 707-420**s in 1960. Took over the giant REAL consortium in 1961, making VARIG overnight largest airline in South America and giving access to further routes in Americas and to Tokyo. Three **Convair 990A**s delivered in June 1963 and first of 11 **L.188A Electra**s in November 1962. Transatlantic routes to Europe added in February 1965 with take-over of Panair do Brasil. Fleet increased with purchase of 10 **HS 748**s in 1967/68 and more 707s, followed by progression of **727** (1970), **737** (1974), and **DC-10-30** (1974). Another major step forward taken in June 1975 with purchase of controlling interest in Serviços Aéreos Cruzeiro do Sul, fully integrated in January 1993. This gave access to more South American destinations and increased domestic market share to more than half. **747-200B** added in January 1981, **747-300** in December 1985, **737-300** in September 1987, **767-200** in July 1987, **767-300** in December 1989, and **MD-11** in November

1991. Removal of international monopoly and intense competition forced major restructuring during 1990s, resulting in elimination of unprofitable services and reduction in fleet.

VARIG today: Brazil's principal airline, operating international network to 30 destinations in 23 countries, and domestic services linking 35 points in conjunction with Rio-Sul. 'Ponte Aérea' air-bridge between Rio de Janeiro and São Paulo shared with Transbrasil and VASP. International routes to North and South America, Europe, Far East and South Africa. Code-share, joint flight/block space agreement with Canadian International, Delta, Ecuatoriana, JAL, LAB Airlines, LACSA, Lufthansa, SAS, TAP Air Portugal and Transbrasil.

Annual revenue: *$3,200 million*
Passengers: *9.7 million*
Cargo: *315,000 tonnes*
Employees: *19,000*
Owned by: *Ruben Berta Foundation*

Associate carrier: *Rio-Sul Serviços Aéreos Regionais SA* (SL), 95 per cent owned, founded 24 August 1976. Provides extensive domestic services mostly in southern states of Brazil with fleet of seven **Boeing 737-500**s, 10 **EMB-120RT Brasilia**s and 10 **Fokker 50**s.

Northeast coverage provided by subsidiary ***Nordeste Linhas Aéreas Regionais*** (JH), founded in June 1976, serving 26 points from hubs at Belo Horizonte and Salvador da Bahia, using nine **EMB-110 Bandeirante**s, four **EMB-120RT Brasilia**s and two **Fokker 50**s.

VARIG fleet

Boeing 727-100F	*c/n*
PP-VLD	20425/824
PP-VLE	19666/480
PP-VLG	20423/810
PP-VLS	19508/457
PP-VLV	19009/374

Boeing 737-200 Advanced	*c/n*
PP-CJN	21012/392
PP-CJO	21013/393
PP-CJP	21014/397
PP-CJR	21015/404
PP-CJS	21016/406
PP-CJT	21017/410
PP-VME	21000/378
PP-VMF	21001/384
PP-VMG	21002/385
PP-VMH	21003/389
PP-VMI	21004/390
PP-VMJ	21005/394
PP-VML	21007/400
PP-VMM	21008/402
PP-VMN	21009/417
PP-VNF	22504/804
PP-VNG	22505/815

Boeing 737-300	*c/n*
PP-VNT	23828/1446
PP-VNU	23797/1416
PP-VNV	23798/1429
PP-VNX	23829/1460
PP-VNY	24864/1918
PP-VNZ	24869/1926
PP-VOD	24275/1637
PP-VOE	24276/1645
PP-VOF	24277/1658
PP-VOG	24278/1660
PP-VOH	24279/1673
PP-VON	24935/1935
PP-VOO	24936/1951
PP-VOR	24093/1727
PP-VOS	25048/2085
PP-VOT	25049/2091
PP-VOU	25050/2125
PP-VOV	25051/2127
PP-VOW	24961/2133
PP-VOX	24962/2139
PP-VOY	25210/2090
PP-VOZ	25239/2100
PP-VPA	26852/2273
PP-VPB	26856/2321
PP-VPC	26857/2326

Boeing 747-300	*c/n*
PP-VOA	24106/701
PP-VOB	24107/702
PP-VOC	24108/703

Boeing 747-300 Combi	
PP-VNH	23394/627
PP-VNI	23395/629

Boeing 767-200(ER)	
PP-VNN	23803/161
PP-VNO	23801/170
PP-VNP	23802/172
PP-VNQ	23804/178
PP-VNR	23805/180
PP-VNS	23806/181

Boeing 767-300(ER)	
PP-VOI	24752/289
PP-VOJ	24753/291
PP-VOK	24843/314
PP-VOL	24844/324

Douglas DC-10-30	*c/n*
PP-VMA	46944/133
PP-VMB	46945/156
PP-VMD	46916/202
PP-VMQ	46941/176
PP-VMV	47843/335
PP-VMW	47844/336
PP-VMX	47845/356
PP-VMY	48282/355

Douglas DC-10-30CF	
PP-VMT	47841/329
PP-VMU	47842/332

McDonnell Douglas MD-11	*c/n*
PP-VOP	48434/476
PP-VOQ	48435/478
PP-VPJ	48404/523
PP-VPK	48405/524
PP-VPL	48406/547
PP-VPM	48439/554

VASP (VP/VSP)

São Paulo-Congonhas Airport
São Paulo, Brazil

History: Founded 4 November 1933, full name Viaçao Aérea São Paulo. Began operations 1 April 1934. **DC-3** introduced in January 1946. Joined in 1950 by first of 15 **Saab Scandia**s. Ordered five **Vickers Viscount**s 10 May 1957, entered service 3 November 1958. World's first non-reservation service established 6 July 1959 over Rio-São Paulo 'Ponte Aérea' air-bridge in conjunction with VARIG and Cruzeiro do Sul. **BAC One-Eleven 400** in acquired (January 1968), **NAMC YS-11A** (October 1968) and **737-200** (1969). **EMB-110C** put on feeder routes 4 November 1973, but transferred to new subsidiary TAM. **727-200** added (April 1977) and **A300B2-200** (November 1982). Privatised 4 September 1990 and started domestic expansion, following removal of VARIG's monopoly. International services started to US in October 1991, and transatlantic flights inaugurated to Brussels. Long-haul fleet now standardised on **MD-11**, first delivered in 1992.

VASP is another Brazilian MD-11 operator and the 325-seat airliner is its primary international type.

VASP today: Brazil's second-largest airline provides comprehensive domestic network to all Brazilian states, together with growing network of international services.

Annual revenue: *$895 million*
Passengers: *2.9 million*

VASP

Cargo: 62,000 tonnes
Employees: 11,000
Shareholders: VOE/Canhedo Group
(60 per cent), São Paulo state
government (40 per cent)

Fleet development: Ten
Boeing 737-300s on order for
delivery starting June 1996.

Associate carriers: Bought
50.1 per cent controlling interest
in dormant **Ecuatoriana** (EU),
founded in July 1974 and once
national airline of Ecuador, for
$32.9 million. Intends to restart
operations in mid-1996, re-establishing network of services
throughout Americas and to
Europe, using seven aircraft
including its sole **DC-10-30**.

Also acquired 49 per cent
holding in Bolivian flag-carrier
LAB Airlines (**Lloyd Aéreo
Boliviano**) (LB) for $48 million,

giving it effective control. Founded 15 September 1925, LAB
serves 13 domestic points and
17 international destinations
within Americas, using two
Airbus A310-300s, one **Boeing**

707-320C, three **727-100**s, three
Advanced 727-200s and two
Fokker F27-200s.

Small 3.34 per cent remaining
shareholding in **TAM Transportes Aéreos Regionais**.

VASP fleet

Boeing 737-200	c/n
PP-SMA	20092/161
PP-SMC	20094/182
PP-SMQ	20155/180
PP-SMR	20157/189
PP-SMS	20159/193
PP-SMT	20160/195

Boeing 737-200C (F)	c/n
PP-SMB	20093/169
PP-SMW	20346/258

Boeing 737-200 Advanced	
PP-SMF	20589/301
PP-SMG	20777/324

PP-SMH	20778/325
PP-SMP	20779/327
PP-SMU	20967/364
PP-SMV	20968/367
PP-SMZ	20971/382
PP-SNA	21094/412
PP-SNB	21095/432
PP-SPG	21616/889
PP-SPH	22070/614
PP-SPI	21476/519
PP-SPJ	21236/461

Boeing 737-200C Adv	c/n
PP-SPF	21073/419

Boeing 737-300	c/n
PP-SOT	25150/2074
PP-SOU	25360/2140

McDonnell Douglas MD-11	c/n
PP-SOW	48413/488
PP-SOZ	48414/491
PP-SPD	48411/453
PP-SPE	48412/454
PP-SPK	48744/592
PP-SPL	48745/596
PP-SPM	48563/593

Virgin Atlantic Airways (VS/VIR)
London-Gatwick and
-Heathrow Airports

*Virgin was the first UK A340
operator but has now also added
the 747-400 to its fleet of earlier
747-100/-200 models.*

History: Founded in 1982 by
Randolph Fields as British
Atlantic Airways, but developed
as offshoot of Richard Branson's
Virgin Group and renamed. Low-
cost high-quality service started
22 June 1984 from Gatwick to
Newark with a **Boeing 747-100**.
Miami service opened prior to
delivery of two **747-200B**s in
1986. Total of eight acquired by
May 1991. Access to Heathrow
granted by UK Civil Aviation
authority in January 1991 and
New York, Los Angeles and
Tokyo services transferred there
in July. New service launched to
Athens in partnership with Greek
airline **South East European
Airways** (SEEA) in March 1993
and with City Jet to Dublin in
January 1994. First **A340-300**
joined fleet in December 1993,
first **747-400** in May 1994.

Virgin Atlantic today:
UK's second-biggest long-haul
airline, providing schedules from
Heathrow to New York, Los
Angeles, San Francisco, Wash-
ington and Hong Kong; from
Gatwick to Boston, Miami and
Orlando; Manchester to Orlando;
London (Heathrow and Gatwick)
to Athens. Johannesburg will be
added in summer 1996, with
Singapore and Sydney to follow
in 1997. Plans European opera-

tion with acquisition of 90 per
cent stake in **EuroBelgian
Airlines**, possibly to be renamed
Virgin Europe. Code-share with
Delta Air Lines, Malaysia Airlines
and British Midland; marketing
alliance with Ansett Australia.

Annual revenue: $730 million
Passengers: 1.65 million
Employees: 4,000
Owned by: Virgin Travel Group

Fleet development: Two
more Airbus A340-300s, at least
one with 10-bed underfloor
sleeping compartment, to join
fleet in 1997, possibly supplemented by two more 747-400s.
Options retained on **Boeing 777**.

Associate carriers: Franchise with Dublin's **Cityjet** (WX),
flying London City-Dublin-Brus-
sels service, terminated in 1996.

Virgin Atlantic Airways fleet

Airbus A340-300	c/n
G-VAEL	015
G-VBUS	013
G-VFLY	058
G-VSKY	016
G-VSUN	114

Boeing 747-100	c/n
G-VMIA	20108/87

Boeing 747-200B	c/n
G-TKYO	21939/449
G-VGIN	19732/134
G-VIRG	21189/274
G-VJFK	20842/238

G-VLAX	20921/241
G-VOYG	20121/167
G-VRGN	21937/419

Boeing 747-400	c/n
G-VFAB	958/1028
G-VHOT	26326/1043

Index to airlines

121